DATE DUE

DE 17 '05			

DEMCO 38-296

Borders, Exiles, Diasporas

CULTURAL SITINGS

Elazar Barkan, Editor

Borders, Exiles, Diasporas

EDITED BY

Elazar Barkan
and Marie-Denise Shelton

STANFORD
UNIVERSITY
PRESS

Stanford,
California

1998

Stanford University Press
Stanford, California
© 1998 by the Board of Trustees of the
Leland Stanford Junior University
Printed in the United States of America

CIP data are at the end of the book

Cultural Sitings

A series edited by Elazar Barkan

CULTURAL SITINGS will present focused discussions of major contemporary and historical cultural issues by prominent and promising scholars, with a special emphasis on multidisciplinary and transnational perspectives. By bridging historical and theoretical concerns, CULTURAL SITINGS will develop and examine narratives which probe the spectrum of experiences that continuously reconfigure contemporary cultures. By rethinking chronology, agency, and especially the siting of historical transformation, the books in this series will go beyond disciplinary boundaries and notions of what is marginal and what is central to knowledge. By juxtaposing the analytical, the historical, and the visual, this challenging new series will provide a venue for the development of cultural studies and for the rewriting of the canon.

Acknowledgments

It is with great pleasure that we thank some of the people and organizations without whom this book would never have been published. First, we would like to thank the participants in the volume. Their essays were selected from about 200 papers given in Claremont, California, at the annual meeting of the American Comparative Literature Association in 1994. The conference was sponsored by the Claremont Graduate School and Pitzer, Pomona, and Scripps Colleges; we thank the deans of these schools for providing the funds and the hospitality necessary to make the occasion as enjoyable as it was successful. The Program Committee, which included Janet Farrell Brodie, Rena Fraden, Joel Lamore, Natalie Rachlin, Arden Reed, Janet Retseck, Michael Roth, and Margaret Waller, deserves special commendation. Winnona Winnet contributed at the initial stages of putting the volume together, and Holly Hauck's administrative assistance and commitment was indispensable, as were the student volunteers, especially Chris Hoene, Lisa Kamitaki, Lisa Kohlmeier, and Heather Wilson.

We would especially like to thank Marjorie Perloff, who, as the ACLA President, initiated the idea of a thematic conference and was closely involved with it at all stages. At Stanford University Press, we are particularly indebted to Muriel Bell, who encouraged the project from its beginning and who made the publication possible, and to Nathan MacBrien, who helped turn the manuscript into a book. We would also like to thank the Claremont Graduate School and Claremont McKenna College for providing some much-needed help in the final stages of producing the manuscript.

As always, special people deserve exceptional gratitude: Lawrence Shelton, Pamela Smith, and Ady and Mulik Barkan.

E.B.
M.-D.S.

Contents

Contributors

ANGELIKA BAMMER is Associate Professor in the Department of German and the Graduate Institute of Liberal Arts at Emory University. She is the author of *Partial Visions: Feminism and Utopianism in the 1970s* (1991), and the editor of *Displacements: Cultural Identities in Question* (1994). Her current work is on issues of ethnic and gender identity in relation to national culture.

ELAZAR BARKAN is Chair of the Cultural Studies Department and Associate Professor of History at the Claremont Graduate School. His books include *The Retreat of Scientific Racism* (1992) and, coedited with Ronald Bush, *Prehistories of the Future: The Primitivist Project and the Culture of Modernism* (Stanford University Press, 1995). His current research topic, "Restitution, National Identity, and International Morality," deals with the growing global trend of using restitution as a compensatory measure in conflict resolution and in addressing historical injustice.

JOAN BRANDT teaches French in the Cooperative Program in Modern Languages at the Claremont Colleges. She has published articles on contemporary French literature and theory and is the author of *Geopoetics: The Politics of Mimesis in Poststructuralist French Poetry and Theory* (Stanford University Press, 1997).

DAVID BRENNER is Assistant Professor of Germanic and Slavic Languages at the University of Colorado, Boulder. He is the author of *Marketing Identities: The Invention of Jewish Ethnicity* (1997) and of numerous articles in journals and anthologies. He is completing a book entitled *Ethnic Entertainment: Pop Culture and German Jews*, from which his contribution to this volume is taken.

RONALD BUSH is David Heinz Professor of American Literature at Oxford University. He is the author of *The Genesis of Ezra Pound's Cantos* and *T. S. Eliot: A Study in Character and Style,* and he edited *T. S. Eliot: The Modernist in History.* With Elazar Barkan he coedited *Prehistories of the Future: The Primitivist Project and the Culture of Modernism* (Stanford University Press, 1995).

ERIN G. CARLSTON received her Ph.D. in Modern Thought and Literature from Stanford University, where she is now an Instructor in the Program in Cultures, Ideas, and Values. Her field is comparative modernisms, and she is the author of *Thinking Fascism: Sapphic Modernism and Fascist Modernity* (Stanford University Press, 1998).

ANNE DONADEY is Assistant Professor of Comparative Literature and Women's Studies at the University of Iowa. She specializes in francophone literature and works at the intersection of feminist and postcolonial theories. She holds a Ph.D. in French Literature from Northwestern University. She is completing a book titled *Palimpsests: Women's Writing Between Algeria and France.* Her articles have appeared in *World Literature Today,* in *L'Esprit créateur, The French Review,* and in the collection *Identity Papers* (1996).

EMILY A. HADDAD is Assistant Professor of English at the University of South Dakota. She is completing a book titled *Orientalist Poetics: The Islamic Middle East in Nineteenth-Century English and French Poetry.*

DANIEL HERWITZ is the author of *Making Theory / Constructing Art: On the Authority of the Avant-Garde* (1993). He works in the fields of avant-garde and contemporary aesthetics, postcolonial studies, and Wittgenstein. He has recently moved to South Africa, where he is Professor and Head of the Department of Philosophy, Natal University, Durban.

JANE HOTCHKISS is a doctoral candidate in nineteenth-century British literature at the University of California, Davis. She is completing a dissertation that examines "wild child" accounts and the literary child-of-nature in the Romantic period and the fin de siècle. She has published on Kate Chopin and has an article forthcoming on Vernon Lee.

RENÉE RIESE HUBERT is Professor Emerita of Comparative Literature and French at the University of California, Irvine. She is the author of six volumes of poetry and of *Surrealism and the Book* and *Magnifying Mirrors: Women, Surrealism, and Partnership.* With Judd D. Hubert, she is at present working on a study entitled *The Artist's Book: The Cutting Edge of Reading.*

FRANÇOISE LIONNET teaches French and Comparative Literature at Northwestern University. She is the author of *Autobiographical Voices:*

Race, Gender, Self-Portraiture (1989) and *Postcolonial Representations: Women, Literature, Identity* (1995), and the coeditor of "Post/Colonial Conditions," *Yale French Studies* (1993) and "Postcolonial Indigenous and Emergent Feminisms," *Signs* (1995).

TYRUS MILLER is Assistant Professor of Comparative Literature, English, and Film Studies at Yale University. He has a study forthcoming on late-modernist fiction and culture, and he is currently writing a book on the concept of authenticity in Walter Benjamin, Theodor Adorno, and Siegfried Kracauer.

RICARDO L. ORTÍZ is Assistant Professor of English at Dartmouth College, where he specializes in Critical and Cultural Theory. He is currently writing a book titled *Diaspora and Disappearance: The Political Erotics of Cuban Exile.*

CATHERINE PORTUGES is Professor and Graduate Program Director in the Department of Comparative Literature; Director of the Interdepartmental Program in Film Studies; and Adjunct Professor in the Departments of French and Communication at the University of Massachusetts, Amherst. She is the author of *Screen Memories: The Hungarian Cinema of Marta Meszaros* (1993) and coeditor of *Gendered Subjects: The Dynamics of Feminist Pedagogy* (1985), and of a forthcoming volume, *Cinema in Transition: Post-communist Cinema in East/Central Europe.* A native of Hollywood, she is working on a book on European filmmakers in Hollywood.

RENA N. POTOK received her Ph.D. in Comparative Literature and Literary Theory from the University of Pennsylvania. She is currently writing a book on literary representations of land and the female body as occupied territories in colonial and postcolonial Irish, Northern Irish, Jewish Israeli, and Palestinian Israeli fiction. She is also a translator of Israeli literature and a writer of short fiction and drama.

WALTER PUTNAM is Associate Professor of French at the University of New Mexico. A graduate of Duke University and the Université de Paris III (Sorbonne Nouvelle), he is the author of *L'Aventure littéraire de Joseph Conrad et d'André Gide* (1990) and *Paul Valéry Revisited* (1995), as well as numerous articles published in both France and the United States. He is currently working on questions of French literary colonialism and postcolonial discourses.

Contributors

LESLIE W. RABINE is Professor of French at the University of California, Irvine. She is the author of *Reading the Romantic Heroine: Text, History, Ideology* (1985) and coauthor of *Feminism, Socialism, and French Romanticism* (1993), and is writing a book on the global circulation of African fashion.

MARIE-DENISE SHELTON is Professor of French at Claremont McKenna College. Her articles on modern French, Caribbean, and African Literature have appeared in critical anthologies and journals including *The French Review, Caribbean Review, Présence Africaine, Présence Francophone, Callaloo, Contemporary French Civilization,* and *World Literature Today.* She is the author of *Image de la société dans le roman haïtien.*

WENDY W. WALTERS received her Ph.D. in literature from the University of California, San Diego. She is writing a book tentatively titled "Landscapes of Identity: figures of Home and Elsewhere Among Writers of the African Diaspora," focusing on the work of Chester Himes, Michelle Cliff, and Simon Njami. She recently published an article on Chester Himes's detective fiction in *African American Review.*

Borders, Exiles, Diasporas

ELAZAR BARKAN AND
MARIE-DENISE SHELTON

Introduction

> First you will come to the Sirens, who bewitch
> everyone who comes near them. If any man draws
> near in his innocence and listens to their voice, he
> never sees home again, never again will wife and
> little children run to greet him with joy; but the
> Sirens bewitch him with their melodious song.
> There in a meadow they sit, and all round is a great
> heap of bones, mouldering bodies and withering
> skins. Go on past that place, and do not let the men
> hear; you must knead a good lump of wax and plug
> their ears with pellets.
>
> — Circe to Odysseus, *The Odyssey*

In *Le Chant des sirènes* (The sirens' song) the Haitian novelist Marie-Thérèse Colimon allegorizes the modern exodus of Haitians to foreign lands in search of freedom and self-redemption. The El Dorado is somewhere else. The voyagers scramble into airplanes, boats, or rafts seeking a Promised Land: "There are those who are simply leaving. There are those who are flying away. There are those who are fleeing. There are those who are escaping unemployment, poverty, failure and defeat."[1] Colimon echoes the goddess Circe, who warns Odysseus of the dangers awaiting him and his men as they sail through the Sirens' isle and face the terrors of Scylla and Charybdis. Circe describes the bewitching power of the Sirens and the fate of those who succumb to the charm of their melodious song: "If any man draws near in his innocence and listens to their voice, he never sees home again, never again will wife and little children run to greet him."[2] To escape a horrible death, the sailors must plug their ears with pellets of wax. Odysseus alone can hear the Sirens' wonderful voices, but to enjoy their song he must have his men tie his body tight to the ship's mast. In a Circe-like voice, Colimon

1

warns those who leave home against the appeal of false gods and the seduction of the winds. The ransom of the journey is also loneliness, separation, shattered dreams, madness, and forgotten love. Without a compass, without a map, the voyager who has tasted the pleasures and displeasures of exile is unable to steer the ship back home.

"Captive people have a need for song," the Jamaican-born writer Michelle Cliff writes in her poetic novel *No Telephone to Heaven*.[3] The reference is not to the throbbing song of Sirens luring travelers away from their homeland but to the beckoning voice of the motherland: "I returned to this island because there was nowhere else. . . . I could live no longer in borrowed countries, on borrowed time. There is danger here."[4]

The call of the toad signals danger. It is heard in the spring and early summer as Gdansk emerges from the thawing winter. Against a pastoral, serene background, an incidental meeting between a middle-aged German and a Polish woman turns into a love affair, unleashing a prosperous industry of exile. In a world infused by memories of past wars, refugees, and mass expulsions, amends are made in establishing a homeland for the dead. The dead bring their live relatives along. Soon, exiled German dead, those who plan their forthcoming death, and younger compatriots crowd into the old homeland, bringing a new prosperity to the city. As the exile economy continues to grow, resuscitating the old borderland, creating the appearance of reconciliation, the personal love affair retreats into the private realm. How do the dead resuscitate a new communal life? Is their prosperity merely a morbid occupation? Gunther Grass's imaginary Gdansk in its early postcommunist days displays a borderland that comes alive through death and prospers through foreigners—Danzig and irony, in four languages, waiting for Hindi to replace Swedish. Or is it Lithuanian? As the Asian presence awakens the industrial life of the city, the German past comes to life through prosperity and a powerful German Mark. New Gdansk, however, is not a place for true believers, who cannot accept the contamination of their ideals by mundane prosperity. The collision of the ideal and the political exiles the lovers to an anonymous Italian cemetery, far from their beloved once morbid industry and away from the toad warning of danger.

We are fond of saying that we inhabit a "global village," an increasingly homogeneous world where people and nations linked by powerful networks of communication are engaged in an incessant process of cultural, political, and economic exchange. "Village" evokes the image of a small, pastoral, stable community, while "global" conveys not only the idea of efficient communications but also border crossings, immigration, and relocation as common experiences. People are transplanted and build new lives away from their homelands but remain part of that global community. Diasporic cultures evolve that are both unlike the home cultures and inseparable from them. The speed of communication through television and cyberspace may encourage the vision of a postmodern world populated by individuals who are no longer citizens of specific countries but humans sharing a common culture. Yet there is the contradictory vision of an utterly heterogeneous world marked by fragmentation, mutilation, and irreconcilable differences. Around the world, countries are torn by civil conflicts, wars, genocide. Fierce nationalisms erect impassable barriers that make brothers, sisters, and neighbors into enemies. Inequality and brutal oppression maintain a great divide between the First World and the Third World. Race, class, gender, and ethnic differences create a widening crater in the discourse on cohesion and global culture. Transplanted, the individual is transformed; the "I" is no longer a speaking subject with a clear history and a distinct voice but rather becomes a composite product of historical antinomies and contradictory impulses. Such are the apparently paradoxical, but not incompatible, explanations of the world in contemporary intellectual discourse. In assembling this volume, we did not seek to eliminate or isolate either of these representations. To do so would create an illusion of coherence that obviously distorts and eludes the complexity of lived experiences.

Within the past decade, discussions of diaspora and transnational cultures, motivated in part by technological advances, have become central to the intellectual investigation of postmodernist culture. Innumerable groups are increasingly categorized as minority cultures, part of an all-encompassing network of diasporas. Initiated in the needs of the displaced and culminating in changed opportunities, diasporic existence in its all-inclusive terms has become culturally and politically affirmed around the globe, albeit as a solution to an impossible situation. Thus James Clifford has recently discussed "diasporas" as a composite: "a history of dispersal, myth/memories of the homeland, alienation in the host (bad host?) country, desire for the eventual return, ongoing support for the homeland, and a collective identity importantly defined by this relationship."[5] But even more important is the focus on ambivalence, on what a diaspora is not, and on the themes the concept replaces rather than the precise substance it conveys. Clifford weaves diaspora as a woof onto the warp of cultural analysis, enriching the critical language on identity formation in its relation to ethnicity and gender.

But can we demarcate in a contemporary cultural system an outside space that will aim at recovering affinities but not be subjugated to exclusiveness, or othering? Understandably such a space would become attractive, opening the possibility for "transnational connections" that link diasporas but "need not be articulated primarily through a real or symbolic homeland" (p. 306). But could such a place exist?

Historically Clifford is happy to adopt "the Jewish diaspora as . . . a *non-normative* starting point" (306, emphasis added). Indeed, in the 1960s, a debate raged in Israel over the very possibility of designating a diaspora as an attractive space, as a choice in contrast to the traditional designation of enforced exile. This semantic debate underscored an intense ideological struggle that permeated political and daily life. The national (Zionist) identity of Israel was challenged by the recognition that Jews may live outside Israel by choice and not coercion. If the images evoked by exile are of suffering, Western and especially American Jewish prosperity did not qualify. This new national autonomous space, a "newly discovered" political reality (Jewish communal memory often considers events of the last century as recent) forced Zionism to ponder its official and widespread belief that Jewish exile resulted from a lack of choice, notwithstanding historical or political reality. Despite significant antecedents, it was only following Israel's independence in 1948 that Zionists faced the necessity of revising their attitudes and understanding of Jewish global dispersion. A working usage emerged which constructed an "ideal type" dichotomy: exile connoted suffering, a negative term evoking displacement, refugee status, and above all the myth of an eventual, and possibly soon, return. In contrast, diaspora came to mean a chosen geography and identity. Exile was largely revered for the cultural stamina of the exiled, their constant loyalty to the historical memory of the communal life, rejection of assimilation, and struggle for authenticity and sacrifice. In contrast, the Jewish diaspora has been envied for its material success and simultaneously denigrated as selfish and failing to contribute to the general good. Building on Jewish guilt, Israeli leaders criticized their brethren in the West, primarily the United States, for succumbing to the temptation of the sirens. Jews who reveled in an affluent (and not so affluent) diaspora were castigated as denying their essential group identity. This was not a manipulated state ideology in the service of foreign policy but a deeply felt national identity, defined as much by those included in the group as those who decided to exclude themselves. Thus Amos Oz, a preeminent Israeli writer, on his numerous lecture tours in the United States, criticized his Jewish audience for not migrating to Israel, for remaining an "audience" instead of joining the "actors" of Jewish history: climb on the stage, he admonished them, migrate to Israel. (In Hebrew the two actions are one verb.) As the conflict with the Palestinians intensified, the Zionist self-justification was further undermined by the unwillingness of Jews around the world to migrate to Israel. The very identity of the nation seemed to be at stake. If exile had been an infliction, diaspora was viewed as a privilege, a solution, a wrong solution, an excess of pleasure which victims cannot afford, not even to witness others enjoying it. This *nonnormative predicament* is engaged throughout the essays in this volume.

The importance of the concept of "diaspora" as an explanatory paradigm stems from its malleable qualities given that it can apply to diverse communities. Dissociated from the historical experiences of a defined group of people, it becomes a universal nomenclature applicable to displaced groups of people. The idea of "diaspora" also creates a "nonnormative" intellectual community, one experienced by numerous contemporary cultural critics and with which they can identify. A global middle voice emerges in the postcolonial context which incorporates the critic as the participant-subject of the discourse on identity. As personal narratives go beyond the autobiographical, they become indispensable guarantors of a theoretical field without a priori borders. Diaspora is a culture without a country, ironically, the exact antithesis of the internal coherence and integration implied by the notion of national culture. Diaspora is about choice. At a political level, the choice is manifested by adopting a voice, which even though ambivalent and fragmented can provide the tools that may serve to dismantle the enduring relations of colonialism. The postcolonial diasporas from Asia, Africa, the Caribbean, and the Americas inhabiting the cities of Europe and the United States by their very desatellized status pose a challenge to the perpetuation of oppressive political and economic structures. The restoration of a collective sense of identity and historical agency in the home country may well be mediated through the diaspora. We know, for instance, that the devastated economies of some Third World countries have been rescued from total disintegration by remittances from the diaspora.

Recognizing the political stakes of diasporic identity, we have chosen in this volume to approach the concepts of borders, exile, and diaspora primarily as themes in literary representations. The essays combine the poetic with the political, while probing the existential consequences of displacement and cultural dislocation. They compel us to examine within a dialogical complex antagonistic but concurrent phenomena endowed with their own internal logic. Rather than a closed structure with finite borders, this collection serves as a canvas reflecting the open-ended, discontinuous, and syncretic nature of the postmodern experience. Rather than finite answers, the essays provide aleatory responses to questions of culture, identity, and language embedded in modern history.

The organizing principle of this volume is an appreciation for complex plural cultures and human experiences. The questions of borders, exile, and diaspora are examined from different personal, political, linguistic, and ideological perspectives. Most of the essays are anchored in the historically determined context of the postcolonial world. Such a presentation begs the question of the place of such a collection vis-à-vis the notion of *grands récits* and metanarratives in which the West has sought to universalize its own experience. Our multifocal approach runs counter to the logic of a hegemonic discourse and surely is not an ornamental attitude that complacently ratifies the status quo, whatever fashionable slant there is today in the celebration of alterity, diaspora, or hybridity (a most frightening word!). We sought to capture the contours of a real or imagined postmodern world in which the ideas of margins and center are simultaneously intertwined and contrasted. In their cognitive strategies, postcolonial and identity theories underlying the essays seem to indicate that all narratives contain silences.

The silences in this volume are in part a matter of selection, at times fortuitous, and to some extent a result of space limitation. Hence the very principle of openness upon which this volume is predicated is somewhat thwarted. We hope that these silences will be viewed as creative, forcing the imagination to draw connections between the essays and other unnamed problematics. Improvisation, repetition, and bricolage seem to be the preferred operational modes of being and creating examined in the essays. "The truth" of the collective endeavor lies in the diversity of experiences contemplated through the prism of race, class, and gender. We invite the reader to explore these issues through our decentered perspective, although we are sure that alternative readings will illuminate the zones of reality and meanings we have left in the dark.

The title of Part I, "Pleasures of Exile," is borrowed from George Lamming's book of essays on the Caribbean condition of uprootedness. As this title suggests, there is a basic irony in the experience of exile which implies at once disconnection and reconnection, gains and losses, screams and laughter. Exile, real or metaphorical, forced or voluntary, is built on anguish, dispossession. But the essays in this section also show that exile carries a potential for salvation as the hope of a possible future instills the urge to speak and reappropriate history. We begin in the abyss.

Why should one give up the anonymity of exile for a German identity and home? The singularity of the German identity is its connection with the evil of the Holocaust. Can it be rejected and then cleansed and sought after? Angelika Bammer in her autobiographical essay embraces Germanness first as a burden of guilt and oppression. She struggles to distance herself from the very identity she is searching for and from its despotic urgency. She seeks to reappropriate and transcend history so as not to be imprisoned only by shame. In David Brenner's essay Germanness is displayed as a fractured identity in which nation, ethnicity, and gender dissolve into nothingness. N. O. Body, the transgendered protagonist of Karl M. Baer's novel, is transformed from a professing self-hater into a willful commodity as he assumes, in his alienated position, an identity that cashes in on xenophobia. A similar gender destabilization intertwined with alienation and political disempowerment informs Reinaldo Arenas's journey from Cuba through Florida to New York to suicide. As Ricardo Ortíz shows in his essay, the existential choice, which is a lack of choice, culminates in Arenas's ultimate sense of imprisonment. The choice exile presents is a facade, an illusory salvation that leads to death.

If the confrontation with injustice or past evil is difficult, the subject positioning of liberal humanitarians within oppressive systems is too fraught with contradictions. Jane Hotchkiss examines the concept of double-consciousness in the work of Doris Lessing and highlights the connection between narrative strategy, white liberal ideology, and colonial oppression. In the postapartheid era, Lessing's voice as a "critic" can be interpreted as that of an "accomplice" and her stories as an apology for "the system." As the critical and the political framework shifts, the text takes on a new meaning, which calls into question the ideological premises of white liberalism. The specificity of the critique underscores the problematic embedded in the instability of home and borders, where identity and politics collide. The liberation of South Africa from white hegemony was predicated, after all, on the recovery of a "useful" past, a different past.

In the socioeconomic matrix of the United States, the experience of exile and diaspora is lived differently and cannot be generalized. In spite of the persistent cult worship of the melting pot idea in the dominant discourse, centripetal forces have led to the affirmation of diversity in the field of culture. Catherine Portuges in her essay shows how the omnivorous Hollywood

ELAZAR BARKAN AND MARIE-DENISE SHELTON

culture, which has globalized identities for decades, was itself shaped by its multiethnic communities effacing the distinctions between the local and the global. For the Central Europeans who came to California in the 1940s, Hollywood had become a home, a global home, always on the border between kitsch and denial. Here the useful past that opens the door to success is a repressed past.

If, for European Jews, immigration meant new opportunities, for the African diaspora life in the United States has historically been characterized by limitations and disfranchisement. A couple of miles away from the Hollywood evoked by Portuges, and a world apart, African Americans in South Central Los Angeles affirm their diasporic presence through a distinct network of cultural codes and subcodes. Culture is in language, food, art, and the reappropriation of something that was already there: the African memory. In her essay, Leslie Rabine examines the dynamics of African American culture in the improvisation of an African-based dressing style. Through the lenses of her camera, Rabine sees the vividly colored African garb and kente cloth as a defiant response to an oppressive history. The appropriation of African traditions and the concomitant desire for "authentic origins" express a yearning for a community, a home. Wearing African dress is not only exotic. It is a political gesture and a symbolic practice. Beyond the artificiality of style, the Afrocentric dresser, a legitimate heir of negritude, poses as an agent of black consciousness. Rabine argues that the politics of black identity in its performative aspects defies the narrow confines of white cultural theory.

Part II, "Modernist Transgressions," explores the notion of the diaspora and the border as a central experience of modern existence. The absence of the home as manifested through language and evident as mimesis is placed at the core of the modernist, postmodernist dilemma. Daniel Herwitz in his essay examines the rhetorical processes by which Wittgenstein attempts to bring words back home and Tyrus Miller brings into focus Walter Benjamin's formulation of a "hedonistic" view of mimesis. In both instances, silence and othering are presented as possibilities that exist only in relation to an accepted, if unavailable, reality. In her essay, Erin Carlston examines Paul Celan's use of the language of the perpetrators to describe the indescribable, to bring forth the aesthetic of poetry in the age of destruction. Celan wrote in German but saw language as the "only one thing [that] remained reachable, close and secure amid all losses." This is an act of reappropriation and also of defiance that can be understood only as mimesis. This use of language and replication carries risks that become especially poignant because the political referent is the physical extermination of the group that is at the center of the absence postulated by the language. Such is the case when the "jews" are a category but also a people, a mimesis of the Jews, of diaspora, of modernity. Marx, for example, a century earlier, sought the real "jew" at the expense of negating the experience of the living Jews.[6] In her essay on Edmond Jabès, Joan Brandt uncovers the troubling affinity between the Nazi description of the Jews as essentially "infinitely mimetic beings" and Jean-François Lyotard's claims that the "jews" signify unnamable otherness. Such affinity underscores the necessity for historical specificity and the risk embedded in global naming.

The modernist project of self-construction is a performance that takes diverse forms. It is certainly marked by the desire to return to the rhythms of a lived, historical past. In a certain way, it also reflects a desire to experience an immemorial present. Deculturation, voyage, and identification with a foreign Other are requisites for this aesthetic pleasure. The tension of reconciliation, of building anew in the midst of death, of diaspora as a model morbid industry, is the very experience that permeates the postcolonial world. In a nonsymmetrical manner, the postcolonial inability to locate an autochthonous identity was anticipated by the modernist appropriation of the exotic and the primordial. Miller describes this in his analysis of how Benjamin bridges the legacy of French ethnography and sociology with the sacred collective behavior and its mimetic faculty, and Renée Hubert locates it in Antonin Artaud's surrealism and escape to exoticism. In both cases, modernist primitivism refuses to identify itself with the primordial construct.

Although it is patently clear that diaspora, borders, and exiles do not lend themselves to a coherent reading, the search for a home produces an anxiety that translates into a yearning for a metanarrative. Home in this case could be language (Wittgenstein), god or the Golem (Celan), or a first order of reality from which one can discuss and transcend the mimesis of the simulacrum (Benjamin, Wittgenstein, Lyotard, Jabès, Artaud). Do these stories indeed produce a global category? The shared experience is of a home that is defined by its absence, a theme expansive enough to embrace global vicissitudes but one that ought not to replace specificities with abstract categories. It is only to be expected that diasporas, borders, and exiles will increase their spell on the contemporary imagination as individuals and communities with multiple identities continuously search for absent homes, homes that exist only in the search itself.

Part III, "Colonial and Postcolonial Encounters," shifts the focus to the ambivalent nature of "transgressive discourse" and cultural resistance in light of theories of representation and identity. Even though dealt with summarily, the complex sociocultural implications of colonialism loom large. The seven essays found in this section analyze conflicts between dominant and oppressed groups in different parts of the world from a variety of perspectives.

Françoise Lionnet examines the current debate in France on immigration and the paradoxes of liberalism's encounters with racism and xenophobia. Through a collection of posters published in France between 1968 and 1988, Lionnet reveals the contradictory nature of purportedly antiracist images and the false "oppositional consciousness" they create. While they extol the value of multiculturalism against the ethnocentric idea of "Frenchness," these images to a large extent reinforce racist stereotypes and the demonization of the foreign "other."

The objectification of colonial subject by the West Orientalist gaze is the subject of two other essays. Anne Donadey shows how the French-Algerian novelist Leïla Sebbar attempts to subvert and transcend the gaze of the other by using his own language and translating his fantasies. Expressing at times a desire for "nostalgic, imaginary return to a prehegemonic world," Sebbar chooses to construct her "imagined community" with fragments, scraps of cultures. In Emily Haddad's essay, the clash of culture leads to tragic misunderstandings and death. In the encounter between the Egyptian and the French, race, nationality and gender confound power relations between colonized and colonizer. Haddad describes how in Sulaymān Fayyāḍ's *Voices* the colonial categorization of people as "us" and "them" has fatal consequences. The colonial space is the theater of violent racial and cultural collision and the source of profound existential malaise. The colonial subject seems condemned to "dwell in-between border, in-between identities." In the pathology of colonialism, there are no innocent oppressors. As Walter Putnam shows in his essay on Jean-Marie Le Clézio's *Etoile errante* (Wandering star), as exile becomes the paradigmatic existence, it often negates the possibility for justice. Dig deep enough and the victor is also a victim, a refugee, in one generation or the next. Death and mourning characterize seemingly endless wars. The home identity becomes its own mourning.

The necessity to define oneself against a hostile hegemonic culture is a source of great anxiety for the postcolonial communities. Questions of voice and language intersect with ideological and political concerns in a balancing act that can be interpreted dialectically as both affirmative and antagonistic. The works analyzed in this section are "métissé texts" which reflect the violence of the historical events that constituted them, thereby challenging certain postulates of contemporary theories of "hybridity." In her essay on

Michelle Cliff, Wendy Walters examines the political and spiritual journey of the displaced Caribbean subject seeking her identity and participation. The diasporic self remains divided but succeeds in reclaiming political agency. The return home is fraught with uncertainty, yet it is a vital condition of existence. There are several ways to translate the postcolonial and postmodern predicament. In his essay, Ronald Bush analyzes it in terms of teratology, comparing Salman Rushdie's experience of exile with the monstrous avatars in the imaginary worlds of Mary Shelley and James Joyce. The political and personal ramifications of Rushdie's literary choice have been enormous and have revealed in a most dramatic way the unexpected fault lines that today striate the surface of the global village. In her essay, Rena Potok considers the situation of Palestinian-Israeli writers who use Hebrew to express their Arab identity. It is a question of the double homeland of language as the writer enriches the language of the "master" with the words and the voices of another home/nation. The choice is political, offering ambivalence as a form of self-empowerment.

From a certain perspective, the experience of displacement and exile can be interpreted as embittering, frustrating, and morbid. From another standpoint, the challenge of fusing or living between different worlds, languages, cultures, and identities is a rich experience. This volume illustrates the broad range of literary and philosophical responses to the centripetal forces of modern history. Diaspora, exiles, or borders offer no generalized definition of the contemporary reality. After all, race, class, gender, and power relations taught us to shy away from reductive explicative schemes. And yet the imagination finds a certain freedom and newness in juxtaposing the memory and identity of such diverse experiences and myriad peoples all in search of home away from home.

NOTES

1. Marie-Thérèse Colimon-Hall, *Le chant des sirènes* (Port-au-Prince, Haiti: Editions du Soleil, 1979), p. 33 (editors' translation).

2. Homer, *The Odyssey*, trans. W. H. D. Rouse (New York: New American Library, 1937), p. 138.

3. Michelle Cliff, *No Telephone to Heaven* (New York: E. P. Dutton, 1987), p. 87.

4. Ibid., pp. 192–93.

5. James Clifford, "Diasporas," *Cultural Anthropology* (Aug. 1994): 305. Hereafter page references are given in the text.

6. Karl Marx, "On the Jewish Question" (1843), in *The Marx-Engels Reader*, ed. Robert Tucker (New York: Norton, 1972), pp. 26–52.

PART I

Pleasures of Exile

1. The Dilemma of the "But"

Writing Germanness After
the Holocaust

*In the spring of 1987 an exhibit entitled "Auschwitz: A Crime Against Mankind,"
co-organized by the Auschwitz State Museum and the International Auschwitz
Committee and sponsored by the United Nations Center for Human Rights, was
brought to Emory University. It was set up in the large, open-space gallery on
the entrance level of Emory's Woodruff Memorial Library. My parents were visiting from Germany that spring, and I suggested that we go to the exhibit together. We met by the entrance to the Schatten Gallery, next to the counter where
book bags are checked as people exit the library. As we were standing there, a
woman with a name tag on her lapel came up and introduced herself to us as
one of the volunteer docents from the Atlanta Jewish women's community.
"Would you like me to take you around the exhibit?" she asked, smiling. I was
about to say, "Yes, thank you, we would like that," when my father answered first.
Flushed with embarrassment, looking down and fumbling with his coat, he said,
"But, we are German." "Oh," our docent answered, "that's all right. . . . Where
are you from?" And, after a short pause, "How do you like Atlanta?" "We are
from Bonn," my father said, and, "yes, we like Atlanta a lot, particularly in the
spring . . . the dogwood . . . and the beautiful azaleas . . ."*

*And then my father, my mother, and I walked with our guide through the
Auschwitz exhibit.*

I shall begin with the dilemma of this "but" ("But we are German"). But it
is the generosity of the "all right" to which I want to respond and to which
my work and this piece here are dedicated.

In his essay "Education after Auschwitz," first read as an address over West
German radio in April 1966 (half a year after the three-year-long trial in
Frankfurt of SS-camp personnel from Auschwitz was finally brought to an
end),[1] Theodor W. Adorno asked what education should mean and what it
could achieve in a Germany after Auschwitz. The goal was clear enough: to

prevent such barbarism from ever happening again. The means to this end, he proposed, were, first, understanding what makes human beings capable of such acts and then learning to recognize the impulses toward such acts *before* they are committed. Such a politics — learning to see, in ourselves and each other, the moves that would enable us to deny the humanity of a person cast as an other to our selves — is what Adorno, in "Education after Ausch-witz," described as a *"Wendung aufs Subjekt"* ("subjective turn"): a politics that engages the self in a process of critical self-reflection.

In light of the resurgence of racist, xenophobic, and anti-Semitic violence in postunification Germany, it would seem as if Adorno's exhortation had fallen on deaf ears. In the early 1990s, as reports of harassment, beatings, and finally killings of people perceived as "foreign" — as ones who "didn't be-long"[2] — became regular, numbing news, the racist nationalism of the new right-wing extremism became all too evident. By 1993, the firebombings of hostels, asylums, and even suburban housing where so-called *Ausländer*[3] lived had left between 30 and 40 women, children, and men dead[4] and spread a pall of racialized terror over Germany. A new list of names — Hoyerswerda, Greifswald, Rostock, Mölln, Eisenhüttenstadt, and Solingen — could be added to the historical map of German shame.[5] This essay looks at some of the reasons why the education that Adorno called for had not taken effect in order to consider what we could do differently. I begin, very simply, with the grammatical subject of my last clause, to ask who this "we" refers to. In short, my questions here turn on how we name and position ourselves as German. Or how we don't. My concern is with the effects of these positionings.

An early explanation for Germans' apparent inability after the Holocaust to engage in a politics of critical self-reflection was advanced by Alexander and Margarete Mitscherlich in *The Inability to Mourn*, published a year after Adorno's "Education after Auschwitz." Drawing on Sigmund Freud's distinc-tion between mourning and melancholia, they proposed that as long as Ger-mans as individuals and the German people as a whole were unwilling to acknowledge that their relationship to National Socialism was marked by desire and narcissistically cathected love, they would never be free to put it past them: "Mourning is a psychic process in which the individual comes to terms with a loss" (Mitscherlich and Mitscherlich 1990:10). Germans had dreamed, after all, of a glorious thousand-year Reich; they had hailed a pow-erful Führer. To the extent that they denied this libidinal investment and were thus unable to own a sense of loss, the Mitscherlichs maintained, they would remain immobilized in a state of melancholia.[6]

In August 1990, after the borders have opened up, I go with my father to Czechoslovakia. We are going to visit the places in northern Bohemia and around Prague where he was born and had grown up, places that had been home until his family, along with the other ethnic Germans in these parts, was expelled in 1945. For him it is a trip to the home he had lost when Germany lost the war. For me it is a trip to foreign places — Rumburg, Leitmeritz, and Schönlinde (or, as they are now called, Rumburk, Litoměřice, and Krasná Lípa) — I had had trouble even finding on the map when we were planning our itinerary. In the car, we talk about home and I mention the sense of loss I sometimes have because "home" is a concept for me that has no place on the map. His response is cutting. He hadn't realized, he remarks, that I was so attached to my German identity; maybe he had failed me by not being more nationalistically German. "It has nothing to do with nationalism," I try to explain. But his response has put worlds of distance between him and me; I no longer know how to say what I actually did mean.

A few years later, during a visit to Bonn, I come closer to the words and the meaning of the loss that, back then, had left me confused and speechless. My parents have rediscovered the letters my father had written my mother during the war and they are reading them aloud. They are embarrassed — and surprised ("We didn't think you'd be interested," they say) — when I ask if I can join them and listen. But they willingly agree. It is difficult for all of us: for me to listen, for them to read. They are ashamed at the ignorance and oblivion of their past selves; they are worried about and afraid of my judgment. I am overwhelmed by the emotional unseemliness of it all. Sitting there, in my parents' living room, beside my mother on the couch, I struggle to take in what these letters are about: love letters from my father, a German soldier, a young man, letters written between 1941 and 1944 to my mother, his bride, a young woman who was not yet twenty when they met in 1941. I am touched and unsettled by the nostalgia that seeps in, past the censors of our critical postwar politics. I see it softening their faces with memories of their young lives and loves and I feel it in myself as I find myself wanting for them what they wanted then: life, happiness, and a future. "But we are German," I think, and my feelings seem shameful to admit as I am haunted by horror-filled memories of the lives and futures that Germans had destroyed.

I am stunned by what the letters say and by what they leave out as I listen to my father read of his patriotic acceptance of the war and his manly duty as a soldier, his love of Heimat (homeland); his romantic fantasies of marriage, family, and home. But as I listen to my father reading, I am stunned even more by the depth of the break between the young man he once was and the old man he has become, compelled to reject or disbelieve some of the most vital beliefs and dreams that his idealism had earlier been fueled by. I realize then that the sharpness of his earlier rejoinder to me on the issue of home ("maybe I should *have been more nationalistic") was marked by the sharpness of his break with this young self, with the young German man who had once believed in the right-ness of his world and the place he was proud to assume in it. It was the loss of that belief, I understood, that both of us felt. Yet we felt it differently, and this difference was one for which we had no words: he as a loss he could not acknowl-edge as loss; I as a never felt possibility.*

In her introduction to the first edition of *Showing Our Colors: Afro-German Women Speak Out* (1986), Audre Lorde traces the destructive trajectory of this denial of loss and its displacement onto guilt to the scene of contempo-rary antiracist politics. "Too often," she notes,

I have met an immobilizing national guilt in white German women which serves to keep them from acting upon what they profess to believe. . . . Because they seem unable to accept who they are, these women too often fail to examine and pursue the powers relative to their identity. . . . Four decades after National Socialism, the ques-tion still lingers for many white German women: how can I draw strength from my roots when those roots are entwined in such a terrible history?

The self-imposed impotence that lies in the "terror of self-scrutiny," Lorde argues, is a waste of energy that we collectively cannot afford, particularly at a time when "the battles against racism, antisemitism, heterosexism, xeno-phobia" demand the most vigilant and energetic intervention (Lorde 1992: viii).[7]

The irony, of course (an irony that is the subject of Freud's essay "On Negation"), is that the *not* dealing with oneself, the repression that the Mitscherlichs analyzed in national terms, is merely the unacknowledged in-verse of an obsessive absorption with that very self. Self-denial is a narcissistic variant.

In August 1990 my father and I spend a few days in Rumburk, the small city in the northeastern corner of Bohemia where my father spent the better part of his childhood and youth until he left to go to Prague University. We stay with a childhood friend of his, Helmut Stein; I sit and listen to the two old men discuss the present and reminisce about the past. Listening to my father, I am struck again by something I have noticed before but never stopped to think about much: the insistence with which he likes to position himself outside the category "Ger-man." "Those Germans," he often says disgustedly, as if he — and I — were not one of them. On an outing to a popular resort area outside of Rumburk we stop at a local restaurant for lunch. Frau Stein, who is Czech, passes on to us a comment by the waitress about "how awful those Germans are" (meaning, pre-sumably, not us but a party of Germans in the adjacent room who have pushed two tables together so they can sit as a group). My father agrees with her assess-

ment. I want to disagree. The group at the large table seems well-mannered and respectful enough, I think. "What's so awful about pushing two tables together?" I ask, knowing full well that this isn't about tables. Yet I am angry over the distancing gesture on my father's part. If Germans are "they," what is he? What am I? What is he to me? What are we to the world and can it be that we are each something different?

Later, reflecting on this incident, I am struck by the historical irony of the fact that my generation seems to have inherited the uncertainty that the generation before us ought to have, the questions and the nonanswers. We — the postwar, post-Holocaust generation — find it hard to place and name ourselves as Germans. Yet the history we inherited makes it hard to escape that place and name.

This, then, is the dilemma of the "but." And its consequences? Central among them is that our difficulty in dealing with our Germanness stands in the way of responding without embarrassment to anyone who calls us by that name or any issue that positions us in that identity. In particular, in Germany after 1945 the dilemma of Germanness has stood in the way of speaking about and acknowledging Jewishness. As the historian Frank Stern documents in *The Whitewashing of the Yellow Badge: Antisemitism and Philosemitism in Postwar Germany* (1992), in the self-absorption of German guilt Jews were effaced once again. Yet the need to ignore something means that extraordinary attention must be paid to that which is supposed to go unnoticed. What we must deny of necessity becomes a perversely obsessive focus of attention. This was the very point that Rainer Werner Fassbinder tried to make in his case for the staging of his play *Garbage, the City and Death*. He insisted that the play should be performed in Frankfurt so that the questions it raised about the city's German-Jewish history could be discussed openly and in public. Yet the perceived anti-Semitism of the play, which was scheduled to be performed in Frankfurt in 1975, provoked such a storm of protest that the city administration canceled the production and Suhrkamp press withdrew the already published text from print. It has never been publicly performed in Germany or, to my knowledge, anywhere else. "When you create a taboo you get a backlash," Fassbinder pointed out, and the reception of his work made his point (1992:19).[8] If Jewishness is made taboo, the ground for anti-Semitism is prepared; if it is national identity, nationalist reaction is predictable.

My argument, therefore, is that we need to own — not deny — being German as the ground for a progressive politics. Progressive intellectuals, people on what we have historically thought of as the Left, cannot afford to cede the terrain of Germanness to the Right while they disclaim affiliation. If Germanness with all that it entails—national identity, a sense of tradition, affiliation with a historical community—is relegated to the Right, then the Left can only situate itself negatively. This is perhaps one of the areas in which the legacy of Marxism, with its insistence on *inter*nationalism as an anti-nationalist move, has left the Left most pathetically, indeed dangerously, unequipped to counter the powerful rallying force of calls for national, regional, and ethnic identities.[9] To a large extent our responses to these positions are still drawn from the polarized politics of the period between the two twentieth-century world wars, in which the alternatives were presented oppositionally: either reactionary nationalism or progressive internationalism. While the Right staked its claim to *Heimat*, the Left opted for or was forced into transcendental (and often literal) homelessness.[10]

In the shadow of the catastrophic wars unleashed in the name of national interests, such a stance has an undeniably compelling force. Yet, equally clearly, the Left/Right polarization of the 1920s and 1930s no longer holds sway now. (Nor, looking back, was it particularly functional in its own time.) In this light, Ernst Bloch's reinscription, in *The Principle of Hope*, of *Heimat* cannot be dismissed as just the regressive nostalgia of a diasporic dream for it is also the concretely utopian recognition of people's need for a place where they belong and are connected to traditions of community. Even Virginia Woolf follows her famous antinationalist credo in *Three Guineas* ("As a woman, I have no country. As a woman I want no country. As a woman my country is the whole world") with an evocative recognition of the emotional pull of what Bloch calls *Heimat*, of the fact that "when reason has had its say, still some obstinate emotion remains, some love of England" (Woolf 1966:109). Or, could we imagine it, Germany?

Within a paradigm in which claiming Germanness was tainted as nationalistic, the progressive alternative was either to become something else or to be as distinctly non-German as possible. In the context of post-Holocaust Germany this alternative also provided a convenient way around the *Vergangenheitsbewältigung* quandary, the injunction to "deal with the past." To motivation (one didn't want to be German) was added an argument (one didn't have to be German), and a solution emerged: one took on a non-German identity. Both the West German new Left and feminist movements of the 1970s and early 1980s present interesting case studies in this regard as their identificatory projections, their icons, and, in some cases, causes (contemporary Palestinians, nineteenth-century Native Americans) mapped out loci of identification—non-German victims of oppression—at a striking double remove from the very position in which their advocates found themselves: postwar/post-Holocaust Germanness.[11]

Such a stance is problematic in several ways, not least in its implications for the kind of communicative ethics that social theorists such as Jürgen Habermas insist is the necessary foundation of a truly democratic public sphere. If I am German, yet disclaim Germanness as a place from which to speak, how can I address issues of national history and politics? When I consign myself either to silence or to some form of appropriation (speaking as or for someone else), dialogue becomes all but impossible. If I can't — or won't — speak for myself, how can I speak with a you? How — as whom — would I listen?

This is precisely the dilemma that Frank Stern charts in his essay "Jews in the Minds of Germans in the Postwar Period." At issue, as Stern sees it, is what he describes as "antagonistic memories": a response to history in which, he claims, "serious attention to the experience of the Jewish people with German politics in the 20th century is less on the German agenda today than ever before . . . [while] an ongoing concern with the brutal nature of this experience is and will remain for generations to come on the Jewish agenda" (1993:5). The reluctance of non-Jewish Germans, even (indeed often particularly) in Left intellectual circles, to deal with German Jewish history or contemporary German Jewish concerns has been all the more striking because this same reluctance has traditionally not been at play when it involved their response to other others. To return to my example above, Palestinians or Native Americans were the perfect others in this regard because they were, first, distinctly not German (in ways that Jews could never be), and second, oppressed in ways that did not immediately engage Germanness.[12] Exceptions to this rule — like the characters in Fassbinder's works — have been accordingly and not surprisingly controversial.[13]

One response to the imbalance that Stern maps out along a German/ Jewish axis is obviously to try to right it. Non-Jewish Germans could be more responsive to the concerns and experiences of Jewish people, beginning with Jews in Germany. Such a response is not only called for, but, two generations after the Holocaust, long overdue. Indeed, the "German fascination with things Jewish" (Zipes 1994) that has recently come to the fore in response to the reemergence of Jewish culture in postunification Germany, is no doubt an attempt to do just that.[14] Yet to be "fascinated" with things Jewish is not enough. Even to be attentive to Jewish life in Germany, both as part of German culture and as a minority culture of its own, does not suffice. The response of non-Jewish Germans to Jews in Germany and German Jews must

21

also be part of a critical engagement with Germanness, with the ways in which this category of identification has been constructed and deployed (culturally, ethnically, racially, and in terms of citizenship) and an understanding of how German/Jewish history has been mapped along the fault lines of this shifting referent. For within German history Germanness and Jewishness have been positioned as simultaneously separate and conjoined, contingent categories that have been inclusive and exclusive of each other at the same time. To look at one has inevitably meant to find the other in one's view, while to avoid either has meant to avert one's gaze from both.

Which brings me back to the dilemma that Germanness presents for progressive German intellectuals and the problematic effects of the averted gaze, the attempt to resolve the dilemma by ignoring it. The critical impulse underlying this strategy is in many ways unassailable, of course, grounded as it is, on the one hand, in the postmodern disbelief in the solidity of identity categories and, on the other, in the equally fundamental suspicion of the manipulative power dynamics inherent in identity politics. Some, like Judith Butler, even argue that this play of unequal power is inherent in the very category of the subject itself as we have conventionally used it: "The subject is constructed through acts of differentiation that distinguish the subject from its constitutive outside, a domain of abjected alterity" (1995:46). Nevertheless, the dilemma remains of needing to come to terms with a given identity even as, or before, one deconstructs it.

This dilemma is perhaps nowhere as evident as in the German case, where the need to come to terms with one's history and the need to deconstruct the identity category by which that history is defined seem so relentlessly in conflict. Frank Stern gives an example of the problem when he describes the imbalance between the attention given German issues from a Jewish perspective and the lack of attention given Jewish concerns from a German perspective, particularly by Germans who have antinationalistically repudiated Germanness. This dynamic, of course, cannot be read only in post-Holocaust terms; it is also informed by the ways Enlightenment ideas of assimilation and emancipation emphasized — indeed, decreed, at a price — the nonotherness of these two identities (a nonotherness perceptually belied, I might add, by the common use of the conjunctive formula "Germans and Jews"). Nevertheless, a twofold task remains: tracing both the differences (in historical memory, lived experience, and cultural positioning) that the conjunction at once erases and inscribes and the commonalities that link us to each other as an uncannily othered same, a historical rendering of Freud's *"Unheimliche."* [15]

This cannot be done, I believe, without a traversal of subjectivity, a *"Wendung aufs Subjekt,"* to return to Adorno's formulation. For me — born into a German, non-Jewish family after the Holocaust and war — this has meant a coming home of sorts to the cultural and familial worlds I left behind when I left Germany, years ago, as a young woman. It is an attempt to write Germanness through an awareness of the exclusions structured into the category that names me: "German." It is an attempt to retrace and, in the process, undo some of the ways these exclusions have been manipulated. It is an attempt, in short, to avoid either conflating the two (Germanness *as* otherness) or opposing them (Germanness *versus* otherness) so as to approach the one through a historical traversal of the other, to understand them together, relationally.

It is in this regard that (perhaps incongruously, at first glance) some of the work being done in the field of postcolonial cultural studies has been particularly helpful to me in my attempt to reconceptualize Germanness. For though there is nothing postcolonial about the German situation per se (apart from the obvious ways in which all of Europe, or even most of the world, can be defined as postcolonial these days), postcolonial cultural studies offer a way of talking about national and cultural identities that points a way out of the dilemma of rejection or affirmation sketched out above.

Although much contemporary work on identity politics and ethnicity has tended to favor affirmative gestures of restoration, postcolonial cultural studies have modeled a counternostalgic move in which identity categories are denaturalized. From this perspective, cultural identity is understood not as given in some essential way (the expression of a national soul or character) but rather as developed in the course of a history in which the terms of this identity are worked out, both internally and in relation to external others. Postcolonial understanding of national and cultural identities is thus predicated on the belief that they are the result of a historically negotiated process and can, therefore, only be understood relationally. Moreover, to the extent that both the categories of analysis and the historical perspective of postcolonial cultural studies are directly informed by the colonial experience to which they are (definitionally, at least) "post," they also begin with the assumption that these relational terms are inherently and in multiple ways unequal. For the historical point of departure is the relationship between colony and empire, in which the one is made subject to the other's rule. At the same time, as Edward Said points out, the "discrepant experiences" of these dominant and subordinated groups eventually overlap and intertwine, forming in the process "contrapuntal ensembles" (1993:31–61). This sameness in difference exposes the notion of static and autonomous cultural identities as fiction, if not deceit: Frenchness is as informed by its relationship to Algeria, in other words, as is Algerianness by its involvement in French history. "We are . . . *of* the connections, not outside and beyond them," Said notes (p. 55).[16]

Said's concept of discrepant experiences that form contrapuntal ensembles maps cultural identity as an inherently contested site: even as we claim, indeed are assigned, a particular subject position ("Germanness," say), the meaning of this position is (re)negotiated continuously. As a result, as Homi Bhabha explains, our relationship to such an identity cannot but be fundamentally ambivalent: "Identification is a process of identifying with and through another object, an object of otherness, at which point the agency of identification — the subject — is itself always ambivalent, because of the intervention of that otherness" (Bhabha and Rutherford 1990:211). Given this condition of hybridity, which Bhabha defines as the recognition that "cultures are only constituted in relation to that otherness internal to their own symbol-forming activity which makes them decentred structures," we can no longer take refuge in the essentialist illusion of a "prior given original or originary culture" (pp. 210–11). Our relationship to ourselves, in terms of cultural identity, is inherently divided, "split at the root." [17]

When one considers not only the centrality of German/Jewish relations to German history but also the multiple, self-contradictory, and constantly shifting meanings of Germanness itself, it is not difficult to see the usefulness of analytical models such as those advanced by Bhabha and Said for theorizing German identity. For "German" can be a category of citizenship, an ethnocultural inheritance, or a racial ascription; it can be one or the other or all at different times. It can be used to *exclude* actual Germans, as in the case of Nazi policies designed to enforce congruence between what had been discrepant in the past (ethnocultural, racial, and legal definitions of Germanness) that stripped Jews of their German citizenship (Brubaker 1992: 167). Or, conversely, it can be used to *confer* Germanness on people who are legal citizens of another country but defined as "German" by descent in terms of the German *ius sanguinis*. In practice, this means that I may be "German in fact" — a second- or third-generation immigrant — but be prevented, by laws and conventions, from becoming "German in law." By the same token, I may be "German in law" but not be perceived as "German in fact" because of my ethnic origin, racial markings, or culture.[18]

Colonial identities, both in the colonies and in the imperial center, were defined by geographical distance, a separation that was structurally bridged by incorporating the one into the other so that they would appear as parts of a whole: the colony was positioned metonymically in relation to the empire. One way imperial power was expressed was by control of mobility: "we" could go wherever we wanted to, "they" would go where they were told. The postcolonial condition, in turn, is marked by the end of separation through distance. As both "they" and "we" can go and be here as well as there, the regulation of mobility as a means of control has become a foregrounded issue. In this respect the German case is curiously homologous in many ways to the postcolonial situation. For one, German identity, defined not as affiliation to a state but to an ethnocultural nation, has always been marked by an inability to separate inside and outside territorially: insiders (Germans) could be outsiders (such as Czech or Polish citizens of German ethnic descent), while outsiders (nonethnic Germans) could live indefinitely inside without ever becoming insiders. As a result, German identity has been inherently bound up with the attempt to regulate internal "foreigners." The prevailing image has been that of a body (the *Volk*) in which foreign bodies (*Volksfremde*), like implants, reside, while, conversely, parts of the body itself periodically move to other bodies.[19]

In this light, Judith Butler's contention that the construction of the subject depends on "acts of differentiation that distinguish . . . [it] from its constitutive outside" must be reframed before it can be applied to German subjects. For, I would argue, in the German case, the defining structure of subject constitution is one in which the other is precisely not perceived as a "constitutive outside" but rather as a "constitutive *inside*." An analogue might be the role of blackness in the cultural construction of Americanness, say, as analyzed by Toni Morrison (1992).

On another, more directly historical, as opposed to systems theory, level, the deconstructive logic of a position like that put forth by Butler makes it difficult to claim a subject position that stands as a point of departure, if not return. And Germanness, for me, is a point of departure in this sense: something deeded to me at birth. Even as its meaning is renegotiated, it is a nonnegotiable fact. And so it is at this point of convergence and difference between Bhabha, Said, and Stern — between "antagonistic memories" and "contrapuntal ensembles," as it were — that my own investigation of Germanness in relation to its historically assumed exclusions begins.

November 1992, in Weimar and Buchenwald with my mother: In the Buchenwald museum, housed in the three-story former storage building at the far end of the Appellplatz, is a mass of material — documents and artifacts — that I can only partially take in. I hold onto details: a typed request by a woman politely asking that the ashes (already paid for) of the persons she names be sent to the above address (a Jewish cemetery), as promised. The letter, we are told, received no response. First, the murder; then, the payment for the cremated remains; then, the plea to keep a promise; then, the agony of no return.

The day has left me drained; I don't want to talk. I want to provoke, cause trouble in the smooth functioning of things, probe the feelings kept at bay under correct postures. I am undone by the despair and grief under the conventional civil forms, and I wonder when this decorum is necessary (to facilitate procedures, help us cope, or provide the thin protection of civility) and when it stifles the responses we need to free if we ever hope to interact humanly.

When we return to Weimar, I go to the Nietzsche house by myself. I am looking for the expression of a response that makes sense to me now: the inability to maintain decorum, to make things cohere, that marked the lucidity of Nietzsche's madness. I am looking, I think, for a counter to Germanness that will undo it from within. In response to the increasingly repressive drive to regulate, control, and limit access to Germanness by essentializing it in ethnic/racial terms, Friedrich Nietzsche broke with his friend and mentor, Richard Wagner. Like other compatriots before and after him, he chose transcendental homelessness, one might say, finally even abandoning his home in language. Wagner, meanwhile, made Germanness his home: building castles and monuments, cultivating German myths, wallowing in the German language.

At the same time, while I am drawn to Nietzsche and repelled by Wagner in this regard, I wonder, again, at the price such homelessness exacts. I see the pain in Nietzsche's early poetry, pressed into satire and sarcasm in his late aphoristic work, expressed in another form in his crippling and fatal illness. I think of Paul Celan, another homeless one who ultimately chose death; of Else Lasker-Schüler's unanticipated and unanswerable grief over the loss of her German Heimat in exile. And I realize that my own movement will inevitably be one back and forth, between the desire to disclaim Germanness and the need to own it at the same time: a critical engagement with its implications.

NOTES

1. On trial were 22 SS-guards from the Auschwitz concentration camp, including the camp commander. The heaviest sentence meted out was fourteen years' imprisonment for the commander in charge. Some of the accused were released with all charges lifted; others were given light sentences of several months.

2. As the mother of one young skinhead involved in an attack on a hostel for asylum-seekers in Eisenhüttenstadt (a town close to the East German–Polish border) put it, "We've got nothing against foreigners. They can come here and then go home, and that's fine. . . . But they shouldn't stay here" (Mehr and Sylvester 1992:138).

3. *Ausländer* literally means "foreigner," "noncitizen," someone coming from the "outside." Connotatively, however, in German usage, it is racially marked, typically used to refer to people living in Germany whose racial and ethnic characteristics are "not German," regardless of where they were born and grew up and even of whether they are actually German. For this reason, Jeffrey Peck proposes leaving the German term *Ausländer* untranslated. On the racial implications of the language that classifies — and ranks — different groups of people in a descending hierarchy of Germanness, see Peck (1992). For a review of the categories of "foreignness" operative in Germany today, ranging from what Dietrich Thränhardt terms "noble foreigners" to those treated as "strange" or, finally, "rejected," see Thränhardt (1989).

4. I have found it difficult to get comprehensive, and thus exact, numbers because each set of statistical data is necessarily partial. Reliable data can be found in Helsinki Watch (1992) and *Hostility Towards Foreigners* (1993).

5. For documentation and discussion of these events, see Funke (1989, 1993), Helsinki Watch (1992), *Hostility Towards Foreigners* (1993), Leggewie (1993), Nirumand (1992), and Stern (1992). For a feminist perspective on the current situation in Germany, see Hügel et al. (1993) and Lennox (1995). This is not an exhaustive list of the available literature but a suggestion of where to begin.

6. Eric Santner (1990) reviews and reengages the Mitscherlich thesis, which he sets against the antinostalgic rhetoric of postmodern critical theory, in his study of the processes of displacement and represssion that marked the cultural negotiation of (West) German identity in the 1970s and 1980s.

7. Lennox (1995) spells out some of the consequences of this stance in her analysis of the relative lack of feminist response to the escalation of racist, anti-Semitic, and xenophobic attacks in Germany in the early 1990s. As she puts it in her description of Alice Schwarzer's response to the deaths of Turkish women and girls in the firebombing attacks in Mölln and Solingen, the popular German feminist position that "Germans are men and women are victims" rhetorically exempts women from responsibility. In an earlier, as yet unpublished, essay, which is part of my book in progress, "Being German," I have examined this position and its effects at some length (see Bammer 1991).

8. Although some of his other work was no less controversial, in terms of the issues I am raising here the debate over *Garbage, the City and Death* is the most pertinent. For the text, see Fassbinder (1991). For documentation and discussion of the controversy surrounding it, see Kiderlen (1985) and the contributions by Andrei S. Markovits, Seyla Benhabib, and Moishe Postone, Gertrud Koch, and Sigrid Meuschel in the special 1986 issue of *New German Critique* on "The German-Jewish Controversy."

9. The shift from national to sub- or supranational group formations in the wake of the global disintegration of traditional nation-state structures was the subject of Eric Hobsbawm's keynote address at the 1991 annual convention of the American Anthropological Association. Both the initiatory premise and the conclusion of

Hobsbawm's talk were that people's need for identification with some larger, communal body is so basic that, postmodernist rhetoric and the transnationalization of politics, economics, and culture notwithstanding, it cannot be argued away or deconstructed. The cultural theorist who has most consistently and attentively analyzed the political consequences of people's libidinal investments in such sub- and suprastate identificatory systems as nation and ethnicity is undoubtedly Slavoj Žižek; see Žižek 1990 and 1993.

10. The return address of correspondence from T. W. Adorno and Siegfried Kracauer to Leo Löwenthal in the 1920s reads "General Headquarters of the Welfare Bureau of the Transcendentally Homeless." See Daniel (1992:32, n. 40). The concept of "transcendental homelessness" was, as Daniel notes, Georg Lukàcs's. In *Three Guineas* Virginia Woolf gave the internationalist position a gender-specific twist by positioning woman as outside nation (1966:109).

11. See Bammer (1991).

12. For a brief but compelling discussion of the relationship between Germans' relationship to Germanness and the strategy of victim identification, see Santner (1990:6).

13. Fassbinder's colleague Werner Herzog, whose concern with the disempowered (the blind, the deaf-mute, dwarves on a desert island, native peoples destroyed by modernity, and the like) is countered by his fascination with conquering heroes, offers a striking contrast in this regard. See, for example, *Even Dwarves Started Small* (1969–70), *Land of Silence and Darkness* (1970–71), and *Where the Green Ants Dream* (1980) and, for contrast, *Aguirre, Wrath of God* (1972) and *Fitzcarraldo* (1980–81).

14. For a deeply engaged and richly informed discussion of this phenomenon, see Gilman and Remmler (1994).

15. I am indebted for this formulation to Susan Shapiro, who is working on the figuration of the Jew as the quintessential embodiment of the *Unheimliche*. For a first sketch of this project, its assumptions, and possible implications, see Shapiro (1994).

16. The dialectic between master and slave described by Hegel in *The Phenomenology of Spirit* is marked by a similar relationship of differential, yet interdependent, power: the master needs the slave in order to be a master, just as the slave needs the master to be a slave. Thus both are bounded and bonded by the terms of the very structure that defines them. Said historicizes these terms in relation to colonialism and imperialism.

17. The term is Adrienne Rich's, taking from her 1983 poem "Sources," about her own hybrid Jewish-gentile-American identity. I am not using the notion of splitting in the Lacanian sense here, although Lacan's psychoanalytic paradigm and its theorizing of division and splitting as critical stages in the formation of a self have played an important role in work on identity constructions within postcolonial cultural studies, notably that of Homi Bhabha. See, for example, Bhabha 1987.

18. The distinction between being German "in fact" and "in law" is Brubaker's. See, for example, Brubaker (1992:121).

19. For a historical and systemic analysis of the strategies by which these internal separations were put in place, see Brubaker (1992). For an example of some of the more curious terms in which these separations were rhetorically cast, see Brubaker (1992:116–17).

WORKS CITED

Adorno, T. W. 1969. "Erziehung nach Auschwitz." In *Stichworte: Kritische Modelle 2*. Frankfurt: Suhrkamp.

Bammer, Angelika. 1991. "Victim Politics: Feminist Constructions in Post-Holocaust Germany." Unpublished manuscript.

Bhabha, Homi K. 1987. "Interrogating Identity." In *The Real Me? Post-Modernism and the Question of Identity*, ed. Lisa Appignanesi. ICA Documents 6. London: Institute of Contemporary Arts.

Bhabha, Homi K., and Jonathan Rutherford. 1990. "The Third Space." In *Identity: Community, Culture, Difference*, ed. Jonathan Rutherford. London: Lawrence & Wishart.

Brubaker, Rogers. 1992. *Citizenship and Nationhood in France and Germany*. Cambridge, Mass.: Harvard University Press.

Butler, Judith. 1995. "Contingent Foundations." In *Feminist Contentions: A Philosophical Exchange*, ed. Seyla Benhabib, Judith Butler, Drucilla Cornell, and Nancy Fraser. New York: Routledge.

Daniel, Jamie. 1992. "Temporary Shelter: Adorno's Exile and the Language of Home." *New Formations* 17. Special issue on "The Question of 'Home.'"

Fassbinder, Rainer Werner. 1991. "Der Müll, die Stadt und der Tod." In *Sämtliche Stücke*. Frankfurt: Verlag der Autoren. [English trans.: *Garbage, the City and Death*. In *Plays*, trans. and ed. Denis Calandra. New York: PAJ Publications, 1985.]

———. 1992. "'I've Changed Along with the Characters in My Films': A Discussion with Hella Schlumberger About Work and Love, the Exploitability of Feelings, and the Longing for Utopia." In *The Anarchy of the Imagination: Interviews, Essays, Notes*, ed. Michael Töteberg and Leo A. Lensing. Baltimore: Johns Hopkins University Press.

Funke, Hajo. 1989. *Republikaner: Rassismus, Judenfeindschaft, nationaler Grössenwahn*. 2d ed. Berlin: Aktion Sühnezeichen Friedensdienste.

———. 1993. *Brandstifter: Deutsche zwischen Demokratie und völkischem Nationalismus*. Göttingen: Lamuv.

Gilman, Sander, and Karen Remmler, eds. 1994. *Reemerging Jewish Culture in Germany: Life and Literature Since 1989*. New York: New York University Press.

Helsinki Watch. 1992. *"Foreigners Out": Xenophobia and Right-Wing Violence in Germany*. New York: Human Rights Watch.

Hostility Towards Foreigners in Germany: New Facts, Analyses, Arguments. 1993.

Bonn: Press and Information Office of the Federal Government, Foreign Affairs Division.

Hügel, Ika, Chris Lange, May Ayim, Ilona Bubeck, Gülsen Aktas, and Dagmar Schultz, eds. 1993. *Entfernte Verbindungen: Rassismus, Antisemitismus, Klassenunterdrückung.* Berlin: Orlanda Frauenverlag.

Kiderlen, Elisabeth, ed. 1985. *Deutsch-jüdische Normalität: Fassbinders Sprengsätze.* Frankfurt: Pflasterstrand.

Leggewie, Claus. 1993. *Druck von rechts: Wohin treibt die Bundesrepublik?* Munich: Beck.

Lennox, Sara. 1995. "Divided Feminism: Women, Racism, and German National Identity." *German Studies Review* 18 (Oct.): 481–502.

Lorde, Audre. 1992. "Foreword to the English Language Edition." In *Showing Our Colors: Afro-German Women Speak Out,* ed. Katharina Oguntoye, May Opitz, and Dagmar Schultz, trans. Anne Adams with Tina Campt. Amherst: University of Massachusetts Press. [German original: *Farbe bekennen. Afro-deutsche Frauen auf den Spuren ihrer Geschichte.* Berlin: Orlanda, 1986.]

Mehr, Max Thomas, and Regine Sylvester. 1992. "The Stone-thrower from Eisenhüttenstadt." *Granta* 42, Special Winter Issue on "Krauts!"

Mitscherlich, Alexander, and Margarete Mitscherlich. 1967. Reprint 1990. *Die Unfähigkeit zu trauern: Grundlagen kollektiven Verhaltens.* Leipzig: Reclam-Verlag. [English trans.: *The Inability to Mourn,* trans. Beverly R. Placzek. New York: Grove Press, 1975.]

Morrison, Toni. 1992. *Playing in the Dark: Whiteness and the Literary Imagination.* Cambridge, Mass.: Harvard University Press.

New German Critique 38 (Spring–Summer 1986). Special issue on "The German-Jewish Controversy."

Nirumand, Bahman, ed. 1992. *Angst vor den Deutschen: Terror gegen Ausländer und der Zerfall des Rechtsstaates.* Reinbek bei Hamburg: Rowohlt.

Peck, Jeffrey M. 1992. "Rac(e)ing the Nation: Is There a German 'Home'?" *New Formations* 17. Special issue on "The Question of 'Home.'"

Rich, Adrienne. 1983. *Sources.* Woodside, Calif.: Heyeck Press.

Said, Edward. 1993. *Culture and Imperialism.* New York: Knopf.

Santner, Eric. 1990. *Stranded Objects: Mourning, Memory, and Film in Postwar Germany.* Ithaca: Cornell University Press.

Shapiro, Susan. 1994. "Ecriture judaïque: Where Are the Jews in Western Discourse?" In *Displacements: Cultural Identities in Question,* ed. Angelika Bammer. Bloomington: Indiana University Press.

Stern, Frank. 1992. *The Whitewashing of the Yellow Badge: Antisemitism and Philosemitism in Postwar Germany,* trans. William Templer. Oxford: Pergamon.

———. 1993. "Jews in the Minds of Germans in the Postwar Period." Bloomington: Jewish Studies Program, Indiana University. [Reprinted as "Antagonistic Memories: The Post-War Survival and Alienation of Jews and Germans." In *Interna-*

tional Yearbook of Oral History and Life Stories. Vol. 1: *Memory and Totalitarianism.* Oxford: Oxford University Press, 1992.]

Thränhardt, Dietrich. 1989. "Patterns of Organization Among Different Ethnic Minorities." *New German Critique* 46: 10–26.

Woolf, Virginia. 1966. *Three Guineas.* New York: Harcourt Brace Jovanovich.

Zipes, Jack. 1994. "The Contemporary German Fascination for Things Jewish: Toward a Jewish Minor Culture." In *Reemerging Jewish Culture in Germany: Life and Literature Since 1989,* ed. Sander Gilman and Karen Remmler. New York: New York University Press.

Žižek, Slavoj. 1990. "Eastern Europe's Republics of Gilead." *New Left Review* 183 (Sept.–Oct.): 50–62.

———. 1993. "Enjoy Your Nation as Yourself!" In Žižek, *Tarrying with the Negative: Kant, Hegel, and the Critique of Ideology.* Durham: Duke University Press.

2. Re-Dressing the "German-Jewish"

A Jewish Hermaphrodite and Cross-Dresser in Wilhelmine Germany

"I was born as a boy, raised as a girl." [1] Such is the self-description of Karl M. Baer, "M" for "Martha," taken from his autobiographical narrative as a person born with stunted male genitalia in late nineteenth-century Germany. Misclassified at his birth in 1885 by a small town doctor, Karl was brought up as a girl despite the signs that he looked and felt "masculine." In 1907, at the age of 22, Baer assumed a masculine identity, a self-revision that was confirmed by the famous sexologist Magnus Hirschfeld, who diagnosed Baer as a "pseudo-hermaphrodite." In the same year, Baer published a memoir under the genial pseudonym of "N. O. Body." *Aus eines Mannes Mädchenjahren* (From a man's girl years — henceforth referred to as "Girl Years") went through at least six printings within the next two years and served as the title for two feature films of 1912 and 1919 loosely based on the story. [2] A recent reprint, edited with a long essay by Hermann Simon, has brought the memoir renewed and deserved attention.

Simon's essay, "Wer war N. O. Body?," the result of twenty years of painstaking research, fills in most of the historical gaps. After his transgenderation in 1907, Baer served as the director of the B'nai B'rith Lodges of Berlin, a Jewish social and welfare organization for both men and women. Baer was by all accounts a gifted and model Jewish functionary. In September 1938 he immigrated to Palestine. Yet despite his importance in Weimar Jewish cultural life, Karl Baer had once been the same legal person — occupied the

This chapter is based on my paper "Cross-Dressing the 'German-Jewish': Androgyny, Hermaphroditism and Ethnicity in the N. O. Body Memoir (1907)," presented at the Annual Meeting of the American Comparative Literature Association, March 3–5, 1994, Claremont Colleges. I would like to thank John Bormanis and Hermann Simon for reading earlier versions of this essay.

same body — as Martha Baer, a highly accomplished journalist, orator, social worker, feminist, and Zionist — before the 22-year-old Martha decided to affect a masculine persona and to marry her female lover. Martha Baer's career paralleled that of her contemporary Bertha Pappenheim, the founder of the League of Jewish Women (Jüdischer Frauenbund) established in 1908. Pappenheim is better known to posterity as Josef Breuer and Sigmund Freud's patient "Anna O.," and it is no coincidence that Baer dubs himself Nora O. Body. In the guise of Martha, Karl Baer had been a Jewish female activist, a leading figure in the fight against the white slave trade (the prostitution of East European Jewish women). In Galicia and the Bukovina between 1904 and 1906, Baer worked tirelessly to uplift Eastern Jewish women economically and politically. She led efforts to organize working women by establishing literacy classes, professional training, employment bureaus, day care, and schools.[3] The Western Jew Baer learned Yiddish and studied Polish and eventually fell in love with a Jewish woman from Czernowitz. Partly because of that woman's difficult divorce, the two were contemplating suicide before Martha consulted the famous Dr. Hirschfeld, who operated on her to correct her anatomical "deficiency." The two thus could marry, though none of Karl Baer's three marriages produced children.[4]

In his narrative, the 22-year-old Karl reveals the ups and downs of a life characterized by mistaken identities, a situation exacerbated by the prudish narrow-mindedness of town life in central-western Germany at the close of the nineteenth century. On the surface, the memoir would seem to be a classic example of ethnic, gender, and sexual self-hatred.[5] "N. O. Body,"[6] the first-person narrator, hides or represses most traces of his Jewishness, his femininity, and any possible gay or lesbian desire.[7] (It is only for linguistic convenience that I refer to the narrator throughout the present study as "him.") Yet when viewed more critically, the elision or alteration of certain facts, a strategy designed to protect N. O. Body and his loved ones, is more a pragmatic decision than it is evidence of shame and embarrassment, a troubled liminality, or a disjunctive doubling. As a result, the memoir tacitly challenges the idea that its author was "self-hating," that is, pathologically split and psychologically overdetermined. Whereas Baer may at times have experienced a tortured ambivalence in leading a double life, the preponderance of evidence points to an incredible resiliency in living multiple roles — gender, ethnic, class, and so forth. Baer's resulting ambivalences, then, need not be viewed negatively, as the inevitable result of internalized antifeminism, anti-Semitism, homophobia, or phallogocentrism.

Instead, Baer's narrative implies that the popular concept of self-hatred is almost always a rhetorical phenomenon, a metapsychological trope that must be located in a cultural-historical context. In the case of the N. O. Body memoir, this trope was designed to appeal to large middle-class audiences that partook of cheap entertainments and sensationalistic books.[8] My approach, then, to personal "identities" in Wilhelmine Germany is original in analyzing minority self-stereotyping as a discourse and instrument of propaganda, not just as a form of bad faith to be explained away as self-hatred, assimilation, or passing. Just because stereotypes of self-hating Jews, hermaphrodites, homosexuals, and other Others were preeminent in late nineteenth-century Europe does not mean that they depicted reality. On the contrary: they were almost always distortions that could not do justice to actual individuals. Precisely because self-hatred was such an effective promotional tactic in the press and in publishing, it took on a dimension beyond its psychopathological definition. "Girl Years" and the history of its reception show that self-hatred is a label, indeed a slander, that can be affixed to any group or individual in any epoch.

To understand the conditions under which Baer's narrative was produced and interpreted also requires drawing on all the generic and intertextual evidence that has inflected readers' responses — from "low, trivial" literature to advertising and book jackets. Intertextuality involves both directly related textual references as well as less directly related cultural expressions, providing an impressive array of potential evidence.[9] An intertextual-generic approach permits us to answer both production- and reception-related questions — why did N. O. Body and his promoters choose the particular subjects they did and why did they present them as they did? What sources did these individuals draw on, what constituencies did they wish to engage, and what approaches did they exclude? In addition, which preexisting intertextual frames did readers use to make sense of the memoir, and were the meanings they produced always in the interest of those social formations possessing more economic, political, or cultural capital?

One intertext Simon does not acknowledge is the social and literary sensation of Adelaide Herculine Barbin, born in the French village of St.-Jean-d'Angely in 1838 and understood to be a girl until she reached the age of 22. At that time, according to his posthumously published memoir, Barbin fell ill and was examined by a doctor who discovered "testicles" embedded on either side of a shallow cul-de-sac that appeared for all the world to be a vagina, together with a rudimentary impermiform penis that could pass for a "voluminous" clitoris. Barbin was then forced to change his civil status. So-called sexual intermediaries (*Zwitter* in German), even though they existed in nature, were held to be impossible under the law. Ordained to live as a man, Herculine, now named Abel Barbin, killed himself eight years later.

It is not unlikely that Baer, or at least his publishers, were familiar with the "tragic" narrative of Barbin as excerpted from his journal and published in 1874. A century later, this "memoir" was reissued with an introduction by French philosopher Michel Foucault.[10] That edition, published in English in 1980, contains excerpts of the autopsy report as well as "A Scandal at the Convent," a fictional account of the Barbin story written some years after his suicide. Foucault was drawn to the material because it illuminates a time when society, reinforced by judicial systems and biological knowledge, began to define and enforce modes of sexuality. Opening his analysis with the now famous question, "Do we truly need a true sex?", Foucault projected his own hopes onto a past where he imagined men and women were somehow less constrained in shaping their sexual identities and desires. At the same time, however, Foucault's case study represents an early challenge to the ideological dogma of "self-hatred." Though flawed, his reconsideration of Barbin's memoir unsettles essentializing categories, and its influence is evident in *The Mystery of Alexina* (directed by René Feret), a feature film of 1986 about Barbin's story.

My approach differs in examining self-hatred as both a discourse that is governed by the sociohistorical and intertextual contexts in which it appears and an effective tool for the promotion and marketing of books. There are several grounds for identifying self-hatred as discourse and marketing in the N. O. Body memoir. These grounds range from the biographical and compositional to the generic and reception-oriented.

Baer's life, as best as we can reconstruct it, substantially challenges the self-hatred thesis. The outstanding features of "Girl Years" are multiple identities, multiple meanings, and multiple modes of address. The evidence suggests that Baer, as both Martha and Karl, was a reasonably well-adjusted person, or what present-day therapists would term "functional." Although this distinction should not diminish the very real, material pain experienced by Baer, even his sensationalizing literary agent, Rudolf Presber (1868–1935), the author of humoristic fiction and editor of a popular magazine, denies the suggestion of self-hatred: "In amazement I listened to her life's story that was presented simply and free of pathos, without the bitterness of an accusation but with the restrained sorrow of an oppressive youth."[11] Baer's biographer, Hermann Simon, also eschews self-hatred as an explanation: "Norbert was not psychologically stunted by his difficult childhood as a girl; he led a normal life as a capable and successful man who was a factor in public life and a prominent figure in the Jewish community" (pp. i–ii). If self-hatred was at issue, why would Baer give us so many clues, playing so dauntingly with fire?[12] Discretion served merely to protect Baer's family because it was clear to his nearest colleagues what was going on. Indeed, even catalogers at the Berlin University library knew the secret, penning in "Karl Baer" next to the author entry "N. O. Body." Finally, Martha/Karl could have settled permanently in Lemberg or elsewhere in Galicia, instead of openly bringing his first two brides back to Berlin.

The careful construction of N. O. Body's memoir also rebuts the idea that Baer was psychologically scarred. "Girl Years" is not only a didactic, instructive narrative that seeks to enlighten its addressees, it is also entertaining, aesthetically pleasing, a quick, fluid read. Perhaps most significant, it is polysemic and multigeneric. For the author proves himself a master of *Trivialliteratur*, drawing constantly on a hodgepodge of nineteenth-century genres: the autobiographical confessional, the narrative of uplift, the romance, the detective story, and the Freudian case history.

The influential possibilities of mass culture are thematized at the beginning of "Girl Years."[13] Later, Baer boasts that as a grade-school "girl," he was writing essays for the pupils who preceded him in social rank. He admires public speakers, debaters, and publicists as "demigods" (p. 106), a factor in his preference for a journalistic career. As Martha Baer he made numerous contributions to the best-selling German-Jewish weekly ever: the *Israelitisches Familienblatt*, a nonpartisan family journal that reached at least 15 percent of the potential Jewish audience in the Kaiserreich. In light of this evidence, it is difficult to have sympathy when Baer, after taking up a masculine identity, laments that he has no career possibilities. In fact, his memoir was contracted before it was ever written, and it was destined to sell well under the tutelage of Presber and Hirschfeld.[14]

Baer's skillful command of popular narrative and understanding of social systems of distinction point to his later successes in public life and as a writer. His journalistic production is still being uncovered, and no one has yet determined under what other pseudonyms he may have published other middle-brow belles-lettres.[15] In "Girl Years" he develops a narrative economy marked by suspense, tension, foreshadowing, and the interplay of desire and fear. The event-driven focus of his technique brings narrative flow and film elements to what might have become a staid memoir. Crucial in Baer's literary apprenticeship were the specific intertexts that informed his literacy. Excluded and shut out by her schoolmates, the nine-year-old Martha responded with a veritable *Lesefieber*, devouring magazines like *Die Garten-laube* and consuming large quantities of loan-library novels by Eugenie Marlitt and Friedrich Gerstäcker as well as adventure stories about Indians, pirates, and the like.

Thirteen years later, in "Girl Years," Karl Baer drew on a variety of popular fictional genres, the most obvious being the redemptional narrative of uplift. Baer's dedication of the memoir to his wife, Beile, the woman who liberates his male heterosexuality (or his butch lesbianism in drag, as the case may be), supplements the trope of the benefactor who uplifts a talented young female or effeminized male.[16] At the same time, the entire scenario is introduced with poetic sensationalism:

> There were such deep wounds
> As a knife could never cut
> One can forget them, dream them away
> To heal them — this one cannot
>
> (p. 7).

Yet Beile soon comes to the rescue, disposing of the initial claim that "Norbert" — as opposed to "Nora" — O. Body is unable to redeem his wounded childhood.

This book is a book of truth. The strangest youth that was probably ever lived, speaks its own language here. This life is to be believed, as strange as it might be. To be strange however is not to tell lies. I want to speak in this book of a life that lay like a burden upon an unknown person, until soft, white women's hands took the weight from him and transformed his sadness into joy. It is the story of the trials and conflicts that grew out of my most inner essence. I was born as a boy, raised as a girl. . . .

And the decision came as *the* woman came into my life. I also want to talk about the love to this woman, who removed the thorns from my path and who transformed my life. . . .

My entire life was like a street filled with thorns — until I met her. (p. 8)[17]

The language and style of these first sentences recall the confessional genre, and the promise of redemption issued here pervades "Girl Years." In keeping with his didactic project, the narrator frequently draws a lesson after each episode, as well as at the opening and close of the book. By alluding to the thorn-crowned, suffering Jesus being comforted by Mary, the narrator embarks on a rhetorical strategy aimed at drawing women into the story. The narrator's constant advice on raising children further suggests that women readers were carefully targeted. For instance, the final insight of the narrative insinuates that Baer's mother should have seen the emerging "tough Jewish male" behind the cross-dressed facade. A good mother, it is implied, would have "enlightened" her child and noticed the growing isolation between ages nine and twelve, the lack of menstruation, and other external markers. In retrospect, the narrator figures himself as a "tomboy" and points out that he preferred to play with boys, use tools, imitate cowboys and Indians, smoke, build treehouses, and climb trees.

While Baer's revisionist, proessentialist argumentation reflects the dominant discourses of Wilhelmine culture, the framing of these discourses in specific genres is meant to appeal to readers.[18] Thus another genre evoked in "Girl Years" is the rags-to-riches story of a poor shopgirl from a declining wealthy family who becomes an academic and women's activist. It is unlikely that Baer was actually apprenticed in a shop. Still, hoping to attract a greater audience, the narrator makes a special effort at reconciliation with the working classes: "Incidentally, young people from educated backgrounds are often only more refined — not better — than those from the lower class" (p. 95).[19] Phrased as afterthought, this statement reinforces a mode of address that conceals the author's class allegiances. At the same time, it suggests a move toward class consensus intended to appeal to readers of varying backgrounds in Imperial Germany.

Two familiar genres even more central to "Girl Years" are the detective story (the *Kriminalroman*) and the romance (the *Liebesroman*.). The former genre is often instantiated in the memoir in the guise of the Freudian case history — a genre that Simon resorts to as well. Then there is the romance genre, to which Baer devotes over a third of memoir (nearly half if we include the narrator's sexual fantasies). The moralizing tone, more prominent toward beginning and end of "Girl Years," yields ultimately to the love story. Anticipating disbelief, Baer props up the authority of the last fifth of the narrative by maintaining that it is based on "diary" entries. In short, success is achieved — Nora O. Body does not lack for suitors, both male and female — but love is lacking. I have dubbed this subgenre the "Tootsie Story" in analogy to the Sydney Pollack movie of 1983 starring Dustin Hoffman. As in the movie, the cross-dressing male of "Girl Years" becomes the voyeur of women's lives and bodies. Two situations offer comic relief to readers. After she has fallen in love with Hanna (read Beile), Nora O. Body receives a series of absurd love letters from a male suitor. Later she punches the young doctor who is treating her for depression when he makes a pass at her.

The modern strategy of diversifying genres to attract readers is reflected in the savvy promotion of "Girl Years." As intimated above, the N. O. Body book was a marketing coup, going through at least six editions within two years. At the price of 2 mark 50, it was affordable even by skilled laborers.

Baer's publisher, Georg Rietz, pandered to a broad readership; his products of the same year included *Das Buch der jüdischen Witze* (The book of Jewish jokes). The book jacket to "Girl Years," illustrated by Lucian Bernhard, an acknowledged leader in graphic design, was also calculated to appeal.[20] It is not surprising, then, that the cross-dressing narrator pays unusual homage to the *Dekorateure* who dress the shop windows and earn a larger salary than the store managers.

Baer's sixth sense for marketing suggests that the discourse of "respectability" (*Sittlichkeit*) in "Girl Years" is feigned.[21] In addition, the emphasis on being "scientific" cannot be taken too literally: popular science was a respectable genre by the late nineteenth century. In "Girl Years" the license to talk openly about sexuality à la Freud is balanced by a perceived need to cloak it in respectability. The openness of this Victorian-era discourse would appear to dovetail with Michel Foucault's account of nineteenth-century western Europe in his *History of Sexuality*: the children know more than the parents, and sexual knowledge is circulated at an astounding pace. This re-visited Wedekindian "Spring's Awakening" is thus replete with N. O. Body's sexual fantasies. Nothing sells like a winner, then, and in "Girl Years" the winners are sex and self-hatred.

I will now explore how the interpretation of the producers of "Girl Years" is at odds with the reception of the book. The consensus of the publishers and agents — "[Baer] didn't write a thriller [*Reißer*]" — rings as false as N. O. Body's closing disclaimer: "I didn't want to write this book, but others suggested that I owed it as a contribution to the psychology of our time and in the interest of science and the truth of humanity" (p. 159). For the individuals behind "Girl Years" set out to achieve the largest readership possible. The memoir was discussed in literary and scientific journals as well as in the popular press (p. 192). The "lively resonance" and "lively portrayal" cited by Simon contradict his position that the integrity of the narrative is preserved. Instead, Baer's novelistic technique plays desire off against repression and assimilation against dissimilation.

As a result, the 1907 foreword and afterword to "Girl Years" "premisread" the memoir, presaging what we know today as the television talk show. One thinks of Oprah, Geraldo, and Donahue constantly circulating so-called expertise on sexuality and gender. Consider the introductory note by Baer's agent, Presber, honored in German literary histories as the epitome of the trivial writer. Here Presber becomes more and more sensationalistic in pitching the book, applauding its "novelistic" qualities: "I had the impression that nature, in league with a humanity enslaved by custom, as well as tradition and fear of ridicule and embarrassment had created one of those novels that varied between tragedy and comedy, a novel that no fantasy-filled narrator would dare to make up" (p. 3). Magnus Hirschfeld, in his contribution, hopes that "Girl Years" "should find an audience far beyond medical and legal specialists" (p. 163). The controversial Jewish sexologist declares the suicide of students and other youth tragedies to be real, not merely the stuff of *Trivialliteratur*. Yet, as his devoted biographer Manfred Herzer has demonstrated, Hirschfeld was himself a public figure and untiring self-promoter. What matters more than Hirschfeld's contradictory ideology, then, is that he gives his own polyvalent spin to the essentialism debate, thereby enhancing the appeal of "Girl Years."[22]

Another interesting reception of the memoir is that of Hermann Simon and his mother. Both are at first taken in by the rumor that Baer was by birth an East European Jew whose parents had him declared a girl so that he might avoid military conscription. Simon contends that Baer formulated (or at least spread) this rumor himself, a problematic interpretation likely influenced by the post-1967 "masculinist" discourse that Paul Breines has analyzed in *Tough Jews*.[23] What Simon sees as a deliberate "mystification of mystification" may ultimately reveal more about attitudes toward the post–Six-Day War Jewish male than about Baer's physical/sexual constitution.[24] Indeed, I question whether Baer was the source of this rumor. Why would he try to control the reception of "Girl Years," which, as we have seen, was already available to much of Jewish (and non-Jewish) Berlin?[25]

The new edition of "Girl Years" is a paperback on high-quality paper reprinted by Edition Hentrich. Although it was a dedicated antifascist publisher located in East Berlin, the Hentrich house chose to market "Girl Years" together with a series of detective and erotic novels by Rudolf Schlichter.[26] It is therefore no accident that one of the first reviews of the newly reprinted memoir appeared in the conservative, but respectable, *Berliner Morgenpost*.[27] The reviewer for the *Morgenpost*, a daily newspaper directed at middle-class audiences, distorted the memoir and thus (further) sensationalized the story. It may also not be an accident that "Girl Years" has been republished in post-Wall eastern Germany and the German print and visual media have capitalized on the issue of "passing" in recent discussions of the GDR past.[28]

The approach to "Girl Years" I have outlined runs counter to current theories which persist in linguistic or ideological suspicion. Rather than reducing everything to the tenuous nature of the sign or a politics of power relations, I have read Baer's memoir in its media context. Suspicionist critics should, for instance, beware of taking the Freudian plunge with this text, fraught as it is with castration imagery that culminates in Baer's childhood fantasy of being the snake Chin-cha-gook from Henry Wadsworth Longfellow's *Hiawatha*.[29] True, Baer explicitly identifies with Oedipus and Achilles, but only insofar as the former was sent off to the mountains and the latter grew up in girl's clothing. We might also recall that Freudian analysis (e.g., *Die Traumdeutung* [The interpretation of dreams], 1900) was itself a well-established genre by the time "Girl Years" was released in 1907. Also, N. O. Body's veiled references to his misshapen penis often make the leap from "kitsch" to "camp," as does the occasional irony in the memoir. Allusions to a headless statue adorning the family's fountain (pp. 16–17) and to cutting his finger when learning to write (pp. 33–34) suggest as much.[30]

N. O. Body's narrative is much too playful in its skein of references to fulfill its goal of being antisensationalist. If anything, I have in this essay underemphasized what might be termed "the pleasure principle" of "Girl Years." N. O. Body, and by extension Baer, indulge in public spectacle, a type of performance intimately familiar to a person engaged in role-reversal and "re-dressing" over the course of three decades. My reading is therefore only one of many possible readings that would examine the pleasure of multiple identities in "Girl Years" with its considerable investment in the activities of identity formation. N. O. Body's representations of desire and masochism[31] in reading, writing, and learning recall a number of postmodernist and postcolonial tropes, such as pleasure and infliction, liberation and alienation, topics addressed in the other essays in this volume.[32]

As "Girl Years" makes clear, autobiography and memoir are themselves narrative tropes. Over twenty years ago, Hayden White pointed out in his *Metahistory* how the necessarily language-bound form of historiography fictionalized its own subject. Particularly within the last few decades, Western academics have undertaken a rigorous interrogation of their own histories, producing accounts and theories that question the possibility of objective historical representation.[33] I would only caution that the rules of evidence still apply when one tries to analyze events and biographies. As a result, my conclusions here are limited by the evidence presently available.

Despite the spectacular, sensationalist qualities of "Girl Years," qualities as evident to Baer's contemporaries as they are to us today, I have endeavored to interpret Baer's memoir with restrained sympathy. This seems to me to stand in contrast both to Foucault's and to Butler's interpretations of Barbin's memoir. Without a doubt, there are many individuals for whom fragmentation is torment, and Butler may be right that Foucault's study of the hermaphrodite tends to gloss over pain and romanticize Herculine's multiple pleasures.[34] At the same time, I cannot fully agree with Butler's counternarrative. Perhaps influenced by the 1986 film or the memoir's fateful "denouement," she is compelled to write: "In the place of univocity, we fail to discover multiplicity, as Foucault would have us do; instead, we confront a fatal ambivalence, produced by the prohibitive law, which for all its effects of happy dispersal nevertheless culminates in Herculine's suicide."[35] For Butler—and, in her opinion, for the "true" Foucault—power and sex are coextensive. That is, because the law generates sex, there is no way that Herculine could be in a limbo of heterogeneous pleasure in some safe realm beyond power.[36] Again, Butler may be correct in her analysis of Barbin and of Foucault's "distortion." Even so (to paraphrase Lloyd Bentson), I know Karl Baer, and Karl Baer was no Herculine Barbin. Butler herself, a year after her critique of Foucault, delivered a long apologia in a different context that recognizes how self-hatred can be as much trope as truth.[37]

"Girl Years," then, should be read not only by conventional intellectual historians but also by "small-c" cultural historians and especially by those interested in cultural studies.[38] Multivalent, multigeneric narratives like Baer's challenge notions of intrinsic textual meaning. In their book on James Bond films, Tony Bennett and Janet Woollacott maintain: "Encounters with texts always have a social function, and the reasons for perceiving one type of encounter as superior to another are wholly external to the text. The process of reading is not one in which the reader and the text meet as abstractions but one in which the inter-textually organised reader meets the inter-textually organised text. The exchange is never a pure one between two unmediated entities, existing in monadic isolation from one another."[39] To do justice to the N. O. Body memoir and its readers, therefore, means to see them as the product of a complicated dialectic between intertextual and social determinants—a dialectic that crosses German, Jewish, and gender borders but that ultimately rejects the canard of self-hatred and the suspicionist discourse of tragic liminality.

NOTES

1. N. O. Body, *Aus eines Mannes Mädchenjahren*, ed. with a prefatory remark and a concluding historical essay by Hermann Simon (Berlin: Edition Hentrich, 1993), p. 8. This is a reprint of the original 1907 edition. Further references are to this

edition with page numbers in parentheses. Further references to Simon's essay "Wer war N. O. Body?" (pp. 167–246) are designated as "Simon's essay" with page numbers in parentheses.

2. See Simon's essay, p. 195.

3. Martha Baer was also an innovator in youth education, the social hygiene movement, and related activities.

4. See Simon's essay, p. 212.

5. For a summary of the literature on self-hatred, see Sander Gilman, *Jewish Self-Hatred* (Baltimore: Johns Hopkins University Press, 1986).

6. The narrator also refers to him/herself as "Nora O. Body" and "Norbert O. Body."

7. The possibility of lesbianism is summarily dismissed on page 94, although it is intimated in the preceding pages.

8. "Girl Years" also appealed to working classes, I argue.

9. William Uricchio and Donna Pearson, *Reframing Culture: The Case of the Vitagraph Quality Films* (Princeton: Princeton University Press, 1992), p. 6.

10. Herculine Barbin, *Being the Recently Discovered Memoirs of a Nineteenth Century French Hermaphrodite*, intro. Michel Foucault (New York, Pantheon, 1980). The original French edition was titled *Herculine Barbin, dite Alexina B.* (Paris: Gallimard, 1978).

11. Rudolf Presber, "Vorwort" to *Aus eines Mannes Mädchenjahren*, pp. 2–3. On Presber, see Simon's essay, pp. 183–87.

12. *Aus eines Mannes Mädchenjahren*, pp. i–ii. On playing with fire (a favorite metaphor of Baer's), see Simon's essay, p. 202.

13. See especially the discussion of the effects of horror fiction on the young Baer and his playmates on pages 15–16.

14. Baer was flexible, able to play a variety of roles, to "live" multiple identities. As a writer, too, he defies easy categorization concerning genre and style, exhibiting a range extending from popular articles and political lectures to scientific papers and historical essays. In addition, Baer's struggle to become a writer is thematized throughout the memoir. In various scenes, he is found scribbling notes on scraps of newsprint.

15. See, for instance, the obituary of Lina Morgenstern signed "N.O." in the Jewish cultural magazine *Ost und West*, January 1910, pp. 33–34.

16. On the trope of the patron in European Jewish culture at this time, see David A. Brenner, *Marketing Identities: The Invention of Jewish Ethnicity* (Detroit: Wayne State University Press, 1997).

17. The statement, "This book is a book of truth," is repeated on the final page of the memoir, 158.

18. For a statement of N. O. Body's essentialist theses, see page 110. Women are, for N. O. Body, not inferior, but different ("*nicht minderwertig*, sondern *anders*wertig"). The difference, moreover, lies in the "method."

19. One may interpret the long episode devoted to the experiences of shopgirls as an attempt to appeal to this audience. Another such appeal to female middle-class readers is the likely fictionalized travel accounts in Baer's memoir, particularly the trips to Norway and Turkey.

20. On the illustrator Bernhard, see Simon's essay, p. 192.

21. For an example of puritanical respectability, see page 29 as well as Hirschfeld's "Nachwort," *Aus eines Mannes Mädchenjahren,* pp. 163–66. On respectability in nineteenth-century Europe, see George Mosse, *Nationalism and Sexuality: Middle-Class Morality and Sexual Norms in Modern Europe* (Madison: University of Wisconsin Press, 1986).

22. Although Hirschfeld had already diagnosed Baer as a "pseudo-hermaphrodite," he refers to N. O. Body in the 1907 "Nachwort" to "Girl Years" as a full, extreme hermaphrodite, an embodiment of the so-called "Third Sex," a true "Zwischenstufe" and not a "Pseudozwitter." His analysis here is based on a legal interpretation of the 1900 *BGB* (*Bürgerliches Gesetzbuch*) [Civil law code], according to which citizens could freely choose their gender. Even so, both N. O. Body and Hirschfeld assess pragmatically that fin-de-siècle hermaphrodites might best choose masculine identities.

23. Paul Breines, *Tough Jews: Political Fantasies and the Moral Dilemma of American Jewry* (New York: Basic Books, 1990).

24. Compare the largely negative reaction in East Germany and Poland to the Six-Day War in 1967.

25. On the rumor that Baer was an *Ostjude,* see Simon's essay, p. 174.

26. See the advertising materials on the final pages of the Edition Hentrich reprint of "Girl Years."

27. Jola Merten, review of N. O. Body, *Aus eines Mannes Mädchenjahren, Berliner Morgenpost,* Jan. 23, 1994, avoids the Jewish dimensions of the memoir, as do others that appeared in the Federal Republic of Germany in 1994. See, for instance, Anita Kugler's review, *die tageszeitung,* Mar. 8, 1994, p. 24; and Susanna Vida's review for *DeutschlandRadio,* Mar. 28, 1994, 4:10 P.M. to 4:30 P.M.

28. For a noteworthy example, see Andreas Sinakowski's narrative of being gay and an informer for the Stasi; Andreas Sinakowski, *Das Verhör* (Berlin: BasisDruck, 1991).

29. On Baer's own confusion regarding Chin-cha-gook, see pp. 39, 47. Cultural historians will make much of Baer's own self-analysis of "masculine" signs, such as a deep voice, irrepressible facial hair, cigar smoking, and hearty beer drinking. In particular, the centrality of his voice change will add grist to the mill of those who focus on stereotypes of the Jewish male voice.

30. See also N. O. Body's first description of his fictional hometown "Bergheim" as located between two mountains. On top of one mountain is "an old predatory fortress-nest in ruins" (*ein altes zerfallenes Raubnest*) that looks down defiantly (*trotzig*) at the valley below (p. 13).

31. On masochism, see esp. p. 85.

32. Let me again emphasize that Baer's memoir is classifiable as "self-hating" if and *only* if we understand self-hatred as a projection of racism onto a perceived inferior other: women, blacks, Indians. Thus, when N. O. Body states a need for German role models instead of Indians, this is only normal — all too normal — for Wilhelminian Jewry and all to dismissible in the post-Holocaust era as the tragic pathology of a wished-for German-Jewish symbiosis. In the ironic context of "Girl Years," then, any diagnosis of self-hatred deserves a large grain of salt.

33. Hayden White, *Metahistory: The Historical Imagination in Nineteenth Century Europe* (Baltimore: Johns Hopkins University Press, 1973).

34. Judith Butler, *Gender Trouble: Feminism and the Subversion of Identity* (New York: Routledge, 1990).

35. Ibid., p. 99.

36. Ibid., p. 4.

37. In a very extensive, unusually personal footnote, Butler contends that "to call another person self-hating is itself an act of power that calls for some kind of scrutiny" (Judith Butler, "Imitation and Gender Insubordination," in *Inside/Out: Lesbian Theories, Gay Theories*, ed. Diana Fuss (New York: Routledge, 1991), pp. 29–30 n. 9.

38. The concept of popular culture for a middle-class audience offers a challenge to the "ideology of mass culture" that posits a dichotomy between "high" and "low" culture. The ideology has been propagated most memorably by the Frankurt School. The legacy of Adorno, Horkheimer, and their allies is, I contend, more of a hindrance than a help in understanding the conditions of production and reception of both minority and majority cultures.

39. Tony Bennett and Janet Woollacott, *Bond and Beyond: The Political Career of a Popular Hero* (London: Macmillan, 1987), p. 56.

3. Accenting L.A.

Central Europeans in Diasporan
Hollywood in the 1940s

From its earliest pioneers more than a century ago to its recent postcommunist wave of émigrés, Hollywood has been the destination of international film artists whose cultural diversity shapes the multifaceted "look" of that most "American" phenomenon, the Hollywood movie. Perhaps more than other contemporary discourses, the art of cinema — its rhetorics and re-makes — has been marked by the globality of these multinational participants, exiles and émigrés traversing linguistic, sociohistorical, and geographical borders of production, performance, and reception. Revitalized by the contributions of so many refugees from the East, Hollywood cinema of the 1930s and 1940s can scarcely be called unqualifiedly "American." Beginning more than a century ago in New York, with the arrival in 1886 of the French cameraman Felix Mesguich, dispatched from Paris to demonstrate the brand-new Lumière Cinematograph, cinema may indeed be said to have been born French and grown up American.[1] Variously constructed as national allegory, colonizing oppressor of otherness, or glamorous dream factory, Hollywood's multiethnic communities warrant renewed attention at a time when its hegemonic products and strategies are seen to threaten the very survival of smaller national visual cultures around the world.[2]

Paradoxically, then, to revisit Hollywood past is to revel in a world of multicultural artistic ferment and cultural exchange, of interferences, and of reciprocal influence — in short, a scene of mutually enhancing oppositionalities that has tended to be marginalized, if not altogether effaced, in contemporary film studies, much as "foreign" actors' accents were sanitized to produce presumably Americanized line readings. In the interest of refocusing attention on that moment, I wish here to evoke the cultural memory of some filmmakers and performers of Central and East European origin working in Hollywood in the 1940s, during and after World War II, an era when the contradictions of collective identity, homeland, nation, and exile were cast in particularly bold relief. Sharpened by the presence of multiethnic practitioners in the film community and the ambivalent reception they received from industry insiders, spectators, and critics, such questions of national, religious, and ethnic difference — not to mention artistic perspective — seem oddly contemporary.

First, I must indulge in an uncharacteristically autobiographical exercise, for "Accenting L.A." is also informed by — and inextricably interwoven with — the parameters of my own life, having been born in Hollywood of Austro-Hungarian (and unacknowledged Jewish) parents who had fled Vienna and Budapest for California in 1939. Their expatriation was sponsored by my father's cousin, a Hungarian physician whose medical practice in a Bauhaus-inspired office on Franklin and Normandie included such movie colony patients as the Hungarians Zoltan Korda, Miklós Rozsa, and Mihaly Kertész (better known as Michael Curtiz, director of *Casablanca*), and by close family friends whose patriarch was Carl Laemmle, the German-born founder of Universal Studios. As a result, Friday night poker games at our house resembled nothing so much as a scene from *Casablanca*, with Viennese actors such as John Wengraf and John Banner (better known later as Schultzie in *Hogan's Heroes*) mingling with Laemmle's descendants, all bidding in German and Hungarian throughout the smoke- and salami-filled evening.

Far from unique, however, my family's diasporan trajectory paralleled and reflected that of innumerable Central Europeans who eventually found refuge in those former orange groves and bean fields. It is their struggle for cultural and national identity that informs my reclamation project: to historicize and restage the scenario of diversity of those actors and directors, directors of photography and technicians, set decorators and costumers who came to America as exiles and experts, volunteers and novices. I seek in this way to reinscribe the distinctly ethnic European "otherness" of those international film industry workers whose contributions to the megalopolis of cinema transformed the back lots of Gower and Vine into what had, by the 1950s, become known as the "dream factory." Among the many responses to their presence, a guidebook to Los Angeles suggests the welcome they received at the hands of local citizens: "Signs reading 'No dogs, no actors' greeted the first movie pioneers to arrive in Hollywood, but the marriage of Midwestern farmers and Eastern entertainers overcame its rocky start, and Hollywood soon became the symbol of glamor and excitement around the world, a mecca for established talent and unknown hopefuls. . . . However seedy the reality, the myth endures."[3]

47

The "marriage" between Hollywood and Los Angeles was, if anything, rockier still, for many of the "Eastern entertainers" to whom the text refers came not from the American eastern seaboard but from Eastern Europe, an ethnographic marker often effaced from their revised autobiographical narratives in favor of names and profiles that conformed more closely to the white Anglo-Saxon Protestant establishment that ruled Hollywood's early dynastic families.[4] Denial, oblivion, disguise, transformation, forgetfulness, reinvention: such were the mechanisms of defense deployed by moguls from the ghettoes of Kiev and Minsk and Warsaw and from provincial towns such as Laupheim and Ricse. Former cloth spongers and junk dealers, glove salesmen and furriers, a pool hustler and a bankrupt jeweler, they became the ruling class of Hollywood.[5] Jack Warner, for example (of the Warner Brothers studio), informed his colleague Darryl Zanuck that only the fact that Zanuck was a gentile prevented Warner, a Jew, from becoming his associate.[6]

Anti-Semitism was rampant in Hollywood in those years, its more benign manifestations extending to remarks such as the contention that the acronym "MGM" stood for "Mayer's Ganze Mespuchah" — the whole (Louis B.) Mayer family.[7] Despite their differences, at most administrative levels there obtained an unspoken solidarity among Jews from Eastern and Central Europe and a discreet tendency to return in kind individual or institutional anti-Semitic practices. Harry Warner was celebrated, among other things, for having refused to do business with Western Electric because of the absence of a single Jewish employee in the firm. The Laemmles and the Laskys became powerful in part at the expense of gentiles who, led by Edison, had rebuffed them completely. Nonetheless, Hollywood was well known for its ambivalent reception of these Eastern entrepreneurs, and even those of us growing up in Hollywood, Los Feliz, and Silver Lake in the 1950s, who could *not*, to our regret, count ourselves as "red-diaper-babies" knew well that the Hillcrest Country Club, so favored among the industry establishment, accepted no Jews.[8]

Yet these groups could not precisely be regarded as constituting a "clan," in contemporary ethnographic readings of ethnicity and nationality, firmly attached to its own traditions, for there were social and class differences between those who had been in America far longer, such as the Selznicks, the Wangers, and the Schulbergs — cultivated, wealthy, liberal, and nonobservant Jews — and the first-generation immigrants whom they regarded with condescension. There were differences, too, between Central Europeans and Germans such as the Hungarian Adolph Zukor, Laemmle, and Irving Thalberg and those of Russian and Polish descent such as Louis B. Mayer,

Lasky, and Warner.[9] (The English Charles Chaplin refused to deny accusations of bolshevism from the Right and apparently took equal pride in refusing to counter claims that he was Jewish, although it seems that he was not. Perhaps still more significant was the intergenerational conflict between producers and their own intellectual offspring who tended to be writers rather than moguls or tycoons.)[10] Retracing their steps reopens generational and ethnic distinctions, linking Jewish identity with geography and marginality.

Deeply desirous of assimilation, many "hybridized" Hollywood Central Europeans retained only vague echoes of the culture they had left behind. Yiddish was hardly spoken by the second generation, and the synagogue on Wilshire Boulevard (an architectural imitation of the Pantheon, in *echt*-L.A. mimetic style), was used primarily for high holy day services. National and regional clannishness, however, was another matter: the French colony, including Jacques Feyder, Françoise Rosay, and Charles Boyer, welcomed war refugees and encouraged their participation in antifascist activities, although their influence had diminished since the 1920s.[11] Those whose politics were anti-Nazi and antifascist especially swelled the ranks and nourished the soul of the Central European community. By 1938, Austria, Germany, and Hungary provided nearly 5 percent of Hollywood's cinematographic personnel. Artists, writers, and intellectuals such as Bertolt Brecht and Thomas Mann, Max Steiner and Arnold Schoenberg, Hanns Eisler and Paul Lukas, Ernst Lubitsch and George Cukor participated in the salon life of this aristocracy of the Left, playing an influential role in the genesis of a more critical spirit in Hollywood marked by the double influence of psychoanalysis and communism.

To what extent, then, can "Europe" be said to have engendered "Hollywood," and what forces impinged upon the repression of that cultural diversity from the American imaginary? There had been, to be sure, earlier influxes of Central Europeans whose Hollywood destinies[12] paved the way for successive waves of "foreign" influence and contributed to the paranoia of McCarthy-era savaging of studio-based "reds" from 1947 to 1953, when my schoolmates' parents from Silver Lake and Echo Park awaited the news of daily subpoenas for harboring copies of the *Daily Worker* in their homes, a distinction that earned them both envy and suspicion. Those producers from the ghettoes of Eastern Europe, rebaptized studio moguls such as Samuel Goldwyn, Louis B. Mayer, Adolph Zukor, and William Fox — founders and patrons of Metro Goldwyn Mayer, Paramount, Universal, and Fox Studios — fashioned their Hollywood from an amalgamated ethnocultural milieu (what Arjun Appadurai has called a "global ethnoscape") that drove the Viennese director Otto Preminger to lament that, to succeed in Hollywood, one ought to be able to do more than just speak Hungarian.

The first wave, from 1923 to 1930, was dominated by Germans, Swedes, Danes, and Hungarians and brought such figures as the Germans Ernst Lubitsch and F. W. Murnau, the Hungarians Alexander Korda and Michael Curtiz, and the Swedes Victor Sjöström and Mauritz Stiller (discoverer of Greta Garbo) to the United States.[13] During the war, and especially after Pearl Harbor, the exiled Europeans contributed powerfully to the Hollywood war effort. After *Confessions of a Nazi Spy*, for instance, the Russian Jew Anatole Litvak joined with the Italian Frank Capra in the cinematographic service of the U.S. Army to concoct several memorable episodes of the *Why We Fight* series. Lubitsch in *To Be or Not to Be*, Curtiz in *Passage to Marseilles*, Fritz Lang in *Hangmen Also Die*, Jean Renoir in *This Land Is Mine*, Alfred Hitchcock in *Correspondent 17*, and Douglas Sirk in *Hitler's Madman* managed, like their post-Stalin East European counterparts, to infuse their comedies, thrillers, and Cold War espionage films with an unmistakable antifascist current. And who can forget the opening (now classic) sequences from Curtiz's *Casablanca* with its polyglot crowds of hopeful refugees awaiting the miracle of an exit visa to a better world?

By the postwar years, however, the shift in anti-Nazi alliances and the beginning of the Cold War transformed Hollywood into the witch-hunt capital, a hotbed of paranoia and denunciation well chronicled in Emile de Antonio's documentary *Point of Order* and Eric Bentley's compendium of the army-McCarthy hearings. Such "typically American" names as the British Joseph Losey and the French Jules Dassin found themselves obliged to leave for Europe, an ironic reversal of the westward migration that had brought them there in the first place, to say nothing of the Hollywood Ten and hundreds of others whose careers and lives were forever compromised, even destroyed. Fritz Lang returned to Germany in 1958, his countryman Bertolt Brecht's Hollywood odyssey but a bitter memory, memorialized in *Contempt* (Le mépris), a 1962 film by Jean-Luc Godard, the postmodern revolutionary of the cinematic apparatus, in which Lang himself appears on screen as a director denouncing the very Hollywood that had betrayed him. As Godard put it with regard to his own complex relationship to Hollywood, "The country of cinema being Hollywood, and my country being that of cinema, I am the only American filmmaker in exile."[14]

The second wave, from the mid-1930s to the early 1940s, was, by contrast, almost exclusively political and brought refugees from Germany, Austria, and France, fleeing first from Nazi Germany and later from Nazi-occupied Europe. They included, among the directors, the Viennese Samuel (Billy)

Wilder, Fritz Lang, and Otto Preminger (who also worked in Prague and Zurich); the Germans William Wyler and Herbert von Sternberg (whose claim to aristocracy was as dubious as that of Erich von Stroheim); the French Jean Renoir and Jacques Tourneur, Julien Duvivier, and René Clair; Max Oppenheimer from Saarbrucken (reborn as Max Ophuls); the British Alfred Hitchcock; the Polish Curt Siodmak; and the Danish Detlef Sierck (better known as Douglas Sirk). Although several returned to Europe after the end of the war, many others stayed to continue their careers in the United States. "I saw myself in my dreams established in that paradise next to Griffith, Chaplin, and all the saints of the worldwide cult of cinema," confessed Jean Renoir.[15] Whereas those arriving in the 1920s came almost exclusively by invitation and had signed contracts with major studios or producers in advance, the wartime immigrants came to America on their own initiative and usually as virtual unknowns who had to work their way slowly through the system. Even relatively well-known figures such as Renoir were forced to make do with what the studios were prepared to offer them rather than having the degree of choice initially accorded to a Lubitsch, a Sjöström, or a Murnau.

By 1940, the studio system was both monolithic and, paradoxically, flexible enough to accommodate a wide variety of talents and approaches. The mostly Germanic arrivals of this period were able to find their niche in a genre that suited their own temperaments and aspirations — usually the melodrama, the thriller, the social problem film, or what has since come to be called the "film noir" — their most distinctive contribution, owing substantially to the aesthetics of German expressionism, which has since engendered a profusion of film-historical and theoretical texts including encyclopedic compendiums and entire issues of the influential French journal *Cahiers du cinéma*. Once they had paid their dues by cooperating with the studio's demands, the more ambitious among them such as Wilder were able to carve out brilliant and distinctive careers by manipulating the system to their advantage, as John Ford, Howard Hawks, and Frank Capra had done before them.[16]

There have, obviously, been successive migrations, most recently another East European wave fleeing the collapse of communism in the former Eastern bloc and the end of state funding for the arts in favor of the "free-market" second economy of the "Wild East." The outstanding Hungarian-born cinematographers Vilmos Zsigmond and László Kovács, trained by the Academy of Theater and Cinema of Budapest, were refugees from another historical trauma: the Hungarian uprising of 1956.[17] The Czech director Miloš Forman, first renowned as an architect of Prague Spring in the mid-1960s and in his "American" phase better known as the director of *Hair* and *Amadeus*, has become the object of both suspicion and envy in his Czech homeland, perhaps also because of his privileged status there as a childhood friend of Václav Havel. Polish-born Roman Polanski admits that "discovering Hollywood was to reach the promised land," and the German filmmaker Wim Wenders contends that "there has always been this great myth for a European filmmaker: to make a film in the USA, the country of unlimited possibilities. The cinema I love and that has most influenced me comes from there." Orson Welles was more circumspect, having been at once lauded by and then marginalized and finally excluded from that promised land: "Hollywood is a golden suburb, perfect for golfers, gardeners, mediocre people and satisfied stars. I don't belong to any of these categories." [18]

Victims of a tormented history, the Central Europeans in particular were fascinated by a Hollywood Babylon that sheltered and even nurtured them. From the earliest pioneers to the most recent wave, filmmakers such as Gyula Gazdag (former head of the Hungarian Film Academy and now teaching in the UCLA Film Department) and the avant-garde director Miklós Jancsó (who taught for two years at Harvard),[19] Central Europeans have marked what we refer to as Hollywood — now "dominant" — cinema with their unmistakable stamp as set decorators, designers, actors, musicians, directors, and craftspeople of every kind. Foregrounding multiple identities and the politics of location, the presence of these Central Europeans in diasporan Hollywood poses the question of identity construction and the importance of belonging, thereby problematizing the filmmakers' positionality and, with it, their different trajectories of travel, exile, and — in some cases — return. A former ambassador to Austria evokes the abundance of internationally renowned Austrians in yesterday's and today's U.S. film industry: "Austria can live without Hollywood, but Hollywood can't live without Austria." [20] These Austrian immigrants included not only artists but also former officers of the monarchy, counts, architects, inventors, and others seeking to make their fortune in California. Jacob Krantz (later Ricardo Cortez) began in Manhattan as an extra in low-budget productions. Karl Freund (co-inventor of the Multicam system) and Rudolf Maté are remembered as top "Hollywood" cameramen. Austrians Wilhelm Thiele, Fritz Lang, and Billy Wilder have been integrated within the Hollywood canon as a result of Hitler's domination of Germany and Austria and the film propaganda machine that followed in his wake, forcing remaining directors to adhere strictly to the doctrines of the Third Reich. Earlier, the Viennese Erich von Stroheim took his place in the company of D. W. Griffith and Charlie Chaplin, while his countrymen Max Fleischer pioneered animated film, Paul Kohner initiated the production of films in several language versions concurrently, and the photographer Franz Planer abandoned the customary use of studio sets to reinstate shooting on location. The Austrian composer Erich Korngold originated the symphonic film music that was to become known as prototypical Hollywood soundtrack throughout the 1940s, and Josef von Sternberg — perhaps best known for having "discovered" Marlene Dietrich — is remembered, among other things, for now classic innovations in the genre of gangster films.

To revisit that formative wartime moment, then, as these few examples attest, is to appreciate, in light of rapidly evolving definitions of European and American identities, the urgent agendas of collective and personal memory, homeland, nation, and exile that fueled Hollywood production and to become cognizant of their impact on all aspects of the film industry from documentary propaganda films made by both Hollywood and European studios to the portrayal of national character and "mentality" in such classic features as *Casablanca* (1942). One of the most popular Hollywood films of all time, its production was paradoxically among the most international: a film about European antifascism, directed by a Hungarian, with a cast composed of Austrian, German, Swedish, French, English, and American actors, it is also a romantic yet trenchant critique of nationalism: in response to the question, "What is your nationality?" Rick Blaine (played by Humphrey Bogart), owner of a nightclub in the unoccupied French territory of Casablanca, famously responds, "I'm a drunkard."

These multilingual accents, too often subjected to the "ethnic cleansing" of a homogenizing cultural imperialism intent on cornering the world's movie market,[21] nonetheless succeeded in maintaining the irreducible particularity of their ethnic and regional voices, resisting, through the polyvocal nature of their discourses and contestatory aesthetics, Hollywood's tendency (its claims to cosmopolitanism notwithstanding) to construct its cultural products as unproblematically "American," intended for a unified group of filmgoers, a homogeneous cosmopolitan audience. For if indeed, as in in Jean-Jacques Rousseau's formulation, "Accent is the soul of discourse,"[22] it remains to be seen whether Hollywood at the turn of the next century will respond to the border crossings of the global cultural market, beyond nationalism and tribalism, even beyond what Freud called "the narcissism of minor difference," toward a reassessment of visual representation as a transnational, multicultural forum. Variously constructed as national allegory, colonizing oppressor of difference, or glamorous dream factory, Hollywood —

and its multiethnic communities—warrants renewed attention now, at a time when its hegemony is seen to threaten the very existence of the national cinemas in which these practitioners once exercised their craft, as witnessed by protectionist debates over the GATT treaty in 1993 and legislation in Germany, France, and Hungary establishing language-based restrictions on audiovisual production, distribution, and broadcasting. As we mark the centenary of the cinematic apparatus and as cultural, geographic, and linguistic borders become increasingly porous, the multiculturality of Hollywood in the 1940s offers a focus for reexamining the ways in which marginalized ethnic subgroups resisted or capitulated to the "ethnic cleansing" of a homogenizing cultural imperialism.

Abbreviated Chronology of the International Film Community and Hollywood

1895   The Lumière Brothers in Paris hold the first public film projection.

1908   Hollywood is founded.

1912   The Hungarian William Fox creates the studio that becomes 20th Century Fox.

1913   The Hungarian Adolf Zukor creates the studio that becomes Paramount Studios.

1914   Chaplin shoots his first film.

1915   The German producer Carl Laemmle creates Universal Studios.

1919   Chaplin, D. W. Griffith, Douglas Fairbanks, and Mary Pickford create United Artists.

1921   The German director Ernst Lubitsch and the Polish star Pola Negri arrive.

1925   The Swedish star Greta Garbo arrives, accompanied by the Swedish director Mauritz Stiller.

1928   Maurice Chevalier arrives from France.

1929   The talkies begin: American films are dubbed in French, German, Italian, and Spanish.

1930   Marlene Dietrich arrives from Germany.

1935   The Austrian actor Peter Lorre arrives in flight from the Nazis.

1939   The Swedish actress Ingrid Bergman arrives, as does the British director Alfred Hitchcock.

1942   The Hungarian director Michael Curtiz shoots *Casablanca*.

1947   Senator Joseph McCarthy instigates persecutions of communists and intellectuals.

NOTES

1. Michel Boujut, "Transatlantique," *Autrement — Europe–Hollywood et Retour*, no. 79 (Apr. 1986): 7.

2. "Zukor annexes Australia," reads an early film journal cover.

3. Richard Saul Wurman, *LA Access* (New York: Access Press, 1987), p. 42.

4. Otto Friedrich, *City of Nets: A Portrait of Hollywood in the 1940s* (New York: Harper & Row, 1986), pp. 141–70.

5. Neal Gabler, *An Empire of Their Own: How the Jews Invented Hollywood* (New York: Crown, 1988), pp. 3–4.

6. Ibid., pp. 131–32.

7. Ibid., pp. 272–73.

8. Alain Masson, "Les Cliques et les castes hollywoodiennes," *Autrement: Hollywood 1927–1941*, no. 9 (Sept. 1991): 139–40.

9. Norman Zierold, *The Moguls: Hollywood's Merchants of Myth* (Los Angeles: Silman-James Press, 1991), pp. 83–90.

10. Lest there be any doubt about the relationship between nation and visual culture, a certificate of gratitude was presented in 1925 to the French director Maurice Tourneur "in recognition of patriotic services for the United States during the period of its participation in the great war for Universal Democracy. The splendid morale of the people, upon which rested the success of the Army and Navy, was in no small measure due to the visualization of the activities of the Nation presented through the medium of the motion picture." (U.S. Government Committee on Public Information, including the secretary of state, secretary of war, and secretary of the navy, as well as director of the Division of Films, from Dominique Lebrun, *Trans-Europe Hollywood* [Paris: Hazan, 1992], p. 21). "La propagande par les rêves, ou le triomphe du modèle américain" conveys the irony and, for that matter, bitterness with which many French critics and industry professionals now regard U.S. domination of the realm of the gaze, confirmed perhaps by Steven Spielberg's comment after a meeting with French president François Mitterrand to the effect that France has the right to its own films, merely an echo of France's protectionist stance in the recent GATT treaty debates.

11. Graham Petrie, *Hollywood Destinies: European Directors in America, 1922–31* (London: Routledge & Kegan Paul, 1985).

12. Ibid.

13. Ibid.

14. Jean-Luc Godard, *Jean-Luc Godard* (Paris: Cahiers du cinéma, 1968).

15. Noel Simsolo, "Impressions Renoir," *Autrement: Europe–Hollywood et Retour*, no. 79 (Apr. 1986): 27.

16. See Mike Davis, *City of Quartz* (New York: Vintage, 1992), in particular "Sunshine or Noir?" pp. 15–98.

17. See Catherine Portuges, "Between Worlds: Re-Placing Hungarian Cinema," in *Before the Wall Came Down: Soviet and East European Filmmakers Working in the West*, ed. G. Petrie and R. Dwyer (New York: University Press of America, 1990).

18. "Special Orson Welles," *Positif*, no. 378 (July–Aug. 1992): 55.

19. I wish to acknowledge Gyula Gazdag and Miklós Jancsó, who graciously contributed several personal communications on this topic in Budapest, 1992–94.

20. As witnessed by the GATT treaty struggles over the conditions of cultural protectionism against global domination by American cinema, most notably on the part of France.

21. The term "ethnic cleansing" is, of course, used symbolically here.

22. Jean-Jacques Rousseau, "L'Accent est l'âme du discours," *Confessions* (extracts) (Paris: Librairie Larousse, 1960), p. 88.

BIBLIOGRAPHY

Baxter, John. *The Hollywood Exiles*. London: MacDonald & Jane's, 1976.

Bessy, Maurice. *Stroheim*. Paris: Editions Pygmalion/Gerard Watelet, 1984.

Bogdanovich, Peter. *Fritz Lang en Amérique*. Paris: Editions de l'Etoile/Cahiers du cinéma, 1990.

Boujut, Michel. "Transatlantique." *Autrement — Europe–Hollywood et Retour*, no. 79, April 1986.

Bojarski, Richard. *The Films of Béla Lugosi*. Secaucus, N.J.: Citadel Press, 1980.

Ciment, Michel. *Passport pour Hollywood*. Paris: Editions du Seuil, 1987.

Cowie, Peter. *Korda*. Paris: Editions de l'Avant-scène, 1965.

Dardis, Tom. *Some Time in the Sun: The Hollywood Years of F. Scott Fitzgerald, W. Faulkner, N. West, A. Huxley, and J. Agee*. New York: Limelight Editions, 1988.

Davis, Mike. *City of Quartz*. New York: Vintage, 1992.

Diamant-Berger, Henri. *Il était une fois le cinéma*. Paris: Jean-Claude Simoën, 1977.

Dietrich, Marlene. *Marlene D.* Paris: Grasset, 1984.

Eisenschitz, Bernard, and Jean Narboni. *Ernst Lubitsch*. Paris: Cahiers du cinéma–La cinémathèque française, 1985.

Eisner, Lotte. *Fritz Lang*. Paris: Cahiers du cinéma–La cinémathèque française, 1984.

"Et l'Europe créa Hollywood." Exhibition Espace Kronenbourg, Paris, July 1992.

Friedrich, Otto. *City of Nets: A Portrait of Hollywood in the 1940s*. New York: Harper & Row, 1986.

Gabler, Neal. *An Empire of Their Own: How the Jews Invented Hollywood*. New York: Crown, 1988.

Haudiquet, Philippe. *Fejös*. Paris: Editions de l'Avant-scène, 1968.

Hirschorn, Clive. *The Columbia Story*. London: Octopus Books, 1989.

Jacobs, Jerome. *Billy Wilder*. Paris: Rivages, 1988.

Korda, Michael. *Des vies de rêve, histoire d'une famille*. Paris: Robert Laffont, 1981.

Lebrun, Dominique. *Paris-Hollywood: Histoire des Français à Hollywood*. Paris: Hazan, 1987.

———. *Trans-Europe Hollywood*. Paris: Hazan, 1992.

Masson, A., ed., *Hollywood, 1927–1941: La propagande par les rêves ou le triomphe du modèle américain*. Paris: Editions Autrement, série Mémoires no. 9, 1990.

McWilliams, Carey. *Southern California: An Island in the Country*. Salt Lake City: Gibbs-Smith, 1983.

Ophuls, Max. *Max Ophuls par Max Ophuls*. Paris: Robert Laffont, 1963.

Palmier, Jean-Michel. *Weimar en exil, le destin de l'émigration intellectuelle allemande antinazie en Europe et aux Etats-Unis*. Paris: Editions Payot, 1990.

Parish, James Robert. *Hollywood Character Actors*. New York: Arlington House, 1978.

Petrie, Graham. *Hollywood Destinies: European Directors in America, 1922–31*. London: Routledge & Kegan Paul, 1985.

Portuges, Catherine. "Between Worlds: Re-Placing Hungarian Cinema." In *Before the Wall Came Down: Soviet and East European Filmmakers Working in the West*, ed. Graham Petrie and Ruth Dwyer. New York: University Press of America, 1990.

———. "Border Crossings: Recent Trends in East and Central European Cinema." *Slavic Review: American Quarterly of Russian, Eurasian and East European Studies* 51 (Fall 1992): 531–35.

———. *Screen Memories: The Hungarian Cinema of Márta Mészáros*. Bloomington: Indiana University Press, 1993.

Rickles, Laurence. *The Case of California*. Baltimore: Johns Hopkins University Press, 1991.

Sorlin, Pierre. *European Cinemas, European Societies, 1939–1990*. London: Routledge, 1991.

Spehr, Paul C. *The Movies Begin: Making Movies in New Jersey, 1887–1920*. Newark: Newark Museum, 1977.

Sperling, Cass Warner. *Hollywood Be Thy Name: The Warner Brothers Story*. Roclin: Prima Publishers, 1994.

Sternberg, Josef von. *Souvenir d'un montreur d'ombres*. Paris: Robert Laffont, 1966.

Taylor, John Russell. *Strangers in Paradise: The Hollywood Emigrés, 1933–1950*. London: Faber & Faber, 1983.

Viviani, Christian. *Michael Curtiz*. Paris: Editions de l'Avant-scène, 1974.

Youngkin, S. D., J. Bigwood, and R. Cabana, Jr. *The Films of Peter Lorre*. Secaucus, N.J.: Citadel Press, 1982.

Zierold, Norman. *The Moguls: Hollywood's Merchants of Myth*. Los Angeles: Silman-James Press, 1991.

Zolotow, Maurice. *Billy Wilder in Hollywood*. New York: Limelight, 1987.

4. Scraps of Culture

*African Style in the African American
Community of Los Angeles*

On Labor Day weekend of 1994, in South Central Los Angeles, *the* place to
be is the annual African Marketplace and Cultural Faire in Rancho Cienega
Park. On its temporary stages, Senegalese dancers, Brazilian musicians, a
Caribbean jazz combo, and a gospel singing group entertain the crowds. But
the main attraction is the 200-odd craftspeople, artists, clothing designers,
jewelry designers, and importers, most of whom live in the inner city.

This essay is based on interviews with 25 such designers and importers,
African Americans as well as immigrants from many countries in Africa and
the African diaspora. I met the people who make and/or sell South Central's
African-inspired clothing and jewelry, at the African Marketplace, as well
as at reggae festivals, cultural fairs at black churches, and African History
Month fairs in shopping malls. Through oral history interviews in their
homes, studios, or shops and more sustained interactions with them in these
places or in the course of my volunteer work with the African Marketplace,
I gathered information about their work and their visions for its future.

Their original, mostly handmade designs, sold to low-income customers,
often in an atmosphere of community celebration, constitute an anomalous
pocket in the world of mass-produced fashion. Their relation to consumer
capitalist appropriation is unusual for subcultural style. African-influenced
fashions are exceptional not only within the commodity system of fashion
but also in relation to the main focus of recent fashion studies. My essay
explores certain questions this exceptionality raises about some basic assumptions of cultural studies.

Recent fashion studies have tended to focus on avant-garde fashions —
especially camp, drag, gender-bending, cross-dressing, and transvestism — as
"subversive" and "radical." These fashions are said to "displace," "challenge," "disrupt," "destabilize," or "unsettle" binary categorizing (Evans and
Thornton 1991; Berlant and Freeman 1992:150; Case 1993:298). They "blur

boundaries" not only of gender systems but of symbolic systems based on binary opposition. In her study of cross-dressing, *Vested Interests*, Marjorie Garber says that these boundary-blurring styles "indicate the place of 'category crisis'" as "the ground of culture itself" (1992:16).

Spectacular, avant-garde, and tongue-in-cheek, they put gender and other symbolic binaries into play because they are themselves extremely playful. Cross-dressing, drag, and camp work through parody and irony. They parody straight, conventional styles and constitute an ironic commentary upon the way clothing constructs conventional identities. Such playful, masquerading styles, especially those associated with gay culture and its critique through parody of straight culture, have made extremely important contributions to radical cultural critique. They have made us pay attention to the constructedness, the fundamental masquerade of all identities, the way we all, and especially straight, white men and women, imitate an artificial ideal in performing our gender, sexual, and ethnic identities.

In comparison to these parodic, playful styles, African-influenced dressing in the black community may seem to belong to a more outmoded, conservative semiotics. The campy styles that parody conventional social identities seem to epitomize practices favored by postmodern culture theory. In undoing the dichotomous structures on which the symbolic order is based, they reveal that meaning, like identity, is constructed and that signs do not have essential meanings but instead produce meaning through a play of differences. By contrast, African-inspired style seems an attempt to signify a bounded, essential identity for its wearer. Many of the designers and vendors say their wares "promote cultural awareness." Bede Ssensalo, an importer of Ghanaian, Ugandan, and Nigerian fabric, clothing, and jewelry, himself an immigrant from Uganda, explains how the style became popular in the United States: "You see, the person in Africa — it's taken for granted. He's in his own culture and everything. The person in America — the African American in America — is in a Eurocentric culture, and he's struggling to get out of that to establish his or her own identity." The use of African style in African American communities may seem to typify unironic, nostalgic yearnings for pure cultural roots, a unified origin, and an authentic tradition upon which postmodern theories have cast a mistrustful eye.

My perspective from within this Eurocentric culture put me in the position of having to try to understand the workings of African style rather than rushing to critique them through a ready-made conceptual grid. This attempt led me to consider some blind spots in our own culture theories. One of these is that the postmodern critique of binary structures has unnecessarily produced its own theoretical binaries — between essential and performative identities, between stable symbolic categories and border-crossing, boundary-blurring floating signifiers. These new theoretical binaries have, moreover, veered dangerously toward becoming value-laden prescriptions for a single "progressive" cultural politics.

One importer of Ghanaian fabrics and clothing, Jon Weber, originally from Brooklyn, articulates the identity politics of African style in a way that complicates our clear-cut, mutually exclusive theoretical categories:

> Having these types of things . . . the outfits, the jewelry, or whatever does not make you culturally aware, but it does make you want to know more about your culture. . . . For instance, I'm a black person, I'm being dogged in a society, right? Now when I put this on, do I wear the heritage of thousands of years of African history? . . . Some people do; it's how you internalize it. Now, instead of being Joe Butler, sanitation worker, you are now, you know, a *kunda*, you know, a prince. . . . When I put on my dashiki, or something, I wear it because it's comfortable, but I also learned that it's a walk that you have . . . it's how you hold your shoulders now. . . . Because you are wearing something that kings have worn.

Weber describes the politics of an identity that is both constructed through performance and grounded in an authentic origin. It is multiple, theatrical, intermittent, and contingent on one hand and essential on the other. Thus it can serve to introduce a study of other ways that this African-inspired fashion challenges a white middle-class bias in our own culture theories, which take avant-garde, campy fashion as the positive ideal.

But first, the African-inspired styles and some of the designers who make them should be introduced. When I first started interviewing the designers and vendors in 1993, the explosive events following the 1992 acquittal of Los Angeles police officers accused of beating Rodney King were fresh in their memories. Some of the people I interviewed expressed anger at the derogatory media treatment meted out to South Central. Their involvement in an urban community that fostered creative ferment contradicted the ubiquitous propaganda portraying gangs-drugs-guns-crime as the sole reality of the black community. Their stories help to set this partial, distorted representation into a larger, more complex context, one in which gangs and drugs are in dialectical relation with the resistance born of creative celebration.

Many colleagues and friends expressed alarm about this fieldwork and urged me not to do it. As a result of the contrast between their warnings and the warm reception I received from the Los Angeles community of African American craftspeople and vendors, the most vivid and certain knowledge that came out of the research does not concern African fashion as such.

Rather, it concerns the frightening extent to which, in spite of our sophisticated critical apparatus, we culture critics have acquiesced to the mass media stereotypes and fear-mongering TV "news" representations of the inner city.

The African American community lies in the center of Los Angeles County's southern region along the north-south spine of Crenshaw Boulevard, from the city of Inglewood in the south through Los Angeles's Crenshaw district at its cultural heart, to the I-10 freeway at its northern boundary. In one relatively well-off area of the Crenshaw district, Leimert Park, African American entrepreneurs and activists are trying to establish a "little Africa" cultural and economic zone. It has attracted designers and vendors of African clothing and thus became a site of my research.

On a sunny Saturday in October, now more than two years after the Rodney King uprising, Leimert Park is crowded with people. Shoppers saunter past the small stores. The storekeepers, who lounge on benches they have placed outside their doors, sun themselves and chat with passersby. Knots of people gather to exchange news. In a parking lot filled with rows of grocery bags, activists prepare to offer free food. On the sidewalk in front of the old Vision Theater, young black men are absorbed in a chess tournament, while Muslims in flowing robes hand out flyers to the passing members of this community. There are no white people — except, of course, for their local pseudo-ethnographer.

Contrary to the warnings of my friends and acquaintances, no one hijacked my car when I parked it. No menacing figures rushed up to grab my purse when I walked away from it. No one glared at me with hostility. In fact, no one paid any attention to me at all, until I recognized in a knot of chatting people a fellow volunteer from the African Marketplace. After greeting me with a warm hug, she whisked me off to the Vision Theater, where community activists had organized a program, "Remembering the Black Panther Party," of films, speeches, and musical performance. The audience of teenagers, older people of an age to be the parents of the former Black Panthers, and mothers with their children dotted the cavernous theater. My friend introduced me to some other mothers and, later, leading me back into the sunshine, showed me the studio where she took classes in West African dance and the clothing and jewelry shops whose owners she knew. It was in the context of settings like Leimert Park, the African Marketplace, Martin Luther King Jr. Boulevard, and the residential areas of South Central that I began an attempt to "read" the meanings of African styles in the African American community.

The styles made by the small-scale designers, tailors, artists, and crafts-

FIGURE 1. Renee Collins displaying
a handwoven kente priest's stole incorporating Ashanti and Christian symbols.

people range from the traditional Senegalese *boubous* (or what Nigerians call *agbadas*) and Nigerian butterfly dresses to the trendy, high-fashion cock-tail suits of African American Ahneva Ahneva or the sweatsuits by Nigerian Christopher Nnadede. Handwoven kente from Ghana (Fig. 1), mud cloth from Mali (Fig. 2), and *séru rábbal* (in French *pagne tissé*) from Senegal (Fig. 3) are used as trims or appliques. Brocades, batiks, tie-dies, starch-resist dies, and fold-resist dies, sometimes with thick, ornate embroidery, are fashioned into original designs combining Western tailoring with flowing West African drapes and cuts.

An infinite variety of changing styles comes from the interaction among immigrants from different cultures on the African continent and African Americans. In learning from each other and exchanging styles and techniques, they constantly invent new looks. The traditional Senegalese and Nigerian garments are imported or made in Los Angeles, either by immigrants or, in rarer cases, by African Americans. The styles are appropriated by Korean manufacturers in the Los Angeles garment district, who produce detailed copies of traditional African robes and knock-offs of the original styles in their sweatshops.

Although the vast majority of hybridizing clothes use African fabric in

FIGURE 2. Synovia Jones selling hand-woven Malian mud cloth and her own designs for children made of West African cloth at the African Marketplace.

FIGURE 3. Bass (Bassiro Lô) and Pam Carter displaying a swing coat trimmed with hand-woven Senegalese *séru rábbal* (*pagne tissé*) at their shop, Khadim of Africa, in Inglewood.

Western cuts, a few rare exceptions go the other way. Sarah Black makes the Nigerian butterfly dress out of a very American leopard print gauze and says she can't keep it in stock. Customers make a distinction between the West African robes, which they wear to church and mosque services, weddings, or dressy events, and the more Western styles, which they can wear to work. A sharply tailored suit with brilliant kente stole and Nefertiti crown serves for formal business events.

The skillful tailors and seamstresses of Inglewood and the Crenshaw district can fashion garments that subtly combine African and Western looks. Wairimu Wachira from Kenya and Bass from Senegal make a sailor collar out of the traditional neck ruffle and modify the flowing robe into a jumpsuit with palazzo pants. Evelyn Kuomontale, a designer who lives in Orange County, describes her syncretic process for business wear: "It's the way you design the sleeves, the puffed-up sleeves that gives it the African look. . . . The skirts, they are normal skirts like the Western skirts. So the pants, Western pants. But it's how I design the sleeves. That changes the whole thing. That brings in the African flavor." Wairimu Wachira has also designed children's clothes in fabric from Côte d'Ivoire, and Synovia Jones's children's designs come with matching West African skullcaps (Fig. 4).

Olujimi King makes a range of styles from traditional damask *grands boubous* to silk-screened T-shirts in his factory in Lagos, Nigeria. He learned the old methods of painting and dying fabric as a child from his Yoruba grandmother in a Nigerian village and now designs his own fabrics and fashions them into "new wave African clothing." Of his designs he says:

Instead of using the machine-printed technique—which is all right, there's nothing wrong with it—but so that the creativity and the technique of our forefathers do not die, I volunteered myself to just go on and carry it, and take it one step farther, you know. Not only the technique of dyeing, but the designs of the clothes, because they already have several designs of clothing from the past. So it's those designs that I've taken one step farther. . . . If they were really traditional, they would probably look square, you know. They wouldn't have any modern touches. Like the baggy pants I'm wearing, normally we stop by the cuff. I've taken it one step farther by taking it all the way down and adding the embroidery . . . so that it looks a little bit different from what our forefathers used to do. And the Tuaregs used to wear a lot of vests in the desert because it was very cold at night. . . . So what I'm doing now is just taking it one step farther by using mud cloth trim on the vests or . . . by mixing the fabric from all over the continent on the vest. So that makes it closer to home. That makes it African.

Like Olujimi, Bass, who learned tailoring from his uncle in a small town in Senegal, also makes everything from *grands boubous* to Western suits in

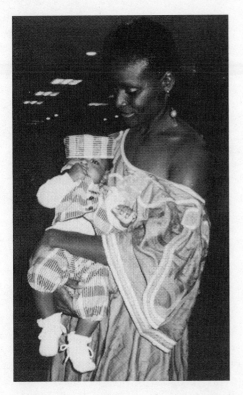

FIGURE 4. Synovia Jones, in a dress from Mali, with her son, who is wearing one of her designs for children.

basin and *légos*, with a range of hybrid styles in between. But his creativity takes a different direction. Whereas Olujimi's fashions combine the flowing lines of West African robes with a chic flair, Bass's fashions are intricately tailored and meticulously lined and shoulder padded. His suits have fitted jackets or swing coats with elaborately cut collars, cuffs, and inserts of *rábbal* or kente. His partner, Pam Carter, a former model from Los Angeles, keeps up with the latest styles in the magazines or on the streets and brings them to him, where Bass, who can conceptualize, cut, and sew a new design without a pattern, incorporates them into traditional Senegalese styles.

Some of the designers, like Aboubacar Sissoko from Senegal or Bakari Santos from Brazil, are artists who work in the media of painting or metal etching. They silk screen their mask paintings onto T-shirts, and Bakari also miniaturizes his metal etchings as earrings. In the hands of Gloria McGhee, the masks become ceramic pins with stylized faces sporting the latest look in dreadlocks, geometrics, or asymmetrical Afros and earrings or nose rings (Fig. 5). The urban mythology masks of Marilyn LaGrone-Amaral draw on her combined Africa, American Indian, and Creole cultures.

FIGURE 5. Gloria McGhee displaying her jewelry at the African Marketplace. Her hip-hop ceramic mask pins are in the foreground.

The economic situations of the designers are as varied as their designs. Some have other jobs. Sissoko is a lawyer, Gloria McGhee is a social worker, Sarah Black is a teacher, Ssensalo is a professor, and Marilyn LaGrone-Amaral is a Hollywood makeup artist and hairdresser. Others, like Wairimu Wachira, Karimu, Synovia Jones, and Christopher Nnadede, are struggling young designers undergoing hardship to establish themselves. They sell their fashions at swap meets and festivals or place them in the African boutiques that dot the Crenshaw district.

A few of the full-time designers have more or less successfully, more or less precariously, established themselves. Bass and Pam Carter have a shop in downtown Inglewood. Olujimi King could be found six months a year at his Jimi King Shango Gallery on chic Melrose Avenue in Hollywood until it closed in 1995. He had another gallery in Lagos. Ahneva Ahneva, who has a shop in the Leimert Park area, designed an Afrocentric tuxedo for President Bill Clinton and does fashion shows for the congressional Black Caucus. She hopes to establish a mass-produced line that will sell in department stores.

But whatever the future holds for a brilliant designer like Ahneva Ahneva, this inner-city creativity remains marginal to corporate mass culture. Even when appropriated by JCPenney and K-Mart, African fashions are sold for the most part only in the inner city where white shoppers do not tread. This marginality gives African-influenced clothing the exceptionality that complicates the current view of postmodern subcultural style within cultural studies.

Some of the styles approach the playfulness celebrated by postmodern fashion studies. For instance, Karimu, a native of South Central Los Angeles, uses scraps of African fabric as complex free-form appliques on southern California sweats. Yet even the more playful of the African styles seem bounded in their semiotic and rhetorical play when compared to the campy styles. Since a comparison of the two kinds of styles in the context of culture theory concerns clothing as a semiotic system, a brief discussion of the semiotics of clothing in general is in order.

If clothing is a social language, if it constitutes a system of signs producing social meaning, pan-African fashion does so through its particular situation within the history and geography of sartorial sign systems. As clothing travels from one historical or cultural context to another, not only its meaning but also, as the quotation from Bede Ssensalo suggests, its mode of signification change. That is, clothing signifiers change not only what they mean but how they mean. They change not only their message but the logic by which signs form and interact to produce meaning.

The African-influenced clothing studied here has changed its meaning and its logic of meaning production as it has moved through the varied symbolic orders of African countries and into those of the United States. In African countries, the uses of this clothing have been transformed by trans-African trading, the slave trade, colonialism and anticolonial movements, postcolonialism, and global consumer capitalism (Barnes and Eicher; Cole 1990; Nielsen n.d.; Pokornowksi n.d.: 104–6, 112; Wares 1981:76–95, 107–8; Wass n.d.). In the United States, these layers of meaning are joined with another historical layering so that African clothing bears the double sedimentation of semiotic systems.

Modern and postmodern modes of sartorial signification in the United States have antecedents in premodern Europe. In feudal culture, symbolic systems other than the sign system gave clothing unambiguous referents;[1] the wearer's position was designated in fixed hierarchies of class and sex and, according to Pearl Binder, "constituted a means of enforcing class privilege in a regimented social structure" (quoted in Ewen 1985:122). With the rise of commodity capitalism and urban mobility, workers could imitate the dress of the wealthy bourgeois, and so clothing communicated more ambiguous messages about its wearer. Instead of *designating* the wearer's fixed place in a scale of positions, it was worn to *signify* a social role. That is, a sartorial signifier designated the signified of a role but not necessarily its referent. Clothing clearly signified gender, class, nationality, and age, as well as various jobs and professions, but did not guarantee that the wearer actually belonged to the social categories signified by the clothing. To take just one example, young immigrant women from Eastern Europe in New York adopted clothing that marked them as "American" as quickly as they could so as to avoid prejudice and find work (Ewen 1985:25–26). In a mobile society, clothing could ambiguously reveal or conceal the social position of its wearer. This modernist mode of signification still operates in many instances, as when fashion magazines advise young working women to dress one rank in the corporate hierarchy above their own as a strategy for promotion. But in postmodern society, clothing has increasingly entered another logic of signification.

By contrast to his modern ambiguity of meaning, postmodern clothing as signifier does not express a stable social identity, and dress becomes costume. Any sartorial signifier — of 1960s hippie, businessman, derelict, priest, prostitute, addict — can be bought and worn by anyone. In both the mass consumer styles and their campy, avant-garde send-offs, clothing is no longer a disguise, as in modernist modes of meaning, but a playful masquerade. Rather than hide a "real" identity, postmodern clothing as masquerade constitutes the identity of its wearer as a fragmented subject. Although African style is costumy, it does not function in this way as masquerade. It maintains an attachment to more stable forms of the social, ethnic, and political identity of its wearer.

Instead of assuming this postmodern subversion of symbolic categories, African style in the United States incorporates a hybridity that does not uproot it from more stable modes of meaning. Yet the African styles do have their own particular semiotic mobility. They differ from the destabilizing subversion of Western avant-garde fashions but are no less significant for a theory of progressive cultural practices, if we want to look at them in global rather than Western terms. The semiotic mobility of pan-African style is related to its geographic mobility. As it circulates from African countries to Los Angeles, it also circulates among different historical and geographically dispersed modes of meaning and coexists in all of them.

Equally noteworthy is that the modes of meaning also circulate with dizzying mobility. In certain places and occasions, African fashions can have a less traditional or ceremonial use in African countries than in Los Angeles. In Los Angeles, it is customary to wear African dress on the last Sunday of the month in black churches or for "Black History Days" at public schools. Immigrants from the former English colonies such as Kenya and Uganda say that the English suppressed the traditional dress. Urban inhabitants there wear West African dress as just another fashion alternative. Wairimu learned to sew as a child in Kenya by making Western dresses, as did Emilie Ngo Nguidjol in Cameroon.

Thus where some of the African American designers say they prefer designing African clothing because, as Karimu says, "it's not going to go out of style," or, as Synovia Jones hopes, it is not a "fad," some of the immigrant African designers see it as indeed another fad. Wairimu Wachira says: "I don't think I'll do the traditional styles for a long time . . . because eventually, like everything else I've been doing, [they] come and go. We have to move on to the next."

Dress in some African countries is dictated by tradition or custom, which may be invented. The market women of Yaounde, Cameroon, wear the traditional flowing *Kaba*. But a photo of the Yaounde market in *Ebony* magazine in 1960, just before independence, shows the Yaounde women wearing Western dress. Traditional dress appears to have been reintroduced by post-independence governments. In another example from postcolonial Cameroon, traditional dress is worn but not in a traditional way. Rather, it recalls Western modernist modes of ambiguity and disguise. Emilie Ngo Nguidjol describes it: "You got better service when you went to a public office [in Yaounde] if you were dressed African, especially like a northerner, because people thought you belonged to that province where the then-president came from." Here the ability of dress to signify identity in a highly mobile society allows the wearer to assume a false identity.

By contrast, Jimi King, speaking in his shop on trendy Melrose, muses about creating clothing symbolism that goes back to the 1950s and to West Africa. His ideas are strongly reminiscent of the anticolonial meaning of hair style in preindependence Senegal as described by author Niang Fatou Niang Siga. Different from the counterhegemonic styles of Western subcultures, whose flamboyant nonconformity signifies rebellion, new styles are named after "shameful events" or popular heroes. Siga writes: "And indeed, the 'NDAR' women plaited their hair in ways that bore witness to their love for a person, their gratitude toward a benefactor, but also as a sign of devotion to a cause. Better still, they made hairstyle into slogans for the masses of people . . . in order to mark shameful events and stimulate the population to action" (1990:7). Such hairstyles, often in combination with distinctive head wraps, had names such as "le salut du Général De Gaulle" (p. 19) or, in 1950, the "'*Kaddu Lamin*' (Woloff for Lamine's speech)," after Lamine Gueye, first president of the Senegalese National Assembly. Siga describes the eponymous hairstyle as a "testimony of satisfaction and gratitude toward the deputy for the just cause he was defending, in his pleadings for the Lamine Gueye Law, to grant citizenship to all people of African origin" (p. 38).

Similarly, King says: "I've been tempted many times to name some designs after some ugly political incidences in Africa . . . so that people would be reminded that some people are taken advantage of and that some things that happened in the past were not right. So that we wouldn't go back and make the same mistakes again, you know. Or, for example, if I did a design and called it 'Steve Biko,' then Steve Biko's name would live forever, you know."

Another example illustrates more generally how African American wearers have succeeded in styling African-influenced fashion into new, and uncommonly enduring, ceremonial uses in the context of the U.S. racial system. Their semiotics, reflecting relatively fixed forms of meaning, point to the bias through which white American cultural theory has developed a narrow view of progressive symbolic practices. The special fifth anniversary issue of *Mirabella* magazine contains an extensive photoessay entitled "*Mirabella's* 100 Fearless Women" (June 1994:45–133). Among the 100 photographs are ones of filmmaker Julie Dash (p. 115), musician, musicologist, activist, and feminist theorist Bernice Reagon (p. 125), and Florence Ladd, director of the Bunting Institute (p. 69). Reagon and the five other members of Sweet Honey in the Rock wear kente weave Nefertiti crowns and large stoles or collars over flowing white outfits. Dash wears a tailored brown jacket with high-style mud cloth collar and cuffs. Ladd wears a simple black top and around her neck a Senegalese or Malian leather amulet box, decorated with cowrie shells. Although the basic outfits, ranging from conservative to flamboyant, are keyed to North American dress codes, the accessories link the three women and distinguish them from the photoessay's other subjects. No other woman among those photographed wears clothing influenced by African style. The clothing signifiers of these three women designate membership in a dispersed community in a way that does not lend itself either to the modernist semiotics of disguise or the postmodern semiotics of parody and masquerade.

In other words, although mass marketed in the black community, the style is not amenable to co-optation in the general consumer market as are most subcultural and ethnic styles. In contrast to punk, hip hop, hippie, motorcycle, or even gang styles on the one hand and the use of Central American, Middle Eastern, or Asian fabrics and motifs on the other, African styles and fabrics resist (or at least have resisted so far) breaking out of the boundaries of their political signification. Their meaning may be diluted by the mass-produced version, but they do not flow into the mass-cultural warehouse of free-floating signifiers and images.[2] How and why do African-influenced styles attain this relative immunity to appropriation by mass culture? And what does this resistance tell those of us in cultural studies about theories of sartorial cultural politics based narrowly on avant-garde fashions that subvert essentializing identities?

In his essay "Black Hair/Style Politics," Kobena Mercer analyzes the ways first the Afro and then dreadlocks, plaits, and weaves helped to "to redefine a diasporean people not as Negro but as Afro-American" (1990:255). African clothing, like African hairstyle, can signify an effort to undo the racial "categories . . . created by binary and dualistic logics from European culture" (p. 256). It can signify a rejection of the white/black hierarchical binary constructed by Western ideologies of race.

An ironically doubled symbolism thus results from the adoption of this style. A self-definition based on differences among cultures of African descent not centered by a dominant white power can function within the black community. But this self-definition alone does not account for the style's relatively stable political meaning. The dominant white culture still constructs itself by defining blacks in oppositional terms as other. Ironically, the persistence of racially opposed categories encloses the signifiers of African difference within a certain stability. Those categories function effectively even in the midst of a postmodern consumer economy that seems able to aspirate everything, including black youth culture, into a commodified flux of mass media signifiers.

The continuing power of oppositional, hierarchical discourses cannot be dismissed by culture theory. The doubled semiotics of African-inspired fashion in a racist society suggests the need to examine the ways in which oppositional logics and logics of flux and fragmentation work together. Perhaps more important, given that African-influenced fashions are used in the United States to symbolize a diasporic difference that conforms neither to dualistic opposition nor to infinite flux, they suggest further the need to examine other forms of semiotic logic working together. In addition, two faces of African-influenced fashion are turned simultaneously toward the dominant, white symbolic order and toward the many cultures of Africa. These two sets of symbolic practices intermingle in its folds.

A first glance at African-influenced fashion from the perspective of culture theory might lead to the conclusion that it merely replicates the logic of an essentialist discourse. The clothing seems to express the desire to identify with a mythic Africa of unbroken genealogies, authentic origins, and intact traditions. As a consumer fetish, it seems to have the power to free its members from dualistic logic, a power that, as sign, it does not possess. But two factors disrupt such an essentializing discourse. The first goes back to the ironic doubling surrounding African fashion in the United States. The second bears on a postcolonial African difference also inscribed in the clothing along with the commodified mythic Africa.

As concerns the irony, the clothing's semiotic stability comes not from the meanings of authenticity, unity, and continuity it expresses as a consumer fetish but from the insertion of those meanings into the context of a racist oppositional logic. Political scientist Manning Marable, novelist Michael Thelwell, and sociologist Robert Blauner all point to the recent social and economic polarization that recreate this logic.[3] Marable says:

Despite . . . obvious symbols of racial advancement, in many respects the state of American race relations reached a new nadir in the late 1980s and early 1990s. . . . Many measures of the social and economic status of blacks began to deteriorate markedly. Black median incomes for families dropped sharply . . . during the 1980s. In higher education, the number of African-American college students declined by nearly one hundred thousand between 1980 and 1986; the number of black doctorates granted annually plummeted from 1,166 in 1977 to only 765 in 1987. (1983:47–48)

In the 1980s, Marable contended, "Blacks are being concentrated in exactly those industries that are undergoing rapid decline and conversely are excluded from the sectors of the economy targeted for growth" (1983:48).[4] In the wake of the 1992 riots, Peter Ueberroth was quoted as telling the Los Angeles Urban League: "For 40 years, corporate America, and I'm part of that, has moved every decent job out of the inner city" (Rivera 1992). The social practices that separate African Americans into abandoned inner cities accompany a symbolic practice that confines them in the category of the other. Ironically, this separation and confinement stabilize the sartorial meanings of freedom that the black community constructs in their context.

An example comes from a televised press conference held by the Damien Williams Defense Committee in Los Angeles in the winter of 1993. Williams had been charged with beating Reginald Denny during the riots that erupted in South Central in April 1992 after the acquittal of Los Angeles police officers charged with beating Rodney King. The Damien Williams Defense Committee, like many spokespeople in the African American community, had continuously charged that a double standard of justice was applied in the two trials. At this televised press conference, the three members of the defense committee wore traditional West African garb. And as is customary on formal occasions in many regions of West Africa, their clothes were made of identical fabric. With their stern, unsmiling faces and their equally stern denunciations of the judicial process, they left no doubt as to the political meaning their clothing expressed. No floating signifiers, neither in parodic displacement of symbolic systems nor in mass market appropriation, were evident here. Their clothing also expressed the meaning of a refusal to be defined within the white/black binary they were criticizing with respect to the justice system. And this meaning could gain a certain force precisely because they were in a situation of being so defined.

But while their clothing drew one set of meanings from its insertion within white cultural logic, it drew another from its place within a network of postcolonial pan-African difference. This difference is not, as in the case of avant-garde, subversive practices, the play of displacing a symbolic system through parodic repetition. It consists rather in the circulation of African fabric and clothing through a double global network. On the one hand, the fashions circulate among the various modes of signification in African countries and U.S. communities — traditional and commodified, ceremonial and decorative — described earlier. On the other hand, the fabric and clothing also circulate through the international network linking small producers, craftspeople, and suitcase vendors, like many of the people interviewed for this study, who travel throughout Africa as well as back and forth from Africa to Europe, the United States, and the Caribbean. Their constant border crossings, unlike those of the gender-bending camp fashions, are literal as well as symbolic. While Western avant-garde fashions cross the semiotic boundaries from one symbolic category to another, the wares of these vendors and designers are constantly crossing from one symbolic system to another, each of which contributes to the design.

For fashion critics to be able to focus on this different form of difference, we would need a shift in global perspective in which the economic and media networks of global corporate capitalism would fade just enough to bring into focus this faint subsidiary caught in its links. This is not so much an alternate network as a fragile, fugitive shadow of the corporate networks, inconspicuously riding their electronic and transportational pathways. The constant migration of the suitcase vendors within their economic subsystem attests to the enormous disruption of traditional ways of life in their homelands. In making available the merchandise for their African

American consumer market, they give yet another ironic twist to its symbolism. The fashions, with their meaning of "traditional Africa," can come about only through the disruption of this tradition. Those stable meanings thus also signify this destabilization of African cultures.

Many of the African immigrants who design the styles and who teach the traditional designs to their African American colleagues have no illusions about the status of that tradition. In postcolonial capitalism, the very forces that destroy the possibility for these immigrants to make a living at home offer the opportunity to sell clothing as a sign of the tradition that has been destroyed. The same economic forces that rob African countries of the ability to sustain the immigrants create "Africa" as a commodity and make this commodity popular.

This constant circulation among various modes of signification and symbolic systems resembles Homi Bhabha's vision of a postcolonial difference, which he distinguishes from "cultural diversity" defined as "a radical rhetoric of the separation of totalized cultures that live unsullied by the intertextuality of their historical locations" (1994:34; see also Gilroy, 1992:188, 191; and Gilroy, 1993:2–8). In cultural difference, by contrast, "cultural interaction emerges only at the significatory boundaries of cultures, where meanings and values are (mis)read or signs are misappropriated" (Bhabha 1994: 35). It is precisely a series of misreadings that produces the interweave of the different meanings in African-inspired clothing.

Some designers reject this misreading. Evelyn Kuomontale, a designer from Uganda, born of a Zairian mother and a Belgian father, works full-time for a missionary Christian fellowship in Orange County and designs as a hobby and for fashion shows to raise money for the fellowship. She criticizes the African American misinterpretation of African clothing: "I think the African Americans here, most of them, need to really go to Africa. Come and see what the real thing is like. Because . . . a lot of styles that they see on the market here, they're not really African in a way. It's okay so long as they are using the African fabric, but they kind of overdo the whole thing. . . . So these are things that develop here and they think it's connected with Africa, and yet it's not. It has nothing to do with Africa." For Wairimu Wachira, an immigrant from Kenya, struggling to build a full-time career in fashion, however, the misreadings are the very point of the designs. She consults *Essence*, a North American magazine for black women, "to see what other designers are doing and how much they've learned in regards to African fashions," and then works off the North American (mis)interpretations of the African clothes to create her own designs.

Bhabha's intercultural misreadings occur not only among African cultures but also between African and white cultures. Emilie Ngo Nguidjol suggests that such misreadings contribute to the ironically stable meanings of African influenced clothes: "There is a perception out there that when Africans wear something, it's OK. They are complimented. When African Americans wear dreads or African clothes, they are not approved or complimented. They are still perceived as threatening."

Her observation can also explain how the semiotic stability of African-influenced clothing accompanies a market stability that is equally unusual in postmodern mass consumerism. Although African-influenced styles are appropriated by consumer capitalism, even these mass-disseminated imitations remain more bounded within the borders of the African American target market than other countercultural and ethnic styles, even those of African American youth. They do not spill over these borders to be absorbed by a white consumer market. (Or at least they have not at the time of this writing. In mass consumerism, *anything* can be — and has been — appropriated.) The recent history of the mass marketing of African-inspired fashions can explain why they are less easily absorbed into the commercial fashion code as just another floating signifier.

Although JCPenney, K-Mart, and Spiegel have co-opted the subcultural, handmade fashions for mass consumerism, they target black consumers. Penney's markets its African-inspired products mostly through a special *Influences* catalog, and only 170 of its 1,300 stores stock the items (Van de Water 1993:1). There is, however, one method by which the corporate distributors can expand their market. Marketing experts note that when the African elements become attenuated enough and removed from the body toward bath and bedding accessories, they become fashionable for white households. White people will use African motifs in their homes but will not wear them on their bodies. The Cox News Service reports: "JCPenney wanted to tap the apparel budgets of African Americans. The expansion into bed and bath linens, however, has had broader appeal. 'We were shooting for the ethnic angle, but it appears we're catching that mainstream customer as well,' said Art Avila, special segment manager for JCPenney's Home & Leisure division" (Van de Water 1993:1). Illustrating the way racial categories are both dissolving and hardening, Avila's words suggest that as long as African-influenced fashions remain too close to the body, appearing as the black body's second skin to the so-called mainstream public, they retain a politically stable meaning. Perhaps this is because these styles are not simply cultural but are also too immediately associated with political identities that white society does not want to be reminded of. Whereas gang style is apolitical, and perhaps therefore more easily co-opted, African style, going back to the late 1960s, connotes a conscious politics that is combined with a bodily presence.

The way white mass culture infuses African-influenced fashion with a politics of opposition brings us back to its comparison with camp, drag, and transvestite fashion and their politics of subversion. The point here is not to pit gay fashion and African American fashion against each other but to look at ways in which cultural studies can admit a multiplicity of symbolic practices as progressive and mutually reinforcing. Current cultural studies tend to see oppositional politics, based on a dialectics of struggle, as outmoded and conservative. A subversive politics, based on displacement of symbolic systems from within, seems the only possible strategy for contesting oppression. For instance, Judith Butler, writing on strategy in *Bodies That Matter*, questions whether mimicry or subversive repetition can always displace symbolic systems, but the book assumes that insofar as it succeeds, this is the only progressive strategy.

Yet in her critique of *Paris Is Burning*, Butler joins bell hooks and Marjorie Garber in questioning the politics of drag in a situation where race and sexuality intersect: "*Paris Is Burning* calls into question whether parodying the dominant norms is enough to displace them" (1993:125). Similarly, Garber's analysis of black men's transvestism in *Vested Interests* complicates her theory of cross-dressing. She analyzes images in which a "feminized black man" is "disempowered and made ridiculous" as an "object of the (white majority) gaze" (1992:269). Here, according to Garber, transvestism "marks . . . the paradox of the black man in America as simultaneously a sign of sexual potency and a sign of emasculation or castration" (p. 271).

Bell hooks's essay on *Paris Is Burning* also criticizes the notion that transvestism is always subversive. Images of "black men in drag," she says, can sometimes help "sustain sexism and racism" (1992:146) when they are shown imitating a feminine ideal that "is the exclusive property of white womanhood" (p. 148). *Paris Is Burning*, according to hooks, "in no way interrogates whiteness" (p. 149) but portrays "the way in which colonized black people (in this case black gay brothers, some of whom were drag queens) worship at the throne of whiteness" (p. 149). She asks: "What could be more reassuring to a white public fearful that marginalized, disenfranchised black folks might rise any day now and make revolutionary black liberation struggle a reality?" (p. 149). The televised stern faces and words of the Damien Williams Defense Committee members are not so reassuring, and their clothing becomes metonymically associated with this demeanor.

For fashion critics, our task is not to choose between the subversive play of drag and the stable meanings of clothing like African-influenced fashion but to examine what both these styles can teach us about symbolic politics at the intersections of race, class, and gender. Whether the more progressive use of clothing is to create stable meanings or to destabilize meaning depends on the context. And in 1990s consumer society the gender or racial context can be unpredictable and slippery. As Marable noted in talking about "the modern racial paradox in American life" (1991:187), oppositional boundaries of race and gender are breaking down on some levels but intensifying on others. TV ads use images of inner-city black street culture to sell a host of products to suburban consumers. Consumers watch these ads from behind the walls of their securely gated, guarded, and electronically surveilled housing developments, designed to protect them from the threat of inner-city youth. In a world of such disjunctures, it is difficult to know when or where discursive parody or dialectical contradiction might better meet a strategic need. And in this world, African-influenced fashion, with its multiple modes of signification, has much to teach cultural critics.

NOTES

1. For an analysis of symbolic systems in Europe that historically preceded the sign system, see Kristeva, "Bounded Text."

2. Another style that has maintained its cultural and market boundaries is the Indian sari in England. According to Naseem Kahn, the sari changed both in India and among Indian women in England in response to the Indian women's movement and the rise to professional status of middle-class Indian women. Within England, however, the market for the new Indian fashions, called East-West (Kahn, p. 68), is mostly confined to Indian women. Saris have been commercialized and internationalized for second-generation Indian women in England. One shop tried to attract Western women, who became about 20 percent of its clientele (Kahn, p. 72). African Marketplace estimates that whites make up about the same percentage of its clientele.

3. Robert Blauner says that "in the last two decades we have seen both a greater acceptance of people of color and a disquieting return of bigotry and racial hatred" (p. 55). For more detailed statistics see Cotton. More recently, novelist Michael Thelwell commented: "Despite this conspicuous expansion of black influence and affluence, diffused and apparently unconnected at the top, our national community

has never in its history been so confused and divided, or so alienated from itself, our working people at greater economic risk, or our inner-city youth in such great jeopardy, mired in such hopelessness, violence, and despair" (pp. 88–89).

4. Eitzen and Zinn similarly report that in the postmodern economic reorganization, four economic factors — new technologies, global economy, capitalist flight, and the dominance of information — have worked to deepen inequality and form new patterns of domination (p. 178). Jeremiah Cotton documents this downward trend in the 1980s by charting economic patterns from 1963 to 1987.

WORKS CITED

Appadurai, Arjun. 1986. "Introduction: Commodities and the Politics of Value." In *The Social Life of Things*, ed. A. Appadurai. Cambridge: Cambridge University Press.

Barnes, Ruth, and Joanne B. Eicher, eds. 1992. *Dress and Gender: Making and Meaning in Cultural Contexts*. New York: Berg.

Berlant, Lauren, and Elizabeth Freeman. 1992. "Queer Nationality." *boundary2* 19, no. 1:149–80.

Bhabha, Homi K. 1994. *The Location of Culture*. New York: Routledge.

Blauner, Robert. 1992. "The Ambiguities of Racial Change." In *Race, Class, and Gender: An Anthology*, ed. Margaret L. Anderson and Patricia Hill Collins, pp. 54–64. Belmont, Calif.: Wadsworth.

Butler, Judith. 1993. *Bodies That Matter: On the Discursive Limits of "Sex."* New York: Routledge.

Case, Sue-Ellen. 1993. "Toward a Butch-Femme Aesthetic." In *The Lesbian and Gay Studies Reader*, ed. Henry Abelove, Michele Aina Barale, and David M. Halperin. New York: Routledge.

Cole, Herbert M. 1990. "Kente: A Meaningful Tradition in Cloth." *American Visions* (Oct.): 18–22.

Cotton, Jeremiah. 1989. "Opening the Gap: The Decline in Black Economic Indicators in the 1980s." *Social Science Quarterly* 70, no. 4: 803–19.

Eitzen, Stanley, and Maxine Baca Zinn. 1992. "Structural Transformation and Systems of Inequality." In *Race, Class, and Gender: An Anthology*, ed. Margaret L. Anderson and Patricia Hill Collins, pp. 178–82. Belmont, Calif.: Wadsworth.

Evans, Caroline, and Minna Thornton. 1991. "Fashion, Representation, Femininity." *Feminist Review* 38:48–66.

Ewen, Elizabeth. 1985. *Immigrant Women in the Land of Dollars*. New York: Monthly Review Press.

Ewen, Stuart, and Elizabeth Ewen. 1982. *Channels of Desire: Mass Images and the Shaping of American Consciousness*. New York: McGraw-Hill.

Garber, Marjorie. 1992. *Vested Interests: Cross-Dressing and Cultural Anxiety*. New York: Routledge.

Gilroy, Paul. 1993. *The Black Atlantic: Modernity and Double Consciousness*. Cambridge, Mass.: Harvard University Press.

————. 1992. "Cultural Studies and Ethnic Absolutism." In *Cultural Studies*, ed. Lawrence Grossberg, Cary Nelson, and Paula Treichler, pp. 187–98. New York: Routledge.

hooks, bell. "Is Paris Burning?" 1992. In *Black Looks: Race and Representation*, pp. 145–56. Boston: South End Press.

Kahn, Naseem. 1992. "Asian Women's Dress: From Burqah to Bloggs — Changing Clothes for Changing Times." In *Chic Thrills: A Fashion Reader*, ed. Juliet Ash and Elizabeth Wilson, pp. 61–74. Berkeley: University of California Press.

Kristeva, Julia. "The Bounded Text." 1980. In *Desire in Language: A Semiotic Approach to Literature and Art*, ed. Leon S. Roudiez, trans. Thomas Gora, Alice Jardine, and Leon S. Roudiez, pp. 36–63. New York: Columbia University Press.

Marable, Manning. 1983. *How Capitalism Underdeveloped Black America: Problems in Race, Political Economy and Society*. Boston: South End Press.

————. 1991. *Race, Reform, and Rebellion: The Second Reconstruction in Black America, 1945–1990*. Jackson: University Press of Mississippi.

Mercer, Kobena. "Black Hair/Style Politics." 1990. In *Out There: Marginalization and Contemporary Culture*, ed. Russell Ferguson, Martha Gever, Trinh T. Minh-ha, and Cornel West, pp. 249–66. Cambridge, Mass.: MIT Press.

Michelman, Susan O., and Tonye V. Erekosima. 1992. "Kalabari Dress in Nigeria." In *Dress and Gender: Making and Meaning in Cultural Contexts*, ed. Rugh Barnes and Joanne B. Eicher, pp. 164–82. New York: Berg.

Mirabella magazine. June 1994.

Nielsen, Ruth. N.d. "The History and Development of Wax-Printed Textiles Intended for West Africa and Zaire." In *Fabrics of Culture: The Anthropology of Clothing and Adornment*, ed. Justine M. Cordwell and Ronald A. Schwarz, pp. 467–98. The Hague: Mouton.

Pokornowski, Ila. N.d. "Beads and Personal Adornment." In *Fabrics of Culture: The Anthropology of Clothing and Adornment*, ed. Justine M. Cordwell and Ronald A. Schwarz, pp. 103–17. The Hague: Mouton.

Rivera, Carla. 1992. "Ueberroth Takes Share of Blame for L.A. Riots." *Los Angeles Times*, July 29, p. A10.

Saussure, Ferdinand de. 1959. *Course in General Linguistics*, trans. Wade Baskin. New York: Philosophical Library.

Siga, Niang Fatou Niang. 1990. *Reflets de modes et traditions Saint-Louisiennes*. C.A.E.C. Dakar: Editions Khoudia.

Smith, Dorothy E. 1987. "Women's Perspective as Radical Critique of Sociology." In *Feminism and Methodology: Social Science Issues*, ed. Sandra Harding, pp. 84–96. Bloomington: Indiana University Press.

Thelwell, Michael. 1992. "False, Fleeting, Perjured Clarence: Yale's Brightest and Blackest Go to Washington." In *RACE-ing JUS-TICE, En-GENDERing POWER*, ed. Toni Morrison, pp. 86–126. New York: Pantheon Books.

79

Van de Water, Ava. 1993. "Home Editors: African Inspirations." Cox News Service. Nov. 23.

Wares, Lydia Jean. 1981. "Dress of the African American Woman in Slavery and Freedom, 1500 to 1935." Ph.D. diss., Purdue University. Ann Arbor UMI, 1984. 8210269.

Wass, Betty M. N.d. "Yoruba Dress in Five Generations of a Lagos Family." In *Fabrics of Culture: The Anthropology of Clothing and Adornment,* ed. Justine M. Cordwell and Ronald A. Schwarz, pp. 331–48. The Hague: Mouton.

5. Coming of Age in Zambesia

When Doris Lessing's collection of African stories first appeared in 1951, white South African reviews revealed the peculiar double vision of colonial settlers. Her sketches of Southern African societies were applauded for their realism, yet the urgent issues they raised were left lying, as if inert, and the urgency was evaluated as a "bitterness" that spoiled her "art." Lessing's work was often regretfully dismissed as "promising but artistically flawed" by her tendency to "standardiz[e] human beings to serve abstract ideas." Her brief return to Africa in 1956 elicited a sharper response. Journalist Oliver Walker confidently claimed, in an article ominously titled "Novelist Given a Tarred White Feather in Bulawayo," that black Africans preferred apartheid to "British hypocrisy" regarding race relations, but Lessing, a "prohibited immigrant" at that time and permitted to cross the border only by mistake, was kept under surveillance throughout her trip and, as Walker put it, "accused of putting ideas into the munts' heads" (47).[1] Her meticulous representation of the monstrous quotidian was recognized, examined in aesthetic terms, and tidily discounted, while her possibly subversive presence stimulated the usual official response of vigilance and control.

More recently, Lessing's work has been found flawed in a different regard; it is neither too bitter nor realistic but rather too "romantic." In her 1991 article "*Veldtanschauung*: Doris Lessing's Savage Africa," Eve Bertelsen cites the need to consider "the ways in which literary tradition and its forms impose upon the writer, defining in advance the range of her creative freedom, and often seriously contradicting or undermining an explicit social or political project."[2] Bertelsen is speaking of the way the romantic/primitivist view of Africa pervades Lessing's early novel *The Grass Is Singing*; specifically, she draws a parallel between Lessing's writing of Africans and Africa and Conrad's in *Heart of Darkness*. Both writers present a "vision of Africa" that relies on "a set of literary conventions and a cultural myth that appears to be stronger than conscious intent" (p. 658). Zimbabwe critic Anthony Chennells has also criticized Lessing's early work for its perpetuation of a romantic view of "darkest Africa." Questioning Lessing's inclusion in the literary canon of Zimbabwe by the *Tabex Encyclopedia Zimbabwe*, Chennells writes: "If one reads Lessing's stories as produced by a European romanticism rather than as the products of a liberal settler, the distinction between herself and writers who wrote Africa as primitive may not be as valid as the Encyclopedia entry assumes."[3]

It is not difficult to find passages that support such a view in Lessing's early stories, collected in the anthology *This Was the Old Chief's Country* and published a year after *The Grass Is Singing*. But I would argue that the early work as a whole demonstrates Lessing's awareness of the problem presented by the literary tradition she is writing her way out of and that many occasions of "romantic primitivism" in that work are deliberately ironic. The story she chose to open the collection, "The Old Chief Mshlanga," confronts the problematic of literary tradition and political intent which Bertelsen finds in the earlier novel. Through its implicit involvement with Conrad's representations of "savage Africa," the text both recognizes and critiques the seductions of romanticism and writes the confrontation with that tradition as integral to the constitution of self-irony in the liberal settler. One might use Homi Bhabha's metaphor of the "tethered shadow" to describe the relationship of Conrad's text to Lessing's — *Heart of Darkness* dogs her discourse, and she deals with its inevitable echoes through parodic repetitions that underline the collusion of belated romanticism in the pathology of colonialism.

In addition, Lessing's African story suggests, *avant la lettre*, postmodern formulations of "identification," in which apparent binary oppositions actually include a third aspect or property, the betweenness itself or "fissure," the reciprocity of difference that both threatens and makes possible the identification. It is this fissure Lessing maps as the territory inherited by the African-born settler awakened to political awareness. Gilles Deleuze, in *Logique de sens*, posits "two readings of the world," the first the mimetic type, which "asks us to think of difference on the basis of pre-established similitude or identity," and a second which "invites us on the contrary to think of similitude and even identity as the product of a fundamental disparity." The first "establishes the world as icon," the second "presents the world itself as phantasm," or, as Walter Benjamin put it, allows "the true surrealist face of existence [to break] through."[4]

In the apparently faithful social realism of Lessing's early work, surrealism consistently breaks through; icons are subverted, phantasms shimmer on the surface of the prosaic. The permeability of the boundary between real and surreal, sanity and schism, was, for Lessing, fundamental: in her own words, "the quintessential eccentricity of the human race was borne in upon me from the beginning."[5] Lessing was no distanced academic observer of the dis-ease of patriarchal imperialism; she learned it at her father's knee. She "concluded at the age of about six" that her father was "mad"; she describes his "splendidly pathological character" as something she "spent a good part of [her] childhood coming to terms with."

It was [my father's] wont to spend many hours of the day seated in a rickety deck-chair on the top of the semi-mountain on which our house was built, surveying the African landscape which stretched emptily away on all sides for leagues. After a silence which might very well have lasted several hours, he would start to his feet, majestically splenetic in shabby khaki, a prophet in his country, and, shaking his fist at the sky, shout out: "Mad! Mad! Everyone! Everywhere! Mad!" (p. 7)

The young Doris May Taylor learned how the skewed double standard of colonial "moral sense" worked. One early lesson, "comparatively uncomplicated, not to say banal," as she puts it, occurred on a windless day when her father was burning a fireguard to protect the cowshed from the wild veld fires common in the dry season in Southern Africa. The fire burned slowly, "yet it was in the nature of things that any small animal, grounded bird, insect or reptile in the 200-yard-wide, mile-long stretch of fire would perish, not presumably without pain." When a large field mouse ran out of the burning grass in front of Lessing's father, the "boss-boy," an African man,

brought down a heavy stick across the mouse's back. It was dying. The boss-boy picked up the mouse by the tail, and swinging the still-twitching creature, continued to stand beside my father, who brought down his hand in a very hard slap against the boss-boy's face. So unprepared was he for this, that he fell down. He got up, palm to his cheek, looking at my father for an explanation. My father was rigid with incommunicable anger, "Kill it at once," he said. . . . The boss-boy flung the mouse into a nest of flames, and stalked off, with dignity. "If there's one thing I can't stand it's cruelty of any kind," my father said afterwards, in explanation of the incident. (pp. 9–10)

This autobiographical anecdote bears some of the hallmarks of Lessing's fiction. She attempts no explication or analysis of the incident; she merely presents it to the reader and moves on to another "more obliquely rewarding in its implications" (p. 10). One is left to imagine the child observing these "lessons" unprotected by the seasoned irony of the adult relating them: the successive shocks to her sensibility, her puzzling over "implications," her gradual deconstruction of rank hypocrisies presented to her as self-justifying truths.

The spatial and verbal structures likewise echo Lessing's fictional strategies and suggest that she must be read with close attention to nuance and gesture. The two men stand side by side watching the controlled destruction of a landscape now inhabited only by "small animals," creatures considered insignificant; yet the narrative voice posits their "presumable pain." The men stand together but are differentiated by their designations as "my father" and "the boss-boy"; then they are once again aligned by the repetition of the phrase "brought down" to describe their actions. The contrast of those actions directly relates to the matter of "dignity." Through the intimacy of the employer's gesture, the blow of hand against face, the suggestion of a father punishing and instructing a wayward child, Lessing extends the figure of her father to encompass colonial patriarchy and the "white enlightenment" of people of color. Through his wordless demand for an explanation and his silent gestures of refusal — "he flung the mouse . . . stalked off, with dignity" — the African man constructs an alternative discourse that rejects the colonizer's language and, to use Homi Bhabha's words, "deflect[s] the dominating ideologies being imposed on him."[6] The farmer's final pompous remark lamely follows the expressive gesture, and Lessing underlines the irony with her repetition of the word "explanation"; this delayed and oblique "reply" to the African's unspoken question inadvertently comments on the white man's actions as much as on the African man's.

In "The Old Chief Mshlanga," Lessing repeats these techniques of juxtaposition and disjunction to construct her ironies. Moreover, the story seems to formulate a delayed response to an earlier male text; one repetition Lessing makes use of that links her text to Conrad's *Heart of Darkness* is the metaphor of the changing map. In setting up what Chinua Achebe has recognized as specifically a critique of Belgian colonialism, Conrad employed as extended metaphor the map of colonial Africa. Marlow's journey takes him not into the sound, red territories of British settlement, but rather through the poisonous yellow of Belgian holdings into the map's terrifyingly blank center, a nonspace inhabited by the blacks he sees as without cultural history — a chaos infected with frenzy, where corruption is contagious. At journey's end, he finds the fatally infected Kurtz, and the lie torn out of him in his encounter with Kurtz's intended shows that Marlow too has, as he feared, been "stained" by his journey into darkness, marked by the contagion bred of what Conrad represents as an intrinsically unhealthy contact between European civilization and the "primitive."

Lessing's story also uses maps and landscapes to symbolize the progress of her protagonist "deeper" into Africa but in ways that critique both European romanticism and British colonialism. Lessing's protagonist is a female child, born into the doubleness inherent to second-generation settlers, for whom the place of birth is nonetheless not one's "native" place. The story, a miniature *Bildungsroman* of a liberal settler, opens with a prospect of the veld farm, which "like every white farm, was largely unused, broken only occasionally by small patches of cultivation. In between, nothing but trees, the long sparse grass, thorn and cactus and gully, grass and outcrop and thorn."[7] This is the "empty landscape" that strained the sanity of whites like Lessing's father; in reality, as the girl in this story comes to know, the land has been "emptied," the people who inhabited it forcibly removed to native reserves far from their ancestral homelands, leaving the country "unmapped." As Chennells puts it, "What Africans saw as places crowded with ancestral associations and spiritual presences, the whites saw as empty spaces waiting to be shaped by their creative will."[8]

The settler child's position lies somewhere between these two perspectives — the veld for her represents both nativity and exile: "Opening [her] eyes curiously on a sun-suffused landscape, a gaunt and violent landscape, [she] might be supposed to accept it as her own . . . to feel her blood running free and responsive to the swing of the seasons." But instead, the white child "could not see a msasa tree, or the thorn, for what they were" (p. 11) because a European template has been uneasily superimposed upon the African land in the child's mind: "Her books held tales of alien fairies . . . she knew the shape of the leaves of an ash or an oak, the names of the little creatures that lived in English streams." Lessing emphasizes the connection to the tradition of romanticism with her inclusion of lines from Tennyson's "Lady of Shalott," which also anticipate the shock of recognition that lies ahead for the child who sings: "Out flew the web and floated wide / The mirror cracked from side to side." For her, the land is "crowded with ancestral presences" transplanted from European tradition, with northern witches, "bred of cold Northern forests," with "a pale willowed river, a pale gleaming castle" (p. 11).

The disjunction between storybook and reality makes the surrounding veld seem "unreal," and to the child, the Africans employed on her father's farm, the only ones she knew, seem "as remote as the trees and rocks. They were an amorphous black mass . . . faceless, who existed merely to serve, to say 'Yas, Baas,' take their money and go"; they are like part of the landscape, dehumanized, not even mysterious; she "was taught to take them for granted" (p. 12).

As the child grows, her range increases; she begins to "inhabit" the farm, to trek for miles a day with her two dogs, her rifle, and her unbreached racism. Here, Lessing presents her female settler, the liberal in her larval stage, so to speak, as a parody of the great white hunter and intrepid explorer whose gun and dogs "were an armor against fear." Yet, like Marlow in the Congo, or like Conrad the writer, the child is aware that all is not right: "Certain questions presented themselves in [her] mind; and because the answers were not easy to accept, they were silenced by an even greater arrogance of manner" (p. 12).

The narrative stance has been third-person up to this point in the story; abruptly it shifts to first person. The occasion for this construction of subjectivity is the farm girl's first encounter — "one evening when I was about 14" — with Africans who exist on the colonial margins. She meets three men, two young, one old, who walk with an "air of dignity, of quietly following their own purpose" (p. 13). When the three do not move off the path at her approach, the girl does not brandish her gun or set her dogs on them — her usual response to what she calls "native cheek"; instead she restrains the dogs and greets the men "a little truculent[ly]." She learns that the old man is the Chief Mshlanga, on his way across the river to visit his brothers, and that this path on the farm's outer margins is an ancient native thoroughfare.

This small incident precipitates the girl's metamorphosis from self-justifying colonizer to self-questioning "white liberal"; Lessing represents its initial phase as an idealism as inappropriate as the blind racism that preceded it.

As the girl follows her newly aroused curiosity about the history of the place of her "nativity" — not its history of conquest and settlement but its African past — she finds, as will Martha Quest, that books can furnish her with little information because "from the British point of view, African history began with their arrival." The sources she does find are linked to exploration and exploitation. An old book locates gold mines in "Chief Mshlanga's country," and an old prospector who passes through the farm still refers to the area as "the Old Chief's country": "That was his name for our district . . . ; he did not use our name for it — a new phrase which held no implication of usurped ownership" (p. 14). Already, this girlchild has far outstripped Marlow, who could no more conceive of Africans "owning" the Congo than of the trees and vines owning the soil from which they spring in strangling profusion.

The child's map is changing again — the fairy-tale map and the map of the farm as white territory have been irrevocably altered by her partial glimpses of the larger map of the veld as a continuously inhabited African place. Paradoxically, her recognition of the original ownership of Africa by free Africans allows her to experience the veld directly, to see and feel it:

"When I saw a native approaching, we offered and took greetings; and slowly that other landscape in my mind faded, and my feet struck directly on African soil, and I saw the shapes of tree and hill clearly, and the black people moved back, as it were, out of my life" into their own African existence (p. 14). She sees a possibility of coexistence, ignoring, with youthful obtuseness, the weight of colonial inequities, and she expresses again the "double" position of the African-born settler, who inherits, but resists, an awareness of exile: "This is my heritage, too; I was bred here; it is my country as well as the black man's country and there is plenty of room for all of us, without elbowing each other off the pavements and roads. It seemed it was only necessary to let free that respect I felt when I was talking with Old Chief Mshlanga, to let both black and white people meet gently, with tolerance for each others' differences: it seemed quite easy" (p. 15). Of course, it is not easy. In what follows in the story, the maps of the colonial present intrude upon the girl's budding political consciousness: first the split map of African space and settler space with its uneasy boundaries and finally, inevitably, the map of power.

To complete her education as a white liberal settler, the girl must lose her idealism, must realize that innocence is not possible in the colonial position. Again, Lessing represents this spatially: the child enters the space of "fissure" as she journeys across the "wild" space of the open veld to visit the Old Chief's village. The impetus for that visit is her romanticization of the African patriarch; her former bigotry has ceded its place to what Frantz Fanon called "negrophilia," a typical progression in the development of white liberal consciousness as Lessing portrays it.

The journey reenacts ironically the invasion of the "structured space" of the African veld by white Europeans. Chennells objects that Lessing's "epiphanies afforded by the veld" belong "to the same discourse as a man discovering his manhood in his encounter with the primitive."[9] But it is difficult to see this girlchild's "epiphany" in that light; it is too self-conscious, too aware of its Conradian resonances. The white child has brought her arrogance with her, expecting to travel free of fear, but she breaks out in "gooseflesh," looks uneasily over her shoulder, and then "realize[s] suddenly that this was fear." Significantly, she recalls that she "had read of this feeling" in books (p. 16); she is having a European experience of the Dark Continent, substituting the "fairy tales" of the literature of colonization for the old ones of witches and oak trees; moving, in effect, from Tennyson to Conrad.

Yet the girl realizes that her experience is "meaningless" even as it completely possesses her; here, Lessing initiates her heroine into the irremediably ironic condition of the politically awakened settler consciousness in a country where colonialism still prevails. The voice moves to second person as she describes the feeling she "had read of": "You move warily, as if your very passing disturbs something old and evil, something dark and big and angry that might suddenly rear and strike from behind" as "the bigness and silence of Africa, under the ancient sun, grows dense and takes shape in the mind . . . , and a deadly spirit comes out of the trees and the rocks" (pp. 16, 17). Lessing clearly signals her satiric intent here: the girl perseveres in her journey "in a divided mind, watching [her] own pricking nerves and apprehensive glances from side to side with a disgusted amusement" (p. 17).

The visit to the village is a humiliating failure; expecting to effect some sort of intercultural meeting of minds, the girl finds instead an "indifferent village." When she intrudes on its patriarchs, she becomes aware of her status as "a white *girl*" (emphasis added): that she is doubly transgressing in their eyes by "invading" their village and by "walking the veld alone as a white man might: and in this part of the bush where only Government officials had the right to move" (p. 18). She spends an awkward few minutes before the "guarded, aloof," and implacably courteous elders and then leaves to retrace her ten-mile journey across open country. But she has learned that this is no romantically timeless enclave of the "primitive." Although the village is picturesque, "not at all like our farm compound, a dirty and neglected place, a temporary home for migrants who had no roots in it," she realizes that its population of "ancients and children and women" reflects colonial exigencies: "The young men were all away working on the white men's farms and mines, and the Chief must depend on relatives who were temporarily on holiday for his attendants" (p. 18). The repetition of the word "temporary" links the village to the compound; both are disrupted by the capitalist colonial enterprise.

Lessing's allegory of a settler's progress has moved from romantic delusion through liberal idealism to liberal self-conscious irony; after her visit to the village, the girl's education goes a step further: "I went slowly homewards, with an empty heart: I had learned that if one cannot call a country to heel like a dog, neither can one dismiss the past with a smile in an easy gush of feeling, saying: I could not help it, I am also a victim" (p. 19).

This "empty heart" predicts white postcolonial angst. The girl has lost her "burden" of arrogance only to discover that it is replaced by displacement. She cannot enter into a new, reciprocal relationship with the colonized: the "other" refuses to mirror her; her attempt at confrontation is deflected by the averted glance. The innocence of one "born" into the role of invader is ended by the knowledge of disparity, and the fallen take up residence in "fissure," with its concomitant anxieties and ironies. This is the territory Lessing pioneers in her African stories. Nadine Gordimer, too, has written of the catch-22 of white liberalism, perhaps most vividly in *July's People*: the only moral choice in an apartheid society is one that can result only in alienation, first from the resistant mainstream society and then, if the desired end of liberation is achieved, from the no longer "oppressed." It remains to be seen how this factor will play itself out in South Africa, where "white liberals" are now simply "whites," part of a political minority no longer empowered by legalized racism.

Lessing's story culminates in a confrontation between two patriarchs — Chief Mshlanga and the girl's father — in which the map of white hegemony displaces all others. Against this absolute fact of colonial power, however, Lessing juxtaposes an alternative, African statement: the story's repeated phrase "This was the Old Chief's country" is finally brought into the present tense, first by the chief in his own language, then by his son in the invader's language.

The dispute is over the tribe's goats' destruction of the farmer's mealie fields, the traditional mode of production in conflict with the colonial cash crop system. When the farmer plays his trump card, telling the Old Chief to "go to the police then," the narrator remarks succinctly that "there was, of course, no more to be said." But the old man says "more"; he stands, faces the farmer, and speaks "once again, very stiffly" in his own language, then turns and leaves. When the farmer insists that the Chief's son, who is the farm's cook, translate this final remark, the young man hesitates, then makes the dual decision to speak and to abandon his servant position: "'My father says: All this land, this land you call yours, is his land, and belongs to our people.' Having made this statement, he walked off into the bush after his father, and we did not see him again" (p. 20).

In the real world of colonial dominion which Lessing "bitterly" insisted upon portraying, discourse is not enough to alter power relations. It is the farmer who "goes to the police," and the policeman, while playing tennis with the Native Commissioner, secures the order for the removal of the "kraal" on the veld to a native reserve some 200 miles from the tribe's ancestral holdings. The young girl visits the village site again, a year or so later, and her thoughts there are decidedly romantic in character: she waxes elegiac over the lush growth of pumpkin vines around the ruins of the mud huts that are returning to the earth. But her final image — of some "lucky" settler sinking a plow into this "vein of richness" in some inevitable future when the land has been opened for homesteading — may be less simplistic than it seems at first reading. Lessing has earlier, several times, remarked on the effects of European agricultural practices imposed upon the veld; "wide green valleys" filled with living creatures become, under colonial "wisdom," farms "largely unused," where "hundreds of acres of harsh eroded soil [bear] trees that had been cut for the mine furnaces and had grown thin and twisted, where the cattle had dragged the grass flat, leaving innumerable criss-crossing trails that deepened each season into gullies, under the force of the rains" (p. 16). This image — the bleak landscape of colonial exploitation — superimposes itself over the "lush warm valley" as in her vision "settler" replaces the Old Chief, and an imagined "mealie field" reminds us of the goats whose grazing triggered the dispute that led to the tribe's removal.

There are no easy resolutions in Lessing's tales of colonial "Zambesia," the fictional name she derived to represent both Rhodesia and South Africa, "two countries . . . similar in atmosphere and political structure" in the time of which she wrote and for some time thereafter.[10] After long struggle, those times have changed, and settlers' stories like Lessing's have become part of history. It is appropriate that even liberal "settler ideologies" be marginalized in an era when Africans write "themselves as subjects of African discourses."[11] The question arises, then, whether it is of any use to retain in social memory — in the literary canon, for example — white liberal stories of the era of white hegemony in Africa and elsewhere. I would reply that, in a postcolonial age more accurately characterized as neocolonial, examples of the art of bearing witness to political oppression are still of value, for that art is one we all must master. It would be romantic to suppose otherwise.

NOTES

1. Eve Bertelsen, "The Quest and the Quotidian: Doris Lessing in South Africa," in *In Pursuit of Doris Lessing: Nine Nations Reading,* ed. Claire Sprague (London: Macmillan, 1990), p. 45. Walker's article is quoted on p. 47.

2. Eve Bertelsen, "*Veldtanschauung:* Doris Lessing's Savage Africa," *Modern Fiction Studies* 37 (1991): 647.

3. Anthony Chennells, "Reading Doris Lessing's Rhodesian Stories in Zimbabwe," in *In Pursuit of Doris Lessing,* ed. Sprague, p. 26. Although I take issue with Chennells's evaluation of Lessing as a romantic primitivist, I want to point out that Chennells places her Rhodesian discourse historically, in the 1940s and 1950s when "the collapse of European empires in Africa was impossible to foresee," and he acknowledges that "her art recognizes equivalent tensions to those which are familiar

today [he means rural-urban and class tensions in Zimbabwe] and her discourse around those tensions refuses closure" (p. 39).

4. Quoted in J. Hillis Miller, *Fiction and Repetition* (Cambridge, Mass.: Harvard University Press, 1982), pp. 5, 6. Benjamin is quoted ibid., p. 10.

5. This quotation and subsequent autobiographical material are from Lessing's *In Pursuit of the English* (New York: Simon & Schuster, 1961). Further references are given in the text.

6. Homi K. Bhabha, from an interview by Brian Wallis in *Art in America* 79, no. 9 (Sept. 1991): 83.

7. Doris Lessing, "The Old Chief Mshlanga," in *This Was the Old Chief's Country: Volume One of Doris Lessing's Collected African Stories* (London: Michael Joseph, 1973), p. 11. Further references are given in the text.

8. Chennells, "Reading Doris Lessing's Rhodesian Stories in Zimbabwe," p. 25.

9. Ibid., p. 26.

10. Claire Sprague's introduction to *In Pursuit of Doris Lessing*, p. 6. In the Martha Quest novels, Lessing named her fictional colony "Zambesia," a change, Sprague notes, which "metaphorically denies" — I would say, acknowledges — "white appropriation of the land and returns it to its owners" (p. 6).

11. Chennells, "Reading Doris Lessing's Rhodesian Stories in Zimbabwe," p. 39.

RICARDO L. ORTÍZ

6. Pleasure's Exile

Reinaldo Arenas's Last Writing

In one of my first statements after leaving Cuba I
had declared that "the difference between the
communist and capitalist systems is that, although
both give you a kick in the ass, in the communist
system you have to applaud, while in the capitalist
system you can scream. And I came here to scream."
— Reinaldo Arenas, *Before Night Falls*

Outside prevailing constructions of nationality organized around the native
and the immigrant, there is the exile. To the extent that Cuban-American
and Cuban-exile writing of the last generation can be said to have fashioned a voice for itself in the larger contexts of mainstream and immigrant-
American literature, it has retained in its own internalized dialectic a profoundly embedded tendency toward self-marginalization and self-alienation.
This is nowhere more apparent than in the work produced by Reinaldo
Arenas in the decade he spent in exile in the United States between his
expulsion from Cuba in the Mariel boatlift and his suicide when he was in
the last stages of AIDS. Arenas's work, more than that of any other Cuban
writer in America, defines the role of a literary production caught in this
"special period," this moment of historical and cultural suspension between
the "end" of the Cold War in most of the world and the tenacious grip of
Fidel Castro's vestigial Marxism on Cuba's, and Cuban America's, political
present.

Particularly in his autobiography, *Antes que anochezca* (translated as *Before Night Falls*), and his less successful "first" American novel, *The Doorman*, Arenas's writing grapples with the simultaneous transition from one

For Pedro Zamora.

cultural and economic environment to another, from one prevailing conception of production and consumption, of labor and pleasure, to its arguably radical opposite. This essay charts this transition, with special attention to that most difficult space of intersection between constructions of simultaneously sexual and political subjects, which marks in the space of the Cuban-exile imagination an aporetic point in its negotiation of especially male Cuban identity as at once masculine, virile, and rigidly anti-Marxist with the stark reality of Arenas's heroic, defiant, and fluid effeminacy.

There is always a temptation to read a culture whose prevailing mythologies have so profound an oedipal cast primarily through Freudian and post-Freudian psychoanalytic categories.[1] That approach is unavoidable here as well; the essay focuses on more "material" effects of Arenas's encounter with the doubled, split history of his people(s) but also analyzes the symbolic construction of Cuban political reality as a function of a quasi-oedipal struggle between the hysterically, murderously hated Fidel, *el hombre, él,* and *Cuba bella, la patria,* the feminine-gendered fatherland to whom Cuban exiles consecrate their deepest loyalty and their most profound fidelity. This is, however, one approach among others in my analysis of Arenas's explicitly literary interrogation of the political stakes involved in the emergence of a definitive literary voice for the Cuban/exile nation(s). Put another way, I hope that asking the question of textual pleasure, as a function of both masculine and feminine, normative and queer sexual/textual praxes, in both semiotic and other terms, will lead us back to more direct political questions of what kind of labor (and by whom) produces politically efficacious forms of pleasure (and for whom).

The Doorman, the Exile, and Threshold Experiences

Arenas completed *The Doorman* as he was falling ill but before his diagnosis, and in this sense the novel stands as Arenas's last major work of fiction before his imagination takes on the intense purgatorial pitch, the queerly undead tonality of his writing under the unequivocal sentence of death. Ironically, however, *The Doorman* shares with the later chapters of the autobiography, which were written well after the diagnosis and well into the progress of his illness, Arenas's hyperbolic vision of freedom, a vision that never lost its appreciation for both abandon and abundance. In general, Arenas's excesses have always seemed to me closer to Jonathan Swift's than to Gabriel García Márquez's.[2] He "screams," and laughs, from a position whose complexity, even impossibility, requires the kind of textual self-immolation one finds in Swift at his most perverse. The figure of Juan, the doorman, recalls the figure of the exiled writer for which Swift has traditionally served as a chief paradigm. Stationed at/on a threshold or border, Juan ministers to travelers, ferrying them from one point to another in a journey in which he plays an exclusively instrumental role. The travelers in this case, however, are only symbolically migratory; they are the New York apartment dwellers living in Juan's building, making their routine, daily journeys between work and home, between the public world and the private fantasy-spaces of their respective cubicles. They are therefore symbolically island dwellers, ensconced in their isolated cells but daily called to the mainland of collective experience; they recall the army of solipsistic projectors in Swift's Academy of Lagado on (perhaps not coincidentally) Gulliver's floating island of Laputa.

To this extent the door functions symbolically as a conduit or channel, connoting in at least the Cuban imagination *el charco*, the watery passage or "puddle" between Cuba and Florida; and in Spanish *la puerta* will always echo *el puerto*, the port, the space of both hopeful departure and safe arrival at the beginning and end of the journey. The doorman is in turn defined according (we might say *reduced*) to the object with/on which he labors, at the same time that that object has only the most tenuous relationship to objecthood. The door is also the eye, the paradigmatic "door" of perception; and thus to have one's protagonist work as a doorman also allows him to work as the paradigmatic subject in a narrative structure, to stand for the subject who works on/processes objects, and others, through its Kantian categories. The door is thus both the doorman's thing and a no-thing, his *objet* in Lacanian terms, at once solid and empty, an obstruction and a space of passage. As such it *is* text, if it is possible to say this; perhaps it is more apt to say the door performs textuality, or, more simply, *texts*, transitively and not. In either or both cases a symbol of promiscuity to be sure, the door allegorizes the promiscuity of the sign, of any symbol, that is, in the hands of a fertile artistic imagination.

Like a doorman keeping vigilant watch on a threshold, in the constant state of having threshold experiences, Arenas writes both in and out of the experience of exile. His name suggests that even symbolically, as well as in more literal ways, he was cursed (implicitly by his mother, who named him) with having to anchor his experience to a shifting surface of sand, between the border-space of the shore, between earth and sea, but also in the arena, the *arenal*, the centralized, localized space of spectacle and performance. It is (t)here that Reinaldo enjoys his uneasy, precarious rein; it is (t)here that "she" is most *la reina*, the queen, of both the arena and the shore. This play with the unmappable space of the border or threshold extends to the anachronistic structure and frame of the two texts of concern here.

Later in this essay I will analyze the last chapters of the autobiography, where Arenas inscribes the dissolution of his last years in the dissolution of reason and sense, a surrender to the forces beyond order which had always governed his life. These include madness, witchcraft, and dreams, words that serve as titles to some of the later chapters. The embodiment of madness is his lifelong friend Lázaro Gómez, who also served as the inspiration for the title character of *The Doorman*. Lázaro served as the sole witness to Arenas's own past, and his occasional bouts with mental instability and his limited education reinforced the quality of childlike innocence necessary to establish a link with childhood itself.[3] Arenas's brotherly tenderness toward his friend recalls the love of the young narrator of *Celestino antes del alba*, Arenas's first novel, for his visionary, poetic cousin. And in the later novel, Juan the doorman, described as "a young man who was dying of grief," suffers from the doubled disenchantment of having been forced to leave his own childhood behind in immigrating to the United States and in having to confront a culture profoundly alienated from its own innocence, its own authentic past or history.[4]

The "million" narrators of *The Doorman*, the Cuban exile community speaking, stereotypically perhaps, with one voice, sum up Juan's predicament thus:

> Ten years ago Juan had fled his native Cuba in a boat, and settled in the United States. He was seventeen then, and his entire past life had been left behind: humiliations and warm beaches, fierce enemies and loving friends whom the very persecutions had made even more special. Left behind was slavery, but the complicity of night as well, and cities made to the measure of his restlessness; unbounded horror, but also a human quality, a state of mind, a sense of brotherhood in the face of terror—all things that, just like his own way of being, were alien here.[5]

While the choice of an (ironically) univocal communal voice raises its own aesthetic and philosophical questions of subjectivity and the force of ideological group-think, in Arenas's hands these questions are always directed back toward the individual and the limits of the collective to "make something" of him. This is clear, for example, in the limited sympathy with which the narrative treats its subject:

> But we, too (and there are a million of us), left all that behind; and yet we are not dying of grief . . . so hopelessly as this young man. . . . He arrived in the United States

an unskilled laborer, like most of us, just one more person escaping from Cuba. He needed to learn, just as we did, the value of things, the high price one must pay for a stable life: a well-paying job, an apartment, a car, vacations, and finally one's own house, preferably near the ocean.[6]

The narrative chorus's summation of Juan as "just one more" of the million they comprise must, I think, be read doubly; the assessment absorbs him into the sum at the same time that it singles him out, makes of him the remnant or remaining one "more" in excess of that comfortable, completed sum. More than an exemplary narrative of immigrant success through hard work and the acquisition of real property, Arenas's impersonation of this community and the ironic take on its values suggested in this passage also undermines the distinction it would place on its own accounting of "value," "price," and "cost." He leaves open the question of whether the inventory of acquisitions signifies either the material comforts of "a stable life" or the "high [spiritual] price" one must pay for that life.

What Remains: The Ghost, the Decadent, and the Death of Desire

Like the alienated, ascetic Juan, never far from his threshold, Arenas occupied a perplexed position in the various "economies" into which he found himself inserted. Both in communist Cuba and late capitalist North America, Arenas, *as a gay man especially*, found himself in excess, existing as the remnant of a corrupt past constructed in the former case as a holdover of bourgeois, in the latter as a holdover of aristocratic decadence. In his study *Gays Under the Cuban Revolution*, Allen Young makes the oft-observed point that Cuban communism simply borrowed from Soviet policy the conviction that homosexuality (and the decadent sensibility it nurtured) was "the product of the decadence of bourgeois society and fascist corruption" in order to uphold a policy of homosexual persecution that for equally cynical reasons the homophobic Batista government did not pursue as comprehensively.[7] The figure of decadent sensibility plays a similarly vestigial role in the classical bourgeois imagination.

Such a figure does make an appearance on *The Doorman*'s stage, but in curiously redoubled form: while Juan himself remains sexually ambiguous, Arenas saves much of his critical commentary on urban gay America for this treatment of the one gay couple in Juan's building, the "Oscar Timeses."[8] They have changed their individual names for the one name that they share and in their years together have come "to resemble each other so closely, both in body and in temperament, that they really appear to be the same person." They are, in fact, distinguished only numerically, going as "Oscar Times One and Oscar Times Two." In this and other respects, they inhabit the extremes of assimilationism and conformity in *The Doorman*. Their homo-sexuality, their erotic orientation toward the same, literally reinforces this, and the fact that one of the Oscars hails from Cuba and the other is a Scottish-American who ironically has taken his assimilationist cues from his lover casts an even more complex irony over the situation. Arenas's attack on North American gay conformity is scathing and organized chiefly around an obsessive pursuit of pleasure which, in its narcissism and material luxuriance, seemed to the philosophically eroticist Arenas as particularly alienated and debased.[9] As he remarks of their frequently failed sex hunts in Manhattan, the Oscars would often "out of boredom, frustration, habit, or just as a last resort . . . end up sleeping together, but at the moment of reaching climax, instead of pleasure they experienced the frustration of possessing or being possessed by repulsive mirror images of themsleves."[10]

This refusal to identify with the already overly identificatory structure of gay male society in the United States exacerbated Arenas's general state of exile; he discovered his chief refuge, understandably enough, in his writing, which for him was always intimately linked with his sexual dispositions. In the autobiography, Arenas makes this connection clear. In Cuban Miami especially, he observes, artists and in particular writers were considered with an odd suspicion: "The sad fact," Arenas tells us, "is that Cuban exiles were not so interested in literature; a writer was looked upon as a strange, abnormal figure."[11] It is impossible not to hear in the Spanish term *anormal* its conventional concomitant, *maricón*, or faggot. What strikes the conventional *machista* Cuban sensibility as culturally suspect immediately also strikes it as sexually suspect. Miami culture seemed to Arenas a distillation of some of the worst features of the Cuban character, especially its sexual politics: "The typical Cuban machismo has attained alarming proportions in Miami. I did not want to stay too long in that place, which was like a caricature of Cuba, the worst of Cuba."[12] It is not surprising, therefore, that Arenas's investments in his writing and in his sexuality so strongly paralleled each other. Cuba, both at home and in exile, treated its writers as badly as it treated its queers; indeed, it seemed not to distinguish one from the other.[13] Eloquently, emphatically, Arenas responds to this imposed disappearance with his own form of transgression through ostentation and excess: he wrote, and fucked, prolifically, promiscuously, with an abandon that looked to him like freedom.

It is, I think, plausible to characterize the limited aesthetic success of *The*

Doorman as a symptom of what Arenas seemed to feel was the suffocatingly commodity-obsessed pursuit of happiness (that is, maximization of pleasure) among all culturally and economically assimilated "Americans," Cuban or not, queer or not. As I have already noted, each of the hyper-insulated apartment dwellers in *The Doorman*'s habitrail universe constructs a "private idaho" for him or herself, each an extension of some idiosyncratic pathology fostered and buttressed by some elaborately commodified fetish system of both possessions and beliefs. Anyone familiar with Arenas's preexile work will recognize in *The Doorman* the allegorized struggle of a literary imagination to break free of the ponderous clutter of simulacra (both material and conceptual), to reaccess the less alienated, mediated relationship with "nature" or "reality" which characterizes that earlier fiction.

Eco-criture

That the narrative of *The Doorman* should also include a culmination in the reaccessing of the infinite (here in the exemplary guise of the sea) also belies the logic of "getting there" via the finite, the particular, the material. Juan's ultimate success in realizing his vision of liberation comes through a rejection of the social, of the human, and the reinvention of language in a discourse with animals, with a renaturalized, reconstituted nature. Arenas's investment in the power of the natural is one of the signature elements of all his work. The biographical sources of this relationship are documented in the early chapters of *Before Night Falls*. In his review of the translation, Roberto Echevarría sums up this relationship nicely: "To say that Arenas grew up close to nature," Echevarría observes, "may sound like a cliché, but in this case the phrase could not be more literal. Among his favorite childhood pastimes were eating dirt, from which he got a big belly full of worms, having sex with various animals and playing with mud in the falling rain."[14] That even his reviewers should take recourse to clichés and literality to naturalize the language with which they describe Arenas's intense familiarity with the natural speaks to the force of this bond. All Arenas's writings contains a radical naturalism that, I argue, earns that writing the curious status of an *eco-criture*.

Juan discovers a method of communicating with the tame, domesticated pets of his tenants and with them plots a strategy of liberation that ultimately reintegrates him, and them, into a "past" even more distant than that of lost childhood or cultural history. In this sense he is a combination of Doctor Doolittle, Gulliver among the Houyhnhnms, and Noah effecting a new creation, a new nature out of the ruins of that murdered by decadent, materialist culture. This culminating vision in *The Doorman* is suggestively apocalyptic in scope; Juan heads with the animals on a transcontinental and eventually global procession, swelling the ranks of his natural army with all imaginable creatures and inanimate objects. Arenas leaves Juan at the conclusion of *The Doorman* on a significant threshold; as they reach "the equator," the "thunderous stampede" of animals "is deafening." [15]

Ironically, *The Doorman* should conclude with the silence into which the deafening roar of nature's rebellion relegates us, but it does not. The last words of the text are given to two competing sets of exiles: one the million narrators, who threaten to use the imminent catastrophe in revenge for their suffering, and the other the doorman himself, whose vision of nature at play, liberated from all structure, from all order except for the promiscuous symbolism of the door, necessarily, perhaps tragically, excludes the very figure of the doorman, whose fate it is to wait, in permanent exile, for no fate at all:

> At the end there would be a door for the dove to enter into her land of dreams. . . . A huge door of green branches and creeping vines in perpetual bloom would await the parrot, the squirrel, the cat and the orangutan, so they could play forever. . . . Yes, doors of sunshine, doors of water, doors of earth, doors of flowering vines, doors of ice . . . tiny doors or immeasurable ones, deeper than the air, more luminous than the sky, would be awaiting the animals to take them to a place where nobody could spy on them through telescopes, or send undercover agents after us. . . . And through these doors everyone, finally, will eagerly rush in.
>
> That is, all except me, the doorman, who on the outside will watch them disappear forever.

The informing wish of Arenas's text returns us to the doorlike space of the metaphor, of language as (trans)figuration, where the writer, the exile, the excluded attendant upon doors awaits, at once witnessing and enacting the rite of liberation for others.

The last chapters of the autobiography extend the apocalypticism of *The Doorman* even further into super-, one might say hyper-, naturalism. Lázaro's madness, which became the type for Juan's in the novel, quickly translates into increasingly poetic and powerful images driven by an eroticized feminine principle. Madness and queerness are semantically linked by the correct Spanish usage, and the idiomatic Spanish deviation, of the term "locura"; Arenas had had occasion in the Cuban sections of the autobiography to inventory the four classes of "locas," of queens he had known in Havana. In the New York section, he turns his attention to the relationship between that other archetype of deviant femininity, the witch, and the erotic

99

principle organizing his life. "The world," Arenas insists, "is really full of witches" of various types, whose "reino" or reign extends beyond fantasy to reality. Arenas's world is indeed saturated by witchcraft; he not only includes most of the prominent women in his life in this category but also his mother, in whose hyperbolic symbolism the list culminates: "the noble witch, the suffering witch, the witch full of longing and sadness, the most beloved witch in the world: my mother . . . with her broom, always sweeping as if nothing mattered but the symbolic meaning of the act." [16] Arenas writes with the same appreciation of the purely symbolic value of the act; the witch extends even beyond the figure of the mother to contain the gender-transcendent figure of the queen, la loca ("Sometimes witches would assume a half-masculine form, which would make them even more sinister") and though he never explicitly identifies himself as such, the momentum of the passage leads us compellingly to Arenas himself, writing as his mother sweeps, the pen replacing the broom as the material locus of a labor whose production is symbolic, magical, but for that reason no less material.

Before Night Falls: AIDS and the Possibility of a Pro-Life Suicide

The autobiography would be incomplete without the suicide note (literally Arenas's "last" writing) to which it inexorably leads, but most of it was written not only well before his death but before the completion of his fictional work. It is preceded by an introduction entitled "El fin," which also came "last" in the chronology of its composition, a text that most directly addresses the issue of the disease that finally destroyed him. "Last words" thus come first, and last, in Arenas's recounting of his life. Time and history work different shifts in both the life and the fiction; in the former Arenas marks the transformation of his literary output by the day of his diagnosis. All his subsequent work operates in the odd, protracted time-space, the chronotope, one might say, of the anticipation of the end; this is most pointedly suggested in the title of the autobiography. It is here, in this inverted, paradoxical space, that we can return as well to the question raised by Arenas's attempt, at the end of his life, in the intimate threshold of his own fatal moment, to understand AIDS, not metaphorically but literally. AIDS stood for Arenas emphatically *outside* the register of the natural, as an unnaturally systematic, all-too-humanly perfect death machine whose only plausible source or origin was for him the closet space of state secrecy, of public conspiracy, of obscene activity perpetrated openly by silent "majorities."

Susan Sontag observes in *AIDS and Its Metaphors* the rarity with which "political metaphors" are used "to talk about the body"; "likening the body to a society, liberal or not," Sontag goes on to explain, "is less common than comparisons to other complex, integrated systems, such as a machine or an economic system." [17] Arenas not only provides one such extended comparison in the introduction to the autobiography, he also employs it in the manner which, as Sontag observes later in her essay, reflects AIDS's readily available capacity to "serve as an ideal projection for First World political paranoia," especially in the way it can stand not only as "the quintessential invader from the Third World," but more so as "any mythological menace." [18] Arenas's own feelings about AIDS, as expressed in the autobiography, suggest something of this paranoia and of the mythological extremes to which it can be carried. At the same time, they remind us of the already mythological cast of the imaginative, ideological, and cultural work done on AIDS by First-World reactionary liberalism.

To quote Arenas:

The actual nature of AIDS seems to be a state secret . . . as a disease it is different from all others. Diseases are natural phenomena, and everything natural is imperfect and can somehow be fought and overcome. But AIDS is a perfect illness because it is so alien to human nature and has as its function to destroy life in the most cruel and systematic way. Never before has such a formidable calamity affected mankind. Such diabolic perfection makes one ponder the possibility that human beings may have had a hand in its creation. [19]

The suggestion that somehow AIDS began as an orchestrated political conspiracy against marginalized communities is certainly not exclusive to Arenas, but in his hands it takes on a particular eloquence, especially given the context of the triple exile into which AIDS throws him.

Sontag herself observes near the end of *AIDS and Its Metaphors* the connection between late-capitalist hyper-consumerism and a prevailing construction of pleasure which at least superficially informs some of the sexual and cultural practices of the gay male communities of urban America discussed earlier. "One set of messages of the society we live in," Sontag argues, "is: Consume. Grow. Amuse yourselves. The working of this economic system," she continues, "which has bestowed these unprecedented liberties, most cherished in the form of physical mobility and material prosperity, depends on encouraging people to defy limits. Appetite is *supposed* to be immoderate. The ideology of capitalism makes us all connoisseurs of liberty — of the infinite expansion of possibility. . . . Hardly an invention of the male homosexual subculture, recreational, risk-free sexuality is an inevitable reinvention of the culture of capitalism." [20] For Arenas, on the other hand, "liberty" predicated on either side of the term "connoisseurship," as either a function of the accumulation or collection of goods or of the hyper-refinement of taste, was perhaps descriptive of a "free," but always of a closed, economy on some level of circulation, but it failed to guarantee pleasure as the effect of a necessarily *open* economy. What "liberty" a closed liberal economy could promise its agents rang of liberal dogmatism to Arenas, to which he would persistently oppose the promise of a liberation from all dogmatism.

This attitude is most clearly reflected in several passages critical of totalitarian dogmatism in communist Cuba. These passages, in effect constituting brief asides within the course of his narrating the events of his life in Cuba, resonate through his subsequent experiences in exile. "All dictatorships," he observes, "are sexually repressive and anti-life. All affirmations of life are diametrically opposed to dogmatic regimes";[21] the simultaneously oppressive and repressive practices of a system as orthodoxly homophobic as Castro's translate fairly directly into the practices of all systems of power predicated on exclusion and closure. As Arenas goes on to observe about AIDS in the context of global politics, "All the rulers of the world, that reactionary class always in power, and the powerful within any system, must feel grateful to AIDS because a good part of the marginal population, whose only aspiration is to live and therefore oppose all dogma and political hypocrisy, will be wiped out." [22] All system, therefore, all dogma, takes on in Arenas's thought the function of *thanatos*, manifests the death drive even as it promises its "free" but limited menu of pleasures to the world. All such economies operate under the principle of scarcity, regardless of the wealth they generate; all such economies restrict, repress, and exclude practices and pleasures based on the antiprinciple, the unthinkable idea of life as limitlessness, as pure abundance.

Arenas thus recognizes the profound distinction between a choking totalitarianism (the aggressive intellectual impulse toward totalities) and the infinite, abundant playfulness of language (the fluid, oceanic fullness of life). His condemnation of all repressive power as life-destroying receives particularly eloquent expression in the nearly symmetrical treatment his text gives to the opposed repressions of the Right and the Left. Arenas observes, for example, the manner in which all tyranny murders laughter in his analysis of the Castro regime's most tragic effect on the once-vital Cuban character:

One of the most nefarious characteristics of tyrannies is that they take everything too seriously and destroy all sense of humor. Historically, Cubans have found escape from reality through satire and mockery, but with the coming of Fidel Castro the sense of humor gradually disappeared until it became illegal. With it the Cuban people lost one of its few means of survival; by taking away their laughter, the Revolution took away from them their deepest sense of the nature of things. Yes, dictatorships are prudish, pompous, and utterly dreary.[23]

Arenas's own profound, proto-Bakhtinian sense of the philosophical dimensions of laughter, its ability to inform our sense of "things," extends equally to his critical evaluation of the more subtle, but similarly life-killing, thing-obsessed materialism of Miami Cubans. "In Miami," he observes, "the obsession with making things work and being practical, with making lots of money, sometimes out of the fear of starving, has replaced a sense of life and, above all, of pleasure, adventure, and irreverence."[24] This disillusionment with the bourgeoisie did not prevent Arenas from feeling an equally strong alienation from the liberal intellectual Left, especially in the academies of North America.[25]

No Conclusions: Pleasure, Politics, and the Art of the Impossible

Arenas's simultaneous and reciprocal condemnation of both conventional Left and Right positions positions him more strategically than ambivalently in the space of politically driven literary and critical discourses, posing against each an alternative critique more accurately representative of his own politics. Judging from her article on Cuban politics and art institutions, "Aesthetics and Foreign Policy," Laura Kipnis would argue against Arenas's collapsing of all restrictive cultural regimes. "If culture is seen as central to social reproduction," Kipnis posits, "it seems to follow that . . . in a society that reproduces itself, in the first instance, politically, as Cuba, artists are subjected to the terrors and rigors of current political policies," and thus "in Cuba, where art institutions are by definition political and politicized, the political meanings of works emerge unmediated, with more genuine potential to be subversive to reproduction."[26]

Later in the article Kipnis turns to a much earlier essay on Cuban culture by Susan Sontag.[27] Kipnis's response to what she feels is Sontag's overaestheticized judgment of the failures of Cuban culture might transfer fairly directly into a response to Arenas's similar views. Kipnis dismisses Sontag's claim for a "triumph of 'erotics' over 'hermeneutics,'" arguing that it merely fulfills "the desire for the self: certainty of a subjectivity outside history, a desire for the immediacy of the unmediated relation, not only to the work of art, but to all the rest of political and social life, as well." [28] Implicit in Kipnis's critique of Sontag is a critique of what she terms the subject of the Enlightenment, particularly "the eighteenth-century aesthetic subject" [29] whose intolerance of any critical dialectic had already been marked by Theodor Adorno and Max Horkheimer.[30] The idea that Sontag's or Arenas's eroticist critical strategies present little more than the retrenchment of the one-note aesthetic subject of the Enlightenment seems dangerously reductive to me, certainly restricted to the limited space of an outdated, and never fully efficacious, ideological polarity.

It is precisely the fate of art subversive to the revolution that Arenas's autobiography charts and his preexile work underwent. Whereas Kipnis concludes that in a cultural environment as radically politicized as Cuba's, "the concept of counter-revolutionary culture . . . does have a reality . . . whereas the possibility of a truly political art or a counterhegemonic art is to a large degree absorbed by art markets and institutions here," Arenas would counter that Cuba's cultural bureaucracy only ironically ensured the political power (especially of art subversive of the revolution) not by absorbing it, that is, at once co-opting it and fostering its life, but by repressing it, indirectly expelling it out of the domestic sphere of cultural exchange. Arenas was an artist in exile long before his physical expulsion from Cuba. As the history of the composition of his masterwork, the novel *Otra vez el mar*,[31] makes clear, the ideology that cultivates the political construction of all art also guarantees the disappearance, via confiscation and destruction, of art construed as politically dangerous, unless it is secreted out of the country like contraband. What "genuine potential to be subversive to reproduction" such art might be said to have, at least in theory, in a system where "the political meanings of works emerge unmediated," seems then profoundly compromised by the system's own paranoid perception of precisely that subversive potential.

A more viable analysis of the political function of art and of the concomitant experience of a subversive, irreverent, laughing pleasure can be found in the work of Slavoj Žižek. Žižek's work seems to me to offer the most opportune articulation of this impossible experience of pleasure; in a section of *Enjoy Your Symptom!: Lacan in Hollywood and Out* entitled "The Subject of Enlightenment," [32] Žižek explains the persistence of the monstrous in bourgeois cultural artifacts by declaring, "You cannot have both meaning and enjoyment." The monstrous, as one embodiment of the limit of meaning or sense, stands then as empty, plastic, promiscuous form, the "objective correlative" for Žižek of "the pure 'subject of the Enlightenment,'" which can no longer be "contained" or "bound" by "the texture of symbolic tradition" and therefore "is a monster which gives body to the surplus that escapes the vicious circle of the mirror relationship." Žižek likens it to both the monstrous and the phantasmatic: "The Phantom" in the Opera or out, "embodies the excess aristocracy has to renounce in order to become integrated into bourgeois society." As such, it is "a kind of 'fossil' created by the Enlightenment itself as a distorted index of its inherent antagonism: what was," Žižek goes on to explain, "a sovereign expenditure, a glitter of those in power, an inherent moment of their symbolic status . . . falls out from the social space whose contours are defined by utilitarian ideology, and is perceived as decadent debauchery epitomized in the bourgeois myth of a corrupted demonic aristocrat." [33] This association is rendered more profoundly ironic by the knowledge that Arenas himself was of the poorest social background, his entry into "decadent," cosmopolitan culture coming at the hands of the very revolution that would consequently persecute him for having taken to it so readily.

In *For They Know Not What They Do* Žižek provides the theoretical basis for the cultural analysis he presents in *Enjoy Your Symptom!* In this earlier text Žižek tries to locate the excessive place of Lacanian jouissance or Barthean bliss in the political imagination, in the political dimensions of the construction of a "subject of Enlightenment." "Where one doesn't (want to) know," Žižek argues, "in the blanks of one's symbolic universe, one enjoys . . . enjoyment [thereby being] the 'surplus' that comes from our knowledge that our pleasure involves the thrill of entering a forbidden domain — that is to say, that our pleasure involves a certain displeasure"; this inverted construction of the subject's pleasure occasions an extended train of deconstructive moves. Totalitarian social order, Žižek argues, reexternalizes, "outs" one might say, the superego; it occupies, as "the discourse of Stalinist bureaucracy" did, a position that, because it stands for "neutral, 'objective' knowledge . . . a knowledge not subjectivized by means of the intervention . . . of some Master Signifier — is in itself mischievous, enjoying the subject's failure to live up to impossible demands, impregnated by obscenity — in short: superegotistical."

Thinking of a discourse that, like Castro's, totalizes the possible by declaring that "the Revolution" defines its practical and conceptual limits ("Within the Revolution, everything; outside the Revolution, nothing"), one can appreciate the fate of the subject confronted with this looming epipsychical image; it inflicts on itself what Žižek calls a "self-torture provoked by the obscene superegotistical 'law of conscience.'" It is precisely this "superegotistical imposition of enjoyment which threatens to overflow our daily life" by thinking *for* the subject and giving the subject no choice but to obey the injunction, "*Carpe diem*, enjoy the day, consume the surplus-enjoyment procured by your daily suffering," an injunction that in turn becomes for Žižek "the condensed formula of 'totalitarianism.'" Žižek's theory thus casts in high relief Arenas's more immediate observations, quoted above, about the "chaste," "anti-vital" character of all "dogmatic regimes," which force-feed the masses "the surplus-enjoyment procured by [their] daily suffering" in precisely the inverted, ironic form of a boredom that saturates everything imaginable.

It is against the murderous boredom of repressive, totalizing systems that Arenas laughs and screams.[34] From the metaphor of the doorman and his door to the witch and her broom, from the metaphoric values that cluster opportunistically around the images of the madman, *la loca*, and the queen, we have to conclude that the limitless expanse of Arenas's imaginative geography is also always and only the "one" fluid space (more nomadic than monadic) of the metaphor, of the gesture of translation, of all metamorphosis in process. This place remains, however, unmappable; it remains the no-place, the aporetic point where all opposition dissolves into mere difference. Aporia does not, however, necessarily translate into atopia or utopia; what position metaphor and transformational narrative may be said to occupy in the cultural imagination of a nation as self-alienated and dispersed as Cuba may be more difficult to map than to situate. It may stand, for example, for the gaps that currently exist geographically, politically, and culturally between Cubas, and Cubans, and continue to widen and proliferate, especially as this "special period" in Cuban history becomes further attenuated. It may just as well stand for the transitional and translational hyphen upon which, as Gustavo Pérez-Firmat has observed, Cuban-Americans may be said most fully to live their own conflicted, individual, and collective cultural dualities.[35]

Although the narrative of Arenas's life begins with a chapter entitled "Las piedras," the stones, in which he recalls his earliest memories, at two, of eating the dirt off the ground of his grandparents' farm, in his final chapter, "Los sueños," or dreams, he will say that his earliest memory is of a dream in which he is about to be devoured by "an enormous mouth" (*una boca incon-mensurable* in Spanish).[36] The consuming incommensurability of these two competing origins, of these two "first," original memories, articulates the general indeterminacy of Arenas's life as textualized, of his text as he lived it, but they also speak to competing histories his people have embraced as the incommensurate, originating narratives of his nation. Even at the point of his death, Arenas seems to have known that the darkness into which he was peering was that of the familiar "confusion" between life and what is not life which had always both cursed and blessed both him and his compatriots. Arenas concludes his suicide note, his "last" writing and the last piece of the text which we call his autobiography, in the temporal mode of an impossible "already." Having laid responsibility for his death at the feet of Fidel Castro and having encouraged Cubans both in and out of exile to continue their struggles for liberty, Arenas casts his suicide in terms of an impossible optimism, in a future certainty only a liberating understanding of the nonrelation of life to death can provide. "Cuba will be free; I already am."[37]

NOTES

1. See Echevarría, "Outcast of the Island." In this review of Koch's English translation of *Antes que anochezca*, Echevarría observes in Arenas's temperament a clinging to transcendent innocence, "a sense of liberation attached" especially to "lovemaking that seems pre-Freudian in its candor." In general, what I term "excess" in Arenas is utopian idealism for Echevarría: "It is as if on some deep level Arenas had innocently believed in Castro's rhetoric . . . and could only measure imperfect human performance against absolute [and therefore impossible] standards of purity." Arenas is therefore for Echevarría "a true son of the revolution and of Castro," and his ultimate disillusionment with and alienation from the law attached to the name of this father translates into a more than familiar dramatic paradigm: *Before Night Falls* is for Echevarría "a narrative linking poignantly the personal and the political levels of [the] family romance, told from the point of view of the abandoned son."

2. This comparison to Swift is anything but incidental. It marks a curious genealogy in the work of political theorists, who, like Edward Said in *The World, the Text and the Critic* (Cambridge, Mass.: Harvard University Press, 1983) and Roberto Fernández Retamar in *Caliban*, trans. Edward Baker (Minneapolis: University of Minnesota Press, 1989) have observed in Swift's thoroughgoing political satires a paradigm for an ironic politics of impossibility. There are undeniable Swiftian elements in much of Arenas's apocalyptic political fiction; in addition to the references in *The Doorman* to *Gulliver's Travels*, one can find in the cannibalistic references in *The Assault*, elements of the genocidal vision of a totalizing rationalism which Swift developed between Part Four of the *Travels* and "A Modest Proposal."

3. Arenas says of his friendship with Lázaro: "In exile Lázaro has been my only link to my past, the only witness to my past life in Cuba; with him I always had the feeling of being able to return to that irretrievable world" (*Before Night Falls*, p. 308).

4. This is precisely Arenas's take on New York as the exemplum of North American culture. In the chapter of the autobiography entitled "Eviction," Arenas discusses his disillusionment with New York at length. Although at first New York had seemed

to him the fulfillment of Havana's promise of cultural and communal richness, that idea of social value was quickly replaced by one bled of its spirituality. Because in the United States "everything revolves around money," even its great cities are rendered soulless. "New York," Arenas argues, "has no tradition, no history. The city is in constant flux, constant construction . . . a huge, soulless factory with no place for the pedestrian to rest, no place where one can simply be without dishing out dollars for a breath of air" (*Before Night Falls*, pp. 293–94, 310).

5. See Arenas, *The Doorman*, p. 3.

6. Ibid., pp. 3–4.

7. Young's text is more readily available even in the United States in its Spanish translation, which is what I use here. Young argues that an emergent homosexual subculture existed in pre-Castro Havana, which fed very directly and very profitably into the larger sexual economy of the pleasure industry for which the Cuban capital especially was justifiably famous. See Young, *Los gays bajo la revolución Cubana*, esp. pp. 29–33. See also Leiner, *Sexual Politics in Cuba*. Leiner, chiefly an education specialist with a deep regard for socialist Cuba's social policy successes, attempts to address the seemingly regressive treatment of people with HIV and AIDS in Cuba by supplying a cultural and political history of Cuban sexual attitudes. Leiner is far kinder than Young to the Castro government's treatment of homosexuals, especially in the last two decades. His book is curious reading alongside Arenas's personal testimony and Young's more distanced study of the same topic.

8. See Arenas, *The Doorman*, p. 8, and all of Chapter 14, which is devoted to the Oscars, whose names are derived from the Cuban Oscar's desire to obscure his ethnicity. Born Ramón García, the character renames himself after "what he considered to be the supreme icons of his new country: the Hollywood Oscar and *The New York Times*" (ibid., p. 69).

9. This distaste partly explains why the gay male community in New York gets precious little direct mention in any of Arenas's work. This latter "culture of desire," as Frank Browning has named it, posed in a marked way for Arenas the equally problematic materialism of the liberal West, which he condemns with a vigor equal to that with which he condemns the bankrupt materialism of Marxist-Leninist-Stalinist Cuba. While Browning's text includes a fairly conventional discussion of Cuban culture's attitudes toward homosexuality (see *The Culture of Desire* [New York: Crown, 1993], pp. 142–48), it serves the larger purpose of my own discussion in its analysis of the assimilationist tendencies characteristic of much of the mainstream commercializing of especially gay male urban culture.

10. Arenas, *The Doorman*, p. 71.

11. Arenas, *Before Night Falls*, p. 290. For Arenas, the philistine attitude of bourgeois exiles toward writers was no more forgivable than the active repression of the communists. No Cuban writer, Arenas finally admits, could escape "the tragic fate Cuban writers have suffered throughout our history; on our island we have been condemned to silence, to ostracism, censorship and prison; in exile, despised and forsaken by our fellow exiles" (ibid., p. 291).

12. Ibid., p. 292.

13. Arenas's descriptions of his alienation from Miami's bourgeois Cuban culture often draws on the figure of the ghost or phantasm: "In exile," he writes, "one is nothing but a ghost, a shadow of someone who never achieves full reality" (ibid., p. 293). Like the exiled individual, the entire exile community, especially in Miami, seemed to Arenas little more than a pathetic, ghastly echo or remnant of an irrecuperably lost Cuba; Cuban Miami was for Arenas "like the ghost of our Island, a barren [*arenosa*, or sandy] and pestiferous peninsula, trying to become, for a million exiles, the dream of a tropical island: aerial, bathed by the ocean waters and the tropical breeze" (ibid., p. 292). It is worth noting how the language in this passage submerges in its semantic resources the whole psychological drama of Arenas's own life. It is the embodiment of the phallic wish to detach itself from a solid but infected body (the infection here also identified with the barren sand [*arenal*/Arenas] of the mainland), and to float/bathe once again in the fluid body of the ocean.

14. Echevarría, "Outcast of the Island," p. 32.

15. Arenas, *The Doorman*, p. 188.

16. Arenas, *Before Night Falls*, p. 296.

17. Susan Sontag, *AIDS and Its Metaphors* (New York: Farrar, Straus, & Giroux, 1989), pp. 6–7.

18. Sontag, *AIDS and Its Metaphors*, p. 62.

19. Arenas, *Before Night Falls*, pp. xvi–xvii.

20. Sontag, *AIDS and Its Metaphors*, pp. 76–77.

21. Arenas, *Before Night Falls*, p. 93.

22. Ibid., p. xvii.

23. Ibid., p. 239.

24. Ibid., p. 292.

25. In scattered passages recounting his time in exile, Arenas makes dismissive mention of "this festive and fascist left," which, he observes, had no better understanding of the complexity of the political experience of Cubans both in and out of the homeland than the most rabidly anti-Castro Cuban rightists. Both sides, in enlisting selectively the elements of his story that could serve their respective political needs, reduced him to a curiosity, a free-floating symbolic presence, a promiscuous political fetish-object, invited to cast its aura at events and functions. "I was surrounded," Arenas tells us, "by gossip and difficulties, and by an endless succession of cocktail parties, soirées, and invitations. It was like being on display, a strange creature that had to be invited before it lost its luster or until a new personality arrived to displace it" (ibid.).

26. See Kipnis, "Aesthetics and Foreign Policy," pp. 207–18. The quoted passage is on p. 215.

27. See Sontag, "Some Thoughts on the Right Way (for Us) to Love the Cuban Revolution."

28. Kipnis, "Aesthetics and Foreign Policy," pp. 216–17.

29. Ibid., p. 212.

30. See Theodor W. Adorno and Max Horkheimer, *The Dialectic of Enlightenment*, trans. John Cumming (New York: Continuum, 1991).

31. *Otra vez el mar* is available in a fine English translation by Andrew Hurley, *Farewell to the Sea: A Novel of Cuba* (New York: Penguin Books, 1986). The last page of the text is devoted to a record of its complex underground existence: "First version disappeared, Havana, 1969/Second version confiscated, Havana, 1971/The present version smuggled out of Havana, 1974/and published in Barcelona, 1982" (p. 413). Arenas also makes frequent reference to the history of this text in *Before Night Falls*.

32. See Slavoj Žižek, *Enjoy Your Symptom!: Lacan in Hollywood and Out* (New York: Routledge, 1992), pp. 131–36. This discussion applies to filmic discourse theories developed in Žižek's earlier work, *For They Know Not What They Do: Enjoyment as a Political Factor* (London: Verso, 1991), esp. pp. 2 and 236–41.

33. See Žižek, *Enjoy Your Symptom!*, pp. 131–32.

34. Arenas's scream should also be heard, I think, as an echo of that Adamic, "barbaric yawp" of Walt Whitman's, the pure noise of an original, still-originating New World poetics; it also echoes the guttural "no" of Retamar (and thus, retroactively, Martí's) insurgent, antitraditional *Calibán*. Since it also marks Arenas as that most stereotyped of subversive homosexuals, the flaming, effeminate "screaming" queen, reading Arenas's work as Adamic certainly puts a subversively sexualized spin on Retamar's and even Whitman's butch constructions of the "new" man.

35. Gustavo Pérez-Firmat, *Life on the Hyphen: The Cuban-American Way* (Austin: University of Texas Press, 1994).

36. Arenas, *Before Night Falls*, p. 311, and *Antes que anochezca*, p. 335.

37. See Arenas, *Before Night Falls*, p. 317, and *Antes que anochezca*, p. 343.

BIBLIOGRAPHY

Arenas, Reinaldo. *Antes que anochezca*. Barcelona: Tusquets Editores, 1992.
———. *The Assault*. Trans. Andrew Hurley. New York: Viking, 1994.
———. *Before Night Falls*. Trans. Dolores M. Koch. New York: Viking, 1993.
———. *The Doorman*. Trans. Dolores M. Koch. New York: Grove Weidenfeld, 1991.
———. *Farewell to the Sea: A Novel of Cuba*. Trans. Andrew Hurley. New York: Penguin, 1986.
Arguelles, Lourdes, and B. Ruby Rich. "Homosexuality, Homophobia, and Revolution: Notes Toward an Understanding of the Cuban Lesbian and Gay Male Experience, Part I." *Signs: Journal of Women in Culture and Society* 9 (1984): 686.
Echevarría, Roberto González. "Outcast of the Island." *New York Times Book Review*, Oct. 24, 1993, pp. 1, 32–33.
Foster, David William. *Gay and Lesbian Themes in Latin American Writing*. Austin: University of Texas Press, 1991.
Kipnis, Laura. "Aesthetics and Foreign Policy." In Kipnis, *Ecstasy Unlimited: On Sex,*

Capital, Gender, and Aesthetics, pp. 207–18. Minneapolis: University of Minnesota Press, 1993.

Leiner, Marvin. *Sexual Politics in Cuba: Machismo, Homosexuality, and AIDS*. Boulder: Westview Press, 1994.

Pérez-Firmat, Gustavo. *The Cuban Condition: Translation and Identity in Modern Cuban Literature*. Cambridge: Cambridge University Press, 1990.

———. *Life on the Hyphen: The Cuban-American Way*. Austin: University of Texas Press, 1994.

Retamar, Roberto Fernández. *Caliban and Other Essays*. Minneapolis: University of Minnesota Press, 1991.

Rozencvaig, Perla. *Reinaldo Arenas: Narrativa de trangresión*. Oaxaca, Mexico: Editorial Oasis, 1986.

———. "Reinaldo Arenas's Last Interview." Trans. Alfred MacAdam, Jr. *Review* 44 (Jan.–June 1991): 78–83.

Sontag, Susan. "Some Thoughts on the Right Way (for Us) to Love the Cuban Revolution." *Ramparts*, Apr. 1969, pp. 6–19.

Soto, Francisco. "*El Portero*: Una alucinante fábula moderna." *Revista de Literatura Hispánica* 32–33 (Fall 1990–Spring 1991): 106–17.

———. *Reinaldo Arenas: La pentagonía*. Gainesville: University of Florida Press, 1994.

Young, Allen. *Los gays bajo la revolución cubana*. Trans. Máximo Ellis. Madrid: Editorial Playor, 1984.

PART II

Modernist Transgressions

7. Defiance and Reconciliation in Paul Celan's *Die Niemandsrose*

For German-speaking Jews in the second part of this century, the question of how, or even whether, to continue to use a language identified with the assassins of the Jewish people has been an anguished one, caught up with the problem of identifying and preserving the polyglot Jewish cultures of the diaspora in the face of assimilation on the one hand and genocide on the other. For Jewish poets in the second part of this century, the question of whether it is possible to write poetry after Auschwitz has also been fraught with difficulty; Adorno's famous assertion to the contrary has stood as challenge, warning, or reproach to many. The poetry of Paul Celan, a Jewish Holocaust survivor writing in German after the war, confronts both these dilemmas. Celan's poetry—the poetry that supposedly changed Adorno's mind—responds to the paradox of its own existence with a gesture of defiance and also a gesture of reconciliation: a defiance of National Socialism, of death, and of God; and at the same time a reconciliation with God, and especially with language, the German language, the words that, as his translator Michael Hamburger has said, Celan "both loved and mistrusted" (Hamburger in Celan 1980:20). But though apparently in tension, the two impulses, of defiance and reconciliation, cannot really be separated. Defiance necessarily constitutes a recognition of the other, and the attempt at reconciliation in Celan's poetry can be the most beautiful, perverse expression of defiance imaginable.

This essay begins with two stories about Prague. This is not merely a scenic detour; it will bring us back to Celan perhaps better prepared to approach certain of his poems. One of these stories took place 50 years ago. The Jewish community of Prague was one of the largest and oldest of Europe, and the Jews of Prague were, for the most part, German-speaking. During World War II Prague was, of course, occupied by the German army, and the Jews were deported. The very few who survived came back to their city after the war, where other Czechs, gentiles, reproached them bitterly for speaking the language of the German invaders whose camps they had just escaped. So the Jews left Prague and went in search of other languages to speak, in the United States, Israel, France — just as Celan, a German-speaking Jew from what is now Romania, moved to Paris after the war and lived there until his death.

And now I step back a few hundred years, to the sixteenth century and the story of Rabbi Löw of Prague. Though a historical figure, the rabbi is now best known for the legend that credits him with the creation of a golem. In the cabalistic tradition, golems were described as quasi-human beings, created from clay by alchemy; the word means "that which is not yet formed, that which is incomplete." Adam is described as *golem* for the first twelve hours of his life, for example. To create a being of human form, gifted with intelligence, one was supposed to take clay and recite over it certain combinations of the letters of the Hebrew alphabet, or write them on the creature's forehead or on a scroll of paper inserted in its mouth. These formulas usually included the secret names of God. To destroy the golem, one had to say the formula backward or remove the scroll from the golem's mouth. There are numerous recipes for the creation of a golem; my favorite specifies that to animate the golem, one wrote "emeth," or "truth," on its forehead and that to destroy it one erased the first letter, leaving "meth," or death.

According to the legend, Rabbi Löw created a golem to protect the Jews of Prague from their persecutors. The golem served him well for a long time, but eventually it ran amok and began killing people, and the rabbi had to remove the name of God from its forehead to destroy it. This myth obviously inverts the Genesis story; God, by naming man, created Adam — who began life as a golem — in His image. The rabbis, by naming God (that is, by pronouncing or writing His names), could create golems in their own image. The myth could also be, if I may permit myself a stretch of the imagination, the formula for the creation of a certain kind of poetry that was possible before the war: take the raw matter of language, mold it into extraordinary, magical combinations, and inscribe it with the name of God, which is "emeth," truth.

It is at this point that we return to Celan. Celan, like the other German-speaking Jews of Europe, like the Jews of Prague, had to confront the question, How does one reconcile oneself with a language? How could one re-speak, recreate the German language so that it would no longer be, or no longer be *only*, the language of murderers? Or, as Jacques Derrida puts it in his book on Celan, *Shibboleth*, "How may one bless . . . ashes in German?" (1986:346).

Celan had great faith in the creative power of language. In his "Speech on the Occasion of Receiving the Literature Prize of the Free Hanseatic City of Bremen," he wrote, "*Erreichbar, nah und unverloren blieb inmitten der Verluste dies eine: die Sprache.*" ("Only one thing remained reachable, close and secure amid all losses: language") (Celan 1986:34). Secure amid all losses, or in the middle of (*inmitten*) loss, is language. And inversely, in the middle of Celan's language there remains loss. He knew that language also had destructive and murderous power. In the mouths of the Nazis, the power to name, to identify, and to distinguish — given to Adam and Eve by God — became the power to annihilate. And the names of Jews, the signs that they belonged to the chosen people, became deadly burdens. In a poem that I will examine more closely below, "So Many Constellations," Celan refers to "the burden of our names" (1980:134–35). (Celan may have found his own surname, Anschel, an unbearable burden, since he changed it to the anagram "Celan" after the war.)

"The burden of names" also evokes the burden of naming, the duty God entrusted to Adam and Eve (which reminds us that all gifts may be poisoned). How is one to assume such a responsibility after seeing how it can be corrupted? One could simply refuse to name, and I think there is a postwar poetry that signals that choice, a poetry that does not name — that, we might say, does not speak, but babbles. This is not Celan's poetry. "*Aber das Gedicht spricht ja!*" he says in "Meridian": "But the poem speaks!" (1986:48). Celan accepts the responsibility of speaking, of naming and creating, but only on certain conditions: most important, that he retain the right, like Rabbi Löw, to destroy his creation before it kills anybody. The rabbis wrote "emeth," truth, on the foreheads of golems; but what kind of poetry could one label with the rubric of "Truth" without betraying the truths of the concentration camps? Celan chose to erase any claim to "Truth," leaving only that of which he was sure: "meth," or death.

We find the moments where Celan destroys his golem everywhere in his poetry. There is one such moment in "Alchemical," a poem that talks about another kind of alchemic transformation, that of human beings into ashes. Celan evokes the image of the smoke rising from the crematoria, in the *Schwestergestalt*, the figure of the dead sister. (The dead sister appears often in Celan's work; she does not refer to an autobiographical sister but incorporates in her insubstantial form all the dead, the dead other with whom Celan maintained what he called a "desperate dialogue." She is the absence always already present in his poems. She is Nobody, the "Niemand" of *Die Niemandsrose*.) Celan indicates the smoke that forms into the figure of the sister, into rings of souls, and into crests or crowns, "around" — and there he puts two hyphens and a stanza break and then returns to a description of the smoke. What the crowns ought to encircle is indescribable; Celan cannot bring himself to name that which has already been murdered by being nominated. At the moment when he approaches it, respect for the dead demands that he return his golem to dust and leave us with death, the space between the stanzas and in the middle of his poetry: the loss in the middle of his language.

So loss, death, and absence are the points of departure of Celan's naming. But he names nonetheless; in fact, except for that which must always remain unnamable, he names liberally, profusely. He accepts the name, the possibility of presence and all that goes with it: subjects, distinctions, boundaries. But he refuses to privilege them. (And let us recall that, in a world where the "privilege" of the chosen people had become a deadly risk, this could easily be a refusal made out of love.) He accepts the responsibility God laid on Adam and Eve, but with a gesture that recalls the story, perhaps apocryphal, that the king of Denmark was prepared to order *all* his subjects to assume the yellow star, as if to say, "If to be marked as a Jew means to be persecuted, deported and killed, then we'll all have to be Jews." And so, as though thumbing his nose at God, Celan seems to say, "Very well: if I must name, I'll name *everything*, I'll make everything a Jew."

Thus we find in Celan's work an enormous number of verbs, past participles, and adjectives transformed into substantives, which are of course equivalent in German to proper names because all nouns begin with capital letters. This transformation of the parts of speech can choose to mark any word as a noun. It is not that at all times everything *is* marked as a noun; that would negate meaning, and Celan says that the poem speaks. It is, rather, that everything *can* become, *risks* becoming, a noun at any moment.

Let us look, for example, at "So Many Constellations." In line 15 the translator has chosen to translate "das Erloschenes" as "things extinguished," so we lose sight of the fact that "das Erloschenes" is a noun that was born as a verb, "erlöschen"; that became a past participle, "erloschen"; and that finally ends up "das Erloschenes," that which is extinguished. This kind of grammatical metamorphosis is fairly common in German, but in Celan's work it is ubiquitous.

In the same way that Celan accords the privilege, or the risk, of a proper name to all parts of speech (which is, obviously, a way of *not* privileging, or perhaps of protecting "real" substantives), he tries to share his privilege — or his responsibility — as a naming subject. Almost always, as soon as he declares himself as a subject, he shares, displaces, or undermines his own authority to control the word—that authority invested in Adam and Eve by God. His passion for conjugating verbs, for example, helps to disperse authority. Consider the third stanza of this poem. "I know," says the poet—the claim of epistemological certitude on the part of the Cartesian subject. But then, immediately: "I know and you know," he grants the possibility of subjectivity and knowledge to the other. Then, "we knew," which introduces an element of doubt—it is possible that we no longer know what we used to know; this is an era when all our certainties have been called into question. And finally, "we did not know"; after all, there was no Truth written on our foreheads. We were there, and we were together, we made our way to each other, but we did not *know*. There is love in Celan, but there is no certainty.

In the context of this poem, indeed, there is not even the certainty that we "were there," if "there" represents a determinate place, because Celan also calls into question the notion of "place" as a present, (de)finite space. This can also be seen as an act of defiance, if we consider the role that concepts of place and boundaries held in Nazi ideology, for instance. The "wandering Jew" has always been posited as that which disturbs frontiers, which is eternally without its own place. There is certainly a notion of "place" in Celan's poetry, but he constantly disturbs its lines of demarcation. The vocabulary of place is so strong that we can often literally draw a map of one of his poems; but we discover, in doing so, that places have a tendency to be displaced, interchanged.

The concept of place in "So Many Constellations," for example, is very complicated. In line 13, there is the place that is Dort, or "there," with a capital letter like the name of a city, and the place that is Nicht-da, or "not-there." Furthermore, in German there is a game going on that we lose in translation, a play between "dort" and "da," two different signs for what could be two different places or could be the same place. (The expressions "hier und da," and "da und dort" both mean "here and there," but in one of them "da" is equivalent to "there," and in the other it is equivalent to "here.") There is also a spatialized time, "Zuweilen," that disappears and returns intermittently. (Inexplicably, Hamburger has inserted a comma before "and at times," so that we do not see that "at times" can be read as the third term in a list of place names: *"Dort und Nicht-Da und Zuweilen."*) And determining the locus of the "I" of the poem, of the "you," of the breath, is almost impossible. "We/were there," the poet says in lines 23–24, "da"; but this "da," which we might be tempted to take as the equivalent of the "Dort" distinguished from "Nicht-Da" in line 13, is not in fact there, "nicht dort."

And if "da" and "nicht dort" are, like the "Dort" and the "Nicht-da" of the thirteenth line, specific place names, then it is possible to interpret line 24 to mean, not that we were there, *da*, rather than there, *dort*, but instead that we occupied all these spaces, we were there *and* not-there: da, nicht-dort, Dort, Nicht-da, and also, and only, "Zuweilen": at times, sometimes absent, sometimes present. We oscillate, the signs oscillate, the nouns and pronouns of the poem absolutely refuse to be fixed in one place. To let oneself be fixed in one place during the Nazi era could be much too dangerous.

In the poem "To one who stood before the door," we find both Rabbi Löw and the golem, as well as another line of demarcation that Celan refuses to fix, that he displaces: that marking the circumcised member of the Jew. The Jew is marked as such by a name, and we have already seen how Celan plays with names, calling attention to and annulling the singularity of names in the same movement. The Jew is also marked physically, by circumcision. As Derrida writes in *Shibboleth*, during his lengthy discussion of "To one who stood before the door,"

a certain tropic may displace the literality of membership in the Jewish community, if one could still speak of belonging to a community to which, we are reminded, nothing belongs as its own. In this case, those who have undergone the *experience* — a certain concise experience — of circumcision, circumcised and circumcisers, are, in all the senses of this word, Jews. Anyone or no one may be Jewish. No one is (not) circumcised; it is no one's circumcision. (1986:340)

The poem poses the question, Who shares the experience of circumcision? Can a golem be circumcised? Or God Himself? Celan refers to the golem as "der Menschlein," the "little human," the "half-human." This half-human has, however, a "bloody sex," he is circumcised; he possesses the mark that signals the entrance of the male individual into the Jewish community. Medieval rabbis agreed that the golem, although gifted with intelligence, was excluded from participation in the minyan, the assembly of ten adult men required for religious services. Women, uncircumcised, are of course also excluded. But Celan refuses circumcision—the determinant of inclusion in, or exclusion from, the community—to no one. He does not even bar God from the circle of the circumcised, it seems, since he has given God's bloody penis to the golem, marking both the subhuman and the divine as human flesh, as Jew: a gesture at once generous and ironic, humorous and blasphemous.

Michael Hamburger says that "negation and blasphemy were the means by which Celan could be true to [the] experience [of being God-forsaken] and yet maintain the kind of intimate dialogue with God characteristic of Jewish devotion" (in Celan 1980:23). Blasphemy is, as it were, a way of being reconciled with a God who cannot be forgiven. Blasphemy admits the presence of One who was absent at the moment when He was most needed. We also cannot exclude the possibility that there is a certain spirit of revenge in the poem, in the act of attributing to God the sign of His own benediction, become a curse: as if Celan said to Him, "Take on Yourself the privilege from which You could not protect us." At any rate, such an inversion would certainly be consonant with the multiple reversals operating between Celan's text and the golem myth of which the poem is, as Derrida has said, the translation.

For another example of these transformations and inversions — between the human and God, God and the golem, golem and Jew — we might consider the translation of the name of God by "Nothing" in line 20. The poet asks Rabbi Löw, instead of inscribing the name of God on the golem's forehead, to write the "living Nothing" in its mind. The significance of the word "living" is clear: Celan's God may be cursed, but He is absolutely not dead. He is reduced to the infinite smallness of Nothing, but this Nothing is, like the "Niemand" of the collection's title, glorified as a proper name. I said above that the *Schwestergestalt*, the dead other, can be characterized as an absence always already present in Celan's poetry, its degree zero. I could also say that the God of his poetry is a presence always already absent, which is perhaps facile but not therefore false. Both are sometimes represented as "Niemand," a word that summarizes everything present in absence, or the inverse, in Celan's poetry.

"Niemand" could also represent Rabbi Löw, in the poem "Psalm," for example. The "us" of the poem is at once the golem and Adam, Adam who was at first golem. The first stanza recalls both creation stories, that of Adam by God and that of the golem by the rabbi. This is, then, a poem about *re-*creations, the quest for a third creation in which we will be molded *again*, *wieder*, from dust and ashes. Celan is searching for the patriarch, whether divine or human, who can recreate something miraculously, not out of nothing but out of nothingness, out of annihilation. And there is no one to do it.

But there is, of course: there is, precisely, No One. (And again we note that "Niemand" in the original poem is a proper name.) And we are going to praise No One, whether He wants us to or not, with praises that are also defiance: a paradox reflected in the word "entgegen" in line 8, a word that means both "toward" and "against." We are going to flower "against" You, against Your will perhaps, if it was Your will that we be annihilated; and toward You, toward a hope or faith that the gesture of love and reconciliation matters, even if there is No One (or only No One) to receive it. We shall remain nothing, but flowering, a rose growing in a desert of ashes. God is absent, but we will praise and blaspheme His presence. Rabbi Löw has been dead for four centuries, but we will go to Prague to lay our pebbles, our poems, on his tomb.

And so here we are, back in Prague. The old Jewish cemetery in Prague, where Rabbi Löw is buried, has been closed for two hundred years. And those who come now to lay pebbles on his grave are not relatives, but only tourists, like us, because the Jews of Prague are dead or in exile. A museum stands next door to the cemetery, displaying the collections of Jewish art, religious artifacts, and personal effects confiscated from the Jews of Prague by the Nazis, who destined them for a museum commemorating the success of the final solution. The site thus represents a sort of "arch-cemetery" with no connection to the living, a place of absolute death, a monument to annihilation. In his poems Celan also goes back to Prague, and his homage to Rabbi Löw might be only a lamentation, an expression of mourning— except that his pebbles are German pebbles. This is his ultimate gesture of defiance and of reconciliation: to come to this place that seems to contain all the deaths of Jews imaginable, in order to sing psalms in German. He holds out his hand to the dead, and in that hand he holds a living, renewed language. Rabbi Löw can summon no more miracles to save his people; God will not recreate them; but Celan will give them back their language. And it is there, with and through language, that every reconciliation begins.

WORKS CITED

Celan, Paul. 1985. *Die Niemandsrose/Sprachgitter: Gedichte.* Frankfurt am Main: Fischer Taschenbuch Verlag.
———. *Paul Celan: Poems. A Bilingual Edition.* 1980. Selected, translated, and introduced by Michael Hamburger. New York: Persea Books.
———. *Collected Prose.* 1986. Trans. Rosmarie Waldrop. Manchester: Carcanet.
Derrida, Jacques. 1986. *Shibboleth.* Trans. Joshua Wilner. In *Midrash and Literature,* ed. Geoffrey H. Hartman and Sanford Budick, pp. 307–47. New Haven: Yale University Press.

8. Mimesis, Mimicry, and Critical Theory in Exile

Walter Benjamin's Approach to the Collège de Sociologie

In the late 1930s in Paris, a short-lived but lively exchange took place between the exiled affiliate of the "Frankfurt School," Walter Benjamin, and the founding members of the Collège de Sociologie — Georges Bataille, Michel Leiris, Roger Caillois, and Pierre Klossowski. This exchange marks an important historical point of intersection between the dominant trends of postwar French theory and the later development of German "Critical Theory." This essay focuses on a single theoretical issue around which many points of contact between the two schools, both direct and indirect, can be demonstrated: the problem of mimesis. During the late 1930s, the issue of imitative behavior, conceived especially in anthropological and ethnographic terms, took on a crucial political charge in these two intellectual circles. It became for them the fulcrum for understanding two associated problems of the non-communist radical Left: the relation of the cultural avant-garde to fascism and the politics of eroticism — the relation of sexuality to social cohesion, history, and religious experience. Although the notion of mimesis had a crucial importance for Georges Bataille, Pierre Klossowski, Max Horkheimer, and Theodor Adorno, I here concentrate on the works of Walter Benjamin, whose exile in Paris and intimacy with French literary circles make his work a particularly intense locus of this theoretical dialogue.

The Frankfurt School is convenient nomenclature for the Institute for Social Research, founded in Frankfurt in the 1920s, then in London and New York during the Nazi years; after the war, it was reestablished in Frankfurt. It was dedicated to Marxist-oriented but noncommunist analyses of culture, social psychology, and social institutions. Its best-known original members include its guiding hand Max Horkheimer, his associate Theodor Adorno, and Walter Benjamin, Herbert Marcuse, and Erich Fromm. The

Collège de Sociologie was far more short-lived and haphazardly organized than the Frankfurt School; until Denis Hollier's compilation of its texts and fragments, it remained little known despite the influence of its major figures. The Collège was founded in the summer of 1937 by Georges Bataille, Roger Caillois, and Michel Leiris. It had three stated goals: to study social structures and activities left out of scientific studies of society (particularly the "sacred"); to develop a "moral community" among the investigators that would have the "contagious" quality of sacred activity, forming a pole of "attraction" for intellectuals; and to found a "sacred sociology," drawing connections between individual psychology and forms of social organization. For a few years, the Collège was the gathering place of many of the most important thinkers in France. Among the speakers in its two years of existence were, besides its founders, Alexander Kojève, Pierre Klossowski, Denis de Rougemont, Jean Paulhan, and the German critic Hans Mayer. Also in attendance were the German exiles Walter Benjamin and Theodor Adorno.[1]

Benjamin had prior contact with members of the inner circle of this group. His interest in surrealism made it likely for him to encounter at least some of these figures, nearly all renegades from André Breton's surrealist orthodoxy. By 1935 he had met Pierre Klossowski, who became Benjamin's French translator; Klossowski's translation of Benjamin's essay "The Work of Art in the Age of Its Technical Reproducibility" appeared in the Institute's Zeitschrift für Sozialforschung in 1936. He developed a close enough relationship to the circle around Bataille to be asked to be on the roster of forthcoming lecturers for the fall of 1939. He was to have presented work on fashion, a major area of investigation in his Passagenwerk, but the Collège collapsed before the lecture could take place. Afterward, when Benjamin tried to flee France, Bataille hid the Passagenwerk papers in the Bibliothèque Nationale, thus preserving them from destruction at the hands of the Nazis.

My exposition of the issue of mimesis begins with two short texts by Walter Benjamin from 1933, "On the Mimetic Faculty" and "Doctrine of the Similar."[2] In these two essays, Benjamin made a programmatic formulation of his ideas on mimesis. The evidence of his letters indicates that Benjamin considered this theory a secularized elaboration of his earlier theological language theory. In his 1918 essay "On Language as Such and on the Language of Man," Benjamin had argued for an expanded conception of language in which not just humans but also things "partake of language."[3] This conception, which formed the theoretical armature of Benjamin's early work on allegory, would also lend a seriousness to his lifelong passion for rather dubious — from a scientific point of view — interpretive practices such as graphology and physiognomics, as well as his more respectable collector's instinct. "All expression," he wrote in this early essay, "insofar as it is a communication of spiritual contents, is to be counted as language. And expression, by its whole innermost essence, is certainly to be understood only as language; on the other hand, in order to understand a linguistic entity, it is necessary to ask for which spiritual entity it is the direct expression."[4] The later notion of mimesis retains Benjamin's early concern with the sacred, but — as with the Collège de Sociologie's "sacred sociology" — it comprehends sacred phenomena as modes of collective behavior and social experience. Following up on his 1933 essays, Benjamin would again attempt to formulate a rigorous, scientifically valid theory of mimesis in his 1935 Referat "Problems of the Sociology of Language," which surveyed a wide range of academic literature, including Lucien Lévy-Bruhl's and Ernst Cassirer's writings on myth, Rudolf Carnap's and Edmund Husserl's studies of logical structure, and psychological studies by Jean Piaget, Karl Bühler, Wolfgang Köhler, and Lev Vygotsky.[5]

"Mimesis" in the 1933 essays designates something broader than the representational and theatrical models inherited from Plato and Aristotle. The "mimetic" here is rather a mode of behavior and even a faculty that comes from the natural being of humans but also constitutes the basis of the human distinction from nature: the ability to appropriate natural forms by means of gesture, language, and concept. Benjamin is thus concerned with a faculty of perceiving and acting *similarly*; this faculty is implicated in the individual and historical development of the modern subject. Benjamin writes: "Nature produces similarities — one need only think of mimicry. Human beings, however, possess the very highest capacity to produce similarities. Indeed, there may not be a single one of the higher human functions which is not decisively co-determined by the mimetic faculty. This faculty, however, has a history both phylogenetically and ontogenetically."[6] The ontogenetic roots of the mimetic faculty are established in childhood, especially in the phenomenon of play. In play, the child not only interiorizes social roles but also learns to live among the world of natural and manufactured things: "To begin with, children's games are everywhere interlaced with mimetic modes of behavior, and their range is in no way limited to what one human being imitates from another. A child not only plays at being a salesman or teacher, but also at being a windmill or a train."[7]

This latter remark is crucial for Benjamin's attempt to historicize the phenomenon of mimetic behavior within specific cultural, generational, and class contexts. The objects imitated, he suggests, have particular historical origins, durations, and significances. The things that surround the world of childhood fantasy and play, as well as their adult analogues, are transfigured by mimetic behavior into concentrated vessels of historical time. The experiences contained in this way can become a vital source of unwritten historical memory, accessible to later recall and analysis, as with Benjamin's own collecting and investigations of material culture.

In his 1933 essays on the mimetic faculty, Benjamin takes up the anthropological significance of mimesis. He argues that the social production and perception of resemblance has changed over time. The crucial locus for this history is the technology of language, especially writing conceived in the broadest sense of *écriture*, inscription both on the page and in social space. Benjamin represents a long historical process, stretching from magical practice to modern language: "This reading is the oldest: reading before all language from entrails, stars, or dance. Later the mediatory elements of a new reading, runes and hieroglyphs, came into use. One may surmise that these were the stations over which that mimetic talent, which was once the basis of occult practice, found its entrance into writing and language. In this way language would be the highest stage of mimetic behavior and the most complete archive of non-sensuous similarity."[8] Clearly, the mimetic practices of modern people are less evident than in those historical cultures in which cultic rites played a dominant role. Yet Benjamin suggests that the mimetic practices may have been transformed rather than eliminated. The task of Benjamin's own form of "sacred sociology," then, would be to designate and investigate the secularized locations of the sacred — the mimetic faculty — within the modern.

During his residence in Paris, Benjamin increasingly considered the mimetic faculty as part of the collective's sensitivity to the signs, objects, and spaces of its environment, especially the metropolis. This collective mimetic faculty, Benjamin argues in his exposé for the *Passagenwerk*, "Paris, Capital of the Nineteenth Century," receives its impulse from "wishful fantasies" out of a collective unconscious.[9] Through these fantasies "the collective seeks both to preserve (*aufheben*) and to transfigure (*verklären*) the inchoateness of the social product and the deficiencies in the social system of production" (pp. 46–47). The wish fantasies "direct the visual imagination" to discover in the city the prefigurations of a classless future in the present. Such "dialectical images," as Benjamin would call them, reveal themselves to the collective in the "thousands of configurations of life, from permanent buildings to fleeting fashions" (p. 47). The collective appropriates these forms unconsciously, *mimetically*, by just doing what it does: walking, shopping, working, taking public transportation. The historical clarification of this faculty and its training into a capacity for the *political* interpretation of environmental signs could, Benjamin suggests, be put in the service of the revolution. Benjamin here conceives a form of political spontaneity — akin to festival and ritual — articulated by the mimetic faculty's implicit knowledge: theory does not provide guidelines to be dialectically realized by collective action, but rather a more explicit, figurative analogue of this action's own mimetic form.

Benjamin believed that the source of the dialectical images lay in the natural and prehistorical foundations of modern cities. In these could be intimated a vast historical span; the mimetic perception of similarities across historical periods was the means by which the collective could lay hands on its own past. Thus Benjamin appealed to an archaeological moment, both as a metaphor for the method of investigation and as a literal model by means of which the anthropology of the modern collective could be reconstructed. In his "Paris, Capital of the Nineteenth Century" exposé of the *Passagenwerk*, Benjamin writes: "What is unique in Baudelaire's poetry is that the images of women and death are permeated by a third, that of Paris. . . . The chthonic elements of the city — its topographical formation, the old deserted bed of the Seine — doubtless left their impression on his work. Yet what is decisive in Baudelaire's 'deathly idyll' of the city is a social, modern substratum. . . . But it is precisely modernity that is always quoting primeval history."[10]

Benjamin's evocation here of the trio of women, death, and the city in relation to prehistory refers his Baudelaire studies to a key essay Benjamin wrote contemporaneously in French on another nineteenth-century author, the Swiss archaeologist and historian of religion Johannes Jakob Bachofen, author of *Mother Right*.[11] I suggest that these essays, the one on Baudelaire in German, the other on Bachofen in French, are linked in a more politically and biographically significant way than has been previously suspected. The juxtaposition of these two essays reveals a radical political conception that Benjamin had embedded in the Baudelaire study but was required to dissimulate because of his shaky financial situation in Paris and his dependence on the Frankfurt School for support. The political position Benjamin had evolved brought him into the orbit of the Bataille group, which had constituted a secret society, Acéphale, dedicated to a new politics of sacred sociology, antifascist in orientation but suspicious from the point of view of even the Frankfurt School's nondogmatic Marxism. The timing was crucial: the Institute for Social Research had just moved to New York; Horkheimer and Adorno were nervous about the threat that a too openly radical stance might pose for their success in establishing themselves there. From his side of the Atlantic, Benjamin hoped that his exposé would convince them to support his research in Paris. Thus walking a fine line between Marxist sensibilities and fears about the status of left-wing Jewish exiles in the United States, Benjamin encrypted his latest political stance.

In the Bachofen essay, Benjamin writes that creation "emerges from matter alone — but the word *Stoff* . . . means dense, thick matter. It is the agent of this general promiscuity whose imprint ancient humanity bore in its hetaeric constitution. Life and death themselves are not exempt from this promiscuity; they combine in ephemeral constellations at the mercy of the rhythm that lulls this entire creation. In this immemorial order death has nothing to do with violent destruction. Antiquity always considered it more or less an aspect of life. The dialectical spirit of such a conception reached its highest level in Bachofen." [12] Bachofen's exposition of what he called the hetaeric phase of human history, before the installation of the patriarchate, served Benjamin as the archetype of a redeemed humanity, living in open mimetic exchange with its material context. It is thus not simply an image of prehistory but of a *gynocratic* prehistory that provides Benjamin with his dialectical image of reconciliation. The most highly developed mimetic contact between modern city dwellers and the natural-historical deposits of the material world presupposes a destruction of patriarchial relations in collective life. The collective subject, with its mimetic anamnesis, would usher in a general "feminization" of social life.

More, Bachofen's work was already charged with a political topicality through its use by fascist and protofascist ideologists such as Ludwig Klages, Alfred Bäumler, and Alfred Rosenberg to legitimate their myth-histories; Benjamin also cites an essay by Erich Fromm entitled "The Social Psychological Significance of the Mother Right Theory (1934)," which Horkheimer had published in Paris in the *Zeitschrift für Sozialforschung*. In polemical passages against fascist interpretations of Bachofen, Benjamin again suggests that the stakes are not simply those of fascism versus communism but also of gynocracy against patriarchy. Thus he writes of such followers of Bachofen as the ethnologist Walter Lehmann, whose lectures on Aztec mythology Benjamin attended in Munich: "They were bold to explore in the famous table of oppositions that formed part of the Pythagorian tradition and of which the fundamental opposition is that between the right and the left. Thus they are inclined to see in the meaning of the swastika that turns to the right a patriarchal innovation that replaced the ancient movement of rotation to the left."[13] In case the implications of that remark remained too occult, Benjamin goes on to assert that for Bachofen, "Communism seemed inseparable from the gynocracy."[14]

The unspoken political message of Benjamin's studies of nineteenth-century Paris brings him very close to the "sacred sociology" of the Collège de Sociologie. Benjamin suggests that fascist myth and symbol — for example, the right-handed swastika — require a mimetic countermobilization of prehistory and of the "sacred." Where fascism looked to an archaic imperial or warrior myth, however, Benjamin counterposed communist gynocracy. Pierre Klossowski's retrospective report on his (and the Bataille group's) relation to Benjamin, published in 1969 in *Le Monde*, suggests in more concrete terms what this politics implied. I quote at length from this text:

I met Walter Benjamin during one of the meetings of Contre-Attaque — the name of the ephemeral fusion of groups headed by André Breton and Georges Bataille, in 1935. Later he assiduously attended the College of Sociology, an emanation intended to make "exoteric" the closed and secret group Acéphale. . . . From this point on he was sometimes present at our secret meetings.

Disconcerted by the ambiguity of "acephalian" a-theology, Walter Benjamin disagreed with us, arguing that the conclusions he then was drawing from his analysis of German bourgeois intellectual evolution, namely, that the "increasing metaphysical and political buildup of what was incommunicable" . . . was what prepared the favorable ground for nazism. . . . There was no possible agreement about this point of his analysis, whose presuppositions did not coincide at all with the basic ideas and past history of the groups formed by Breton and Bataille, especially Acéphale. On the other hand, we questioned him even more insistently about what we sensed was his most authentic basis, namely, his personal version of a "phalansterism" revival. Sometimes he talked about it to us as if it were something "esoteric," simultaneously "erotic and artisanal," underlying his explicit Marxist conceptions. Having the means of production in common would permit substituting for the abolished social classes a redistribution of society into *affective classes*. A freed industrial production, instead of mastering affectivity, would expand its forms and organize its exchanges, in the sense that work would be in collusion with lust, and cease to be the other, punitive, side of the coin.[15]

It was on this basis, the vision of communism not just as an economic reorganization but as a revolution of the passions as well, that Benjamin and the Collège members found common ground.

Benjamin's advocacy of an antipatriarchal libidinal politics caused him difficulties with one member of the Collège, Roger Caillois. Caillois had recently made a major contribution to the debate on mimetism. His two-part essay on mimesis and mimicry, "The Praying Mantis," had appeared in 1934 and 1935 in the renegade surrealist journal *Minotaure*; it was reprinted in full in *Le mythe et l'homme* in 1938. There, in strong contrast to Benjamin's anamnestic conception of mimetism, Caillois interprets it as a profoundly regressive phenomenon. In Caillois's view, it follows from a derangement of the individual organism's relation to its surrounding space and consequent relinquishment of its difference from its environment. Thus, for example, the leaf bug takes on the characteristics of the leaves upon which it sits immobilized. In mimetism, the living individual surrenders a part of his vitality to the death drive, the impulse to return to an inorganic state.

"The Praying Mantis" was reviewed by Adorno in strongly critical tones for the 1938 *Zeitschrift für Sozialforschung*; in the same issue Raymond Aron reviewed the book in which Caillois's essay was reprinted, *Myth and Man*. A third review of another work by Caillois, "L'aridité," also appeared in this issue; the reviewer was "J. E. Mabinn (Paris)."[16] Although Caillois had declared himself antifascist, "L'aridité" exhibits at least strong authoritarian leanings. It is a sustained call for the discipline of "voluntary servitude" against the slack disorder of the desire for liberty. This voluntary servitude, however, has a sexual — or more properly, antisexual — dimension, too, since it represents precisely the suspension of pleasure and passion under the function of intellect. As Denis Hollier notes about the sexual politics of this position: "The hierarchy of beings [masters and slaves] is . . . above all a political sublimation of the sexual, the overcoming of the sexual by the political. It produces the political as nonsexual. But . . . this overcoming itself is described according to the pattern of sexual difference. The difference between the sexual and the nonsexual occurs along the lines of sexual difference itself. Power — which the masters find beyond pleasure — is a phallic desublimation."[17] The reviewer "J. E. Mabinn" takes up, in his own unique style, substantially the same points in his 1938 notice as Hollier does in his more recent essay. In Caillois's essay, the reviewer comments, "It is striking how the historically conditioned character traits of today's bourgeois come together in a remark, outlined with elegant style, on the margin of the age. The terse strokes of this design carry all the characteristics of pathological cruelty."[18] If it is not already clear, "J. E. Mabinn" was Walter Benjamin — the pseudonym anagrammatized his name.

If, with his conception of mimetism, Benjamin had called for a collective liberation of the senses and a feminization of society, Caillois projected an opposed vision: the formation of a "dry," masculine, disciplined elite, whose power would lie in its resistance to the seductions of liberty and pleasure. This position represented the political activation of Caillois's antithetical view of mimetism. The hard, dry qualities which he valued would be won through a kind of willed devitalization, a deliberate chastening of mind and body to deaden sensual and affective response. Assimilating itself to the harsh, lifeless nature of the desert and the winter wind (another of Caillois's favorite metaphors at this time), the elite projected by "L'aridité" would sacrifice "life" for increased self-control and power.[19]

Benjamin, who was trying to leave Europe and come to America, personally feared Caillois's "dryness," his expressed penchant for cultivated cruelty, and explained to Horkheimer in a letter: "As I learned a few days ago through a lucky accident, Caillois is close friends with and says 'du' to Rolland de Renéville. Renéville has till now taken up my matters in his capacity as secretary in the naturalization office of the Justice Ministry; but he would above all be able to work for, and hence also against, them if he ever went from the prefecture to the Justice Ministry. Under these conditions, my naturalization could in fact be endangered if the notice on 'L'aridité' appeared under my name."[20] Unfortunately, as we know, Benjamin's efforts at disguise were to have little effect, either for good or for bad: he was forced to flee from the Nazis, and when that flight was blocked he took his own life. But his mimicry — his adoption of the pseudonym — seems in retrospect to foreshadow that fatality. It is as if, in masking himself, he had capitulated to Caillois's ascetic view of mimetic phenomena: "The assimilation to space is necessarily accompanied by a decline in the feeling of personality and life. It should be noted in any case that in mimetic species the phenomenon is never carried out except *in a single direction. . . . Life takes a step backwards.*"[21]

NOTES

1. The most recent and comprehensive history of the Frankfurt School is Rolf Wiggershaus, *The Frankfurt School: Its History, Theories, and Political Significance*, trans. Michael Robertson (Cambridge, Mass.: MIT Press, 1994). The documents and related materials of the Collège de Sociologie can be found in *The College of Sociology, 1937–39*, ed. Denis Hollier (Minneapolis: University of Minnesota Press, 1988).

2. Walter Benjamin, "Lehre vom Ähnlichen" and "Über das mimetische Vermögen," in *Gesammelte Schriften* (hereafter cited as *GS*), 2, ed. Rolf Tiedemann and Hermann Schweppenhäuser (Frankfurt a/M: Suhrkamp Verlag, 1977), pp. 204–10, 210–13. A translation of the former appeared in *New German Critique* 17 (1979): 65–

69 under the title "Doctrine of the Similar." An English translation of "On the Mimetic Faculty" can be found in *One-Way Street and Other Writings*, trans. Edmund Jephcott and Kingsley Shorter (London: Verso, 1979), pp. 160–63.

3. GS 2:140–41.

4. GS 2:141.

5. See "Probleme der Sprachsoziologie," GS 3, ed. Hella Tiedemann-Bartels, pp. 452–80.

6. GS 2:210.

7. GS 2:205, 210.

8. GS 2:213.

9. "Paris, die Hauptstadt des XIX Jahrhunderts" in *Das Passagenwerk*, ed. Rolf Tiedemann (Frankfurt a/M: Suhrkamp, 1982), pp. 45–59. For further discussion of Benjamin's conception of collective wish-images, see my article "From City-Dreams to the Dreaming Collective: Walter Benjamin's Political Dream Interpretation," *Philosophy and Social Criticism* 22, no. 6 (1996): 87–111.

10. *Passagenwerk*, p. 55.

11. J. J. Bachofen, *Das Mutterrecht*, ed. Hans-Jürgen Heinrichs (Frankfurt a/M: Suhrkamp, 1975). A translated selection from *Mother Right* and other works by Bachofen can be found in *Myth, Religion, and Mother Right: Selected Writings of J. J. Bachofen*, trans. Ralph Manheim, Bollingen Series 84 (Princeton: Princeton University Press, 1967).

12. GS 2:223.

13. GS 2:228.

14. GS 2:230.

15. Pierre Klossowski, "Entre Marx et Fourier," excerpted in *The College of Sociology*, pp. 388–89.

16. Roger Caillois, "L'aridité," *Mesures* 4, no. 2 (1939): 7–12. Adorno's, Aron's, and "Mabinn's" reviews appeared in *Zeitschrift für Sozialforschung*, ed. Max Horkheimer, Vol. 7, 1938; I refer to the facsimile reprint by Kösel-Verlag, Munich, 1970.

17. Denis Hollier, "Mimesis and Castration," *October* 31 (1984): 7.

18. GS 3:549.

19. The influence of the fashion for Sade among the circle around Georges Bataille is evident. Yet unlike Caillois, Pierre Klossowski — Benjamin's friend and translator — recognized the contradictions any attempt to actualize Sade's literary conceptions of freedom in political reality would entail. In his study of Sade published shortly after World War II, *Sade mon prochain*, Klossowski noted that Sade's conception of freedom evolved, by a rigorous progression, from a "materialist atheism" toward a "transcendental fatalism." To free his ego from dependence on God (still in effect in blasphemy) and on his victims (still in effect so long as he enjoys their torture), the Sadean libertine had to become as indifferent as nature itself. Yet this becoming like nature — in its vast destructiveness — negated the libertine's absolute freedom at the moment it was realized. His freedom becomes indifferent

through his pursuit of absolute distinction, and its sole expression can be a purely destructive violence. Klossowski's conclusion resonates as a profound and devastating criticism of Caillois's attempt to activate mimetism as a political concept.

20. Benjamin to Horkheimer, November 17, 1938, quoted in GS 3:695.

21. Roger Caillois, "Mimicry and Legendary Psychasthenia," *October* 31 (1984): 30.

9. "Sharing the Unshareable"

*Jabès, Deconstruction, and the
Thought of the "Jews"*

Compromised by Martin Heidegger's silence on the issue of the Holocaust
and by Paul de Man's early collaborative essays, deconstruction has been
denounced in recent years for its failure to come to terms with the socio-
political, particularly in regard to its supposed inability to respond to the
imperative to speak out on the Nazi atrocities. Jean-François Lyotard, for
example, claims in his relatively recent *Heidegger and "the jews"* that Heidegger's failure to speak out against the Extermination even after his break
with National Socialism was due not simply to a "deconstructionist lapsus,"
as he calls it, but rather to a flaw within deconstruction itself, for in focusing
too persistently on the philosophical question of Being, deconstruction remains tied to a tradition that refuses to think the possibility of nothingness,
of something "unpresentable" or ungraspable within Being itself.[1]

As Lyotard points out, this is all the more curious given that it was Heidegger's own critique of the metaphysical tradition, of its focus on being's
"thingness" while forgetting the fundamentally enigmatic essence of Being
as such, that taught us to think the unthinkable, to preserve the memory of
what is necessarily missing, forgotten, and utterly unrepresentable in both
language and thought. In failing, however, to push his deconstructive project
far enough, preferring instead to embrace notions of the authenticity and
ultimate "destiny" of Being, Heidegger's thinking remains complicitous, according to Lyotard, not only with the Western philosophical tradition but
also with its politics, whose rejection of heterogeneity and otherness, or indeed of anything that disrupts conceptual, representational, or social homo-
geneity, can have Nazism as one of its possible consequences. Although that
politics is obviously not always identical with that of National Socialism and
does not necessarily authorize such monstrosities as Nazism's "final solu-

This essay is from Joan Brandt, *Geopoetics: The Politics of Mimesis in Poststructuralist French
Poetry and Theory* (Stanford: Stanford University Press, 1997).

tion," it nevertheless finds a place within a conceptual framework that can always permit such a possibility. For if the Jews were to be eliminated without leaving a trace or memory, it was because of a "politics of absolute forgetting" made possible by the Western philosophical tradition in its effort to eliminate the unrepresentable from thought.

In making such a claim, however, Lyotard reveals the extent to which his own critique is derived from the very deconstructive analyses he criticizes. Despite his claim that writers such as Jacques Derrida and Philippe Lacoue-Labarthe are too closely tied to a philosophical/representational problematic, their rigorous questioning of traditional notions of mimetic representation and of the precepts of identity that underpin it provides the basis for Lyotard's own critique of Western metaphysics by allowing for an examination of the very modes of thought that make the totalitarian discourses of fascism possible and by pointing to the ways in which politics is by its very nature dependent on the metaphysical notions of identity and representational language that Lyotard also calls into question. Indeed, the writings of Lacoue-Labarthe and of Jean-Luc Nancy as well, who have written extensively on the mechanisms of fascism and its totalitarian logic, have provided insights that clearly inform Lyotard's argument.[2] In claiming that traditional mimetic principles (manifested most directly in representational language but also evident in the sociopsychological identificatory mechanisms shaping psychic and communitarian identity) are at the very root of National Socialism, where the formative or fashioning power of the German myth constitutes national identity, they underscore the extent to which the unifying logic of mimetic representation, with its subsumption of difference under a structure of sameness and identity, provides the basis, in its most extreme manifestations, for the formation of a totalitarian politics. The political fiction of the German myth, which involves the projection of a model, image, or type (i.e., the Aryan type) with which one identifies and through which the identity of a people or race is fashioned and ultimately realized takes as its point of departure the structure of mimesis itself which, when understood in its traditional sense as an infinite repetition of the same, involves the appropriation of some predetermined model or originary concept (thus indicating that self-identity is dependent on the existence of an other), while denying the contradictory and destabilizing elements that the relation to otherness implies.

This is why Lacoue-Labarthe claims that mimesis is not simply a philosophical or linguistic problem but a political problem as well. The philosophical condemnation of the duplicitous structure of the mimetic (which has prevailed, according to Lacoue-Labarthe, throughout the history of the Western philosophical tradition up to and including Heidegger), its refusal to recognize the "impropriety," the "lack of being-proper" that comes from the mimetic relation to the "other," is essential to any process of national identification. Given that the contradictions implied in the mimetic relation serve to undermine self-contained identity and thus to destabilize the identificatory mechanisms essential to the self-formation of the political community, people, or race, the "law of the proper" must prevail; there can be no admission of duplicity within the mimetic process itself. As Lacoue-Labarthe argues, "mimetological law," which posits an original plenitude to which subsequent reproductions are to remain ideally subordinate, "demands that *imitatio* rid itself of *imitation* itself, or that, in what it establishes (or has imposed upon it) as a model, it should address something that does not derive from *imitatio*" (*HAP* p. 79).

Thus if Lacoue-Labarthe is right in saying that fascism is "the mobilization of the identificatory emotions of the masses" (*HAP* p. 95), it can be looked upon as one of the possible consequences of this attempt to overcome or erase mimetic paradoxality whose duplicitous logic is one in which the Jews themselves are implicated. If the Jews were eliminated for posing a threat to national identity, it was not because they were seen as the enemy in the traditional sense, for they could hardly be said to have constituted an organized political or military force that challenged the authority of the German state. It was instead because they were perceived to be entirely without identity. They were "unlocatable," functioning neither as an integral part of the community nor as an adversary standing outside it. Citing the anti-Semitic writings of a leading Nazi theoretician, Alfred Rosenberg, Lacoue-Labarthe points out that the Jew was not seen by Rosenberg as standing in opposition to the Nazi dream of self-realization in the form of a superior Aryan *type*; the Jew figured instead as its "contradiction," "the very absence of type," a "formless, unaesthetic 'people,'" which by definition [could] not enter into the process of self-fictioning and [could] not constitute a subject, or, in other words, a being-proper (*être-propre*)." The Jews thus represented for the Nazis the process of "destabilization" itself. Their capacity to insert themselves into every culture and state defined them as "infinitely mimetic beings," as the site of the "improper," of an "*endless mimesis*, which is both interminable and inorganic, producing no art and achieving no appropriation" (*HAP* p. 96).

Interestingly, and paralleling Lacoue-Labarthe's remarks, it is indeed "the jews" who come to signify, in Lyotard's text, this problematic of the "improper."[3] And yet, despite Lyotard's acknowledgment of his indebtedness to certain aspects of Lacoue-Labarthe's analysis, it is this focus on the mimetic as a fundamental component of the political that he finds particularly objectionable in Lacoue-Labarthe's work because it neglects what Lyotard believes can never be inscribed in a representational determination. By remaining too preoccupied by the Heideggerian question of Being and its relation to the mimetic, Lacoue-Labarthe forgets, according to Lyotard, the question of "the jews" and the possibility that the West, whose history Lacoue-Labarthe traces in essentially philosophical terms, might be "inhabited, unknowingly, by a guest . . . that is neither 'Western'" (H, pp. 83–84) nor reducible to what can be represented conceptually. For Lyotard believes that the "West is thinkable under the order of *mimèsis* only if one forgets that a 'people' survives within that is not a nation (a nature). Amorphous, indignant, clumsy, involuntary, this people tries to listen to the Forgotten" (H, p. 94). In placing his term in lower case, however, as well as in the plural and in quotation marks, his aim is not to designate the Jewish people alone, or some form of "political . . . religious . . . or philosophical . . . subject," but to signify that unnameable otherness, the forgotten "unrepresentable" that the West has tried to eradicate from thought.

Despite Lyotard's claim, however, that the term should not be confused with real Jews, there are obvious parallels between the two, for both have become objects of a radical exclusion. Given that the condition of being Jewish is one of continual "emigration" and "dispersion," the Jews are seen to "'thwart' every program of mastery" (H, p. 81). They are never at home even within their own tradition because it includes, in Lyotard's words, "exodus as its beginning, excision [and] impropriety" (H, p. 22). If the specter of anti-Semitism has, as a consequence, haunted the West, it is not simply because of Western xenophobia, according to Lyotard. It is rather the means by which the stabilizing structures of Western culture and thought try to protect themselves by actively forgetting the "impropriety" that "the jews" (in both lower and upper case) have come to represent.

Although there are moments in Heidegger's writings that touch on this thought of unthinkable "impropriety," there are others, in Lyotard's view, that miss entirely this problematic of the unpresentable, certainly during his association with the Nazi party but even after the break, when his discourse on art and technology ignored for the most part what Lyotard calls the "thought of 'the jews,'" taking it "to the point of suppressing and foreclosing to the very end" the Extermination itself (H, p. 4). And while both Lacoue-Labarthe and Derrida have tried to respond to this question of Heidegger's silence and have, over a period of many years, attempted to distance them-selves from the more "mythical" aspects of Heidegger's thinking, their effort has done little to satisfy Lyotard. He claims that the fault lies with the decon-structive approach itself, which is still too philosophical, too "respectfully nihilist" (i.e., too forgetful of the oblivion of Being) to ever address what constitutes the very epitome of unrepresentability, the event for which no discourse can ever be adequate, that is, the Holocaust itself.

Indeed, if the Holocaust is to be addressed, and with it the thought of "the jews," it cannot be done through a philosophical critique, from which de-construction, in Lyotard's view, has not succeeded in liberating itself, nor can it be done through the more traditional forms of representational discourse. For in transforming the event into images and words, we forget that there is a forgotten, that there will always be something that eludes the structures of language and thought. This something can, in fact, as Lyotard indicates, never be inscribed within a representation or concept because it is in reality nothing that can be stored in memory. One can only remember it "as forgot-ten 'before' memory and forgetting" (H, p. 5), as an absence that is there nonetheless, residing within the "deep unconscious" where, according to Lyotard, "there are no representations" (H, p. 11).

In this sense, then, Lyotard's notion of "the jews" takes on a significance that extends far beyond the physical reality of the Jews as a people. Related by Lyotard to Freud's notion of the "unconscious affect," the term refers to something that exceeds the powers of the human psyche, to a kind of "ex-cess" that in the Freudian context takes the form of an "initial" shock to the system that the psychical apparatus is unprepared to deal with and of which it is unaware. Although Lyotard does not locate the source of this "initial" trauma in any particular event or situate it within a specific stage of psychic development, this notion of a past as forgotten but whose repercussions are still felt as a symptom or phobia in the present is suggested by Lyotard's no-tion of "the jews." In its relation to the interminably deferred, the term des-ignates what Lyotard calls an "originary terror," an origin without origin that the Western philosophical and literary tradition, in its obsession with foun-dational thinking, has worked actively to forget.

What Lyotard calls for, then, is a thinking of a different sort, one that acknowledges the inescapable necessity of representing the "forgotten" while remembering that what it "represents" can never be represented in writing. To reinforce his point, he offers a list of writers who, in his view, give voice to the forgotten "unrepresentable"; it includes such "great non-German Germans, non-Jewish Jews" as Freud, Benjamin, Adorno, Arendt, and Celan, who not only question but also "betray the tradition, the *mimèsis*, the immanence of the unfolding, and its root" (*H*, pp. 92–93). Although Lyotard's list is hardly exhaustive and is even expanded elsewhere in the text to include other writers such as Kafka, Celine, Bataille, and Char, it is interesting to note that one important non-French French, non-Jewish Jew is conspicuously absent from Lyotard's text. That writer is Edmond Jabès. As a nonpracticing Egyptian Jew who first confronted the condition of being Jewish in his early forties when he and the other members of the Jewish community were forced by the Nasser regime to leave Egypt, Jabès, from the moment of his exile in France, never ceased addressing the very questions that preoccupy Lyotard. And though Lyotard's "forgetting" of Jabès may not have been deliberate, it was clearly convenient, for Jabès, who died in January 1991, was, as one critic put it, a "deconstructionist by his own admission,"[4] one who not only addressed the question of the Holocaust but who also lent a forceful voice to what Lyotard refers to as "the thought of 'the jews.'" Indeed, through a reading of the works of Jabès, I shall argue in opposition to Lyotard, who stresses the political inadequacies of Lacoue-Labarthe's (and indeed the whole of deconstruction's) focus on questions of the mimetic, that it is, in fact, this very interrogation of traditional mimetic precepts that allows for a thought of what Lyotard describes as the "forgotten," "unthinkable," "immemorial dispossession" that is inscribed within the very heart of representation itself. For Jabès' texts show that, far from avoiding the political questions raised by the experience of Auschwitz, the issue of the holocaust in the two senses of the term, as Lyotard's "originary terror" and as that singular, never completely representable but most terrifying of historical events, is at the very "center" of their preoccupations.

It should be pointed out, however, that while it is possible to argue that a certain remembrance of the unrepresentable can be found in the deconstructive texts of Jabès, his work, like that of other writers associated with deconstruction, has been criticized for its presumed silence on the Extermination. Berel Lang, in his "Writing-the-Holocaust: Jabès and the Measure of History," claims that the "question of whether writing centered in the Holocaust, in the Nazi genocide against the Jews is even possible: literally and morally *possible*" is never uttered in Jabès' *The Book of Questions*.[5] It is, according to Lang, "unhappily repressed," dissolved into a more generalized problematic of language which makes it disappear as a unique historical event. Lang is, of course, correct when he points out that the question of writing and of language in general is a major preoccupation in the work of Jabès. It, in effect, propels the work through the production of volume after volume — all of which testify to the inadequacy of representational discourse. Beginning with the seven texts that constitute *The Book of Questions* and continuing through the three-volume *The Book of Resemblances* and the four-volume *The Book of Limits,* Jabès' work accentuates on the most basic structural level the problematical nature of language, for the work takes on the character of a seemingly endless proliferation of words with a total of fourteen volumes circling around one another, each repeating and trans-forming the other in continuous search of its elusive center. Incapable, how-ever, of establishing a totality, the writing of the book becomes an activity that can never be finished; the rupture that is necessary to the very dissemi-nation of the word prevents the constitution of a unified entity. For this rea-son, the work itself remains for the most part unclassifiable, offering no pos-sibility of determining its status as either poetry or prose. Although each text bears a superficial resemblance to the novel in terms of length at least, there is only the barest existence of a plot. The first cycle (The Book of Questions, The Book of Yukel, The Return to the Book) is concerned in part with the Nazi Holocaust and with the separation of two lovers, Sarah and Yukel, which occurs when Sarah is placed in a concentration camp. The madness and eventual death of Sarah and the suicide of her lover Yukel are suggested, but they are never developed in a logical, orderly sequence, for the events and the characters themselves are often confused. Three different versions of the arrest of Sarah are given with no clear indication as to which is correct; the circumstances of Yukel's suicide become interwoven with the death of the narrator himself. We are told that we will be given a portrait of Sarah and Yukel, and yet there is no portrait. Memory fails and stories are never told.

In the context, then, of this constant questioning of the powers of repre-sentative discourse, Lang's critique seems legitimate. And yet, to accuse Jabès in particular and deconstruction in general of erasing or "repressing" the memory of the Holocaust and thereby leaving us vulnerable, unable to pro-tect ourselves against its possible recurrence, is to cover over, once again, the problematics of representation that not only Jabès but the Holocaust itself brings into particularly sharp focus. Berel Lang has himself described this problem most convincingly. He writes:

We understand here the dilemma that Jabès — and any writer who takes the Holo-caust as subject — confronts. On the one hand, it is difficult, perhaps impossible, for a writer to meet the Holocaust face to face, to re-present it. The events themselves are too large for the selective mirror of fiction, too transparent for the unavoidable conceits of literary figuration; linguistic representation is in any case redundant, thus an impediment, when the events that converge on a subject speak directly and clearly for themselves. On the other hand, to write about the Holocaust obliquely, by assumption, leaves the task that had been declined by the author to the reader, who can hardly — if the *writer* will not — hope to find a passage from personal emotion and imagery to artifice. Where then is the work of literary representation to be done? (*Sin of the Book* 194)

Clearly, the "work of literary representation" can only be done in the context of a Jabesian questioning, which in acknowledging the impossibility of writing about the Holocaust becomes at the same time the only means by which its memory can be preserved. While it is true that the names or dates representing the event may ultimately annihilate what they save, they also, as Jabès' texts clearly show, save what they annihilate, permitting, as Derrida writes, "alliances, returns, commemorations, even if there should be no trace scarcely an ash of what we thus date" or thus name.[6] The failure of the Holocaust "to write itself," as Lang puts it, in Jabès' work cannot therefore be attributed to Jabès' failure to assume his "moral responsibility." Indeed, the inscription of the Holocaust as that which resists conceptualization and the limiting representations of traditional discourse requires an investigation of the concept of representation itself. Although almost no one, least of all those who embrace deconstructive theory, denies that the Holocaust is an issue that must be addressed, one cannot avoid asking how it is possible to fulfill that responsibility without reaffirming the concepts of representation that the Holocaust itself calls into question. And, more important, how does one *impose* such an imperative without reinforcing the oppressive and dictatorial logic that the imperative itself was meant to counter? And even if one were to affirm the naive notions of history and representation that Lang calls into question, does a detailed elaboration suffice? Does it give us a greater understanding of the significance of that horrific event? Not according to Jabès: "For the Jews, unfortunately, after all the camps and all the horrors, it is an all too banal story. It isn't necessary to go into details. When you say: they were deported — that is enough for a Jew to understand the *whole* story . . . if these are things that cannot be expressed, they are also things that cannot be emptied of meaning" (*Sin of the Book*, pp. 18–19).

If, then, we are to address the issue of Auschwitz, and we must, it perhaps can never be done directly. It requires, in Derrida's words, "another rhythm and another form," a kind of writing that leads not to the formulations of condemnations and imperatives but to a questioning of the modes of thought that make atrocities such as the Holocaust possible. For the Nazis, according to Jabès, were not an aberration, or as he puts it, "some brutes descended from another planet." Their activities must be considered in the context of a culture that allowed fascism to flourish:

How does one forget that [the Nazis] were supported by a large majority of the German people, including, with a few exceptions, its intellectual elite? It is therefore the culture in which we live that must be interrogated. We must try to understand *how* it could have given birth to the worst and not only *in what ways* it revealed itself as incapable of preventing it; because is it possible to separate man from his culture? The most important texts written since Auschwitz are engaged in this interrogation.[7]

The oblique references to the Holocaust in Jabès' texts, which Lang finds far too elliptical, are not, therefore, signs of Jabès' failure to assume his moral responsibility. Jabès' response to Adorno's injunction against the writing of poetry after Auschwitz, in fact, states just the opposite; he claims that "we must write," while acknowledging that "we cannot write like before."[8] One could indeed argue that rather than repressing the question regarding the possibility of writing on the Holocaust, Jabès gives that question a place of prominence in his work; it takes the form of an almost obsessively recurring but necessarily indirect reference whose very obliqueness raises Lang's question: "Is writing centered in the Holocaust even possible?"

It can be shown that in spite of Jabès' constant questioning of language's capacity to represent history, the Holocaust is a haunting presence/nonpresence that reverberates throughout the Jabesian corpus. It is manifested in the piercing sound of a scream whose shrill echo resonates in all fourteen volumes, carrying with it not only the fragmented memories of the Holocaust itself but the resonances of two thousand years of Jewish history. It is a scream of madness—that of the Jewish woman, Sarah, who loses her sanity upon returning from the concentration camps. It is the collective scream of a people deprived of a communal or national identity and who, perhaps for that very reason, were persecuted for an identity of vileness that had been imposed by others. It is the cry of the newborn which, as it is ejected from the womb, is already a cry of "pain" and "exile"; it is also the cry of God, whose withdrawal was made known to the world at Auschwitz; and lastly, it is the scream of the book, which, in perpetuating itself in the course of its own destruction, has a destiny that becomes intertwined with that of the Jew. Indeed, if a history of suffering and persecution is contained in this screaming excess of language, which, as the "effect of a shock" (Lyotard) or of an "immemorial wound" (Jabès), remembers without re-

membering what both the mind and language are too overwhelmed to syn-
thesize, it is because the Jew in Jabès' texts harbors within his very being
everything that the Western tradition has tried to purge from thought, destabilizing all of our accepted notions of nationhood, of the individual subject,
and of his language.

This occurs first of all because the Jew in Jabès' texts has no self-contained
identity. One can never be entirely Jewish because one is never wholly oneself: "With, or for, others I am never *me* — I am *the other of me*," someone
says in *The Book of Resemblances*.⁹ "Are you Jewish?" another asks. "Will I
have been? Only as the void torments the void?" ¹⁰ Dispersed throughout the
five continents, condemned to a life of homelessness, wandering, and exile,
the Jew can never serve as a stable model, a fixed image or type with which
one identifies and through which the identity of a people is fashioned or
realized, for his very existence problematizes such a traditional mimetologic.
Indeed, it is the Jew in Jabès' texts who forces us to confront the mimetic
impropriety that resides at the heart of every being, for he shows that self-
identity is dependent on the existence of an other, of an other's perception
or of an other's language without which no presencing, no manifestation of
being would even be possible but which at the same time sets in motion the
processes through which that presence is also destroyed: "You can free yourself of an object, of a face, of an obsession," says one of Jabès' imaginary
rabbis. "You cannot free yourself of a word. The word is your birth and your
death." ¹¹ What is ultimately revealed, however, is not that Being simply *becomes* language, for Jabès is not creating a self-enclosed, purely linguistic
universe here, but rather that Being cannot become *at all* without the aid of
a supplement. Its existence depends, in other words, on the operations of a
mimesis, which fill up the void, complete an originary deficiency, so that
Being can be brought to light. For this reason, the specificity of the Jew is
throughout Jabès' fourteen volumes indissolubly linked to that of language,
revealing an interconnectedness of Being and the word that undermines the
self-contained status of each:

So, with God dead, I found my Jewishness confirmed in the book, at the predestined
spot where it came upon its face, the saddest most unconsoled that man can have.
Because being Jewish means exiling yourself in the word and, at the same time, weep-
ing for your exile.¹²

every letter in the book is the skeleton of a Jew.¹³

This relation between the letter and the Jew is thus what brings them both
into existence, but it is also what allows them to tear each other apart. In fact,

every being bears the traces of that tearing; the echoes of its painful cries reverberate throughout the Jabesian universe, which for Jabès has become "un univers juif," a "Jewish universe," in which "the suffocated screams of our words of flesh" reveal "the entire extent of human misery." [14] The Jew in the Jabès' text thus unwittingly becomes the ultimate subversive, for he undermines our most cherished assumptions about the absolute integrity of individual identity, with the very presence of Being at the origin of its discourse clearly finding itself contaminated by the secondariness of the word that represents it. The scream in Jabès' texts can thus be seen as a reaction to the loss of originary presence, to the sudden "flare-up of an ancient terror," [15] which not only brings Lyotard's "'initial' shock" immediately to mind but which in the Jabesian corpus is linked to the scorching flames of fire, carrying with it all of its frighteningly holocaustal implications. [16] For it is in the reflection of a cracked mirror that we see the "origin in flames," a "fire-God" who burns Himself up in His own simulated image. Thus, because God, this divine "Master of mirrors," is Himself traversed by mimetic duplicity, He becomes a "God of flames," a self-incinerating, holocaustal nonorigin that functions in a manner not unlike that of Derrida's differential trait. For God, as a sage writes in *Le Livre de l'hospitalité*, who is nothing but "difference," can "only create difference; a world estranged from the world and yet faithful to itself through its very strangeness" (73). God's word, referred to variously in Jabès' texts as the incendiary "trace of a trace" (E, p. 188) or as a "parole différente," becomes a point of convergence and also conflict, bringing together both being and language and thus giving each some measure of existence, while allowing neither to stand in its full presence, sending nothing that has not been touched by the scorching flames of fire. As Jabès writes: "To the incendiary letter we have granted the right to set fire. The word is a world in flames. God burns forever in the four fires of His Name." [17] The image of God, through its inevitable withdrawal, thus comes to stand for the emptiness of this self-incinerating origin. In naming the originary "forgetting of God" out of which "God emerges," He is the one who allows us to remember what Lyotard refers to as "that which is without memory" and thus to "think the unthought" as it arises through the "inaugural" confrontation with language.

While this may be seen as a form of response to Lyotard's call for a writing that exposes the forgotten nonorigin, Lyotard would likely object, as did Berel Lang, to Jabès' excessive focus on questions of the mimetic. It must be recognized, nevertheless, that this very problematization of mimesis in Jabès' texts brings us closest to the Lyotardian perspective, for the forgotten "unrepresentable" at the "origin" of thought, which is neither pure Being nor pure Language but rather the condition of the relationship between the two, becomes in the Jabesian context a "deep chasm without memory," an "unfathomable Nothingness" that unveils while still veiling the catastrophic (non)presencing of Being.

Existing only in their "relation to the space of an articulated word" (E, p. 163), God, man, and the universe are thus drawn together in their fatal encounter with language, joined in a shared state of incompletion and finitude that is rendered particularly explicit by Jabès' "univers juif." Although "we all suffer from this absence of identity," it is the Jew in Jabès' texts, as one who has been historically deprived of a fixed point of origin or ultimate point of reference, who is perhaps more aware than others, according to Jabès, of this exile in language. As the following oft-cited comment reveals, the entirety of the Jewish experience, which is so central to Jabès' work, is assimilated to the structure of writing, with both the word and the Jew wandering aimlessly in exile with nothing to ground their movement. "I talked to you about the difficulty of being Jewish, which is the same as the difficulty of writing. For Judaism and writing are but the same waiting, the same hope, the same wearing out" (BQ, p. 122).

What this means, however, is that rather than constituting a self-contained, purely linguistic and therefore ahistorical universe, as so many critics of deconstruction would have us believe, this assimilation of the exile of language to that of the Jew, which is based on the loss of the referent, is what ultimately reinstates referentiality. In opposition, then, to Lang, who sees in Jabès' critique of representational discourse a certain bracketing of the event of the Holocaust itself, it can be argued that Jabès' focus on the interconnectedness between being and language and on the fundamentally duplicitous structure of their sharing is what allows history and the memory of the Holocaust to be preserved. For though the process of representation becomes nothing more than a series of substitutions and replacements that ultimately undermine the unity of what it seeks to represent, it also provides our only possible contact with the world and with ourselves. As Jabès writes in The Book of Shares, every book is a book of history whose pages are "weighed down with centuries." It is also a "book of ashes" whose words do not simply testify to the loss or destruction of the outside world and its history but become, like the smoldering remains of an earlier conflagration or the wrinkles in an aging face, ineradicable traces of the past. Indeed, the memory of the Holocaust is indelibly embedded in The Book of Shares' burning pages which refer repeatedly to ashes and fire: "We were a people," Jabès writes. "But this people scattered. We are a book at the heart of the fire" (73). "How can we read a page already burned in a burning book unless by appealing to the memory of fire" (95)? In this case, both the Jew and the book, or the Jew *as* book, carry the indestructible traces of their history, bearing within their fragmented corporality the charred residues of an originary conflagration (and thus recalling Lyotard's "terror without origin") whose ties to a later, more terrifyingly brutal incineration are also unmistakable.

Jabès stresses repeatedly throughout his work the interconnectedness between these two fundamentally unrepresentable "events" (i.e., between the holocaustal nonorigin and the Holocaust itself), beginning with his first volume, *The Book of Questions*, in which the burning pages of the book are linked specifically to the burning of "a human being near the common grave." And later, first in the *Book of Yukel*, where the fumes of a forgotten nonorigin appear alongside the gas chambers' blackened emissions, and then in "Elya," with its reference to the "flickering barbed wire of nothingness." What accounts for the interconnectedness between these two seemingly unrelated "events" is clearly the inability to tolerate the possibility of nothingness within Being, the desire to eradicate the "lack of being proper" in whatever form it might take through a movement of repression that culminates at Auschwitz. For Auschwitz, as Jabès writes in his last work, *Le Livre de l'hospitalité*, is the "ultimate erasure," the "erasure of Nothingness" and impropriety that the "jews," in the Lyotardian sense but also in the Jabesian sense, have come to represent. By giving bodily form and substance to this continual confrontation between being and language, the Jew in Jabès' texts carries with him the indestructible memory of that "nothingness" and becomes, as a consequence, the victim of a far more radical extermination.

And despite Jabès' constant questioning of the adequacy of representational language, the memory of that extermination permeates the Jabesian corpus. A cursory examination of merely two pages of *The Book of Questions* suffices to counter the objections of those who suggest that Jabès focuses excessively on the textual. Although historical events are never developed in a logical, orderly sequence, the reference is nonetheless unmistakable:

"We both have the number of our expiration tattooed on our forearms," a voice in *The Book of Questions* affirms. "At that time, barbed wire grew like ivy, but round, round and deep. . . . At that time, evidence was queen . . . the ashes of Jews sent to the ovens were used to season her meals. 'Close your eyes,' advised the sensitive souls. 'Do not look away,' pleaded the victims. The door which opened onto the mass grave or onto life was the triangle formed by our conquerors' legs. You had to get down on all fours to go through it. Honor to those who were trampled there. Honor to those whose skulls were cracked by the boots of the enemy parading in rhythm to his hymns of glory. . . . And Serge Segal shouted at the prisoners around him, who would soon be scattered in the various extermination camps prepared for them, shouted as if in the name of the Lord to His assembled people (au nom du Seigneur à Son peuple rassemblé): "You are all Jews, even the anti-Semites, because you are all marked for martyrdom. Your future is mine, docile pain for those who are prepared. I pity and kiss you, brothers. Your eyes recite in chorus the prayer of the mornings of misfortune." (162–163)

With echoes of the SS resonating both visually and audibly in some of the paragraph's somber lines and thus reinforcing the horror of its content, it is clear that rather than subsuming the memory of the Holocaust under a more generalized problematic of language, as Berel Lang seems to suggest, Jabès is not only *not* prevented from speaking out against the Holocaust, but his very foregrounding of that problematic ultimately subverts the logic upon which the Holocaust, and indeed all acts of intolerance, are grounded. For to exterminate the Jews in the name of racial purity is to exterminate the thought that no pure identity is possible. That thought, however, is what Jabès repeatedly resurrects. The fate of the book, which is never to be constituted as a unified entity, and the fate of the Jew are intertwined in such a way as to make the constitution of a purely textual world just as impossible as the purity of national or racial identity, for Jabès' many volumes bring both the racial and the textual together in their experience of ashes and fire, joining both being and language in a paradoxical structure of sharing which, as the term implies, divides as much as it unites, carrying with it the recognition that no identity is safe from contamination by that which presumably remains outside it. Indeed, the very word "Holocaust," as the "all-burning," is caught up in the duplicitous structure of that sharing, gathering together the multiple experiences of that atrocious event and permitting us to share in its memory while consuming it in its full presence, reducing it to ashes, leaving traces that nonetheless testify to the existence of a holocaustal fire.

It is thus through this "pyrotechnical writing" of fire and ashes, which marks the limits of representation, that Jabès addresses the issue of the holocaust in the two senses of the term, as Lyotard's "originary terror" and as that never completely representable but most horrifying of historical events; he arrives, in other words, at what Lyotard has referred to as the "thought of the 'jews.'"

JOAN BRANDT

NOTES

1. Jean-François Lyotard, *Heidegger and "the jews,"* trans. Andreas Michel and Mark Roberts (Minneapolis: University of Minnesota Press, 1990), pp. 75–77. Hereafter cited in the text as *H*.

2. See Philippe Lacoue-Labarthe and Jean-Luc Nancy, "The Nazi Myth," trans. Brian Holmes, *Critical Inquiry* 16 (Winter 1990): 291–321. See also Lacoue-Labarthe's analysis of Heidegger's endorsement of Nazism in *Heidegger, Art and Politics,* trans. Chris Turner (Oxford: Basil Blackwell, 1990). Hereafter cited in the text as *HAP*.

3. The word "improper" or "impropriety" is derived from the French term "propre" signifying property or the state of being in possession of one's own and proper identity.

4. See Eric Gould's introduction to *The Sin of the Book: Edmond Jabès,* ed. Gould (Lincoln: University of Nebraska Press, 1985), p. xv.

5. Ibid., pp. 191–92.

6. Jacques Derrida, "Shibboleth," in *Midrash and Literature,* ed. Geoffrey Hartman and Sanford Budick, trans. Joshua Wilner (New Haven: Yale University Press, 1986), p. 327.

7. Edmond Jabès, *Du Désert au livre: Entretiens avec Marcel Cohen* (Paris: Pierre Belfond, 1980), my translation.

8. Quoted by Jason Weiss in "The Questions of Edmond Jabès," *International Herald Tribune,* July 21, 1983. See also Warren F. Motte's discussion of Lang's critique of Jabès in *Questioning Edmond Jabès* (Lincoln: University of Nebraska Press, 1990), pp. 89–91.

9. Edmond Jabès, *The Book of Resemblances,* Vol. 1, trans. Rosmarie Waldrop (Hanover, N.H.: Wesleyan University Press, 1990), p. 110.

10. Edmond Jabès, *The Book of Resemblances: Intimations, The Desert,* Vol. 2, trans. Rosmarie Waldrop (Hanover, N.H.: Wesleyan University Press, 1991), p. 44.

11. Edmond Jabès, *The Book of Questions,* Vol. 1, trans. Rosmarie Waldrop (Hanover, N.H.: Wesleyan University Press, 1991), p. 101. Hereafter cited in the text as *BQ*.

12. Edmond Jabès, "Elya," in *The Book of Questions,* Vol. 2, trans. Rosmarie Waldrop (Hanover, N.H.: Wesleyan University Press, 1991), p. 143. Hereafter cited in the text as *E*.

13. Edmond Jabès, "Aely," ibid., p. 216.

14. Edmond Jabès, *Le Livre de l'hospitalité* (Paris: Editions Gallimard, 1991), p. 43; my translation.

15. Edmond Jabès, *The Book of Shares,* trans. Rosmarie Waldrop (Chicago: University of Chicago Press, 1989), p. 66.

16. Here the word "holocaust" is used in its etymological sense as the "all-burning," i.e., all "holo" is burned "kaustos."

17. Edmond Jabès, *The Book of Margins,* trans. Rosmarie Waldrop (Chicago: University of Chicago Press, 1993), p. 37.

10. On the Exile of Words in
the American Simulacrum

A Free Exercise in Wittgensteinian
Cultural Critique

In *The Man Without Qualities*, Robert Musil shows us a society whose sense of historical destiny is matched by its provincial self-importance, whose social roles are empty frames propped up by pomp and theatrical self-exhibition, whose capacity for duplicity and self-deception is the perfected work of centuries, a society capable of dissipating the greatest qualities into boredom, flatulence, and staleness. An enormous day-old Sacher torte, this society, of course Vienna on the brink of disaster, is one in which the language is sugar-coated with a sickly sweet and stale decadence. Ulrich, the novel's main character, comes to realize that he can no longer think of himself as a "man of promise" when he reads an anecdote about a horse. Musil puts it thus:

The time had already begun when it became a habit to speak of geniuses of the football-field or the boxing ring, although to every ten or even more explorers, tenors and writers of genius that cropped up in the columns of the newspapers there was not, as yet, more than at the most one genius of a centre-half or one great tactician of the tennis court. The new spirit of the times had not yet quite found its feet. But just then it happened that Ulrich read somewhere . . . the phrase "the race-horse of genius." It occurred in a report of a spectacular success in a race. . . . Ulrich, however, suddenly grasped the inevitable connection between his whole career and this genius among race-horses. For to the cavalry, of course, the horse has always been a sacred animal, and during his youthful days in the barracks Ulrich had hardly ever heard anything talked about except horses and women. That was what he had fled from in order to become a man of importance. And now . . . he was hailed on high by the horse, which had got there first.[1]

In this passage Musil shows us a use of language that has been hyped by the media (here the Austrian newspaper) to the point that its integrity begins to be shattered. What genius is may be the subject of debate, the question of who is and who is not one may be in some cases unsolvable, but to call an animal a genius is to lose one's grip on the fact that genius is essentially, paradigmatically human, being the manifestation of cognitive and imaginative powers residing as deeply in the human person as, say, the soul does. Such exaggerations of language are (perhaps) even more notoriously rampant in our own time, when Stephen Soderbergh's film *Kafka* can be called "a mega-masterpiece" by one critic, as if being a mere masterpiece (like Kafka's work itself) is no longer a good enough term for mass consumption. The production of meaning by the forces of advertising, the unhinging of language in a world of decadence, the regulation of meaning by the theater of presentations tie us to fin-de-siècle Austria in spite of many differences between then and now. When language goes haywire, the things we do with words go haywire, the language games we play with them, the pattern of beliefs and attitudes that underlie our uses of them, which condition their applicability and restrict their sphere of reference, go out of control.

The Austrian avant-garde wished to think of such an inflation in the use of language as essentially correctable. As the writers of *Wittgenstein's Vienna* have taught us, Karl Kraus, Adolph Loos, the Vienna Circle, and the work of Ludwig Wittgenstein each in its way aimed to return language from a state of decadence to its bare-boned authentic structure.[2] Assuming that language, architectural form, and the rest have essential structures, the avant-garde countered inflation by a minimalist claim to find the unornamented, essential structure of language, architectural form, science, or whatever and to return each to its purified sphere of authentic use.

This claim that language was in exile from itself, living in the form of some decadent, Baroquified dessert, and that it could be disciplined, returned to its essential structure and authentic self, was modernist in the sense that it assumed that language, architecture, or whatever had an essential, bare-bones structure that regulated authentic use. The early Wittgenstein's *Tractatus* aimed, in this modernist vein, to exhibit the essential form of the linguistic proposition, a form rooted in logic, and thus to show the limits of language.

The later Wittgenstein famously gave up his early belief in linguistic essence — referring to it as a former fixation — yet retained something approaching the concept of language in exile from its authentic use, or at least from the language games in which it has a genuine use, however "authentic" this use may be (and from whatever perspective "authenticity" might be measured). "Language on holiday" must return to the world of the everyday, where it accomplishes genuine work in our language games. Words must be returned to the common, public practices shared by communities of persons in which they have meaning and roles in the commerce of life. Of crucial importance is that these are common practices shared by communities of persons to which words are returned. It is not to my own special use that a word is brought back, but rather (in anything like the standard case) to a we: call it Hegel's "I" that is "we." Wittgenstein's emphasis is on shared linguistic practices in which words find their home; he presupposes that words belong in common language games backed up by shared values, modes of training, and styles of life.

Should we doubt this presupposition? Postmodernists and poststructuralists have shared Wittgenstein's antiessentialist perspective but have posed related challenges to the presumption that language has an authentic set of shared public uses to which it ought to be returned. Challenging the metaphor of a linguistic home, both Lyotard and Derrida have raised questions about whether Wittgenstein's claim to circumscribe a set of "proper," "ordinary" uses for words of a communal "we" is not a tacit essentialization both of language and of the people who speak it. For what is being asserted is that a set of rules govern (however loosely) a common linguistic practice, rules which both Lyotard and Derrida believe as often as not prescribe the most profound marginalization of those whose styles of life and complex identities differ from the terms of the mythically imposed (logocentric) "we." The poststructuralist suspicion is familiar, and many have addressed themselves to uncovering the worst attitudes of cruelty, castigation, and victimization lurking behind the most ordinary and docile of common linguistic practices, finding sadism and masochism in the most elegant of (linguistic) homes (not to mention disciplinary power at the background of haute/liberal forms of linguistic training).[3]

Indeed for Lyotard, there is nothing called "society" (and by extension, social practice) to which our words could be returned because the concept of the social order has broken down into that of an interrelated set of fragmentary language games, none of which can be legitimated by the old master narratives. Rather than bringing words back home, postmodern knowledge practices are defined as the remaking of these fragments into new modes of application. The key is not to return to a community of common use but rather to witness and work through what Lyotard refers to as the "differend": a difference between persons and their beliefs, attitudes and styles of life which communal rules have ignored or repressed, with the result that at least one party is consigned to the indignity of silence. Postmodern justice is for Lyotard the opening up of mutual speaking and listening such that all voices will be in play in the conversations of justice, freeing postmodern art and culture to invent new forms of speech that will, by stages, allow both speaking and listening to occur. This might hardly look like the return of words to their origins and homes but rather the freeing of them from social constrictions so that they might allow new perspectives on difference to arise. Are these new perspectives to be thought of as new language games with new communal rules — say, better and more humane ones? Yes and no: Lyotard leaves this unclear. For on one hand he claims that the point is to invent new concepts and rules (read: new linguistic homes), while on the other he claims that the point is to avoid the calcification of language into systems of address and representation that will be, inevitably, as lacking in the flexibility required for new conversation (and witnessing) to happen as the old rules were — and therefore as unjust.

Derrida also endorses the call of global, linguistic homelessness when he famously announces: "There will be no unique name, even if it were the name of Being. And we must think this without *nostalgia*, that is, outside the myth of a purely maternal or paternal language, a lost native country of thought." Derrida goes on to say in "Différance" that we must "*affirm* [this condition] . . . in the sense in which Nietzsche puts affirmation into play, in a certain laughter and a certain step of the dance."[4]

Derrida's call to homelessness is abetted by his attack on the assumption behind ordinary language philosophy that key regions of ordinary linguistic practice are prephilosophical sites of linguistic meaning.[5] "What we do is to bring words back from their metaphysical to their everyday use," Wittgenstein asserts.[6] But for key words such as metaphor, truth, reality, experience, text, man, woman, west, or orient, Derrida argues that philosophy is so deeply implicated in the construction of their meanings that we have no way to pry apart the everyday from the metaphysical. Indeed, in his cultural writings, Wittgenstein may appear to come close to endorsing Derrida's suspicion. For in these writings, Wittgenstein asserts that many of the ordinary linguistic practices of the late modern Europe of his time are so overwhelmed by metaphysics that one cannot even tell in what direction their home might lie (as if we were in the land of Oz and wished to get back to Kansas).

There is the thought that language must typically and unproblematically be brought home from the wilds of its metaphysical corruption to some mythical "we" who will recognize themselves in it and come to use it, dare one use the phrase, authentically, the romanticized nostalgia of a philosopher who many times claimed that he belonged in the vanishing world of Beethoven, Schubert, and Goethe. Is there a home with Auntie Em in a place called Kansas for words to return to when they tap their shoes together three times and whisper: "I want to go home, I want to go home?" Or should we rather take the claim that words ought to be returned to a common "we" — with the philosopher assuming the privilege of speaking in the name of this "we" — to be a last vestige of a modern mentality which contemporary theorists have made a racket out of dismantling?

Of course, Lyotard's ambivalence about just how far old homes, new homes, or homelessness will be the result of contemporary practice is perhaps right because it is unclear before words are worked through in particular contexts what will and ought to happen to them, especially since homing and homelessness, rules and the lack of them, are interdependent conditions. If there were no homes, then there could be by definition no homelessness. If persons were not rooted in common practices with commonly accepted rules of use, then their own critical twists on language, meaning, and practice, their own rewritings of the rules or suspension of them could never occur. One can stand at odds with one region of culture, seek to change or liberate one region of the language, only because one is sufficiently in agreement with culture overall, because one agrees in linguistic use sufficiently with others to make these quarrels intelligible. The very possibility of difference requires underlying modes of similarity that will, as the philosopher Donald Davidson puts it, serve as a frame against which differences become coherent and capable of articulation.[7] Similarly, between two completely different uses of a word there could be no recognition of difference and hence neither *différence* nor dissemination of meaning, *différance*, in Derrida's sense. A person who exists in a diaspora is also a person very much of a place, time, and culture — perhaps of multiple cultures. And insofar as we are rooted in common linguistic practices, it is to be expected that such practices might become disfigured with the result that we experience common modes of alienation from the "we" that is also "I." This is Marx's subject and it is also Wittgenstein's.

My point in this essay is to appropriate Wittgenstein to the purpose of cultural critique by suggesting that although there is much truth in various theorizations of the condition of homelessness and its creative dance, there are also — there *must* also be — significant places for the integrity of some "we" whose common languages have lost their power and whose words require returning home to those language games from public exile and alienation. The question then becomes for a particular case: how much is linguistic alienation to be construed as a situation requiring the postulation of a common home to which we should endeavor to return our words, and how much is this alienation rather to be understood as calling forth the breakup of this idea and the assumption of creative affirmation in which words are given new uses in a never-ending diaspora. A great deal hangs on the answer in a given case, although answers will no doubt differ greatly from case to case.

The case I discuss here is that recalcitrant Baudrillardian simulacrum — alive and well somewhere in America if not also elsewhere — in which the word "genius" is unhinged, the word "ethnicity" essentialized with both becoming figures of overcapitalization and advertising. In the frenetic and desultory state of affairs called the simulacrum, racehorses become adulated as geniuses and films as mega-masterpieces. These are familiar critical ideas that require clarification.[8] My contribution is to bring Wittgenstein to the discussion. Mine is not so much an attack on Baudrillard's ideas (which I in many ways admire) as a way of reading the simulacrum that does not (contra Baudrillard's own pronouncements) preclude the possibility of a cultural critique of it. The question is how far various tropes of home and homelessness have application in the critique of the simulacrum: to what extent, that is, the words "genius" and "ethnicity" are in linguistic exile in the simulacrum and must be brought, in Wittgenstein's sense, home to prior linguistic practices that lend them more genuine use, and how far these words must be liberated from the simulacrum into a state of free homelessness. To work out an answer, some legwork about what Wittgenstein means by bringing words to the ordinary or everyday must be done, and it will occupy the first part of the essay. The second part will take up the extent to which Wittgensteinian critique — critique by appeal to the ordinary — has application in the contemporary American context.

Wittgenstein speaks of philosophical problems in a number of distinct ways, one of which is this: A philosophical problem takes the form of being lost: "I don't know my way about" (*PI*, #123). Finding one's way in the language means bringing words back home from the philosophical to the ordinary. "What we do is bring words back from their metaphysical to their everyday use" (*PI*, #116). And "When philosophers use a word — 'knowledge,' 'being,' . . . and try to grasp the *essence* of the thing, one must always ask oneself: is the word ever actually used in this way in the language-game which is its original home?" (*PI*, #116). This returning of words from being "on holiday" to their actual place in the shared language games that are their home restores their genuine uses to the practices in terms of which words have use and therefore, genuine meaning. There is an underlying romanticism in this conception of return which Stanley Cavell has noted: "Words are somehow 'away,' as if in exile, since Wittgenstein's word seeks its *Heimat* . . . as if it is up to us to seek their return." Cavell goes on to say:

It would a little better express my sense of Wittgenstein's practice if we translate the idea of bringing words back as *leading* them back, shepherding them; which suggests not only that we have to find them, to go where they have wandered, but that they will return only if we attract and command them, which will require listening to them. But the translation is only a little better, because the behavior of words is not something separate from our lives, those of us who are native to them, in mastery of them. The lives themselves have to return.[9]

This is the crux of the matter and the reason why the *Investigations* has the design it has, for it is a book designed not simply to shepherd words back to their original homes in the language but to shepherd back people with certain urges to make words wander into the domain of the metaphysical. Life must be led back for words to be led back because words are given meaning and integrity only through our practices (in the broader context of our form of life). When words are "away" it means in the first instance that we are engaged in philosophico-cultural practices that require adjustment. This shepherding of life back to itself brands the *Investigations* a Christian book, one inspired by the very St. Augustine whose philosophical picture of language the book aims to dismantle.[10]

Since my interest is in the relevance of Wittgenstein's idea of bringing language back home to the everyday for cultural criticism, it is crucial to note that according to my reading of the *Investigations*, the concept of the ordinary is a complex and modulatory notion, subject to what poststructuralists call "slippage" of meaning and therefore difficult to grasp. In the first instance the concept of the ordinary emerges *by contrast to the philosophical*. *Investigations* #1 to at least #308 involve the retrieval of words from their philosophical (mis-)uses back to acknowledgment of their roles in the practices that give them their home. This home is so basic, so deep, that it may remain wholly unnoticed. We come to discover (having repressed this knowledge or been unable properly to claim it) that the activity of rule-following and understanding is coherent only in terms of the practices in which rules are set, practices that supply us with criteria, however plastic or indecisive, for correct rule-following. We come to learn that there are in general (perhaps always) no essences to language, no essential definitions for the meanings of our words. Rather, there is a family of things which fall under our concepts (a family of different things meant by the terms "game," "house," "thinking," "philosophy," and "person"), and this family is linked together into a conceptual whole through its pattern of interconnections, which have in turn been established through the history of our practices. In the *Investigations* we thus come to learn about the dependence of words on the language games in which they play roles. The rule-governed character of language games leads to a recovery of the knowledge that a rule is established and determinable only in the context of a practice, and in the light of this ineluctable piece of knowledge, we come to learn about the most basic links between pain language and the "characteristic forms of pain behavior." Words are thus returned to their most basic homes through the dismantling of those philosophical pictures (of meaning, rules, solipsism, and so on) that have "bewitched" us.

Wittgenstein thinks of the philosophical as a mode of seduction residing in the language itself, hence as eternal in its pressure on human thinking. In the remarks collected under the title *Culture and Value*, he asserts:

People say again and again that philosophy doesn't really progress, that we are still occupied with the same philosophical problems as were the Greeks. But the people who say this don't understand why it has to be so. It is because our language has remained the same and keeps seducing us into asking the same questions. As long as there continues to be a verb "to be" that looks as if it functions in the same way as "to eat" and "to drink," as long as we continue to talk of a river of time, of an expanse of space, etc., etc., people will keep stumbling over the same puzzling difficulties and find themselves staring at something which no explanation seems capable of clearing up.[11]

The ring of Kant is clear here, for Wittgenstein is telling us that the very nature of language, the very possibility of its use, is internally connected to its capacity to generate philosophical misuse. Philosophical misuse is identified as grammatical confusion that seduces us into believing that words with different grammars have the same grammar (as in "I see the cup on the table" vs. "I see your thought clearly"). We fail to follow through and acknowledge their paths of difference, which are deeply buried in the language yet obvious to the point of triviality in retrospect. The philosophical returning of words from exile may be described as bringing us back to acknowledgment of those features of the meaning and use of those words that are so obvious that no one really notices. Were philosophy to try to make assertions about language and linguistic practice, everyone would find its assertions trivial to the point of absurdity and none could possibly disagree, once, that is, such persons were correctly led to see what is what with our words. "The clarity we are aiming for is *complete* clarity. But this simply means that philosophical problems should *completely* disappear" (*PI* #133).

Again, such knowledge is so basic that stating it in the form of theses would be utterly trivial. Yet philosophy's work of returning words from their states of displacement is hardly a trivial matter. Indeed, it can take the greatest genius to work out and bring to light the significance of basic features of words that have been repressed: the significance of characteristic forms of behavior for sensation language, of interpretation for various kinds of perception, of language games for the meanings of words, and so on. As in Lacan's famous use of Alexander Poe's Inspector Dupin, the obvious is least noticed simply because it is right in front of our eyes, and it may therefore require the greatest act of "deduction" or "intuition" to acknowledge it. The philosopher who tries to recover the obvious can get it wrong, as Wittgenstein probably did when he discussed mathematics as opposed to psychology. Yet a great deal hinges on getting it right because when words are in exile from their most basic levels of meaning, they *really are in exile,* an exile perhaps unnoticed by entire cultures. Where exile from this degree of obviousness obtains, *it really obtains.* For the level of meaning ordinary language philosophy seeks to recover is so basic that no one could possibly speak a language without it, hence its apparent "triviality."

Wittgenstein's thought that philosophy is an eternal mode of seduction residing in the language we speak informs his extension — or modulation — of the concept of the ordinary to the study of our daily linguistic practices from the grammatical point of view. Convinced that psychology, mathematics, and other disciplines have infected our ordinary concepts of thought, imagination, emotion, calculation, proof, and so on (his is a disease metaphor), the work of the latter sections of the *Investigations* Part 1, of much of the *Investigations* Part II of the *Remarks on the Foundations of Mathematics,* and of the last writings on psychology (along with the work on aesthetics, ethics, and the like) aims to return us to acknowledgment of the grammar of our ordinary concepts, concepts we acknowledge every day by using them, yet which, once we try to stop and think about them, are rendered obscure. In mapping grammatical paths of intersection and difference between ordinary psychological concepts, for example, Wittgenstein aims to retrieve psychological concepts from the clutches of behaviorism, introspectionism, and other psychological theories that he believes have projected metaphysics onto the mental. He provides the reader with long discussions of the grammar of how thinking is and is not distinct from picturing and imagining, imagining from feeling, feeling from believing, thinking from that half-perceptual and half-conceptual state/activity called "seeing-as" or "aspect seeing."

This work of acknowledgment is intended to be purely descriptive, that is, absolutely nontheoretical, nonexplanatory, and nonevaluative. For the features of meaning Wittgenstein aims to recover are — again — so basic that nothing could be asserted about them: again, they are supposedly obvious to the point of triviality. Hence they are important in the highest degree because they show us what our actual concepts of thinking, imagining, feeling, and the rest are. Through a process Wittgenstein refers to as the "assembling [of] reminders for a particular purpose" (PI #127), philosophy shepherds us back to this ordinary conceptual network without itself asserting anything at all. "Philosophy simply puts everything before us, and neither explains nor deduces anything. — Since everything lies open to view there is nothing to explain" (PI #126).

While the claim to decisively separate (mere) grammatical description from normative explanation, theorization, or causal analysis surely does hold for those very basic features of ordinary meaning and use discussed in the *Investigations* Part 1 (the fact of general connections between pain and pain behavior), it is less likely to hold when Wittgenstein turns to the intricate and robust description of ordinary concepts and practices in psychology, mathematics, and other regions of life. For when philosophy approaches linguistic practices in all their complex social plenitude, it finds itself in a terrain of fragmentary language games, which it must assemble into coherent narratives whose subjects may be matters of great controversy. When it considers the concept of pain in a robust sense, what is ordinary language philosophy to say about the practices of gendering pain language in our society, about the connections between medical language and psychological language that Foucault made a racket out of exposing, about the legal practices surrounding our use of that term? Can these features of meaning and use be described independently of normative, theoretical, and causal commitment? What would a "purely descriptive account" of them be like, and who would presume to give it? Again, what of a description of the concept of money, of its use in society, and of the dolorous connections between money, consumption, and the concept of art? What of the "grammar" of the rules of justice? In describing these language games, the ordinary language philosopher is faced with a mass of interconnected fragments of meaning and use, whose grammatical paths are obscure, deep, and in need of narrative elaboration — no doubt from several perspectives. In the construction of these narratives, it is no longer clear where description ends and theorization begins, where conceptual analysis yields to genealogy and genealogy to causal explanation, or where explanation leads to evaluation, evaluation to critique, and critique to redescription. This is, I take it, a conceptual point about the family of different things we call "description," some of which lie further from theory than others. Was it not Marx who famously asserted that philosophers have (so far) only interpreted the world, whereas the point is to change it, leaving us to surmise that interpretation can go only so far in the absence of a critical and revolutionary attitude? And is it not the same Marx who stakes his volumes of *Capital* on the claim that a description of the role of money in the capitalist world — a description of the practices in terms of which the concept of money acquires its meaning and the word "money" is given a use — requires the deepest theorization and the most revolutionary conviction? It is an anomaly in Wittgenstein that while he rethinks most every other distinction in terms of a host of intermediate cases and blurred intersections, he never rethinks along similar lines his own distinction between conceptual description and these other modes of characterization. No doubt this reveals his own presuppositions about philosophical practice.

We can now understand the slippage of meaning in Wittgenstein's concept of the ordinary as it is applied from case to case. Whereas the concept of the ordinary is introduced to refer to features of words that are so basic that no one could seriously challenge them once they are revealed in the right light, the concept gradually modulates into that of the intricate grammars of our current practices as they are socially situated in the everyday — for better or worse, richer or poorer. The ordinary therefore modulates from being a basic ground of meaning and use to which all must agree so as to raise debates about other features of meaning (all must agree that pain is connected to pain behavior to discuss the gendering of pain), into what Pierre Bourdieu calls the region of the "habitus": the basic fabric of our everyday linguistic practices, the things we do with words in our current social world (like gendering pain language).[12] What a "grammatical" investigation recovers in the first instance is that to which everyone must agree, while what it brings to light in the second instance is the actual work our words do in our daily practices, work we may detest and wish to challenge. In such latter cases, returning words from exile to their home in the everyday is like Freud's delivery of the neurotic to reality. Freud never promised the neurotic a rose garden, a picnic out of the pictures of Renoir, when he or she performed the work of replacing the id by the ego and came to see the world as it is. Rather, Freud promised the capacity to face the difficult recalcitrances of reality without recourse to illusion or to the mechanisms of de-

fense. Call that an existential face-off with the everyday rather than an acknowledgment of its inevitable power, and call reality that which is the whirl
of one's embodiment, a whirl that is neither perfect nor avoidable. In a similar vein, Wittgenstein would claim that his delivery of words (and persons)
back to their everyday practices hardly glorifies those practices but rather
allows us to see them with a clarity undiluted by philosophical illusion so
that the work of facing off to our practices — of analyzing them, criticizing
them, theorizing them, accommodating ourselves to them, accepting them,
rejecting them — may begin. Thus the ordinary in the latter sense is not adulated but returned to, and where this philosophical return stops is exactly
where cultural and political critique may commence.

As the concept of the ordinary modulates from the first sense to the latter,
the notion of a grammatical description of practice similarly becomes more
deeply theory-laden, more fully explanatory, and more profoundly normative. The nature of description changes with its subject. And it is crucial that
there are a host of intermediate cases between the ordinary in the first and
latter senses. I therefore do not think there is a fully clear distinction between
those features of words that are "basic" (to which everybody must agree because they are the features of words that make language use possible) and
those that are not, between those aspects of linguistic practice that cannot be
criticized and those that can. One proceeds through a series of intermediate
cases, and it is the degree of "obviousness" that counts. Then, to the degree
that one can discover with conviction that a sociolinguistic practice has displaced these basic features of the word, one has always discovered something
deep, something as deep as a transcendental condition on language use.[13]

It should be evident that a culture that treats racehorses as geniuses (Musil's
"Kakania," which bears more than a little resemblance to Austria) is one for
which the term "genius" is in exile because it is absolutely basic to the concept of genius and the history of our practices of using that term that geniuses
be human beings (genius being a paradigmatically human capacity). No
doubt there is much to debate about what genius is and where it is to be
found. And the subtlety in Musil's passage is that as the term is extended
from one domain to the next it passes through a set of intermediate cases of
so-called geniuses (businessmen, sportsmen) that Ulrich finds himself at
least able to entertain before packing it in when confronted by the racehorse
of genius. It is at that point, when in a feat of equestrian dressage, the term
has leaped over the fence from the human into the animal kingdom, that we
have finally arrived at a point where a feature so basic to the meaning and

use of the term has been violated that we can unproblematically speak of language in exile. Racehorses may display something like talent, virtuosity, and brilliance, yet as Wittgenstein would put it, to be a genius one must participate in the human form of life in a way that the horse ultimately fails to do. Even a calculating prodigy who cannot string five words together can at least calculate (and should we rest comfortably in even calling her a genius?).

Similarly, a culture that has bounded from the domain of the master-piece into that of the mega-masterpiece ("mega" carrying so much weight of tonnage, wattage, voltage, and manpower that an Arnold Schwartzenegger would need to master the mega in the piece) has placed the word "master-piece" in exile. For whatever there is to debate about the meaning of the term "masterpiece," about its domains of application and about the complex (and prominently debatable) practice of speaking of masterpieces, canoniz-ing them, and so on, we would all agree that the term is meant to suggest that there is nothing better, a masterpiece being an example of its kind that is both prima and ultima. If Soderbergh's work had been called a mere mas-terpiece, I would have quibbled with the inflated extension of the term to his well-constructed but hardly magisterial film. In my own view, such a practice of inflating the term would already bespeak the exile of the term (although I suppose this is debatable). It is "mega" that really hurts, for it signifies a practice which obliterates the "ultimate" feature of the masterpiece in a blaze of language racing out of control in a state of hyperinflationary energy. Call this the energy — the practices — of advertising, of the media, and of a culture that has lost all sense of comparative language (i.e., "good," "better," "best"), and with it all sense that present judgments are conditioned through their connections to a repertoire of past judgments that cannot simply be viewed as material to be superseded.

With racehorses and mega-masterpieces, we have entered the world of Baudrillard. If Baudrillard is correct, these inflationary practices are not iso-lated but rather indicative of the everyday — the habitus of America, America being the sign of the future of the world — in which we now live. This simu-lacrum has colonized our linguistic unconscious; we have no more memory of the exile of words from their home. Such a culture is no longer capable of working through its inner disturbances; its way of life is no longer even, Baudrillard will tell us, to be thought of as in exile. For there is no coherent way to imagine a route back out of exile, no liberation is possible. The revo-lution has already happened, Baudrillard famously tells us, and what you see is what you get.

DANIEL HERWITZ

Baudrillard speaks of this condition as that in which "the real" has dropped out, in which there is no longer a distinction between inner and outer life that would substantiate the presence and conception of reality, reality now having metastasized into an "ecstasy of communication," a manic production of meanings on the basis of simulated models (hence the term, "simulacrum"): "We no longer partake of the drama of alienation, but are in the ecstasy of communication." . . . Our private sphere has ceased to be the stage where the drama of the subject at odds with his objects and with his image is played out. We no longer exist as playwrights or actors but as terminals of multiple networks."[14] Wittgenstein also believes that modern culture (by which he means European culture) has gone through a process of decline, and he is dubious that its cultural practices can be returned to their homes in ordinary, prephilosophical, use.[15] Baudrillard, by contrast, attributes this deformation in the form of life to the forces of media technology in which realities have been replaced with models provided by advertising, television, sociological studies, and so on. The self is a product of these models, not to mention of plastic surgery, psychobabble, and skin cream; the person has become a nexus of capitalization. And the world is a figment of the media, an enormous media event. In this world, people overcapitalize on money, looks, youth, ethnicity, color, religion, or whatever, turning the self into a figment of advertising. Improvising on Baudrillard's ideas with the help of Andy Warhol's, everyone gets fifteen minutes of fame, and they prepare by turning their personae into salable stereotypes, items that can be bought and sold on the market. Essentializing the self, its sexuality, identity, and ethnicity, allows all persons to package themselves and to exploit the racy, juicy features of their personae: those the media, the arts, or the academy currently favor. In a peculiarly American perversion of a peculiarly American ideal, the concept of democratic populism is rewritten as that of mass homogenization, meaning if one person can overcapitalize on ethnicity — say as a white male preppie East Coast son of a banking family whose ethnicity ensured him a place in the sun — then everybody else can. So we all now overcapitalize on ethnicity. If one person can be a victim, then everybody else can be a victim, so we overcapitalize on victimization. And if one person can be a genius, then everybody else can, so we get National Public Radio with its endless homilies by people who sermonize about "life and its tribulations," convinced of the boundless depths in their gelatinous platitudes.

To unpack the deformation of the real in any or all of these cases is hardly simple. For there is something right in each. Traces of victimization *can* be found in numbers of the population. And if Kant is right, every human being possesses some capacity for genius in virtue of having taste. Finally, even the gelatinous can sometimes voice the true, albeit in an unappetizing form.[16]

If Baudrillard is correct, the displacement of the terms "genius" and "ethnicity" could hardly be more complete, for the real itself has dropped out, leaving us using these terms wholly in the absence of that context in which even the inmost basic features are, it appears, preserved. The habitus of ordinary use in the United States has wholly alienated these terms from their grammatical functions, from the most deep and obvious features of their use. Thus the ordinary in Wittgenstein's first and most basic sense has been lost. In the sphere of genius, the concept of genius is controlled by the forces of high-speed, high-concept production values which inflate films into mega-masterpieces and racehorses into geniuses. The model of genius is the super-model.

Behind this replacement of the real by its models is an inchoate analysis of what it is to possess a relation to the real: "We no longer invest our objects with the same emotions, the same dreams of possession, loss, mourning and jealousy" (EC, p. 12). On my reading of Baudrillard, this amounts to the unhinging of our ordinary practices of construing reality, our ordinary modes of interfacing with it, our ordinary modes of attention to it, our ordinary evaluations of it, our ordinary feel for it and way of acknowledging it. To find in oneself and in one's culture a relation to reality is to feel toward people, entities, and events in a certain way, to interpret and respond to them in a certain way, to play certain games with the world as opposed to others, for example, the game of collection and recollection as opposed to that of modeling and remodeling. There is no reality, no real to be known, apart from our language games, apart from our modes of treating objects, our ways of knowing them. Our words do not otherwise refer to things, nor do we otherwise know things.

On my reading, then, Baudrillard's vision of the real is congenial to Wittgenstein's. This reading implies that for the real to "drop out" is for us to remove ourselves from this pattern in which reality is respected, in which we interface with it in our language games. That is, the forms of practice in which we relate to and acknowledge the world in certain ways have dropped out, and with the defacement of these practices comes the estrangement of words in the simulacrum.

It might be thought that Baudrillard is a radical conventionalist for whom there never was a real to begin with — reality having from the beginning been an artificial construction of social practice. In the section of *Simulations* called "The Orders of Simulacra,"[17] however, Baudrillard makes clear that before the current, third stage of simulations now in place in the West, the orders of simulacra did allow a place for the real in the sense in which I describe it. These former orders of simulation did not efface the real, but rather imitated it (the first order) through a kind of counterfeit, or produced new regions of it through the forces of mass production and replication (the second order). It is only in the third stage of simulation, that in which the real is replaced by models, that the real is effaced altogether.

Yet all of this depends on the plausibility of the claim that we no longer recognize even the most basic features of our words, our language games, and the reality they construe. Surely, it will be retorted, we by and large do know that racehorses are not geniuses and masterpieces are not superseded by the mega in mega-culture? Daily life — the life in which people struggle to earn livings, pay their taxes, drive their cars, and play with their children — is a life in which people by and large use words in basic and stable ways and are therefore in control of the real in equally stable ways. No doubt these modes of interpreting reality are themselves fraught with ideology, aggression, and victimization, but they also hang on to the world and do not replace it by models. Even in Los Angeles, known to its intimate enemies (of which it has many) as La La Land, people, it will be retorted, by and large know how to acknowledge the real in the usual ways. Most people do not live as if they were on a talk show, or on display in a catalog, or speaking from a screenplay. Well, perhaps by and large they do not, but to what extent has the simulacrum invaded their fantasies of success, their images of happiness, their patterns of consumption? To what extent do they instinctively conflate politics with television, thinking of political candidates as mere products that can be discarded after two-year intervals when they fail to "deliver" the goods (as if a society could be changed in the way that a television set can be fixed)? To what extent do Americans conflate the world with the media events presented on their local network news? To what extent is the simulacrum especially present in dominant forms of American culture (Hollywood films, the art world, the media generally)? Can one provide clear answers to any of these questions?

Baudrillard's vision of near-total simulacrification is ultimately incoherent. For to analyze what the real is and how it has been replaced by models, Baudrillard must retain a memory of the real, a sense of its otherness from what is happening now. For were he left with no concept of reality, the concept of a model that replaces it would become equally meaningless. So in claiming that the real has dropped out, Baudrillard proves that it has not dropped out of him. Not that he must be able to define or essentialize this reality; its form might arise through a negative dialectics: through the conviction of something negated by the simulacrum that demands restitution. Baudrillard acknowledges the fact of exile because he is capable of providing the diagnosis of loss. He has a concept and a memory of the real, as do we.

Baudrillard will counter that there is small consolation in this attribution, for his own grasp on the real is a last vestige of a pre-postmodern mentality that the culture will soon succeed in evaporating. Nor does he search for this lost presimulacrized reality, in the manner of some contemporary Mr. *Kennst-du-das-Land-Wo-die-Citronen-blüh'n* type of guy. He would claim that his knowledge that the simulacrum is a simulacrum is, as in Wittgenstein's case, "impotent" to counter the forces of power. Things will inexorably get worse. But what substantiates his bleak prophecy other than his particularly French desire to scandalize Europe by claiming that America is the land of the future (according to his own futuristic construction: the American of *America*)? Baudrillard, loving every moment of it, manages to aestheticize this figment of his own construction — a figment also rooted somehow in reality — and he is at home on the freeway and in the shopping mall. (Perhaps only French poststructuralists can enjoy this simulacrum of freeways and shopping malls, usually because they can retreat to their drizzling, gray patina of a linguistic home which is Paris for one-half of the year. Theirs is a mere *dacha* in the simulacrum.)

Baudrillard's claim is modernist in mentality: it is the Hegelian claim of transparently discerning the diagnostic structure of the age, its basic shape, and the intoxicated claim the European avant-garde makes when it reels on about the future that looms on the horizon like a perfect diamond, except that instead of a diamond we will inherit its zirconium look-alike version, which, as the Home Shopping Channel might tell us, will be distinguishable from the real thing only by your jeweler. How is that arch-modernist claim to transparency and prophecy substantiated? What do we really know about an age, about its so-called shape and its future? To what extent does the Hegelian metaphysics of ages with clear and uniform shapes apply? Who is to tell the extent to which the everyday, the ordinary, has become Baudrillard's lunar landscape, with no earth and world to return to? And for whom?

The domain of the simulacrum is clear in places and obscure in others. Not everybody in America dresses and acts as if they were characters in *Melrose Place*, and there is plenty of room in America for all kinds of people, all kinds of communities, and all kinds of values, Let us think of the simulacrum — contra Baudrillard's unsubstantiated, monolithic vision of it — as a tendency within the space of America, one far more pervasive in certain areas of American life than others, but in some sense generalized into all domains of life, if only in the guise of a threat or a haze of possibility. Let us think of it as a profound mode of pressure, a free-floating seduction, a training ground for the young. How profound is its effect on the young, on those who have grown up in an age in which history is defined through the fact of television? Surely we cannot claim the epistemological presumption actually to *answer* this question, as if we could render completely determinate judgments about the possibilities and flexibilities of others. History has proved the old wrong about the resources and interests of the young too many times for that. Crucially, cultural critique need not require that kind of certainty to proceed seriously with its work. Indeed, it cannot require it because it will never be forthcoming. We do not need to produce a determinate picture of how far and in what ways the simulacrum is in place in order to resist it. All we need do is to point to significant instances of it, significant regions of its pressure on persons, to make our work plausible. For the point is that insofar as it is in place, then words are in exile, and the work of critique is required. We need never be able to tell just how far it is or was in place in order to perform this work. For to speak from the concepts of Stanley Cavell, ours is the work of acknowledgment — of acknowledging what is at stake in the simulacrum — not of telling exactly where it is. We speak of a tendency, a mode of seduction.[18]

Let us now map some further relations among genius, ethnicity, and subjectivity or identity as they are played out within this Baudrillardian space, wherever it may be found. We have already seen that as genius is inflated in value, it is thereby vulgarized. It becomes practiced as the genius of the capitalist and the advertising agent whose creations of ever new products are regulated by principles of association and seduction. The whirl of concepts, attitudes, values, and relations, which define the identities of things, are exploited when they are used to generate the auras of new products. In short, the real becomes in the end a mere aura, a mere material to be used for these products. Just imagine Madonna dressed up as Rosa Luxemburg and you get the picture. This kind of genius, this capacity for using the real as an aura attached to new productions, is beautifully exhibited in Robert Redford's *Quiz Show.* The two producers of the quiz show (which becomes the subject of criminal investigation following allegations that the contestants were given the questions in advance, allegations proven true), have a natural and absolute indifference to moral norms of all kinds. Their indifference, their incapacity to be shamed in any way or made to feel guilty, yields them a special adaptability, a capacity to slide endlessly from one position to the next, endlessly to seduce, rewrite, alter the face of reality. They are, Redford suggests, perfectly suited to their medium, namely television. Redford's fine movie, about the days when the simulacrum was just rearings its ugly head on the scene of late modern life, is about our defeat before this power and energy, a power whose slippery, aquatic plasticity and pleasure for mass audiences makes it nearly impossible to face. The frenzied way television turns reality into events of fixation — into a succession of inflated media events — and then drops each story, each piece of the real, when its particular frenzy can no longer be visually presented with the speed of white light — can, like capitalism, cheerfully thrive on its own self-criticism. An example is the glee with which the very newscasters who deformed the O. J. Simpson trial turn from time to time against "the media," uttering exclamations about its potentially damaging role in recording reality, yet leaving this discussion abstract enough so that it does not return to them. Their five-minute sequences devoted to criticizing their own media thus end up being yet another five-minute television sequence that continues the frenzy of the particular media event by continuing the fast talk about it and keeping audiences fixated on it. This endless rewriting of the real with the speed of lightning is the free play of "genius," so called, within the simulacrum.

Actual examples from advertising are clear. "Don't blend in/the Beverly Center" the sign says at La Cienega Boulevard, near the Beverly Center itself (a large Los Angeles shopping mall). This sign, one of whose versions is composed in the off-white of designer clothes and presented in a sleek, designer type font, sells difference through product conformity. "Don't blend in" suggests the blended materials of designer clothing: the silk/linen or cotton/poly combos described on Armani or Vittadini labels. Thus you — and thousands like you — avoid blending into the American melting pot by buying these blended products that make you unique. Which is to say that you can affirm your uniqueness only by speaking in the language of product variety, by blending in. Americans no longer need the mythology of the melting pot because they are unified by their shared language of product variety and self-itemization. We are homogenized through shared (self-)production values.

This discussion of self-production must inevitably lead to the topics of ethnicity and multiculturalism, as these too are played out within the simulacrum (as opposed to "outside" of it, where they are also played out). For the replacement of the myth of the melting pot by the language of not blending in through blending in is nothing other than multiculturalism played out within the simulacrum. This particular sign was off-white, but it also appeared in green and other colors. It could have been black, Hispanic, Jewish, or cast in the slinky shape of the new, aerobicized woman. For in the simulacrum all items of difference, uniqueness, and genius, all works of art, literature, and music, all ideas, opinions, and events are rewritten as products, as items that can be consumed and propagated in the marketplace. America — for this is what Baudrillard is talking about, television and the media having quite different formats and effects in other parts of the globe — is indeed capable of deforming its most precious values in the simulacrum. Thus the magnificence residing in American multiculturalism is turned from a great and crucial idea into a simulacrum of itself. Real difference is essentialized, turned into an aura, a product difference to be consumed and exploited in the marketplace of persons. The difference between a Jew and a Chicano becomes that of a caplet versus a tablet, a gel versus a powder, a cream versus an ointment, a solid versus a spray, a dress from the Tweeds catalog versus one from the J. Crew catalog, a lawyer versus a lawyer from L.A. *Law*, an actor, or a president. Indeed, at the level of gender I would suggest that the androgynous or bisexual clothing and physique often favored by the worlds of advertising and entertainment is part of the same attempt to market genuine body difference as mere product difference, thus replacing desire for the heterosexual other (whose body is different from yours) by the glamour and allure of one who is now different from you only by virtue of product variety. Gender is replaced by allure. Insofar as gender difference is a disadvantage, this is an advantage; but the advantage comes at the cost of replacing desire for the other with an expression (through clothing) of the shared value of product allure. This can be witnessed in the current tastes in Hollywood for eighteen-year-old fashion models with no personality traits and little actual eroticism to play leading roles: they exist in the netherworld of film as products, not people, and the days of Irene Dunne, Grace Kelly, and Anna Magnani are long gone. Now the language of blending is at the basis of American sex — blending in to an androgyny and thus reclaiming the illusion of one's uniqueness and desire by the glamour of being desirable in the marketplace. Is this what we wrote the Declaration of Independence for? America seems to have a special talent for replacing desire with product desirability.

The academy, keen to be skeptical of everything but itself, has not been spared a place in the simulacrum. Consider its consumption of theoretical buzzwords, its production of endless theoretical agendas, its fashions, according to which suddenly everyone in a discipline suddenly works on topic X (cultural studies, deconstruction, and so on). No doubt the academy is as complex as the rest of America, and its shifts in discipline, its production of theories, all have their multiple goods (which are the topic of another paper). But when viewed from the present perspective, the sociology of the academy cannot help but suggest that of mass capitalism generally, with its procedures of advertising, stardom, its practices of turning objects (here, texts of study) into mere product differences (mere objects of various theorizations). Students learn theories with the lightning speed and grandiose power of television media events, as if every text were to be thought of as a media event. This strategy turns the text into a simulacrum of itself. Of course, the text always was framed, some parts of it centralized and others marginalized, yet the irony is that the very work of uncovering and deconstructing these past processes of marginalization is also the work of instituting the power of the media into academic discourse. Speaking in a Foucauldian vein, one could say that the very discourses of resistance (discourses identified as theory, cultural studies, and the like) end up further sedimenting the very forms of power they claim to resist by turning academic study into a television approach to the text. This kind of power is very hard to resist, yet it demands the most profound acknowledgment. Even (and especially) Foucauldian language, with its tendency toward monolithic exposure, quickly becomes disseminated in the zone of the avant-garde with the vast speed and exaggeration of advertising campaigns, the seductiveness in Foucauldian cinematographs of sexuality and horror being as salable on the intellectual market as the sleek bisexual silk black garment is at the Beverly Center, perhaps because the same people are buying in each case. This process is seduction by those products that create one's self-image in terms of a commodity — call it the creation of a discipline called Foucault INC, a discipline that glosses over Foucault's eccentric genius and turns his work into a mass market academic product. (Then am I, as the writer also seduced, say, by the aura of "serious cultural critique," an aura fabricated through Theodor Adorno's hyperintellectualized and hyperserious concepts, romanticized through an equal dosage of Walter Benjamin, and complexified beyond all requirement through a discussion of Wittgenstein? This cannot be discounted.)

Since the very idea of the multicultural is the manifestation of the same America whose tendency is to turn all ideas into brand items, multiculturalism must resist its own deep tendency toward simulacrafication. The very commitment to multiculturalism therefore presupposes a capacity to resist the simulacrum in which real difference is rewritten as product difference. And what can legitimate our belief that the world is not merely a simulacrum other than what comes from our capacities to write, show, lead, and assert? What can remind us of this fact other than the recollection of what we cannot fail to know about genius, about people, and about ethnicity? Call this the recollection of the ordinary in Wittgenstein's most basic sense. *Our* collective capacity for genius is proven good by such work. National Public Radio ought to celebrate *this* capacity.[19]

America has its own talents for serious resistance to this state of affairs (even if serious resistance may turn the resisters into media events in spite of themselves). When some television reporter asked Richard Rodriguez what it is like to be a Chicano writer, he responded that at the moment he was feeling Chinese. He lived, after all, in San Francisco, shopped in Chinatown, ate Chinese food, had Chinese friends, and so on. This was, I take it, his way of refusing to be turned into an ethnic stereotype by a country which demands that all concepts be processed in microseconds, that all persons be comprehensible in milliseconds, and that the self become the figment of a magazine called *Self*. Rodriguez was, I take it, refusing to turn his identity into an essentialist fact that could be bought and solid in the way that Ralph Lauren consumes and sells British upper-class "ethnicity" as an auratic fashion reconstruction. No doubt being Chicano is manifested in broad regions of Rodriguez's work, yet its presence is obscure as well as obvious, uncircumscribable as well as clearly delineated in places, a web of beliefs, attitudes, styles of relations, modes of intimacy, and tastes whose domain and range are everywhere and nowhere, a home that is evident in the self yet also diffuse. In short, it would take the work of genius to give appropriate representation to Rodriguez's ethnicity, to do the work of what Wittgenstein would call its showing.

So far, I have claimed that genius and ethnicity are words that exist — in some obscure yet significant way — in a simulacrum in which genius is made hyperbolic, and ethnicity essentialized. Both are, that is, redefined through practices that recruit the pattern of concepts, attitudes, values, and practices lending each its meaning; turn this pattern into an aura in the case of advertising and an essential set of market properties in the case of ethnicity; and use this aura or these properties to invest the new product with market value. Insofar as ethnicity is also advertised, it is turned into an aura as well as a set of marketing properties. Now it is time to return to the group of questions posed at the opening of this essay about the extent to which bringing words out of the simulacrum ought to be construed as bringing them home to a "we," a "we" now understood as a set of basic features of words that all speakers who know the language and participate in its practices must share. To what extent are these words really in exile demanding to be brought home, and to what extent should we rather think of liberating them from the simulacrum into a postmodern and free practice that accepts and celebrates their homelessness?

This question has already been answered in part because insofar as genius and ethnicity are displaced from their most basic features (that humans are geniuses, that ethnicity is not an essence) the Wittgensteinian picture of bringing these terms back home — put the other way, of remembering the practices that give these words their meanings — is in order. How much further does the Wittgensteinian picture go in picturing what it is to bring words out of the simulacrum?

Insofar as having an ethnicity (or religion, or nationality, and so on) means sharing a background with others, bringing one's ethnicity out of the simulacrum is bringing it home to this "we." No doubt the common features shared by members of an ethnic group fail to add up to an essence, no doubt this "we" is constituted more along the lines of Wittgenstein's family of overlapping features, no doubt ethnic groups are held together in various ways (through third-person stereotypes, shared rituals, styles of life, beliefs, attitudes, and common modes of remembrance). Nevertheless, my point is simple. The term "ethnicity" loses its coherence if no common heritage and mode of being in the world is presupposed. What would it mean to speak of having nothing in common with others yet speak in an ethnic voice? (What would it mean to speak of having nothing in common with others period?) The term "ethnic" becomes incoherent here. There is no ethnicity consisting of only one person (although one person could be the sole survivor of an ethnic group — a last Jew writing in the name of a lost people). I take it that such obvious features of this word's meaning and use are Wittgenstein's domain of the ordinary: part of the grammar of the word "ethnicity."

There is also, however, an equally central place for an existential relation to one's ethnic self, and at this point, the retrieval of ethnicity may become a dialogue of the self with itself, an acknowledgment that what ethnicity means to me is not to be also glossed unproblematically as what it means to the "we." In affirming (or denying) one's ethnicity, one may merely claim to speak for oneself. One may end up speaking purely for others as well, but that depends on whether they take your acknowledgment to speak in their name as well. Nothing can guarantee that this will take place, or for how many people constituting the "we." In any event, here the idea of bringing the ethnic name home to a common practice gives way to the concept of rewriting this term in a way that leaves the "we" indecisive. This point may be developed by referring to the work of Akeel Bilgrami.

Bilgrami develops the concept of an affirmation of ethnicity (in his case of a Muslim identity that is both religious and cultural) by distinguishing what he refers to as the first versus the third-person perspectives on identity. The third-person perspective is that from which others have beliefs and attitudes toward oneself as an ethnic (or religious or cultural) type.[20] These third-person beliefs and attitudes are, it has been the task of much postcolonial (and other) writing to show, often distorted, essentializing, and cruel. Bilgrami contrasts the third-person perspective to a first-person one, that of the agent's own perspective on his or her ethnicity (or religion, or nationality, or gender, these things often being nearly impossible to sort out[21]). A third-person perspective need not be essentializing, but when it is, it requires a special negotiation from the first-person perspective, the danger being that the person either internalizes the third-person perspective whole cloth or rejects it whole cloth. In this context we may speak of abjection as the state in which the cruelty of the third-person perspective is wholly internalized in the self, such that one views oneself through the glaring and incisive gaze of the other. Grandiosity, by contrast, is the state in which one views oneself through the lens of an inflated third-person representation: that of the British colonizer who views himself as a royal subject of a nation born to rule in virtue of its liberal-cum-monarchical traditions, its rational cunning, its ruddy cheeks, and four-part, Anglican songs *senza vibrato*; or, in Bilgrami's case, that of the moderate Muslim who compensates for his underlying sense of abjection through an equally intransigent embracing of the very qualities the colonizer has exaggerated and essentialized in castigating him.[22]

As Bilgrami points out, it is a condition of knowledge about oneself that one can assume the third-person perspective on one's own ethnic/religious beliefs, attitudes, and practices. The third-person perspective provides the possibility of truth, not simply of distortion. For from the "outside," agents may take perspectives on their ethnicity that will modify or otherwise correct their own distortions in self-image and will also supply them with material to affirm. The agent will affirm himself or herself against the stereotype, or in favor of the objective viewpoint. The agent will acquire a perspective of otherness from which the agent's own self will look different. In the light of this dialectic, a more authentic and worldly self-affirmation will occur.

Bilgrami's discussion focuses on moderate Muslims, who ought, he believes, to redefine their relationships to scriptural texts so as to replace orthodoxy with openness, threat with internal criticism. Bilgrami urges moderate Muslims to question the totalizing authority of their script and tradition; he desires that they rewrite the terms of their identity and allegiance, not that they simply return to some romanticized Mecca of the mind where the word "Muslim" has its home. Their reaffirmation of being Muslim will be a parting from the old linguistic home and the old practices as well as to return to a rediscovered home, a rewriting of the old identity, the old texts, the old practices, which at once preserves and selects them, at once sublates and refuses them. This affirmation will place the community up for grabs, render the linguistic home existentially insecure.

We are no longer in the space of Wittgenstein's picture of returning words home from exile, but rather in the space in which a play of affirmations and denials takes place in a fragmented "we." Naomi Scheman was among the first to interrogate Wittgenstein's trope of bringing words back home to their *Heimat* (homeland) on the grounds that it presupposes a common practice, a "we" acceptable to all in which words belong, a community of persons who ought to now use the word in this way.[23] Writing nicely of the importance of a diaspora whose language games remain at odds with those in the sociolinguistic center, she is attentive to the element of domination implicit in the blithe claim of a common home for all. This element is surely present in the claim to bring genius or ethnicity entirely home — as if someone could decide for everyone else what genius and ethnicity are, as if the fact of the postmodern, with its debates about canonization, identity, and the like, could be magically obliterated.

I have suggested that ethnicity implies the common as well as the differential. If there were no overlap in style and practice between persons in an ethnic community, then ethnic terms would have little real application other than as third-person — usually prejudicial — ways of lumping people together as "those damn Xs." Sometimes there is little more binding people together than the prejudices of others, but our self-descriptions tend to assume that there is often far more to being a Jew, a Chicano, a whatever, that there is far more in common between these people than that. Yet my ethnicity is not (quite) yours, even if we are both called an X and both call ourselves Xs, nor is my own process of affirmation yours. Hence the overall meaning of the ethnic name must arise through the movement between positions of affirmation and acknowledgment in the public sphere. (Derrida famously signifies both rewriting one's identity and the play between public positions by his adoption of Freud's "Fort/Da" as an image of knowledge.)

Here we have clearly surpassed the fruitfulness of Wittgenstein's picture.

Our *common* practices are practices in which bringing words home and re-making their use are interconnected processes, impossible ultimately to pry apart. We live both at home and diasporically, in the center of the "we" and at its margins, together and individually — all at once. This is a reminder to the philosopher who would be bewitched by the trope of bringing words back home or by any claim that a single trope is adequate to picture how words work when they are used well or freed through the process of critique. We can no more get away without the metaphor of a proper home for words than we can get along entirely within its conceptual domain.

The metaphor of language in exile, with its connections to leading, re-turning, and *Heimat*, both does and does not work as a picture of how words work in life. Affirmation and acknowledgment are ways of returning our words home in Wittgenstein's sense, of returning our practices and beliefs to a home we cannot fail to know in virtue of knowing and inhabiting our-selves. But these are also at the same time language games that go beyond the metaphor of *Heimat* into those of renegotiation, recreation, differentia-tion, and the play between various conflicting affirmations. Perhaps this is what Nietzsche meant by the dialectics of affirmation when he felt the need to speak of affirmation as "becoming what one is." [24]

NOTES

1. Robert Musil, *The Man Without Qualities*, trans. E. Wilkins and E. Kaiser (London: Picador, 1979).

2. Stephen Toulmin and Alan Janik, *Wittgenstein's Vienna* (New York: Simon & Schuster, 1974).

3. The locus classicus being Nietzsche's work, *The Genealogy of Morals*, in *The Birth of Tragedy and the Genealogy of Morals*, trans. F. Golffing (Garden City, N.Y.: Doubleday Anchor Books, 1956).

4. Jacques Derrida, "Différance," in *Margins of Philosophy*, trans. with Additional Notes by Alan Bass (Chicago: University of Chicago Press, 1982), p. 27.

5. The question Derrida sets to Wittgenstein, Austin, and "ordinary language phi-losophy" — a philosophy he also adores — concerns the ultimate distinction between ordinary and philosophical uses or words, that is, the philosophical assumption that there is a pristine sphere residing somewhere in the form of life and our language games which is not yet philosophical and therefore authentic and to which words can be shepherded. This question, a deep one, is indeed forced by Wittgenstein's belief that European culture is so overwhelmed by metaphysics that it is perhaps played out. But if Wittgenstein believes that language has become thoroughly perpetrated by metaphysics, then where is its prephilosophical home to which words can be re-

turned? Or better, how can this metaphysics be cleared away so that words can be returned to a home that we do not yet know but know must be there (for we do use words with reasonable success often enough to know that we know them well enough for them to have meanings given by language games, and we do share common senses that they have been on occasion violated). Wittgenstein's romantic philosophy of return to a not yet known home, reminiscent of Novalis, exists in sharp contrast to Derrida's claims that "perception does not exist" because the word "perception" is so perpetrated by philosophy that we do not know what it is to speak of "seeing." Derrida moreover harps on the idea that whenever someone claims to ascertain the sphere of the ordinary, he or she is artificially restricting the natural plasticity and dissemination of words and contexts, a free play of openness that forecloses on our having very much to say about what the ordinary is. By contrast, Wittgenstein is convinced that in some basic way we know not only how to see; we also know what the word "seeing" means and have language games in which we ordinarily and successfully use this word without the perpetration of philosophy. See Jacques Derrida *Limited INC*, trans. Alan Bass, Samuel Weber, and Jeffrey Mehlman (Evanston: Northwestern University Press, 1993).

6. Ludwig Wittgenstein, *Philosophical Investigations*, trans. Elizabeth Anscombe (New York: Macmillan, 1968), #116. Hereafter quotations from the *Philosophical Investigations* will be followed in the text by *PI* and the section number.

7. See Donald Davidson, "On the Very Idea of a Conceptual Scheme," in *Inquiries into Truth and Interpretation*, ed. A. Bilgrami (Oxford: Clarendon Press, 1984), pp. 183–98.

8. I refer to theorizations of the postmodern by Jameson and Harvey (Frederic Jameson, *Postmodernism, or, the Cultural Logic of Late Capitalism* (Durham: Duke University Press, 1991); David Harvey, *The Condition of Postmodernity* (Cambridge, Mass.: Blackwell, 1990). Lyotard, Harvey, and others theorize the postmodern on the basis of different regions of culture that are taken to be paradigmatic of it. On the various perspectives from which postmodernism has been construed, see Harvey, Part 1, and Daniel Herwitz, "Postmodernism: An Overview," in *Encyclopedia of Aesthetics*, ed. M. Kelly (New York: Garland, forthcoming).

9. Stanley Cavell, "Declining Decline," in *This New Yet Unapproachable America* (Albuquerque: Living Batch Press, 1989), pp. 34–35.

10. See Ray Monk, *Ludwig Wittgenstein: The Duty of Genius* (New York: Free Press, 1990).

11. Ludwig Wittgenstein, *Culture and Value*, trans. Peter Winch (Chicago: University of Chicago Press, 1984), p. 15e.

12. I owe this formulation of the concept of the ordinary in terms of the "habitus" to conversations with Marjorie Perloff. For Bourdieu's discussion, see Pierre Bourdieu, *Distinction: A Social Critique of the Judgement of Taste*, trans. R. Nice (Cambridge: Harvard University Press, 1984).

13. For the Kantian reading of Wittgenstein, see the writings of P. M. S. Hacker,

for example, his *Wittgenstein, Meaning and Mind*, Vol. 3 of an *Analytical Commentary on the Philosophical Investigations, Part 1, Essays* (Oxford: Backwell, 1993).

14. Jean Baudrillard, *The Ecstasy of Communication*, trans. B. and C. Schutze, ed. S. Lotringer (Brooklyn, N.Y.: Semiotext(e), 1988), pp. 22, 16. All further quotes from this text will be cited in the text as *EC*.

15. See his *Culture and Value*, where he stresses again and again his belief that European culture is so utterly permeated by metaphysical thinking that it is played out, incapable of return. See also G. H. von Wright, "Wittgenstein in Relation to His Times," in *Wittgenstein and His Times*, ed. B. McGuinness (Chicago: University of Chicago Press, 1982), pp. 108–20.

16. National Public Radio can also be seen as an expression of America's Quaker/Protestant roots, as if it were playing out an enormous town meeting where everyone who is moved to speak is to be listened to, for the art of listening, which thereby means the art of waiting, openness, and silence, is the route to a social and spiritual justice that is communal. I take John Cage's art to address itself to the inculcation of such a spirit. But then, if National Public Radio were really dedicated to the free conversation of all, its conversations would include everybody. Then where are the intellectuals, the artists, the conductors, the true geniuses? Why are they not asked to be included? Do they always refuse, or are they marginalized by those who play out a simulacrum of all-inclusiveness that really represents the denial of the talented and the intellectually serious? Does America really hate those who exhibit a level of talent, whose words present a level of complexity that challenges the homogenized claims of each and every citizen to the mastery of knowledge and genius in each of its forms? Or is it rather that in an arch-colonialist gesture, we allow only fancy Europeans and elegant postcolonials with Cambridge accents to be geniuses, to be creative, interdisciplinary, and original and seldom afford Americans the same status? Ours is the ambivalence of the colonial toward the colony. In one voice we reject all things non-American, claiming as President Clinton did that this is the "greatest country in history" and that it has no prototype except in the populace, while in another voice we ape the European, believing that only he or she is capable of sophistication and talent.

In this regard see Stanley Cavell on the repression of the American transcendentalists and on the fact that Hollywood's geniuses had to market themselves as cowboys to be taken seriously by America. He has written about such things in several places.

17. Jean Baudrillard, "The Orders of Simulacra," *Simulations* (New York: Semiotext(e), 1983), pp. 81–152.

18. For a discussion of this most central concept in Cavell's work, see his "Knowing and Acknowledging," in *Must We Mean What We Say?* (Cambridge: Cambridge University Press, 1969), pp. 238–66.

19. Both genius and ethnicity share the condition of outrunning rules, and both are similarly deformed within the American simulacrum. Genius is the talent for making things in a way that outruns the rules it also depends on. As for ethnicity, in

spite of its many codifications, conformities to rules, and modes of institutionaliza-
tion, *authentic* ethnicity, like a poem, a joke, or a work of philosophy, is a way of
inhabiting things that is both rule-governed in its practices (Jewish bar mitzvahs, Irish
wakes, rituals of scarification or circumcision, rules about what women are allowed
and not allowed to do or become) and that is a cultural style going beyond all rules,
a creative way of posing the world and inhabiting it, a style, a way of becoming a
collective "we." (I am sympathetic to the nineteenth-century's concept of ethnicity
as the genius in this case residing in the various people who variously comprise a
people. I take it that this is what the nineteenth century knew, that this is what Herder,
in spite of his many problems, knew. But one need not believe this to secure the more
modest — and obvious — point that both genius and ethnicity share the condition of
ourunning rules.)

20. See Akeel Bilgrami, "What Is a Muslim? Fundamental Commitment and
Cultural Identity," *Critical Inquiry* 18 (Summer 1992): 821–42.

21. Again, it has been the point of much postcolonial writing to show how categories of ethnicity, religion, and gender are superimposed onto one another into a
synergized picture, such that in being a colonial subject, one is "feminized" by the
gaze of the colonizer, while from one's internal perspective, one is male, and so on.
See, for example, Sander Gilman, *Differences and Pathology* (Ithaca: Cornell University Press, 1985).

22. Bilgrami, haunted by the lack of support for Salman Rushdie by moderate
Muslim intellectuals in the United States and abroad, argues that their refusal to
criticize actual examples of "Arab fanaticism" such as the Fatwa pronounced by the
Iranian clergy against Rushdie and their uncritical identification with fanatical Arab
leaders (Saddam et al.) represents a compensatory adulation of the very qualities the
West attributes to all Arabs: fanaticism, cruelty, grandiosity, intolerance. As such, it is
a stance that betrays an internalized vision of oneself as the other sees one: as essentially fanatical, grandiose, and the like. Grandiose identification with the fanatical
then serves to conceal a deeper sense of abjection about oneself. Bilgrami argues that
this postcolonialist stance prevents moderate Muslims from critically rethinking their
own relations to the Muslim faith, and thus bringing that faith into the modern
world. See Bilgrami, "What Is a Muslim?"

23. Naomi Scheman, "Forms of Life: Mapping the Rough Ground," in *The Cambridge Companion to Wittgenstein*, ed. Hans Sluga and David Stern (Cambridge:
Cambridge University Press, forthcoming).

24. Friedrich Nietzsche, *Ecce Homo*, trans. W. Kaufmann (New York: Vintage
Press, 1974).

11. Antonin Artaud's Itinerary
Through Exile and Insanity

Insanity is complete otherness; it distorts and
transports, rousing the other scene.
— Michel Foucault, *L'Histoire de la folie*

Antonin Artaud articulated through his diverse writings the exile imposed
upon him by outside authority. This reaction on his part did not result from
political or ethnic displacement, for he lived among people whose language
he had always shared and which he had completely mastered. Exile for him
meant not only a cutting off of communications with others, but finally with
himself. Condemned to live in a no-man's-land, Artaud simultaneously experienced the plight of imprisonment and the impossibility of changing his
condition as though he had committed an irreparable crime against society.
This situation appears all the more tragic because Artaud needed even more
than most writers to belong to a congenial group, as his career as actor and
theater director, as well as his active participation in the surrealist movement — from which he was banished — show so clearly. In his mind, exile
and imprisonment resulted entirely from the institutional pressures of the
Third Republic.

Artaud's writings have been considered by some as unclassifiable. They
do not fit into any mold and could be labeled as "non-genre literature."[1] He
practiced poetry, composed plays and essays about the theater, entertained a
vast correspondence, acted and created film scenarios, left many scattered
drawings, rushed into anthropological adventures on which he reported,
and published letters of protest. Most of his works, more often than not
autobiographical, bear the stamp of a tortured mind attempting in vain to
uncover the causes of exile and imprisonment and, through creative effort,
to reverse an intolerable situation and effect a cure. Overtly or covertly, contestation characterizes the vast majority of his texts and even his contorted

self-portraits, thus implying his constant involvement in a conflict against outside forces and against himself.

Although surrealists, and André Breton in particular, often dwell on cultural and social alienation, they rarely if ever expose, as does Artaud, spiritual mutilation. Breton describes himself as surrounded by an impermeable zone of boredom that distances him from the everyday life of the bourgeois and shelters him from bureaucracies. By decontextualizing objects and focusing on the dream, Breton reaches for the surreal, which he attains, if only momentarily, through illumination. Basic definitions introduced into the manifestos, *Surrealism and Painting,* and other key texts proclaim both a reconciliation and a division. Projection into an undetermined future and the adoption of a credo that alternately inscribes and erases mitigate any propensity toward alienation. Dreams and anthropological ventures into non-Western cultures serve mainly to confirm the utopian visions in which the surrealists had sought salvation.

In one of his early texts, *Umbilical Limbo* (1924), Artaud immediately sets himself up against others and thereby proclaims his difference. The territory of this otherness is not confined to writing, since he claims that his goal is not the text, the poem, or the book, but his very existence. This autobiographical text brings to the surface cleavages in identity, unbridgeable divisions of the self: "I suffer because the spirit has no place in life, and because Life has no place in the Spirit; I suffer from the Spirit-voice, from the Spirit-translation or from the Spirit-intimidation of things to make them enter into the Spirit." [2] Self-awareness attained through suffering from such incompleteness and isolation is tantamount to exile and results in alienation. When reconciliatory gestures toward the outside world and the recovery of inner stability appear doomed to failure, such a loss of identity becomes irreversible.

Like most surrealists, Antonin Artaud took a strong antibourgeois stand throughout his life, but whereas they acted in the name of a movement, he engaged in a solitary struggle. He opposed the establishment because of its materialistic concerns, its static lifestyle, and its rigid adherence to oppressive forms of institutionalism. The growing influence of the state as opposed to individual freedom, as implied in Artaud's polemical writings, would become a major thesis in Michel Foucault's *Discipline and Punish* (1975). Early in his career, Artaud engaged in anarchistic behavior and aggressively maintained controversial positions. Whereas Breton in his manifestos first imposed a surrealist model and later attacked members of his group, including Artaud, who had allegedly betrayed it, the latter's diatribes were primarily directed against institutional leaders or administrators without explicitly proposing an alternate solution. Although Artaud did not regularly speak in the name of surrealism, Breton, in *La Révolution surréaliste* (1925), eagerly reprinted his two "Open Letters," the first to the "Presidents of the European Universities" and the second to the "Heads of the Insane Asylums." In the former, Artaud declares university administrators guilty of denying the potential vitality of the spirit, the secret rules of the heart, the power of language. He accuses the academics of mummifying the Western world by reducing it to tribunals and factories that "manufacture" doctors, magistrates, and false scientists. A similar indictment recurs in various guises in Artaud's writings, though the accusations are not necessarily directed against the same establishments. In later texts, he will continue to insist on the failure of institutional structures and the dignitaries who uphold them. Nonetheless, he occasionally discovers within them vestiges of a positive creative force whose dormant power he can still detect. Conversely, he condemns their propensity to embalm as a deliberate denial of humankind's natural state.

In his "Open Letter to the Heads of the Insane Asylums," he speaks as a victim of repressive incarceration, humiliation, and alienation. He opposes those in authority to outsiders, who have no voice or function within the institution. When Artaud wrote this text, he had already been subjected to a limited stay in an asylum. In spite of differences in style and tone, it anticipates attitudes expressed in later autobiographical fragments dealing with the confrontation between the insane and institutional forces. The second letter addresses mainly social and legal issues. Artaud vehemently insists on the guilt of the bureaucratic heads. He labels doctors as prison guards and policemen. These early anarchistic manifestos only marginally involve personal grievances. Later in his career, after long periods of internment, Artaud accused the psychiatrists, under whom he suffered for much longer stretches of time, of tyrannizing their patients and practicing unjustifiable invasive methods: "One does not know, — one does not know sufficiently — that *asylums*, far from providing asylum, are dreadful jails where prisoners supply free and convenient labor and where maltreatment is the rule; and this is what you tolerate" (1956:267). Artaud attacks the very foundation of society when he reveals the repressions committed by doctors who arrogate powerful positions, cast themselves in dignified roles, and are credited by the bourgeois establishment with healing powers and a talent for uncanny communication. Artaud thus reduces the alleged intellectual powers of psychiatrists to a brazen fraudulence condoned by society. He contests the doctors' assumed right to probe into the minds of their patients, thus questioning the

very basis of psychiatric treatment and policy. By proclaiming the psychiatrists' guilt, Artaud, in these epistolary manifestos, shows how their attitudes
are determined by fear of the unsettling ideas and challenging views arising
from madness and delirium. Consequently, he comes to the defense of those
declared mad and insists on putting an end to the indignities and spiritual
mutilations to which they are routinely subjected. He puts particular emphasis on the value of illumination attendant upon delirium. He argues against
internment, an exile from the world inflicted upon the mentally ill against
their will. Artaud's letter not only attacks authority but also formulates a first
apologia for the wisdom and knowledge of the insane, whose often astounding abilities and inspired achievements he stresses. This radical revision of
the status of the insane eventually reached fulfillment in his text on Vincent
van Gogh. Artaud's assessment of the remarkable contributions of the so-
called insane would invalidate the contentions of psychiatry. Indeed, he distinguishes the authentic *aliéné* from those designated as mad by the bourgeois establishment. Artaud did not attack authority only in his writings but
also in public outbursts. Although he may not have proposed a program for
changing the pattern of European politics, culture, and tradition, he repeatedly revealed to French youth, frustrated in their hope of transforming the
world, the evils of a static society fostering exile and slavery, a society that
should be held responsible for widespread alienation.

As actor, director, and playwright, Artaud came to grips with another
powerfully entrenched institution, the theater and its official representative,
la Comédie Française, dominated by bourgeois psychology and so-called realism. To counter this oppression, Artaud proposed various non-Western
models, notably the performances of the Balinese. The conventional European stage, an enclosure open only on the side of the audience, evokes spatial imprisonment. Developed under and with the encouragement of the
autocratic Richelieu, it provides an admirable setting for characters victim-
ized by fate and their own inescapable passions. Artaud had participated in
the liberating theatrical adventures of Aurélien Lugné-Poe, Sacha Pittoëff,
and Charles Dullin before assuming the direction of the Théâtre Alfred
Jarry, which ceased operations in 1930, the year before the Balinese theater's
Parisian engagement. Lavishing praises on the innovative generic transgressions practiced by the Balinese, Artaud relied on a non-Western culture to
reduce the estrangement and denial of the self caused by an authoritarian
establishment. Thankfully, the Balinese theater had escaped the psychological trends that, in his opinion, had brought ruin to the European stage. From
the very first sentence, Artaud confronts European and non-Western expres-

sion: "The spectacle of the Balinese theater, which draws upon dance, song, pantomime — and a little of the theater as we understand it in the Occident — restores the theater . . . to its original destiny . . . in a combination of hallucination and fear"[3] (1964a:64). Artaud does not merely praise an alternative form of entertainment but suggests a model for rejuvenating our beliefs and our need to regain the fundamental unity we have forsaken. He proposes replacing the false order of an imprisoned identity inherent in Western theater by unleashing the primitive forces of nature and exorcism, thus uncovering deep-seated inner secrets. A double that hides behind its own reality provides a surrealist gloss opposing all reliance on conventional identity. Artaud also blames the false values of European society on injuries and deprivations inflicted on the self. Thus he warns his readers of the various modalities of exile: a feeling of having become different from, as well as incompatible with, others, a sense of alienation from the self, and the resulting awareness of a threatening inner void leading to a loss of identity. By thus explaining societal and cultural as well as personal and psychological divisions in terms of exile, Artaud implicitly reveals an almost Manichaean obsession with duality.

Like most surrealists, Artaud in his dissatisfaction with Europe was drawn to other continents and sought new visions of the world. Rich in cults and myths, Mexico offered a life free of materialistic strictures. Breton chronicled his political trip to Mexico in "Souvenirs du Mexique," published in *Minotaure* (1939). Wolfgang Paalen organized expeditions to British Columbia and Alaska even before World War II. Like Artaud, he ventured off the beaten track to penetrate the secrets of Indian tribes. But unlike Artaud's, Paalen's goals and motives were duplicitous because he illegally acquired artworks at bargain prices.

Artaud saw Mexico as exemplary long before he contemplated a trip there. In *The Theater and Its Double* (1938), he included the scenario of a play as a model for his revolutionary program in the theater. In *La Conquête du Mexique*, Cortez, the oppressive colonizer, opposes Montezuma, the colonized victim. The Spanish invader abundantly displays all the negative characteristics of modern Europeans. His inflated and dictatorial self contrasts with the peaceful spirituality of the Aztecs. Artaud shows how the colonizer instills in the colonized feelings of alienation, which their leader tries to dispel. Called "roi astrologue," he is endowed with extraterrestrial powers. In this early scenario, Artaud already contrasted the pathological behavior of the Spanish with the healing powers of the Indians.

Artaud planned his trip to Mexico with a clear sense of mission and a determination to distance himself from the isolation he attributed to French authoritarianism. Before his departure, he familiarized himself with its cultural life and its revolutionary commitment. Intent on exploring the areas most immune to Western culture, he succeeded in participating in the secret peyote rites, a feat almost impossible for an uninitiated white man. Artaud states that his Mexican experience brought about a reversal of the feeling of exile and alienation produced by French institutions, notably mental hospitals. From the vantage point of this totally foreign but remarkably congenial civilization, Artaud had good reason to accuse those who had humiliated him in Europe.

In 1936, Artaud addressed an open letter published in *El Nacional* to the governors of the Mexican state. Interestingly enough, it provides a counterpart to the open letters published in *La Révolution surréaliste*. Once again opposing one group to another, Artaud takes an outspokenly partisan position by addressing an appeal full of praise for the Mexican government and accusations of the French state: "In my opinion, European culture is bankrupt; I believe that in the unbridled development of its machines Europe has betrayed true culture. In response, I insist on betraying the European conception of progress" (1973:228). Whereas he believes that French institutions fabricate the notions and conditions of sickness and paralysis, he claims that Indian tribes have power to heal the soul. His trip to Mexico can be interpreted as a search for a cure, a recognition that his sanity was still threatened, and a trust that assimilation, however momentary or partial, to other customs, together with the practice of primal rituals, would restore unity and health instead of increasing rift and division. He stresses the superiority of Mexican culture, immune to modern consumerism, industrial progress, and European hierarchical divisions. Mexican cults advocated a return to the earth and considered the harmonious relationships between human organism and nature as the true sources of vitality and energy, sources he felt thoroughly lacking in Western culture. In short, he attempts to substitute primeval antecedents for a fabricated Gallic past based no doubt on Cartesian rationalism, so often propounded by French pedagogues. The metaphor of the body and the allusions to basic elements, notably fire, play a significant role. Life is characterized by fluidity, which may suggest the flow of blood or the movement of sap within a plant. Based on multiple forms of transmission, all of them mysterious and occult, all of them facilitating communication between individuals as well as between humans and the earth, Indian rites remain incompatible with organized exploitation. Refusing to view the country as a tourist or even as a scholar, Artaud saw himself as a participant capable of penetrating mysteries intuitively rather than conceptually. He aspired to produce a quasi-magnetic interaction that would restore man as a whole, as a unity, and not as the fractured being produced by doctors in hospitals. He sought salvation in the emotional unanimity of tribal life — in the vital pursuits of a group. His participation consisted in sincerely playing a part in a real rather than a make-believe situation. He had at last found the ritualistic performances he had so vainly sought as theater director.

Benjamin Péret, one of the most dedicated political activists among the surrealists, expressed similar views in his *Air mexicain* (1952). Strongly committed to revolution and political action, Péret lived among the Indians of the Amazon and spent the war years in Mexico. In his epic, the Aztecs emerge as an exemplary people. He, too, celebrates the conjunction of natural and human forces far removed from the contaminated institutions of the Third Republic. He indicts empire builders mainly because they deny human rights. Like Artaud, he equates present-day European authoritarianism and repression with the conquistadores' persecution of vitalistic tribes.

Artaud's major texts on Mexico are unquestionably the essays collected under the title *Au Pays des Tarahumaras* [In Tarahumara land], much of it written during his internment at Rodez. For this reason, his Indian experiences inevitably interacted with his responses to, and reflections on, cultural and institutional life in France. In each of his texts, Artaud established links between the effect of confinement, its ever-increasing process of alienation, and the opening up of spiritual channels resulting from Mexican rituals. After having undergone electroshock, he felt that the psychiatrists had deprived him of any possibility of self-control, thus confirming his belief that far from corresponding to a natural state, mental disease was no more than a degeneration produced by doctors: "If there had not been any doctors, there would never have been any sick people" (1974b:57). Accordingly, medicine in Western civilization has always fostered an aberrant view of the human being. The doctors' alleged cure by electroshock inevitably leads to and compounds violence and destruction. In *Artaud le Mômo*, Artaud argues that treatment deprives the patient of his human shape — "fleshy state pulverizing state" — and identity. The patient must confront not only suffering but separation from reality as well as cruel and violent descents into nothingness and emptiness. The result is a deathlike state in all patients — a false death that perpetuates itself.

This enforced destructive exposure contrasts with his voluntary taking of peyote in the land of the Tarahumaras. Artaud had tried drugs before, especially opium, some of which had produced hallucinatory or delirious effects.

He regarded peyote as a positive drug and those he had previously taken as negative. Although this Indian drug disrupts normal relations with everyday life, it does not produce irreversible effects: "But one arrives at such a vision only after one has gone through a tearing and an agony, after which one feels as if turned around and *reversed* to the other side of things, and one no longer understands the world that one has just left" (1972:32).[4] The Mexican experience gives a collective meaning to individuality and identity. It opens up into the unlimited: "Peyote leads the self back to its true sources ... and one no longer doubts what one is" (34).[5] Since the peyote rites belong to a collective experience, they cannot be defined in terms of personal needs or described as a venture into a private domain. Because the utter loneliness that encroached upon Artaud disappeared when he joined the leaders of a tribe, he claimed that, by means of an initiating passage, the "endangered" Tarahumaras could conceivably help him to recover from his European trauma. Michel Leiris stated in *L'Afrique fantôme* that in his expedition he, too, sought rejuvenation, but his involvement was of a totally different nature: "As for me, I continue my work as supervisor, examining magistrate or bureaucrat" (1951:73). He never questioned, let alone rejected, his fundamental identification with European institutions.

The most crucial pages of "Le Rite du peyotl" were written while Artaud was at Rodez. Unfortunately, the sequestered, isolated, suffering man labeled as mad did not succeed in regaining his identity by reliving his Mexican venture through his writing. At Rodez, Artaud attempted to "reactivate" an experience that had brought him further away from exile and nearer to the possibility of self-mastery. But his eventual awakening to the reality of insanity with its cruel divorce from ordinary existence inevitably worsened his situation, for he felt that his sense of being had been torn away from him at Rodez more brutally than before his Mexican adventure. Dr. Ferdière had encouraged him to write and draw, as had Dr. Toulouse during a very early internment many years previously. Although Artaud produced drawings as well as such major texts as *Au pays des Tarahumaras* (1945), *Les Lettres de Rodez* (1946), *Artaud de Mômo* (1947), and *Van Gogh, le suicidé de la société* (1947), and although he remained in constant contact with major literary figures such as Michel Leiris, Jacques Rivière, and Jean Paulhan, he failed to regain his self-mastery. Even at the time of *L'Ombilic des limbes* and *Le Pèse-Nerfs* [Nerve scales] (1927), he had complained about his inability to express his thoughts and his fear that words eluded him. At the age of nineteen, he had angrily destroyed his manuscripts, thus early in his career associating writing with violence. He wrote Paulhan: "Don't even include initials" (1967:226), thus denying his identity as author. Although writing did not restore his mutilated being at the time, he had nonetheless shifted the inevitability of madness from his exiled self to the world, to the civilization to which he had physically if not spiritually returned.

Thus Artaud pictured himself as exiled from the world but also from his own creations. He refused to sign so major a work as *D'un voyage au pays des Tarahumaras*. As he explained to Paulhan, a signature would entail identification with a being that no longer existed. By this refusal, he symbolically relinquished his involvement in his own text. Haunted by cultural, historical, and personal crises, the writer no doubt felt that adding an empty signature would compound an initial confusion and alienation. The gesture involving *D'un voyage au pays des Tarahumaras* undoubtedly goes beyond his relationship to this particular text for it addresses the fundamental experience underlying writing. Artaud's perception of exile and his confrontation with the void, which cut him off from any feeling of belonging while depriving him of that sense of continuity indispensable to recognition, could no longer be mitigated by the "completion" of a text or a drawing. By suppressing the signature, by publishing a text of which the author was to remain anonymous, Artaud insisted on the total separation of the self from the other. Jean-Michel Rey states: "Situating himself outside the boundary of what he has written, renouncing his name and signature, . . . Antonin Artaud is exiled from the emplacement of discourse" (1991:8, 9). The renunciation of name and signature may have had little effect on the work of art or its message, but it must have had a devastating impact on the creator, whose exile from the self removed him from the domain of written as well as spoken communication while contributing to the dissolution of identity rather than helping to restore it. The secretive author must have wished at times that writing and drawing could remain strictly private. The official language he was forced to use had affinities with a straitjacket.

Not exclusively a writer, Artaud intermittently resorted to drawing as a means of expression. After sporadic attempts in his youth, he completed a voluminous portfolio in his later years. He often produced on the same page substantial interactions between the pen and the brush, repeatedly alternating between the verbal and the visual as though they required each other's support, all the more so because their creator was perpetually haunted by the fear that the word, the line, and their articulation would elude his control. In 1988, Jacques Derrida and Paule Thévenin published Artaud's drawings, thus giving a new dimension to his production and showing the irrelevance of setting conventional borderlines between types of texts and images. Artaud did not consider his drawings perfected artifacts and made no claims for their professionalism. What mattered to him was their linear pulsation and vigor together with the immediacy of their relation to the self as well as their distancing from the viewer.

Some of the problems so far discussed are reflected at least in one of Artaud's late self-portraits (Fig. 1). Thévenin in her comments on the portrait relies as much as possible on remarks made by Artaud himself. The artist's emaciated face with its tight and intense expression, rising above all other elements in the frame, seems to have lost its grounding. Without establishing a visible contact with anything else, the eyes in particular accentuate the proximity of the void. In spite of its physical closeness, a female face turned in the same direction as Artaud's likeness does not belong to the same world. Although it is not possible to identify all the objects and figures in the drawing that surround the portrait that rises above them or to postulate how they contribute to the undercutting of identity, the most striking feature is the oversized hand. No less than the face, it evokes a displacement. Its monumental enthronement, which distances it from the self-portrait rising above it, nonetheless precludes any form of interdependence or unity. The hand and the face appear equally emaciated. The head includes stretched-out and bent figures reduced to a cramped posture. Indeed, the rupture between the hand and the face is duplicated by the failure of the hand to assert its unity or of the fingers to show their autonomy. The cohesion of the self is seriously put in jeopardy. Thévenin mentions that Artaud sometimes burned drawings he had worked on for a long time (1986:25). Whether his destructive gesture expresses his failure to attain professionalism or, on the contrary, chastises his desire to reach perfection, it can also be considered analogous to the refusal of his signature.

This schizophrenic personality trait, this deliberate effort to split himself off from himself, also sheds light on his text on van Gogh. As early as 1925, Artaud brought up the issue of suicide: "I have been dead for a long time, I am already suicided. *They* suicided me, so to speak. . . . But what would you think of an *anterior suicide*, of a suicide that would make us retrace our steps, but on the other side of existence, and not on the side of death" (1956b:246).[6] In this passage, he expresses his ideas in the same terms as in *Van Gogh, le suicidé de la société*. Suicide is not characterized as a self-reflexive, unilaterally subjective gesture but as an objective impact: "I am already suicided. They suicided me" — the verb becomes passive or active instead of reflexive,

FIGURE 1. Antonin Artaud, *Self Portrait* 109, © 1997 ADAGP, Paris / Artists Rights Society (ARS), New York.

expressing either a state or an aggression by some hypostatized power. The proximity with nothingness has become so overwhelming that resurrection or reunification is out of the question.

Suicide is often considered the supreme self-inflicted wound, often an almost sacrificial act. But in Artaud's essay, it corresponds to the victimization that society inflicts on those it has declared mad and against whom it feels compelled to protect itself so as to safeguard its beliefs and institutions. On more than one occasion, Artaud labeled the eventual infliction of death as vampirism, for it reduces the victim to anemia and weakness. Suicide committed by others, not by the self, results from a passive state or gesture on the part of the person who embraces death. The title of the essay is somewhat misleading insofar as Artaud treats van Gogh's turbulent creativity almost as if it were his own. Suicide, however, was a subject in which he had long had a personal interest and on which he had published two essays some twenty years earlier in *La Révolution surréaliste* (1929) and, as already mentioned, in *Le Disque vert* (1925). Thus his choice of title is in keeping with the general thrust of his oeuvre.

Artaud compares suicide to a power of regeneration occurring at the very moment when his self, his being, has reached a point of inertia and his identity is, so to speak, decentered. When he reaches a state of total exile, when he feels completely shaped by others, when he has lost the mastery of his own territory, only then does he seek to emerge from this limbo: "Suicide will be no more for me than a means to reconquer myself violently, to burst brutally into my being" (1956b:221). To burst out violently from a state of negation, gaining through suicide ultimate self-possession, is Artaud's goal, so that his early definition of suicide is not completely unrelated to his crucial experience with peyote.

Artaud's concern with the victimization of the insane and the exile imposed on them by institutional tyranny is nowhere more powerfully developed than in his essay on van Gogh. The dichotomy between the restrictions arbitrarily imposed on the sick by those in power and the potential for ideological transgression, penetration, and adventure of the interned is stressed repeatedly in this text. Artaud frequently alludes to the analogies between his own situation and that of van Gogh. Like the painter, the writer had been repressed and mistreated in several hospitals until Dr. Ferdière accepted him as a patient at Rodez. He repeatedly acknowledged his gratitude to this physician: "Not only did you help me live, but you *invited me* to live when I wilted" (1974a:197). This good doctor administered electroshock, a controversial treatment condemned by others and regarded as pernicious by the author in his *Artaud le Mômo*, but surprisingly condoned by him in some of his *Lettres de Rodez* (1946). The term "envoûtement" (maléfice) applied to the prisoner's condition personifies solitary imprisonment, implacable alienation, forced inertia, total separation from others, and spiritual deprivation. Mentioned in relation to van Gogh, "envoûtement" clearly evokes a state within which Artaud was only too familiar and against which he desperately struggled. Despite short interruptions, his madness was almost continually accompanied by extraordinary lucidity and self-evaluation. While stressing these alternations, the essay on van Gogh analyzes once again the humiliation and reductions caused not so much by insanity itself as by society, primarily by doctors. Artaud pleads for the need and practice of exorcism, since "vous délirez" (you are raving) is the answer a person receives who speaks about experiences reaching beyond the everyday, invisible to the naked eye, pertaining to the occult, the hermetic, the magical, the apocalyptic, and opening on to the supernatural or the infinite. "Vous délirez" could have been the answer given to van Gogh, to Gérard de Nerval, to Friedrich Hölderlin by anyone to whom such revelations were confided. Frequently these revelations are addressed to physicians who, in their eagerness to prevent further transgressions, intellectually and physically restrain their patients, going so far as to force upon them protracted states of isolation and inertia.

This sense of failure and the urge to overcome it by restoring one's identity had been discussed by Artaud at various moments. In a letter to Dr. Ferdière, written from Rodez, he further articulates the need to overcome his fundamental crisis. Any letter that he would write to his doctor would necessarily focus on possible alternatives to internment whether in the physical, mental, or psychological sense. Inertia, laziness, passivity are the signs of man's downfall. Artaud admits in more than one document that he is seriously afflicted by these evils, even if initially he had not caused them. He concentrates on the image of what man should be or should strive to become in fostering the creation of his soul. Most men are oblivious to or unaware of this act of self-creation, essential to the regeneration of society. In this letter, the impulse toward creative vitality transcends the questions about who is mad and who is not and whether madness leads to productivity or threat.

Artaud was at least temporarily saved by the sympathetic care he received from Dr. Ferdière. In his attempt to counter Artaud's helpless sense of "envoûtement" and exile, Ferdière took seriously the link his patient had established between madness and genius as well as contacts outside the ordinary world and supported his desire to give free play to his talents. While undergoing a necessarily interrupted process of liberation thanks to Ferdière's support, he did not lose sight of the more general problem posed by psychiatrists. *Van Gogh, le suicidé de la société* contains a diatribe against the painter's physician, Dr. Gachet. Artaud attributes van Gogh's suicide to society as represented above all by Dr. Gachet and to a lesser degree by Theo van Gogh, who had attempted to calm his brother rather than allow his delirium full power of expression. Physical and psychological causes are usually given as explanations of the suicide. Gachet sent the agitated van Gogh to the fields to paint. But since his allegedly twisted, but in reality penetrating, thoughts and dreams had been discredited, his painting, deprived of its exploratory thrust and frenzied vitality, would result by reversal in an act of death. Gachet treated van Gogh according to conformist concerns without taking into account his identity.

Van Gogh's suicide was not a voluntary act on the part of the painter but was caused by his victimization by society. Artaud makes it clear, however, that in spite of the mutilation society inflicted upon van Gogh, he showed greater lucidity concerning his state than did his doctors. Exonerating the painter from violence, from the self-inflicted wounds on his hand and ear, Artaud attributes to him the power of self-illumination. Although van Gogh was not insane until society forced him into that state and erroneously labeled him as mad, his paintings nevertheless deeply disturb the viewer. In spite of Artaud's familiarity with the painter's letters to his brother, the greatest revelation comes to him from the paintings. Although the paintings created by an artist alienated from society may not have provided an escape, they can be viewed as an aggressive and avenging gesture against those who had segregated him because they had misunderstood his behavior. Defying description, the paintings cannot be reduced to representations of a safely circumscribed reality, for they express the exiled artist's and, indeed, humanity's, despairing plea for human solidarity. Artaud suggests that for him as well as for van Gogh a hopeless distanciation from reality takes place when others or outside forces attempt to impose a deathly calm. Although Artaud does not express this idea directly, the reader is given to understand that in his paintings van Gogh translated an experience and related to human exchanges of which he had been deprived. His trees are not immobile but convulsive (like the features in many of Artaud's self-portraits), for the painter penetrates below the surface and dislocates the center of gravity. Van Gogh's objects — Artaud mentions shoes, candlesticks, birds — seem to lay bare nerve endings and hostile flesh. They convey the painter's irreparable alienation. His nature provides a direct, unmediated contact and may propel forces that attain the infinite: "There is enough infinity on earth" (1974:60). The access to and penetration into nature is, according to Artaud, not primarily or exclusively a psychological act or the result of a psychological device. Although he declares that each canvas constitutes "an event," this expression could be ambiguous and merely suggest that none of van Gogh's artworks should ever go unnoticed. An event pertains to a happening, contrasting by its very terminology with bourgeois inertia and pointing toward change and even upheaval. The event is unique; it has political connotations of great importance to Artaud. For the work of the artist to have an impact, it must assert its revolt, thus transforming each brush stroke into a significant act, an event. A brush stroke should not lead merely to an element of painting because the iconographic or pictorial representation cannot be self-sufficient even if it remains experimental. Taking his point of departure in the paintings alone, Derrida reaches conclusions similar to those of Artaud, who had so completely identified with the artist: "That he does not utilize painting for any other purpose than itself, that he recognizes it for what it is with its own specific means and in accordance with its essence, insofar, so to speak, as this essence is excessive. This essence is an act and an energy" (1994:171).

Before the painter had been belittled, before he had been told "vous délirez," before others had tried to tranquilize him, he had produced by his art a "staggering blow," generating a force disturbing to bourgeois conformism and institutions. If van Gogh in his paintings, like Artaud in his texts, pleads for violent transformations, it is by means of their writing and brush strokes, which do not owe allegiance to any defined or definable concept of painting or literature. Both Artaud and van Gogh were torn from society, but their exiles do not coincide with the alienation others imposed on them — those who by certifying them as mad inflicted upon them a cruel injustice. Artaud retold his unforgettable grievances by pleading the case of van Gogh's art. He not only identified with the painter but with his art, for his text consists not of ordinary prose but of rhythmic pulsations, the poetic equivalent of van Gogh's convulsive brush strokes. His *Van Gogh, le suicidé de la société* abundantly confirms André Breton's assertion that "beauty must be convulsive or not be at all." Although Artaud often powerfully communicates the state of suffering, of nervous and psychological disturbances, his own painful alienation manifests itself most strikingly when he embraces the plight of others: the Indians who take peyote or van Gogh the artist or the certified insane.

In his rejection of institutions, Artaud is remarkably ahead of his time, for he propagates ideas and ideals relevant to problems crucial to our times. As he characterizes the ruling forces in terms of the asylum, he comes close to castigating them as a colonizing force.[7] His study on van Gogh provides the image of the repressed, while his comments on Indian tribes propose models far more open and vital, but even more endangered, than the enfeebled European institutions claiming omniscience. As a writer, he contributed to the liberation of the word from its authoritarian straitjacket, yet he could never overcome the feeling of exile generated by his own creativity.

NOTES

1. For use of the term "non-genre," see Culler, "Towards a Theory of a Non-Genre Literature," pp. 255–63.

2. Unless otherwise stated, all translations are by J. D. Hubert. Dates in parenthesis refer to the original publications. Those in "Works Cited" are to the more accessible *Oeuvres complètes*, published by Gallimard.

3. Translation from Artaud, *The Theatre and Its Double*, p. 53.

4. Translation from Artaud, *Peyote Dance*, pp. 36 and 38.

5. "Le Rite du Peyotl chez les Tarahumaras" and "D'un voyage au pays des Tarahumaras," originally published separately, are included in the collected essays *Au Pays des Tarahumaras*.

6. This text was originally published in a special issue of *Le Disque vert* (1925) on the subject of suicide.

7. In his recent article "Dans le cercle de la cruauté: *Les Tarahumaras* d'Antonin Artaud," Carlo Pasi discusses the problem of colonization extensively.

WORKS BY ANTONIN ARTAUD

1956a. *Correspondance avec Jacques Rivière, Oeuvres complètes*, vol. 1. Paris: Gallimard.
1956b. *L'Ombilic des limbes. OC*, vol. 1.
1956c. *Le Pèse-nerfs. OC*, vol. 1.
1956d. "Lettre aux Recteurs des Universités européennes" and "Lettre aux Médecins-Chefs des Asiles de Fous." *OC*, vol. 1.
1958. *The Theatre and Its Double*. New York: Grove Press.
1964a. "Sur le Théâtre balinais." *OC*, vol. 4.
1964b. *La Conquête du Mexique. OC*, vol. 5.
1967. *Les Nouvelles révélations de l'être. OC*, vol. 7.
1971. *The Peyote Dance*. Trans. Helen Weaver. New York: Farrar, Straus & Giroux.
1972. *Au Pays des Tarahumaras. OC*, vol. 9.
1973. *Lettres du Mexique. OC*, vol. 8.
1974a. *Lettres de Rodez. OC*, vols. 10 and 11.
1974b. *Artaud le Mômo. OC*, vol. 12.
1974c. *Van Gogh, le suicidé de la société. OC*, vol. 13.

OTHER WORKS

Breton, André. 1939. "Souvenirs du Mexique," *Minotaure* 12–13.

———. 1948. *Martinique charmeuse de serpents.* Nevers: Sagittaire.

Culler, Jonathan. 1981. "Towards a Theory of Non-Genre Literature." In *Surfiction: Fiction Now and Tomorrow,* ed. Raymond Federman, pp. 255–63. Chicago: Swallow.

Derrida, Jacques. 1994. "Maddening the Subjectile." In *Boundaries: Writing and Drawing, Yale French Studies* 84:154–75.

Foucault, Michel. 1972. *Histoire de la folie à l'âge classique.* Paris: Gallimard.

———. 1975. *Surveiller et punir* [Discipline and punish]. Paris: Gallimard.

Leiris, Michel. 1951. *L'Afrique fantôme.* Paris: Gallimard.

Pasi, Carlo. 1995. "Dans le cercle de la cruauté: *Les Tarahumaras* d'Antonin Artaud." In *Nouveau monde autres mondes,* ed. Daniel Lefort, Pierre Rivas, and Jacqueline Chénieux, pp. 129–47. Arles: Lachenal & Ritter.

Péret, Benjamin. 1952. *Air mexicain.* Paris: Arcanes.

Rey, Jean-Michel. 1991. *La Naissance de la poésie: Antonin Artaud.* Paris: Métailié.

Thévinin, Paule, and Jacques Derrida. 1986. *Artaud, dessins et portraits.* Paris: Gallimard.

PART III

Colonial and Postcolonial Encounters

12. Immigration, Poster Art, and Transgressive Citizenship

France, 1968–1988

Will we still be French thirty years from now?
— *Le Figaro-Magazine*, October 26, 1985

The minorities, who have marginalized
themselves . . .
— An eminent Sorbonne professor at an elite U.S.
institution, April 4, 1993

The French Senate voted today to approve a bill that
gives the police wide-ranging powers to make spot
identity checks as part of a Government crackdown
on illegal immigration. The bill created an uproar
when it was first presented last month because it
specified that any other criteria than race could be
used by the police. The amended text, passed by a
vote of 228 votes to 88, will allow the police to ask
anyone to present identity papers.
— Paris, July 10, Reuters, as reported by
New York Times, July 11, 1993

The student revolts of 1968 sparked grass-roots movements of solidarity and resistance in which the poster was used as a powerful vehicle for spontaneous and organized communication. It appeared on the walls of all the major cities with the initial purpose of galvanizing workers and students. In the 1980s, the poster became a catalyst in the fight against racism. It was used to mobilize public opinion and served as an instrument of information about new laws and the rights of citizens. It spurred debate about the nature of

French society and the place of culturalist ideologies within a tradition rooted in the concept of universal rights.

Posters generally combine stylized visual messages with short, provocative statements. They mirror the conflicts simmering within popular culture and trace the evolution of *mentalités*. My purpose in this essay is to look at the discursive universe that emerges from a series of posters assembled in 1989 by Mehdi Lallaoui and the Association Black Blanc Beur in the book *20 ans d'affiches antiracistes*. This collection colorfully foregrounds the social and cultural anxieties related to historically unresolved issues of identity in France. These posters are a symptom of the acute discomfort that occurs cyclically at important junctures of French history, especially when a sense of loss pervades the national imagination. The 1980s and 1990s have been a period during which the presence of large numbers of visibly "different" immigrants from the Francophone areas of Africa has both threatened and reinforced the idea of Frenchness painstakingly constructed since the Revolution.

France's experience during the last decades of the twentieth century is not an isolated phenomenon. Most industrialized countries have had to face similar crises of identity following the influx of large groups of migrants from the poorer areas of the world. This migration has sparked heated public discussions about the nature of citizenship in a multicultural world, the rights of individuals to cross borders seeking political asylum or economic advantages, and the role of history and continuity, race and culture in the definition of a nation. At the heart of these concerns is the question posed by the title of an article in a 1993 issue of *L'Evénement du Jeudi:* "Le droit à l'immigration est-il un droit de l'homme?" (Is the right to immigrate a human right?) (1993:11–12)

France has always prided itself on being a *terre d'accueil,* a land of freedom and human rights. Since the Revolution, however, the ability of French citizens to welcome or simply accept the arrival of large groups of foreigners—let alone tolerate their own regional minorities—has been severely tested during three specific periods of crisis. Historian Gérard Noiriel has pointed out that contemporary debates need to be understood within the context of similar events that occurred during the 1880s and the 1930s. These two periods of intense and massive immigration from Italy, Portugal, Belgium, and Poland provoked crises similar to those of the 1970s and 1980s, resulting in virulent attacks on foreigners and their children. There were incidents against Belgian mine workers in the Pas-de-Calais in 1892 and against Italians working in the salt mines in Aigues-Mortes in 1893. In the

1920s, Spanish miners were attacked by striking French workers in the North, whereas in Valence, striking Armenians were singled out by French union organizers. In Lyons in 1934, an argument between Moroccan and French workers ended in the death of a Moroccan, and in 1938 a Polish foreman was killed by striking workers (see Noiriel, 1988:247–94). During the "été meurtrier" of 1973, more than a hundred Algerian workers were assassinated, prompting the Algerian government to halt emigration temporarily. Some ten years later, in 1983, 1984, and 1986, several Maghrebian adolescents became casualties in the racist wars against the children of immigrants. Whereas the 1890s were marked by the Dreyfus affair and the 1930s by the rise of fascism, the 1980s will be remembered as the decade that witnessed the emergence of Jean-Marie Le Pen's National Front. The political and cultural history of modern France is thus inseparable from the immigration "problem," which has repeatedly been invoked as the source of grave economic, social, and cultural destabilization. The measures voted by the French Senate in July 1993 to give the police broad powers to engage in identity checks (as indicated in my third epigraph) appear to be the culmination of this history of right-wing contestation of the idea of *accueil* and the ideals of the Revolution.

In the three decades since the end of the Algerian war and the beginning of decolonization, the question of African (Maghrebian or sub-Saharan) immigration has been front-page news because of many criminal incidents and the cultural and political rhetoric accompanying them. The radicalization of popular culture since 1968 has helped to encourage resistance to the historical recurrence of xenophobia and the political agenda of the Right. Just as Emile Zola, who was the son of an Italian immigrant, spearheaded the campaign against anti-Semitism in support of Colonel Alfred Dreyfus, publishing his famous manifesto *J'accuse* in 1898, many intellectuals in the 1960s joined forces to support the rights of minorities and immigrant workers to enjoy decent working and living conditions and equal justice.

The book 20 *ans d'affiches antiracistes*, published to commemorate the bicentennial of the Revolution, reproduces 300 posters from more than 40 French cities. It presents a collective visual history of contemporary struggle against the exploitation of immigrants and racist attacks on their French-born children. As Lallaoui puts it in the blurb on the back cover, "We intend this work to be a reminder of the events that have occurred around immigration for the past twenty years." But the book also bears witness to a material practice — the sometimes subversive, always informative, act of *affichage*. This act of posting notices on the walls of cities creates a social space that is inscribed with multiple meanings. Within this space oppositional consciousness can begin to be created and the voices of new social actors be heard. The space can thus become multivocal and relational, showing how new imaginary relations of identification and new articulatory practices are produced. The poster is a repository of popular memory, and at its best, it creates a dialogical moment in which new definitions of community, new configurations of "Frenchness" can begin to be glimpsed. But it is also a space that reveals *how* oppositional discourses are recuperated by the ideology of integration and citizenship, by a benign form of multiculturalism that insists on consensus and the celebration of differences with no room for the productive tensions caused by contestation and conflict. It is significant that many of the posters chosen were produced by associations and organizations financed by institutional monies (be it the Communist Party, labor unions such as the CFDT, the Comité de Liaison Anti-Racisme, or France-Ethnicolor, an organization sponsored by the Fondation Danielle Mitterand, wife of the president). The posters thus trace the evolution of public opinion as well as the ways in which this evolution is influenced by political and civic organizations.

Lallaoui's book is particularly interesting because it reveals with candor and clarity the paradoxes at the heart of "official" discourses about volatile issues such as racism and immigration. Although the intention of these social and political organizations is to fight virulent forms of prejudice, the images they endorse suggest various forms of ideological containment. This is not surprising because posters are a medium for propaganda and proselytism. To reach its target audience (the "average" French citizen, whose drives and perceptions are rooted in the "white" collective unconscious perceptively defined by Frantz Fanon in *Black Skin, White Masks*), the iconography of the poster has to speak a language that can be immediately recognized, interpellating the viewer with elements of a dominant ideology that it nonetheless tries to destabilize. While proclaiming the value of difference, many of the images actually contain difference within parameters that are safe and familiar for the "average" citizen. It is as though an illusion of consensus can be produced by reassuring the public that diversity is an easily embraced project. This suggests the disturbing ways in which the idea of diversity — which could not become a reality without profound and irreversible social changes — can be diluted down to a trite and simplistic celebratory message full of good intentions but naively blind to the ideological underpinnings of representation.

Arranged in chronological order in the book, the posters of the 1960s and

FIGURE 1. "A bas le racisme!" (Down with racism). Silkscreen. Marseilles, 1969.

early 1970s are heavily influenced by the French Communist Party's (PCF) ideology of worker solidarity. The message is simple and direct. The aim is to include all nationalities, in the spirit of the *Internationale:* one 1968 poster bears the inscription "Equal work for equal pay" (Lallaoui 1989:10) in six other languages: Italian, Spanish, Portuguese, Greek, Turkish, and Arabic. During that period, the enemy of the worker is clearly defined. He is a caricature of the *patron* drawn in the style of the *Pieds nickelés* comics, cigar-smoking, rapacious, and greedy, but not invincible. The bilingual text (French and Arabic) of a 1969 example, in bold red letters on a simple white background, frames the drawing of a handshake, one hand white and the other dark, squeezing the body of the discomfited boss who is forced to let go of his ill-earned profits. The alliance between African and French workers is promoted as the most effective means of jeopardizing the boss's status and bringing about the revolution (p. 11, Fig. 1). Other well-defined enemies are the *flic* and the *préfet,* both represented as lackeys of the oppressive capitalist French state personified by an enormous rooster, the *coq gaulois,* whose claws are enslaving and destroying the worker and his family (p. 12, Fig. 2). These images seem to carry the legacy of the 1930s. Many of the posters in that genre were sponsored by the daily *L'Humanité,* the news organ of the

FIGURE 2. The French state personified as *le coq gaulois*. Silkscreen. Marseilles, 1969.

PCF. They establish a binary framework, encouraging and universalizing class struggle in authentic communist style. The workers represented are exclusively male; brotherhood, peace, and equality are promoted within a traditional framework tied to workers' demands. Class identity is the only form of belonging that is recognized, and the claim of the PCF to speak for a large constituency of workers remains unchallenged. One does not hear the voices of immigrants in these texts. The captions address them and attempt to enlist and organize them using an authoritarian political rhetoric that emphasizes economic struggle and unity of purpose, often bordering on paternalism.

On July 1, 1972, a strong new law against racism took effect (see Lallaoui 1989:14). It paved the way for organized campaigns against all forms of hate speech and discrimination in the workplace or in real estate practices. It also provided a legal framework for dissolving racist organizations. Around the same time, the oppositional rhetoric of the Left began to change, moving toward espousing the democratic rights of workers of all races and against arbitrary expulsions of foreigners or enforced isolation of workers in substandard hospices. "Identical rights for the French and the immigrants," proclaimed several posters of the mid-1970s in support of the demands of immigrants striking "for open, decent, and affordable housing" (pp. 20, 21). The "enemy" is no longer a clear-cut figure but an abstract social and cultural problem: "Racism divides, racism distracts, racism kills," the slogan now says (p. 15, Fig. 3). Human dignity, living conditions, and the right to education and cultural specificity increasingly have become the nodes around which narratives of integration are constructed. The language of liberation and revolution has been released from its class-based European origins. Greater awareness of the Third World, its presence at home, and the nature of its problems has displaced the moral and political dilemmas of the Left toward more ambiguously defined areas: questions of identity, equality, and citizenship. "The rights of man are indivisible: All have the right to live with their family" (p. 39) is the leitmotif of several well-organized campaigns aimed at educating both the French public and the new immigrants.

Some posters are addressed specifically to the good French citizen, appealing to rational and altruistic motives in the face of continued harassment by racist extremists: "Next to you, foreign workers want to learn. With them, let's fight ignorance," one poster by the Liaison Committee for Literacy urges (p. 16, Fig. 4). The drawing of two outstretched white hands supporting a smaller, darker hand that holds a pen while attempting to write the ABC's suggests a "father knows best" attitude on the part of the support organization. The hierarchical framework appeals to an ethics of responsibility that promotes literacy as a means to full citizenship under the law. This poster also constructs the "foreigner" as an infantile figure within the social sphere: smaller, ignorant, in need of guidance. The goal is inclusiveness based on shared cultural values that can be acquired through education and whose importance, in a process of peaceful integration, is stressed as a fundamental principle of democratic republicanism. Yet the ideology of colonialism surfaces in the imaginary register of the appeal: the white man still bears the burden to provide for those less fortunate, less civilized. This poster is an excellent example of postcolonial paternalism and of its survival to this day in the language of some French educators such as the one I quoted in my second epigraph at the beginning of the chapter.

The year 1973 marked another turning point. The outbreaks of murderous violence against Algerians galvanized the immigrant community into creating its own Committee of Algerian Workers. A sense of communal identity began to develop as a means of self-defense. Equal rights for all as well as

FIGURE 3. "Le racisme divise / le racisme fait diversion / le racisme tue" (Racism divides / racism distracts / racism kills). Paris, 1973.

PRÈS DE VOUS DES TRAVAILLEURS ÉTRANGERS
VEULENT S'INSTRUIRE
AVEC EUX
COMBATTONS
L'IGNORANCE
abc

vous pouvez être moniteur
adressez-vous:

FIGURE 4. "Combattons l'ignorance" (Let's fight ignorance). Silkscreen. Paris, 1973.

respect for cultural differences were stressed. On a simple white background, a large black coffin with the white crescent of Islam bears the caption: "Don't let them bury our freedoms" (p. 18, Fig. 5). It is the first appearance of an allusion to Islam as part of the imagery of contestation. No direct verbal reference to Islamic groups was made, but four years later, in 1977, in Compiègne, a meeting was announced about "Islam within immigration" (p. 31). The poster is trilingual—French, Arabic, and Portuguese—suggesting that the meeting was aimed at a large constituency of workers from Africa, the Maghreb, and Portugal. Religious differences began to be recognized in the public sphere, but at the same time, the right-wing government in power between 1974 and 1981 took extreme measures to enforce expulsions in the face of growing public concern about the limits of peaceful coexistence.

FIGURE 5. "Ne laissons pas enterrer nos libertés" (Don't let them bury our freedoms). Nationwide, 1973.

FIGURE 6. "Vers une société multiculturelle" (Toward a multicultural society). Paris, 1978.

Acculturation and assimilation were called into question by people on both sides of the issue, conservatives and immigrant families who desperately wanted to hold on to what Dominique Schnapper has called "the 'hard core' of their culture" (1992:126) for fear that their children would forget their identity.

To counter this polarization, multiculturalism was encouraged. In 1978, the first defense of multiculturalism appeared on the walls of Paris: "It is possible to live together. Down with racism, let's cultivate our differences" (Lallaoui 1989:33, Fig. 6), proclaims a yellow, purple, and pink drawing of a diverse group of bright-eyed and smiling adults and children, all colored in deep pink. The tone has become hopeful, optimistic, almost utopian. Despite the reference to racism, diversity in this image is not racially coded. What is stressed is diversity of interests, professional or otherwise. One man wears a miner's helmet, another carries a guitar, yet another looks like a busi-

FIGURE 7. "Journées des différences" (Celebration of differences). Cannes-Écluses, 1983.

ÉCOLE SUPÉRIEURE
DES INSPECTEURS DE LA POLICE NATIONALE
CANNES-ÉCLUSE (Seine-et-Marne)

JOURNÉES DES DIFFÉRENCES

23 et 24 avril 1983 de 15 à 19 heures

exposition artistique · peintures -- sculptures -- photographies
présentée par l'Association des Artistes Originaires de l'Immigration (A.A.O.I.)

nessman with a folded newspaper in his hand. A mother carries a baby, and a young girl with a doll in her hand is standing in front of the woman; a young boy is playing with a hoop. Traditional gender roles are unquestioned, revealing the enormous gap between the representation of women in this popular medium and the dynamic feminist movement of the 1970s that was reaching only a small percentage of highly educated middle-class women, bypassing the rest of the population. Thus in 1976, a black-and-white poster announces: "Algerian women in the struggle" (p. 21), but the line drawings of female figures represent them as faceless, wearing the chador, and covered from head to toe. Concession is made to the traditional appearance of women within Islam, despite the contradictions embedded in the caption.

Several "festivals" were organized during the late 1970s. An atmosphere of carnival pervaded many of these events and the posters that announced them: "Arab music, songs, and poetry" (p. 34), "French-immigrant get-

FIGURE 8. "Gagnons ensemble" (Let's win together). Nationwide, 1984.

together" (p. 36), "Fourth festival of immigrant workers" (p. 43), "Day of black peoples" (p. 49), "Festival of unity" (p. 52), "Intercultural childfest" (p. 65), and "Cultural encounters" (p. 86). Some of these posters from the late 1970s and early 1980s are attractive, colorful, with great eye appeal. Multiculturalism as a form of spectacle suddenly gained visibility within the public sphere, becoming a productive category, affirmative and celebratory, and the word "differences" began to appear regularly after 1983 (pp. 71, 80, 82; Figs. 7, 8, 9, respectively). But in 1984, an astonishing poster was published by the secretary of state for immigration. The caption reads: "Living together: the immigrants in our midst," and the black-and-white drawing of the interior of a subway car shows eight people standing around a single metal pillar, holding on as the train moves. The immediate impression is one of overcrowding, belied by the happy smiles on everybody's face. Each of the passengers represents a racial stereotype. The man in the felt hat has a

FIGURE 9. "Vivons ensemble avec nos différences" (Let's live together with our differences). Sticker. Nice, 1984.

hooked nose, the two blacks have exaggerated simian features, the Asian man has buckteeth, the Arab wears a djellabah, another Mediterranean type has curly hair and a thin black mustache, and the remaining two are white. They have no "distinctive" cultural or racial characteristics (p. 78, Fig. 10). This poster, Mehdi Lallaoui is compelled to explain, "was barely distributed." A government representation of the "other" clearly intended as "humorous," this poster merely succeeds in creating a grotesque counterpart to the playfully stylized messages of Figures 8 and 9. It is a racist caricature that exemplifies the "official" presupposition that there is such a thing as a degree zero of representation, a French or white norm from which all others depart. Distance from this norm produces phenotypical "difference," and whiteness is the implied universal standard. Under the guise of encouraging peaceful cohabitation, this poster reproduces and reinforces all the tenets of nineteenth-century racial science.

The Socialists were in power between 1981 and 1986, and several mea-

Vivre ensemble: les immigrés parmi nous

Secrétariat d'État chargé des immigrés

FIGURE 10. "Vivre ensemble: les immigrés parmi nous" (Living together: the immigrants in our midst). Secretary of state for immigration, 1984.

sures favorable to immigrants were passed, including a moratorium encouraging clandestine or illegal immigrants to come forward and regularize their situation. Yet the political unconscious of French politicians was still mired in blatant ethnocentrism. The stereotypes in Figure 10 fix meaning and reinforce the proverbial *idées reçues* of racial ideology and the anthropological fictions that serve to consolidate the French subject in opposition to his or her exotic colonial other. By contrast, the staging of the "other" in Figures 8 and 9 generates a carnivalesque body, masked, multiple, unstable, and capable of disarticulating the logic of institutional racism. The indeterminate, inclusionary identity that emerges from the collage or bricolage of Figure 9 in particular is a powerful reminder of the ideological contradictions simmering during the 1980s.

In their study of carnival as political discourse, Peter Stallybrass and Allon White have shown how cultural hierarchies that are fundamental to the mechanisms of ordering in European culture are played out in representations of the human body. They argue that in "domains of transgression . . . place, body, group identity and subjectivity interconnect" (25). The face in Figure 9 is such a transgressive site where the logic of identity formation according to the hegemonic discourse present in the drawings of Figure 10 is turned upside down. The message here is that the other and the self clearly share a space and an intersubjective realm in which hair, eye, and skin color are secondary to the ability to engage in another form of identification: that which is mediated by the geographical space of France, allegorized in the shape of the earring hanging from the left ear of this composite model with a female face. This image is echoed by another colorful poster from 1987, "Ethnicolor festival: Plural culture week" (p. 115, Fig. 11), in which the computer photograph of a black face multiplied six times has been superimposed with purple, red, yellow, white, and green paint suggesting ritual masks. Among the faces are green and orange drawings of palm leaves and a stylized Eiffel Tower. The Eiffel Tower functions here the way the earring in the shape of the hexagon does in the previous image as a mediating sign, a focus of solidarity and the symbol of shared citizenship. The idea of "Frenchness" implied by the Tower is transgressed by the black faces while consolidating the ideals of democratic participation and cohesion. In other words, this "Ethnicolorfest" suggests the energies and potentialities of almost unlimited cultural and social transformation. The human face, reproduced so as to be identical yet different from itself, is the prototype of a new society, a new nation, apparently widening the options for all citizens while simultaneously reaffirming traditional symbolism and stable hierarchies. Indeed the Tower is inscribed on the whitewashed face in the middle. As Stallybrass and White point out, "The underlying structural features of carnival operate far beyond the strict confines of popular festivity and are intrinsic to the dialectics of social classification. . . . Transgressions and the attempt to control them obsessively return to somatic symbols, for these are the ultimate elements of social classification itself" (1986:26). In other words, the heterogeneous symbolic material of the collective imaginary (the suggestiveness and foreignness of exotic and primitive masks) is first reinforced by the multiplicity of faces and their racial difference, but then this difference is subverted as racial categories, having been recognized, are put under erasure by a process that succeeds in achieving the categorical self-identity of the French citizen as first and foremost "French," yet retaining traces of an archaic, vaguely menacing tribal identity. This classification thus does not question, let alone undo, the validity and legitimacy of a very traditional symbolic system belonging to Fanon's "white" unconscious and anchored in a national site or monument, namely the Eiffel Tower. Moreover, the Tower as a symbol of technical know-how, development, and progress is set in opposition to the "jungle fever" connoted by the masked faces, implying a teleological historical

FIGURE 11. "Festival ethnicolor: Semaine culture plurielle" (Ethnicolor festival: Plural culture week). Paris, 1987.

development from tribal to "modern" republican identity, thus reinforcing simplistic oppositions between tradition and modernity.

During the mid- to late 1980s, many posters used the children of immigrants to represent the new faces of French youth. Along with Harlem Désir's powerful lobby SOS Racisme, these images served to remind the old-style nationalist forces that lily-white Catholic France was but one facet of a society rapidly undergoing profound but irreversible changes. The cultural debates increasingly turned on the ability of the state to "reconcile individual freedom and full possession of the rights of citizenship with the right of minorities to enjoy their own cultural identity" (Giraud and Santamaria 1991: 8). These anxieties were replayed throughout the major crises of French history during the modern period. Indeed, the 1993 bill passed by the French Senate indicates that in the present conjuncture, the answer to the question posed in the *Evénement du Jeudi* article is, for a majority of French nationals — of whatever background — that immigration is not to be considered a fundamental human right.

This concern echoes and predates many heated debates about immigration in other European countries. The presence of large groups of foreigners as well as regional minorities has been an integral part of French exceptionalism since the Revolution; more than ever the question now revolves around the relationship of cultural specificity to national identity. Attention is continually focused on the need for successful integration of immigrants from the south and on the relationship between their everyday practices, their individual identity, and the ideals of citizenship.

The events of the 1970s and 1980s and the popular visual and discursive commentaries I have briefly discussed reveal the ambiguities that currently surround the ideals of republicanism and the contested terrain it shares with multicultural objectives. In France, as Dominique Schnapper has stated, "Multiculturalism in private life and the social realm is a reality, a democratic ideal, and a right. But political multiculturalism — in other words, the juridical recognition of this right in the public sphere, whether in the schools or other aspects of political life — cannot be inferred logically or politically from the de facto multiculturalism of the social realm" (1992:183). This position presupposes an unexamined separation between public and private identities. In this view, political rights can be seen as independent of the private dimensions of our political unconscious, an attitude that can arguably be described as naively similar to the one that subtends the institutional production of the posters. Public opinion in Europe and in the United States tends to subscribe to this view, and a theoretical consensus seems to be developing around the idea that the political rights of all immigrants, once installed in their new social space, are to be respected.

During the 1980s, the aim has been, as Didier Lapeyronnie (echoing Schnapper) puts it, to "link the demand for cultural specificity to the idea of a political integration rooted in republican universalism" (1991:44). Does this mean that the social and ethnic "difference" of minorities, that is, their freedom to practice their religion and their right to fashion a private cultural identity based on their collective historical memory, should not be in conflict with their right to full citizenship under French law? The cultural evolution traced by social scientists points in that direction. But it is also clear that some "private" cultural practices (such as the wearing of the scarf by Islamic young women or female genital excision of the children of Malian immigrants—see Fourny 1991, and Lionnet 1992, respectively) come into conflict with the public realities of republicanism and the ideology of freedom and equality it is supposed to uphold. The images in *20 ans d'affiches antiracistes* underscore these contradictions and the possibilities as well as the responsibilities that constitute any multicultural society worthy of the name.

The question will thus remain of the legitimacy of the distinction that social scientists like to draw between the "private," the "social," and the "political." Does the political reality of the 1993 bill guarantee that "social" multiculturalism will continue to flourish within the confines of the law? Shouldn't we rather worry that this bill is a harbinger of greater curbs on the private and social freedoms of French citizens whose outward appearance does not correspond to familiar stereotypes of Frenchness? The "fête" of the 1980s with its transgressive potential is clearly over, contained by the normative ideals of democratic solidarity that construct the citizen in opposition to a "foreigner" or an "enemy" whose presence threatens the social order (see Alexander 1992).

This enemy, it seems to me, is already implicit in the "Ethnicolor" poster, lurking through the jungle foliage, eyes averted but features disciplined by the white mask. This face is threatening: it suggests that beneath a thin veneer of "Frenchness" an exotic, archaic, and untamed presence might suddenly take over. The poster thus plays dangerously on French citizens' unconscious fear of the irrational and the primitive in its attempt to be open and inclusive. It sadly predicts the turn to the Right that began in the 1990s, prefiguring the demonization of the "other" that the 1993 law enforces.

WORKS CITED

Alexander, Jeffrey C. 1992. "Citizen and Enemy as Symbolic Classification: On the Polarizing Discourse of Civil Society." In Michèle Lamont and Marcel Tournier, eds., *Cultivating Differences: Symbolic Boundaries and the Making of Inequality*, Chicago: University of Chicago Press.

L'Evénement du Jeudi 451, June 24–30, 1993.

Fanon, Frantz. 1967. *Black Skin, White Masks*. Trans. Charles Lam Markmann. New York: Grove Press.

Fourny, Jean-François. 1991. "Introduction: La Paille et le grain." *Contemporary French Civilization* 15 (Summer–Fall): 167–84.

Giraud, Michel, and Ulysses Santamaria. 1991. "*La démocratie politique en Europe et les minorités ethniques.*" *Les Temps modernes* 540–41 (July–August): 4–9.

Lallaoui, Mehdi. 1989. *20 ans d'affiches antiracistes*. Paris: Association Black Blanc Beur.

Lapeyronnie, Didier. 1991. "La France et la Grande Bretagne face à leurs minorités ethniques." *Les Temps modernes* 540–41 (July–August): 10–45.

Lionnet, Françoise. 1992. "Identity, Sexuality, and Criminality: 'Universal Rights' and the Debate Around the Practice of Female Excision in France." *Contemporary French Civilization* 16 (Summer–Fall): 294–307.

Noiriel, Gérard. 1988. *Le Creuset français: Histoire de l'immigration: XIXe–XXe siècle*. Paris: Seuil.

Schnapper, Dominique. 1992. *L'Europe des immigrés*. Paris: Ed. François Bourin.

Stallybrass, Peter, and Allon White. 1986. *The Politics and Poetics of Transgression*. Ithaca: Cornell University Press.

13. Michelle Cliff's No Telephone to Heaven

Diasporic Displacement and the Feminization of the Landscape

But my island is a pebble. . . . Seeds will not take
root on its cool surface. It is a duck's back of water.
A knife will not snap it open. It will slay giants but
never bear children.   — Edward Brathwaite

Migration is a one way trip. There is no "home" to
go back to. There never was.   — Stuart Hall

The fictional narratives of writers of African descent allow us to study the
ways that diasporic subjectivities challenge modernist categories of nationality as a basis for identity. Novels by African diasporic authors such as
Michelle Cliff, Chester Himes, and Paule Marshall participate in the destabilization of such modernist binaries as home/not-home, homeland/
adopted land. Modernist visions of the homeland as a fecund, nurturing
mother, as the site for resolution of a fragmented diasporic subjectivity
into the full self, are deconstructed by feminist postcolonial narratives like
Michelle Cliff's second novel, *No Telephone to Heaven*. R. Radhakrishnan
states that "in our times, whether we like it or not, the dominant paradigm
of identity has been 'the imagined community' of nationalism" (1993:752).
The following analysis of *No Telephone to Heaven* suggests, however, that
nationality as a means to describe identity reflects a modernist agenda that is
called into question by diasporic narratives existing in a postmodern world
marked by the transnational flows of people and capital.

The protagonist of *No Telephone to Heaven* is Clare Savage, a light-
skinned, upper-middle-class Jamaican who struggles with her multiple na-

tional and racial identifications. Clare immigrates to the United States and subsequently to London but also struggles with her longing for her Jamaican birthplace, tracing a path Cliff has described as "her movement toward homeland and wholeness," "this landscape of her identity" (1990:265), Cliff's novel ultimately questions notions of wholeness and complicates the ways in which the nation and subsequently the landscape (terms not always coextensive) can generate subjectivity or be equated with the main character's identity. As a young girl, Clare is left in the United States with her near-white father, "abandoned" (as she sees it) by her darker mother and sister, who return to Jamaica, the narrative implying that the lighter-skinned father and daughter are better suited to the demands of assimilation made by U.S. institutions. Her mother, disgusted with U.S. racism and ill at ease in the urban northeast, chooses the darker daughter, "the one who favored her," and returns to Jamaica (Cliff 1987:84). The loss of her mother and of Jamaica profoundly shapes Clare's sense of self. When news of her mother's death reaches Clare and her father in the United States, Cliff writes, "She woke at twenty to find herself a motherless child — plainly" (p. 104). My analysis will show that this condition of being a motherless child and the analogous one of being a childless woman are important metaphors structuring Cliff's complex and provocative narrative. Throughout the novel the island of Jamaica stands for both mother and motherlessness, ultimately resisting a stable symbolic role as womb or home.

Clare's transatlantic movements describe a particular postcolonial diaspora. When she immigrates to the former colonial metropolis, London, to begin a study of European art history, the narrator describes her as "student of the motherland. Motherless" (p. 88). The choice of London was made "with the logic of a creole. This was the mother-country" (p. 109). Clare's postcolonial hybridity here is expressed in national terms: as a privileged Jamaican schoolchild her education has been steeped in the culture of the colonizer, Britain. Her early adult trajectory is to delve deeper into this dominant discourse as represented by "European art history." These oceanic crossings from Jamaica, to the United States, to London constitute part of Clare's postcolonial position and that of the New World itself, which Stuart Hall characterizes as "the place of many continuous displacements: of the original pre-Columbian inhabitants, the Arawaks, Caribs and Amerindians, permanently displaced from their homelands and decimated . . . the displacements of slavery, colonisation and conquest." As a young Jamaican woman, Clare is displaced from both land and self-image. Hall continues, "[The New World] stands for the endless ways in which Caribbean people have been destined to 'migrate'; it is the signifier of migration itself — of traveling, voyaging and return as fate, as destiny; of the Antillean as the prototype of the modern or postmodern New World nomad, continually moving between centre and periphery. (1990:234)

Clare's nomadism is a shuttling between national locations that forces her to confront the racial *métissage* of her own genealogy. Travel to the "centre" brings her into contact with members of other diasporas, immigrants from across "the Empire." Upon her arrival in London, "she was not prepared for the dark women in saris cleaning the toilets at Heathrow. She tried to put them out of her mind" (Cliff 1987:109). Though part of Clare identifies with these women as displaced subjects of empire, the lightness of her skin exempts her from being racially identified with them. When she applies for legal resident status the clerk assures her, "'Then again, you're not at all like our Jamaicans, are you'" (p. 117). Continually faced with such exemptions, Clare is less and less willing to accept the superficial comfort they may afford her. On complaining to a schoolmate about the racist proclamations of a National Front demonstration she is told, "'But you needn't take it personally, you know. . . . I mean, you're hardly the sort they were ranting on about.'" Clare responds, reflecting her growing political awareness: "'That doesn't make it at all better. . . . Besides, I can never be sure about that . . . and I'm not sure I should want . . . ah, exclusion'" (p. 139). While in graduate school in London, Clare travels back to Jamaica on school holidays, staying with her aunt and uncle and spending time with her friend Harry/Harriet. Harry/Harriet, the son of an upper-class Jamaican and his maid, increases Clare's awareness of the class stratifications on their island, the ways in which neocolonial elites (potentially like herself) maintain the structures of colonialism that oppress most of the island's population.

For Clare, who is born into upper-middle-class Jamaican society, spends her teenage years in the United States and early adult life in Britain, to name her identity in national terms requires negotiating the various nationalities that claim *and* exclude her. Clare's time in Europe is marked by her increased self-identification as Jamaican, by her growing association of Jamaica as her homeland as well as her mother's land. She rejects the colonial "motherland" as a "borrowed country" and turns instead toward the country of her mother and grandmother. Clare is not only nationally hybrid but also of mixed race and class — her father's ancestors were slave owners. For Clare the choice of her mother and grandmother over her father is a political one, a choice of the nation as island and landscape, not the nation-state of Jamaica as controlled by neocolonial elites.

In describing her own hybrid identity as "a writer of Afro-Caribbean (Indian, African, and white) experience and heritage and Western experience and education (indoctrination)," Cliff has written that "underneath it all, [is] the granddaughter of Sycorax, precolonial female, landscape, I(s)land: I land" (1991:40). This reference to *The Tempest* is a particularly telling convergence of terms, revising New World "discovery" myths and giving the "precolonial female" ownership of and identification with the geography of Jamaica. She performs Columbus's journey: "I land," and claims her rightful possession, as Sycorax, not Prospero, was the rightful, original possessor of Caliban's island. In act 1, scene 2 of *The Tempest*, Caliban tells Prospero, "This island's mine by Sycorax my mother, / which thou tak'st from me" (Shakespeare 1964:54). In both Shakespeare's and Cliff's figurations, ownership of the land as nation is based on matrilineal descent. The title of Cliff's article in which this passage appears, "Caliban's Daughter: The Tempest and the Teapot," points to a dichotomy Cliff speaks about often: wildness and civilization. She has said that her own colonial education (the teapot) attempted to civilize wildness out of her. In this article she states, "My wildness had been tamed, what had been defined as wildness: a wildness that embraced imagination, emotion, spontaneity, history, memory, revolution, flights of fancy, the forest. Flesh was replaced by air, Caliban by Ariel" (p. 39). And yet this wildness, this identification with the landscape and forest remains, and it wars with colonial indoctrination until, like a tempest in a teapot, the postcolonial female is ready to explode. This pressure on the self, the boiling point Clare reaches, can be better understood in light of recent feminist and African diasporic identity theories. Teresa de Lauretis writes that "self and identity . . . are always grasped and understood within particular discursive configurations. Consciousness, therefore is never fixed, never attained once and for all, because discursive boundaries change with historical conditions" (1986:8). Clare's encounters in London clearly reveal to her the linguistic basis of shifts in her racial and national identities. Because of her light skin, in verbal encounters with "white" people, her identity is coded as nonblack. Stuart Hall emphasizes the discursive nature particularly of racial identification: "'Black' . . . has always been an unstable identity, psychically, culturally and politically. It, too, is a narrative, a story, a history. Something constructed, told, spoken, not simply formed" (1987:45). Steeped as she is in the modernist agendas of the colonizer, Clare at first seeks a resolution to her "multiple, shifting, and often self-contradictory identity" via what is termed a racial/political *choice* (de Lauretis 1986:9). She is uncomfortable with multiple subjectivity.

Because Clare's father, Boy Savage, is extremely light-complected and makes every attempt to pass for white when the family emigrates to the United States and also because he emphasizes the importance of European education, he represents the colonial "civilizing" process, the life in captivity against which Clare eventually rebels. In Clare's eyes, her mother and the Jamaican natural landscape represent wildness; staying in the United States with her father she has felt like a wild thing held captive. Cliff suggests that her father's indoctrination has bleached the past from Clare's mind "just as the rapes of her grandmothers bleached her skin" (1991:45). Boy Savage's insistence on his own and Clare's whiteness is based on the erasure of histories of rape and oppression throughout his family line.[1] He denies the "fundamentally relational nature" of his own hybrid identity and enforces "the negations on which the assumption of a singular, fixed, and essential self is based" (Martin and Mohanty 1986:196). In America, "Boy had no visible problem with declaring himself white. It was a practical matter, he told his wife. There was no one to say different. . . . He told people he was descended from plantation owners — and this was true. Partly. With each fiction his new self became more complete" (Cliff 1987:62). In underscoring the scripted nature of race identification, Cliff calls to mind Françoise Lionnet, who reminds us that racial categories are only semantically constructed and locally significant: "In the absence of scientific experiential grounding, it is language that conditions our concept of race. . . . The boundaries of that concept change according to cultural, social, and linguistic realities" (1989:12). Though the narrative repeatedly points to this semantic construction, it does not deny the *material* power of such constructions to enforce economic and physical oppression. For example, Boy's ability to manipulate these linguistic codes barely enables him to protect his immigrant family from a southern U.S. motel proprietor who is also a Ku Klux Klan member. The edifice of Boy's whiteness is built on denial and the partial fictions he substitutes for his actual life histories. "Through all of this — this new life — he counsels his daughter on invisibility and secrets. Self-effacement. Blending in. The uses of camouflage" (p. 100).

Kitty Savage, Clare's darker mother, who returns to Jamaica, soon becomes identified in Clare's mind with the landscape of the island itself. As an immigrant to the United States, Kitty "didn't hold to metamorphosis and felt but homeless" (p. 54). Kitty seeks out "shops from *home*" in the Bedford-Stuyvesant section of Brooklyn, indulging her bittersweet homesickness among the sensual memories of food from Jamaica: "In these shops she broke her silence, here she felt most the loss of home, of voice, even as she brushed the loose dirt off the yam-skin, imagining its origin in the bush, stroked the rough green lips where the cho-cho split, stuck her finger in the sap where the mango had been joined to the tree, remembering how it could burn and raise a sore. Resisting a desire to rub the sharp stickiness into her nostrils and around her mouth" (p. 65). Here island produce, the fruits of the landscape, are figured in terms of female sexuality, strengthening the female gendering of the Jamaican natural geography promoted by the narrative. Later, after her mother's death, Clare studies Aristotle's *Physics*, analyzing the definition of *place*. Cliff writes, "Each thing exists in place. Each thing is described by place. Would this new knowledge have pleased her mother?" (p. 117). When Clare returns to Jamaica, relaxing by a river on her grandmother's property, "her mother's landscape," she thinks of her mother: "I was blessed to have her here. Her passion of place. Her sense of the people. Here is her; leave it at that" (p. 174). The mother's identification with place becomes literal and complete in Clare's mind. Cliff's novel thus enacts a remapping of the Jamaican landscape in feminized, perhaps nostalgically maternal terms. In an article titled "Decolonizing the Map: Post-Colonialism, Post-Structuralism and the Cartographic Connection" Graham Huggan argues that "the proliferation of spatial references," "the redisposition of geographic coordinates" in much postcolonial writing "stresses the provisionality of cartographic connection" in a "reaction against the ontology and epistemology of 'stability' promoted by colonial discourse" (1989:127). Clare's remapping, then, denies the colonial cartographic ordering of her father's side and reclaims the Jamaican landscape for Sycorax, the precolonial female, and for her mother (the inheritor, the rightful — original — possessor) who "'knew every bush . . . its danger and its cure. She should have stayed here. In America she was lost . . . the tree with the sweetest mango seemed her cherished goal . . . and she always managed to find it in deep bush'" (Cliff 1987:173).

Part I of *No Telephone to Heaven* is titled "Ruinate," defined by Cliff as a "distinctive Jamaican term . . . used to describe lands which were once cleared for agricultural purposes and have now lapsed back into . . . 'bush'" (p. 1). For Cliff, *ruinate, bush,* and *wildness* are equivalent terms to which she opposes the terms *civilization, colonialism,* and *cartography*. It is important to see, however, the slips in these binarisms. For example, ruinate and bush are controlled and ordered not only by colonizers but by the colonized as well. Clare's maternal grandmother, for instance, imposed her own order on the wildness of native vegetation as a gift to a Christian God. Paradoxically, this order becomes apparent to Clare only at the moment of its disap-

pearance: when Clare returns to reclaim her grandmother's land, the garden
is gone:

Her carefully planned flowers, a devotion of fifty years, a way, she said, of giving
something back to the Almighty . . . these flowers, chosen for color and texture
and how each would set off the next, revealing splendor and glory, her order, her
choices . . . had been haphazardly supplanted by wilder and brighter ones, exploding
disorder into her scheme. A wild design of color was spun through her garden and
across her grave, masking the stonecutter's spare testament to her devotion: SERVANT
OF GOD. A flame-of-the-forest sparked the disorder, as the heavy jasmine scented the
ruination. (p. 8)

Cliff's novel emphasizes the pre-Christian power of ruinate, of wild vegetation, as the garden here overwrites not only the grandmother's natural
scheme but her linguistic remains as well, the written discourse of her self-
identification, carved in stone. Her efforts to serve a Christian God by manipulating wild nature into order are baffled by the colorful plants that ob-
struct the language on her gravestone. This powerful natural profusion also
bears signs, which her mother can read, as we have seen her mother reading
the location of hidden mangoes. Edouard Glissant says of Caribbean literature, "Din is discourse" (1989:123). Thus ruinate itself is a site where meaning is inscribed in seeming chaos. Eventually Clare too learns to read history
in the landscape. J. Michael Dash expresses the view that "it is not the rational mind that restores the past, but that the past resides in material objects
that only release their hidden meanings when encountered imaginatively or
sensuously. Landscape in the imagination of New World writers functions in
the same way. In its uncharted profusion it translates the intricate and polysemic nature of collective experience[2] (Glissant 1989:xxxv). For Kitty Savage
in Bedford-Stuyvesant, the sensuous encounter with a Jamaican mango re-
leases her past to her consciousness and imagination.

It is important to emphasize, however, that Cliff's novel goes much further than providing an empowering remapping of the Jamaican landscape as
precolonial female. The novel reads Jamaican geography in terms of *post-*
colonial geopolitical realities and transnational power linkages, bearing out
Adrienne Rich's observation that "a place on the map is also a place in history" (1986:212). If the narrative only constructed an idyllic natural space —
one clearly marked also as maternal — then it would be nostalgically compli-
cit with a modernist aesthetic. We would see Clare as a woman who seeks to
escape her difficult postcolonial racial positionings in Britain by returning to
the womb, to a prelapsarian identity as her mother's blissful child. The power
of Cliff's novel lies in its refusal of simple nostalgia and modernist notions of

the homeland as site for the resolution of "fragmented" subjectivity, the restoration of the full individual. Part of what draws Clare back to Jamaica is the prodding of her friend Harry/Harriet, who writes to her in Europe, keeping her updated on the decay and despair of her island home. Harry/Harriet continually reminds Clare of her own belonging to Jamaica, as well as her accountability. The idea of responsibility or accountability has been split in Clare's upbringing. Her father's construction of home and family "was repressive space built on the surrendering of all responsibility" (Martin and Mohanty 1986:198). Her father purposely avoids driving past scenes of Jamaican poverty, whereas her mother stops to give people money. Clare's mother gives her a sense of responsibility toward "her own people," here implied to be darker, poorer members of Jamaica's population. One of Kitty's last letters to her daughter, then still in the United States, contains the postscript: "'I hope someday you make something of yourself, and someday help your people,'" which Clare reads as "A reminder, daughter — never forget who your people are. Your responsibilities lie beyond me, beyond yourself. There is a space between who you are and who you will become. Fill it" (Cliff 1987:103). Clare's lover in Europe, a Vietnam veteran named Bobby, ill from excessive exposure to Agent Orange, encourages her to see that her mother's people are her people, her mother's homeland her homeland (p. 152).

The pressure on Clare's need for self-identification becomes acute as she moves from passivity, from moving between racial identifications, toward agency and political strategy. Though Benedict Anderson reminds us that "'exile is the nursery of nationality,'" Clare's diasporic movement nurtures race identification as the dominant signifier of nationality (Anderson 1994: 315). In seeing her mother's people as her people, Clare aligns herself racially with darker-skinned Jamaican citizens. In a nation of mixed-race peoples, she is moving toward claiming her Jamaicanness, her home in Jamaica, as her blackness. Along this path, however, Clare is pressured by an either/or ultimatum, urging her to *choose*. She explains to Bobby, "'You know, there are people who look one way and think another, feel another. We can be very dangerous, to ourselves, to others. Got to quell one side, honey, so I was taught'" (Cliff 1987:152). At this point Clare feels pushed to settle, in some way, the shifting, hybrid elements of her self-construction. Harry/Harriet, a gay man who himself shifts between gender identifications by cross-dressing, warns Clare, "'The time will come for both of us to choose. For we will have to make the choice. Cast our lot. Cyaan [can't] live split. Not in this world'" (p. 131). Harry/Harriet, who by the novel's end calls him/herself only Harriet, again anchors discursive subjectivity in material conditions of oppression. When s/he says one can't live "split" in "this world," s/he alludes to homophobic oppression as the condition that erects boundaries around her/his own self-construction.

The potential for individual agency exists within a web of sociocultural rules constraining the various "choices" that may or may not be open to Clare. Can she be a legal resident of London? Can she pass for white? Can she even enroll in the appropriate grade in school? When Boy Savage takes Clare to enroll in a high school in New York, the principal informs them that all "foreign" students must start a year behind, despite Clare's proficiency in Latin and French, her skill in algebra and geometry, and her knowledge of Dickens, Shakespeare, and Milton. Pressing Boy to "admit" his blackness, the principal disbelieves his assertion that they are white. She calls them "white chocolate," saying, "'We have no room for lies in our system. No place for in-betweens'" (p. 99). It is very important, then, to see the cultural, social, political, and economic constraints that work against a naively or apolitically free-floating subjectivity. Though race may be discursively constructed, those discursive boundaries are overdetermined in each local situation. Their power, in fact, obviates *choice*. That is, despite what Harry/Harriet says, it is not simply (or only) that Clare must *choose*. In the high school, before the National Front, and other places, the choice was made before she entered the scene. "The system" (in the form of institutionalized racism) has codified its rules and thus circumscribed the choices available to Clare. Clare's *political consciousness* of blackness, however, creates her as a subject who "has agency (rather than 'choice'), the capacity for movement or self-determined (dis)location, and hence social *accountability*" (de Lauretis 1990:137; emphasis added). As Clare's political consciousness develops, her sense of accountability, first instilled by her mother, strengthens. Warning of the terrible conditions in Jamaica, Harry/Harriet writes to Clare, "'Come home. . . . Come back to us once your studies are finished. Could help bring us into the present. . . . Jamaica's children have to work to make her change. It will be worthwhile . . . believe me" (Cliff 1987:127). Here Harry/Harriet posits Jamaica as mother, whose *children* are accountable for her condition. This important reversal of a typical nurturing (or disciplining) relationship persists throughout the book. If we read Jamaica here as nation-state, represented by a neocolonial ruling class, we could see Harry/Harriet calling for a rebel consciousness among the youth to overturn a stubborn hierarchy. Or if Jamaica here stands for the impoverished sectors of society, s/he is asking the nation's children to help heal a sick country.

Although both implications are present, I think the narrative pushes us (and Clare) to read Jamaica as Jamaica's poor.

Cliff presents the landscape of Jamaica as lush, maternal, and sensual, but so too does she inscribe it with the marks of oppression. The fantasy of a precolonial Eden is not allowed to remain intact in the postcolonial milieu. Thus the history of slavery, poverty, and capitalist industrial waste everywhere scars the island landscape. On a vacation in Jamaica, enjoying sun and sea with Harry/Harriet, Clare is reminded by her friend of the history of slavery: "'There is a vast canefield right behind us. Less than ten yards from our blessed bodies is cane. Do you know what went on, what happened along those avenues? In the buildings at the center of the piece? . . . Some of our people, girlfriend . . . some of our ancestors" (p. 131). But at this stage in her education by Harry/Harriet—which parallels the indoctrination she received from her father and the colonial education system—Clare's silent thought is, "And what am I supposed to do about it?" (p. 133). Clare's father's historical fictions served to obscure Clare's connection not only to these "others who were made invisible to her as a child but also the suppressed knowledge of her own family background" as slave owners (Martin and Mohanty 1986:198).[3] Clare is slowly "learning at what price privilege, comfort, home, and secure notion of self are purchased, the price to herself and ultimately to others" (p. 203). She is moving toward a sense of responsibility to her homeland, an accountability to her mother's request that she help her people. The Dungle, a ghetto of shacks and extreme poverty in Trench Town, appears throughout the novel as a reminder to Clare and Harry/Harriet, who says, "'Cyaan [can't] live on this island and not understand how it work, how the world work. Cyaan pass the Dungle, cyaan smell the Dungle, and not know this island is the real world . . . in the worst way. . . . It nuh stand as a warning for all a we—no matter how light? how bright?" (Cliff 1987:123). Thus Jamaica cannot exist as a nostalgic escape for Clare or an idealized womb space, a fantasy homeland. Instead it is a microcosm of the oppression of Third World peoples everywhere.

The narration of No Telephone to Heaven is structured around Clare's final participation in resistance struggles, in her full acceptance of her accountability to Jamaica. Toward the end of the book her commitment is articulated in her conversation with a South African woman, perhaps a leader of the movement. Clare has been back in Jamaica for two years, teaching schoolchildren the history they do not learn in the colonial education system. She no longer asks what she can do about present and historical oppression because now she sees its connection to herself. She explains to the unidentified woman,

"I am in it. It involves me . . . the practice of rubbing lime and salt in the backs of whipped slaves . . . the ambush tactics of Cudjoe . . . the promised flight of Alexander Bedward in rapture back to Africa . . . cruelty . . . resistance . . . grace. I'm not outside this history — it's a matter of recognition . . . memory . . . emotion. When I study Tom Cringle's silk cotton tree, I wonder about the fact that I have never been able to bear a necklace around my throat . . . not even a scarf." (p. 194)

For Clare to come to knowledge of her personal connection to Tom Cringle's silk cotton tree used for hanging slaves, for her to feel the historical pressure around *her* neck, she has had to learn to reinterpret "her experience within the family . . . in relation to the history of race relations in an 'outside' in which the family is implicated" (Martin and Mohanty 1986:204). These familial connections and implications were formerly suppressed by her father, who told her that, like lynching in the southern United States, Tom Cringle's silk cotton tree was "'a form of punishment for wickedness'" (Cliff 1987:55). The geography of the island, the natural plant life, now signifies for Clare more fully the particular histories of oppression in the nation. She can read the discursive din. And now Jamaica no longer functions as fecund mother in Clare's mind.

Instead, the nation refuses to mother, and one consistent reminder of this throughout the novel is the presence of orphans. Early in the narrative we meet the murderous Christopher, orphan among many orphans inhabiting the Dungle. Clare herself is motherless at twenty and, having rejected her father, is in some ways an orphan. On one of her visits back to Kingston on school holiday from London she observes a Christmas pageant of orphaned children:

She was confused. Orphans, foundlings, abandoned babies, fatherless children, little wanderers, were no novelty to the island, of course. And Clare knew that. She remembered how her father, as they left Kingston for her grandmother's place in St. Elizabeth, long time ago, how her father had avoided passing through Trench Town, Denham Town, the Dungle. How, when he could not avoid that passage, due to detour, rain, accident, the children swarmed around the car, beating the hood, and she felt shamed. But these children below her were not the same children at all. Even from a distance she could make out their lightness, was startled by it — this thing that in Jamaica was significant of origin, expressive of expectation. (pp. 119–20)

Again Clare is faced with an excess of information above and beyond the facts suppressed by her privileged upbringing. She had seen and accepted the fact of orphanage among the poor, felt shame and sympathy. The very lightness of these Christmas orphans, their resemblance to herself, shocks her into a more politicized awareness of orphanage. But there are other ways too that Cliff's narrative does not allow the island to function as nurturing womb. And this refusal is paralleled by Clare's own physiology.

She returns to Jamaica for the last time in a scene that deliberately recalls the middle passage of slavery: "She had arrived in Kingston with a high fever, in pain, entering the city on the sea as her ancestors had once done. Some concealed below. Some pacing above, bonnets protecting their finely complected faces from the brutal sun. Windward Passage. Spanish Main. Contrary images" (p. 168). This passage alludes not only to the mixed racial lines of Clare's genealogy but also to the class stratifications in her history. After she arrives and is hospitalized, Clare's illness is diagnosed as "a raging infection in her womb" that will most likely leave her sterile (p. 169). This infection is born of chemical/industrial poison distributed by imperialist militarism because it is the result of her becoming impregnated by Bobby, the victim of Agent Orange. Though she miscarries in Europe, the chemical scars her womb, denying her future progeny. Clare's infected womb is mirrored by the womb of Jamaica, the motherland, which is also polluted, infected by the chemical wastes of capitalist enterprise. In "A Borderless World? From Colonialism to Transnationalism and the Decline of the Nation-State," Masao Miyoshi states that "environmental destruction is a major consequence of the development of TNCs [transnational corporations]" (1993:748). The resistance leader, alluding to the transnational linkages that create Jamaican oppression, reminds Clare,

"You know then that the rivers run red . . . and the underground aquifers are colored . . . from the waste of the bauxite mines and the aluminum refineries? . . . Children drink from this water every day of their lives. Women wash in it. Men fish from it. Brew coffee. Clean tripe. Immerse believers. The waste leaches into the land. And people for miles around are covered with a fine dust which invades them. Do you have any idea of the power of such things . . . for future generations . . . for the future of your homeland? Do you not realize that this is but one example of contamination from the outside? And you are but one infected nation?" (Cliff 1987:195)

Previously Clare saw Jamaica as a mother. Here, her infected, now infertile, womb is likened to the infected Jamaican nation which cannot nurture its children. And capitalist imperial industrialism is named as the culprit, the oppressor replacing slavery but causing a similar effect on the institution of the family. In "Mama's Baby, Papa's Maybe," Hortense Spillers explains that because the slave system so often denied the privileges of maternity to female slaves by usurping rights of ownership over newborns, the Western construct of family "becomes the mythically revered privilege of a free and freed community" (1987:74). Clare, who can no longer reproduce, donates her birthright, her grandmother's land, to the resistance movement which aims to fight against imperialist destruction of Jamaica, to help ensure a future for Jamaica's children. Amid the rupture of vertical, genetic familial ties, Clare constructs multiple horizontal relationships, similar to the found family of slavery implied by Spillers. Spillers adds, "The captive person developed, time and again, certain ethical and sentimental features that tied her and him, *across* the landscape to others, often sold from hand to hand, of the same and different blood in a common fabric of memory and inspiration" (p. 27). This union of same and different blood, tied by common memory and inspiration, is echoed in a description of the resistance fighters very early in the novel:

These people — men and women — were dressed in similar clothes, which became them as uniforms, signifying some agreement, some purpose — that they were in something together — in these clothes, at least, they seemed to blend together. This alikeness was something they needed, which could be important, even vital to them — for the shades of their skin, places traveled to and from, events experienced, things understood, food taken into their bodies, acts of violence committed, books read, music heard, languages recognized, ones they loved, living family, varied widely, came between them. That was all to be expected, of course — that on this island, as part of this small nation, many of them would have been separated at birth. (Cliff 1987:4)

In aligning herself with this horizontal "family," Clare has exercised political agency, (dis)locating herself from a (superficially) secure position as privileged, educated, light-skinned Jamaican. The unity of the rebel group is not based on sameness (of blood and the like) but on work, struggle, experience, and history. In returning to Jamaica, then, Clare has not come "home" because we have seen the ways that her former location of home was based on repressed histories both within and without herself, histories she can no longer repress, which she now sees as essential to her self-construction. Once she has "given herself to the struggle," she reclaims these parts of herself: "She is white. Black. Female. Lover. Beloved. Daughter. Traveler. Friend. Scholar. Terrorist. Farmer" (p. 91). This is a rich and varied identity which she has reclaimed "from a history of multiple assimilations and that [she] insists on as a strategy" (de Lauretis 1986:9). Against the either/or choice emphasized by Clare's family and Harry/Harriet, the narrator allows Clare a more hybrid, compound self. For Clare, "'not being home' is a matter of realizing that home was an illusion of coherence and safety based on the exclusion of specific histories of oppression and resistance, the repression of differences even within oneself" (Martin and Mohanty 1986:196). The rebel community, then, is not a "home" but a coalition.

In her essay on coalition politics, Bernice Johnson Reagon explains that coalition work is done with people who are not like you, and therefore it may not be comfortable. She states that "coalition work is not work done in your home. Coalition work has to be done in the streets. And it is some of the most dangerous work you can do. . . . It's very important not to confuse them — home and coalition" (1983:359–60). For the diasporic subject, New World displacement creates an "endless desire to return to 'lost origins,' to be one again with the mother, to go back to the beginning. . . . And yet, this 'return to the beginning' is like the imaginary in Lacan — it can neither be fulfilled nor requited" (Hall 1990:236). The narrative function of *No Telephone to Heaven* is to destabilize and undercut the endless desire for home and to allow for a postmodern subjectivity that problematizes a modernist binary of home and not-home. As bell hooks says,

The very meaning of "home" changes with the experience of decolonisation, of rad-icalisation. At times home is nowhere. At times one knows only extreme estrange-ment and alienation. Then home is no longer just one place. It is locations. Home is that place which enables and promotes varied and everchanging perspectives, a place where one discovers new ways of seeing reality, frontiers of difference. One confronts and accepts dispersal, fragmentation as part of the construction of a new world order that reveals more fully where we are, who we can become, an order that does not demand forgetting. (1989:19)

Jamaica can no longer function for Clare as womb space, secure home, or nurturing mother. She sees that the histories of slavery and colonialism and the present realities of imperialist industrial capitalism are all con-nected and that they disrupt the narrative of Jamaica as idyllic Eden. Clare's naming herself in national terms now as Jamaican is a political and opposi-tional definition, aligning herself against a neocolonial elite linked to inter-national capital. Radical activist political engagement is demanded from Clare, just as it was demanded from her ancestors Nanny and Cudjoe, who formed horizontal alliances among other slaves as they led guerrilla resis-tance movements on the island. Clare learns to forge a similar alliance with the South African woman who asks her to think of "Bishop. Rodney. Fanon. Lumumba. Malcolm. First. Luthuli. Garvey. Mxembe. Marley. Moloise" (Cliff 1987:196). Such struggles are dangerous and often deadly. hooks de-fines this "space of radical openness" as risky, not safe, and dependent upon a "community of resistance" (1989:19). Biddy Martin and Chandra Mohanty write that giving up secure home space is a (necessary) giving up of self (1986:209). And Bernice Johnson Reagon writes of coalition work, "Most of the things that you do, if you do them right, are for people who live long after you are long forgotten. That will only happen if you give it away" (1983:365). Clare's trajectory in the novel has been toward a relinquishing of her desires for a stable, socially privileged self-positioning. Rather than agree to work in her upper-middle-class aunt's antique shop, she has taught schoolchildren "indigenous" Jamaican history. Radhakrishnan describes a Gramscian program by which "the production of subaltern identity has to go through (albeit critically and adversarially) dominant discourses before it can seize agency as its own" (1993:759). Clare has moved through the discourse of the colonizer, through a variety of hegemonic educational institutions, to come to this point where she constructs her politically oppositional consciousness. But those traces of dominant discourse are not erased, and they contribute to the multiply positioned subjectivity Clare has adopted: scholar/terrorist . . . traveler/farmer.

Clare's political act, however, not only requires her to give up a fixed sense of self, it obliterates her self and person as she dies, literally burned into the Jamaican landscape, the entire rebel community the victims of a "Quashee," someone who gave away the rebels' plan to attack a Hollywood movie production crew filming in Jamaica. How are we to read this paradoxical defeat at the moment of agency? Cliff has written elsewhere that though Clare is burned into the landscape by gunfire, "she is also enveloped in the deep green of the hills and the delicate intricacy of birdsong" (1990:266). Cliff describes this as "an ending that completes the circle, or rather triangle, of the character's life. In her death she has complete identification with her homeland; soon enough she will be indistinguishable from the ground. Her bones will turn to potash, as did her ancestors' bones" (p. 265). These statements are problematic on several levels. Cliff envisions for Clare only a physical "identification" with her homeland, which is here figured in naturalist, not geopolitical terms. I have tried to show instead how the entire narrative charts Clare's progress toward political agency, toward identification as radical political strategy. This seems to me a much more complex process, one not reducible to the simple triangular (Jamaica, United States, Britain, Jamaica) movement of Clare's physical body. On Cliff's terms as expressed in her essay, Clare's death might complete this physical triangle. But I think the book's power, its politically oppositional dimension, is obscured by such a reduction. Clare's return is diminished to an atavistic bond with Jamaica as natural Eden if we accept such an easy completion. Similarly, the idea that Clare is now "enveloped in the deep green of the hills and the delicate intricacy of birdsong" also seems idealistic. How will her dead eyes perceive the lush green, her dead ears hear the birdsong? Mary Lou Emery has suggested that the Hollywood reality of the U.S. movie crew filming in Jamaica *overwrites* rebel identity, and this is an important point because it reminds us of the transnational corporate linkages that support the exploitation of the island and most of its people. We have seen the limits of agency, the power of "the system" to codify Clare's racial identification. Cliff's ending reinforces the hegemony of this institutional, systemic power. Miyoshi reminds us that in our era of multinational capital, "the nation-state . . . is thoroughly appropriated by transnational corporations" which are much more immune to local guerrilla resistance movements (1993:744). But another way to read Cliff's ending may retain several of these meanings. Perhaps it is not only the gunfire that overwrites but the landscape itself. The last lines of the book are all bird and animal noises, with the final sentence, "Day broke" (Cliff 1987:208). As in the burial ground of Clare's grandmother, here the natural environment has the last "word." Thus multinational capital in conjunction with corrupt militarism, as well as the wildness of ruinate, all exert their irrevocable, final pressures on Clare's newly reclaimed political identity.

NOTES

1. This essay is part of a book manuscript on African diasporic writing and displacement. In another chapter, on Michelle Cliff's *Abeng*, I develop this discussion of the father's history.

2. Dash credits Glissant with this observation, which he must be paraphrasing.

3. Martin and Mohanty discuss the writing of Minnie Bruce Pratt. Though the personal pronouns in this and other quotes from this article refer to Pratt, they are equally applicable to Clare Savage.

WORKS CITED

Anderson, Benedict. 1994. "Exodus." *Critical Inquiry* 20 (Winter): 314–27.

Brathwaite, Edward. 1988. *The Arrivants: A New World Trilogy.* Oxford: Oxford University Press.

Cliff, Michelle. 1987. Reprint 1989. *No Telephone to Heaven.* New York: Vintage International.

———. 1990. "Clare Savage as a Crossroads Character." In *Caribbean Women Writ-*

ers: Essays from the First International Conference, ed. and intro. Selwyn R. Cudjoe, pp. 263–68. Wellesley: Calaloux.

———. 1991. "Caliban's Daughter: The Tempest and the Teapot." *Frontiers* 12 : 36–51.

de Lauretis, Teresa. 1986. "Feminist Studies/Critical Studies: Issues, Terms, and Contexts." *Feminist Studies/Critical Studies,* ed. Teresa de Lauretis, pp. 1–19. Bloomington: Indiana University Press.

———. 1990. "Eccentric Subjects: Feminist Theory and Historical Consciousness." *Feminist Studies* 16 (Spring): 115–50.

Emery, Mary Lou. 1993. "Language beyond Language: Michelle Cliff and Visual Art." Paper presented at the annual meeting of Multi-Ethnic Literatures of the United States, April 30, Berkeley, Calif.

Glissant, Edouard. 1989. *Caribbean Discourse: Selected Essays,* intro. J. Michael Dash. Charlottesville: University Press of Virginia, Caraf Books.

Hall, Stuart. 1987. "Minimal Selves." *ICA Documents* 6, *Identity: The Real Me? Post Modernism and the Question of Identity,* pp. 44–46. London: ICA.

———. 1990. "Cultural Identity and Diaspora." *Identity: Community, Culture, Difference,* ed. Jonathan Rutherford, pp. 222–37. London: Lawrence and Wishart.

hooks, bell. 1989. "Choosing the Margin as a Space of Radical Openness." *Framework* 36 : 15–23. Special issue, "Third Scenario: Theory and the Politics of Location."

Huggan, Graham. 1989. "Decolonizing the Map: Post-Colonialism, Post-Structuralism and the Cartographic Connection." *ARIEL* 20 (Oct.): 115–31.

Lionnet, Françoise. 1989. *Autobiographical Voices: Race, Gender, Self-Portraiture.* Ithaca: Cornell University Press.

Martin, Biddy, and Chandra Talpade Mohanty. 1986. "Feminist Politics: What's Home Got to Do with It?" In *Feminist Studies/Critical Studies,* ed. Teresa de Lauretis, pp. 191–212. Bloomington: Indiana University Press.

Miyoshi, Masao. 1993. "A Borderless World? From Colonialism to Transnationalism and the Decline of the Nation-State." *Critical Inquiry* 19 (Summer): 726–51.

Radhakrishnan, R. 1993. "Postcoloniality and the Boundaries of Identity." *Callaloo* 16 (Fall): 750–71.

Reagon, Bernice Johnson. 1983. "Coalition Politics: Turning the Century." In *Home Girls: A Black Feminist Anthology,* ed. Barbara Smith, pp. 356–68. New York: Kitchen Table, Women of Color Press.

Rich, Adrienne. 1986. *Blood, Bread, and Poetry: Selected Prose 1979–1985.* New York: Norton.

Shakespeare, William. 1964. *The Tempest,* ed. Robert Langbaum. New York: Signet-NAL.

Spillers, Hortense, J. 1987. "Mama's Baby, Papa's Maybe: An American Grammar Book." *Diacritics* 17 (Summer): 65–81.

Walters, Wendy W. 1996. "Landscapes of Identity: Figures of Home and Elsewhere Among Writers of the African Diaspora." Ph.D. diss., University of California, San Diego.

14. Monstrosity and Representation in the Postcolonial Diaspora

'The Satanic Verses,' 'Ulysses,' and 'Frankenstein'

A man of mature years finds himself a permanent outsider in what appears to most of his fellows to be a homogeneous cultural community. To them he (whose father was born in the East) is inescapably Oriental: exotic, licentious, and unsettling. He, however, imagines that he lives by the most modern Western standards and bends over backward not to be different, to the extent of telling off-color jokes about his own group. (His audiences applaud his tales and turn them back at him.) Even in his subconscious, his family ethnicity seems grotesque, so much so that to represent it, the narrator of his story must shift from sympathetic psychological realism to a surrealistic black comedy that threatens to take over the show. In a crucial moment, the central figure finds himself transformed into a monster possessing the features of a comic stage version of his ethnic stereotype. Nevertheless, as monster, both to himself and to his tormentors, he possesses powers well beyond the comic. Like Mary Shelley's Frankenstein monster, he provokes real fear without feeling himself in the least bit menacing. (Unable to reconcile his treatment with the universal standard of rational justice he has internalized, he is then strongly tempted to inflict evil of the kind he has suffered.) And like the rough beast in Yeats's "The Second Coming," he bears an apocalyptic religious significance — as both destroyer and creator, he seems to be part of a large historical cycle of revelation, orthodoxy, and corruption. But unlike Yeats's ominous presence, he has conscious glimmerings — perhaps portentous, perhaps delusional — of his destined place in apocalyptic history.

My account of the progress of Salman Rushdie's divided hero in *The Satanic Verses* has a calculated purpose. It was constructed to display the affinities between Rushdie's novel and a work not usually associated with it—James Joyce's *Ulysses*—with the hope of clarifying the intersection between concepts that are as omnipresent as they are difficult to define: modernity, modernism, postmodernism, and postcolonial.

Rushdie's novel conforms readily to our emerging sense of postmodern fiction and the postmodern condition. A comedy rooted in the international world of advertising and popular culture, it represents what Rushdie elsewhere calls a condition of "hybridity, impurity, intermingling"[1] in the denizens of a polyglot, multicultural fictional diaspora who are as comfortable in London as in Delhi. For Rushdie's characters the West's dream of a rational, universal culture has been clouded by the energies of religious revivalism, and the West's imperial claims exchanged for the comfortable commodifications of a multicultural global market. This market-driven yet religiously haunted condition speaks, to appropriate Anthony Appiah, of the worldwide frustration of both rationality and (in the Weberian sense) rationalization. What we currently experience, Appiah suggests, is "the incorporation of all areas of the world and all areas of even formerly 'private' life into the money economy. Even in domains like religion . . . modernity has turned every element of the real into a sign, and the sign reads 'for sale.'" This explains something, Appiah continues, about why religions have not faded away in an apparently disenchanted and secularized world: "What we have seen in recent times . . . is not secularization—the end of religions—but their commodification."[2]

For Appiah, "modernity"'s global commodification also frames and interrogates postcolonial authenticity. In recent African writing, he contends, the great theme of the postcolonial—the legitimation of a national or nativist culture distinguished from the culture of the colonial powers—has turned sour. An apparently liberating postcolonialism now seems merely the coin in trade of "a *comprador* intelligentsia: a relatively small, Western-style, Western-trained group of writers and thinkers, who mediate the trade in cultural commodities of world capitalism at the periphery. In the West they are known through the Africa they offer; their compatriots know them . . . through an Africa they have invented for the world, for each other, and for Africa" (p. 348). African novels that refuse to continue the realist tradition of nationalist legitimation, Appiah maintains, might more usefully be considered postmodern than postcolonial so long as we remember that their turn against realism has a specifically Third-World twist.[3] Alternatively, we might reconstruct our understanding of postcolonial writing so that it incorporates postrealism, "postnativist politics, a *transnational* rather than a *national* solidarity," "pessimism," and a necessary "challeng[e to] earlier legitimating narratives" (p. 353).

Thus for Appiah, postcolonial writing, far from offering a Third-World alternative to the self-reflexiveness of postmodernist fiction, inevitably incorporates its sophistications. In so doing, he argues, it differs from the fiction of "modernism," a theory that "saw the economization of the world as the triumph of reason." "Postmodernism," Appiah contends, "rejects that claim," along with modernism's claim to judge both Western and "primitive" art "by putatively *universal* aesthetic standards." On the contrary, postmodernism refuses to legitimate aesthetic constructs "by culture- and history-transcending standards" (p. 347). In Appiah's view, modernism is either to be associated with "Weber's account of [rationalized] modernity" or with a response like that of T. S. Eliot, who "shares Weber's account of modernity" but nostalgically rejects it in favor of a naturalized and pernicious reconstruction of a prerational past (p. 344). Against either an optimistic or a pessimistic modernist reading of historical dynamics, postmodernism's response is skepticism and subversion.

The discussion of *The Satanic Verses* that follows uses and seconds the substance of Appiah's sensible coupling of postmodern and postcolonial fiction. But it also questions the hard distinction he makes between modernism and postmodernism. By teasing out the affiliations between a characteristic postcolonial/postmodern narrative like *The Satanic Verses* with one of the foundation stones of international modernism, I wish to suggest that postmodern fiction extends a project begun in the early twentieth century not only in its technical procedures but in its derivation from the crisis of European colonialism.

The notion of diaspora, an international community of necessarily hybrid identity (and one that attaches itself as readily to the exiled Irish as to the exiled Jew), provides a useful wedge here, as Rushdie acknowledges. In his critical prose, Rushdie is forthright about the importance of Joyce's precedent in his view of the nontotalized vision of modernist fiction. He speaks of himself, for example, as "a modern, and modernist, urban man, accepting uncertainty as the only constant, change as the only sure thing" (*IH*, p. 405), and he associates the "language and literary forms" of this modernism with an effort through which "the experience of formerly colonized, still disadvantaged peoples might find full expression" (*IH*, p. 394). It is essential, he insists, that "Indian writers in England" continue to have access to this international history of exiles, "quite apart from their own racial history. It is the culture and political history of the phenomenon of migration, displacement, life in a minority group. We can quite legitimately claim as our ancestors . . . the Irish, the Jews; the past to which we belong is . . . the history of immigrant Britain. Swift, Conrad, Marx are as much our literary forebears as Tagore or Ram Mohan Ray. . . . We are inescapably international writers at a time when the novel has never been a more international form" (*IH*, p. 20).

The Satanic Verses, the Postcolonial Diaspora, and Postmodern Style

In midlife, Bombay-born Mr. Saladin Chamcha (whose name was short-ened and anglicized from Salahuddin Chamchawala with the unfortunate by-product of taking on the Hindi meaning of "spoono": a sycophant, toady, or suck-up) has "constructed [a British, 'somewhat sour, patrician'] face." It "had taken him several years to get it just right — and for many more years . . . [he thought of it] simply as *his own* — indeed, he had forgotten what he had looked like before it. Furthermore, he had shaped himself a voice to go with the face, a voice whose languid, almost lazy vowels contrasted dis-concertingly with the sawn-off abruptness of the consonants" (p. 33).[4] Until the day of crisis recounted on the first page of Rushdie's novel, the necessary but almost forgotten ventriloquism of Chamcha's voice has enabled him to make his living. He had been trained as a classical actor, and the mimicry required of every aspiring immigrant enabled him to become "the Man of a Thousand Voices and a Voice" on TV — a voice-over artist par excellence. ("If you wanted to know how your ketchup bottle should talk in its television commercial, if you were unsure as to the ideal voice for your packet of garlic-flavored crisps, he was your very man.") With his "female equivalent," a Jew-ish actress named Mimi Mamoulian, he has achieved TV stardom projecting his accented virtuosity as the lead on *"The Aliens Show . . .* a situation comedy about a group of extraterrestrials ranging from cute to psycho, from animal to vegetable, and also mineral, because it featured an artistic space-rock that could quarry itself for its raw material . . . there was also a coarse, belching creature like a puking cactus" (pp. 60–62). Saladin, in other words, along with one of the Jews he "was brought up to have views on" (p. 60), uses the memory of his native culture to popularize a show that caricatures the disagreeable otherness of aliens. When challenged about its stereotyping, his answer is that "'the damn show isn't an allegory. It's an entertainment. It aims to please'" (p. 63). In fact, he cannot quit the job, for there is no market in England for his native face and his native voice on the traditional stage. Nor do serious Indian roles exist.

Alas, even Saladin's accommodation fails. Eventually, his producer informs him that ethnic audiences "want fucking *Dynasty*, like everyone else. Your profile's wrong . . . *The Aliens Show* is too big an idea to be held back by the racial dimension" (p. 265). In the event, leftist political protest has provided a pretext for the producer's racist resistance to even self-caricaturing aliens, and there remains no place for Saladin on the air. Saladin's performance has worked too well. Later his imitations, developed to pass as British and then to "entertain" his hosts, will find voice only in the work of malice. Forced into hiding and apparently forsaken by Gibreel Farishta, his partner in crisis, Saladin will use his voice in locker-room phone calls to inflame Farishta's jealousy and drive him to madness and suicide.

Saladin's ethnic self-hatred is all too familiar from life, but it has literary antecedents as well. The most important of these is James Joyce's modern-day Ulysses, Leopold Bloom, the grandson of Lipoti Virag (of Szombathely, a Hungarian town psychologically at the Oriental reach of the Austro-Hungarian Empire but in fact just over the border from Austria proper), and the son of Rudolph (Virag) Bloom (once of Hungary and later a suicide in his adopted Ireland). In Joyce's Dublin, Bloom, technically Protestant by virtue of his father's postmarital conversion and Catholic by virtue of his own, finds himself perceived, despite every effort to assimilate, as a stage Jew of Oriental exoticism by Protestants and Catholics uneasily pretending to share a common culture. In the cemetery or "Hades" chapter of the book, which contains his closest descent into despair, Bloom approaches a funeral cab and three Dubliners who, having queried, "Are we all here now?" (p. 72)[5] let him enter. Epitomizing Bloom's cultural alienation, the chapter reaches its first epiphany when the carriage passes an apparently Jewish loan shark named Reuben J. Dodd and Bloom's companions erupt in anti-Semitic curses. Bloom's self-protective reaction is to swell the chorus by beginning a joke about Dodd's legendary cheapness, which concerns his miserly tip to the boatman who saved his son's life. Bloom, though, is unable to finish the joke before one of his companions interjects that the reward was too much by half. Nor does Bloom's own generosity at the occasion of the funeral protect him, nor, in the "Cyclops" or pub chapter, does his adopting the role of cagey Jew to help the dead man's widow swindle an insurance company out of its share of a previous loan. To even the most sympathetic of his countrymen, he remains the envied consort and tormented cuckold of licentious "Madame" Molly and "a perverted jew . . . from a place in Hungary" (p. 276).

The vicissitudes of national identity, in other words, which Anthony Appiah understands as of the essence of Third-World postmodernism, were already present in 1922 in the conditions of exile and diaspora in which Joyce set *Ulysses*. Given its historical context, this is not surprising. As Vincent Cheng among others has recently pointed out, Ireland at the time of Joyce's writing had, after centuries of colonial English rule, reached a stage of national emergence.[6] Joyce's self-exile, enacted against a literary effort of national legitimization now known as the Irish Renaissance, was to prove paradigmatic. Frightened by the chauvinist energy of early censorship of cosmopolitan writing, Joyce dramatically left Ireland for good, sensing that only card-carrying nationalists would be allowed to thrive. Even after Ireland achieved independence, Joyce kept his British passport, and, commenting on passages concerning his support of the Irish break from England written by his first biographer, Herbert Gorman, he both insisted on his patriotic sympathy and confessed that he had been fated to become independent Ireland's first dissenter.[7] Finally, he dedicated his last and most arduous labor, the writing of *Finnegans Wake*, to exploring the construction of cultural identity in Ireland and in Europe, making his hero an Irish Protestant under great duress in a suburb of Dublin and his focus the creation of Irish English in the caldron of European language formation from Celtic rune to American slang (and notoriously including all the languages of polyglot Europe from Serbian to Finnish).

Ulysses was begun in the polyglot countercurrents of Trieste amid a virulent Italian irredentism already roiling the fatigued tolerance of the Austro-Hungarian Empire. One of Joyce's models for Bloom, Teodoro Mayer, the publisher of the principal newspaper, *Il Piccolo della Sera*, was, like many other Triestene Jews, a passionate irredentist because Austria tolerated anti-Semitism in the city.[8] Yet the Jews were later to suffer from Italian nationality under Mussolini, and Joyce with prophetic intuition during his stay in Trieste modulated his politics from a Dubliner's sympathy with the oppressed Italians to a grudging appreciation of the cosmopolitan empire in decline.[9] In *Ulysses* he fused the provincial city of Dublin with its pan-European counterpart, Trieste, and explored the contradictions of cultural identity in a multicultural context from the perspective of an outsider defined by those contradictions. If Leopold Bloom, moreover, lacks the television voices that allow Saladin Chamcha to make a life, he is no less the product of the first moment of mass culture. An advertising canvasser, he happily breathes the air of the first decades of mass production and mass communication.[10] And like Saladin Chamcha he thinks of himself as a saint of emergent Western universalism — in the fantasy of his subconscious, a proponent of "New worlds for old. Union of all, jew, moslem and gentile. . . . Esperanto the universal language with universal brotherhood. . . . Free money, free rent, free love and a free lay church in a free lay state" (p. 399).

Nevertheless, Bloom like Chamcha is forced into the stereotypes of the society he strives to enter, and the stylistic gyration necessitated by that compulsion opens the literary post- or surrealism of literary modernism and its successors. In neither *Ulysses* nor *The Satanic Verses* do these stylistic procedures embrace difficulty for its own sake. Both involve the fabrication of identity in psychosocial spaces unsuited to the unified perspective of literary realism. In the words of Rushdie's criticism, "black and white descriptions of society are no longer compatible. Fantasy, or the mingling of fantasy and naturalism, is one way of dealing with [this situation]." Indian writers in Britain, he adds, have a special entrée into such procedures because they write "from a kind of double perspective: because they, we, are at one and the same time insiders and outsiders in this society. This stereoscopic vision [essential to postmodernist fiction] is perhaps what we can offer in place of 'whole sight'" (*IH*, p. 19). But as Rushdie acknowledges, the insider/outsider condition and the stereoscopic vision are shared with other and earlier immigrants: the chronicler of "Joyce's abandoned Dublin . . . Isaac Bashevis Singer and Maxine Hong Kingston and Milan Kundera and many others. It's a long list" (*IH*, p. 15).

What seems "real" about the Jew or Muslim to an ordinary citizen of Dublin or London will be perceived by the self shoehorned into that "reality" as something outrageous, grotesque, darkly comic. Charles Dickens was among the originators of this generic expansiveness in the English novel to accommodate the conflicting realities of the industrial city, and Rushdie is eloquent about the importance of his innovation. The catastrophe of *The Satanic Verses* is an extended recreation of *Our Mutual Friend*, and Rushdie in his prose acknowledges that "the city as reality and as a metaphor is at the heart of all my work. 'The modern city,' says a character in *The Satanic Verses*, 'is the *locus classicus* of incompatible realities. . . . As long as they pass in the night, it's not so bad. But if they meet! It's uranium and plutonium, each makes the other decompose, boom'" (*IH*, p. 404).

But it was Joyce who gave the postcolonial urban diaspora literary form. In *Ulysses*, Bloom's subconscious and dialogical apprehension of ethnicity emerges in a hallucinatory and (were it not for its painfulness) hilariously exaggerated perception of his family. A mild example is the Oriental fantasy he entertains of his wife, Marion (Molly), during the novel's "Circe" or Nighttown chapter, where late-night exhaustion facilitates the eruption of subconscious mentation:

(He looks up. Beside her mirage of datepalms a handsome woman in Turkish costume stands before him. Opulent curves fill out her scarlet trousers and jacket, slashed with gold. A wide yellow cummerbund girdles her. A white yashmak, violet in the night, covers her face, leaving free only her large dark eyes and raven hair.) . . . (A coin gleams on her forehead. On her feet are jewelled toerings. Her ankles are linked by a slender fetterchain. Beside her a camel, hooded with a turreting turban, waits. A silk ladder of innumerable rungs clings to his bobbing howdah. He ambles near with disgruntled hindquarters. Fiercely she slaps his haunch, her goldcurb wristbangles angriling, scolding him in Moorish.) (p. 359)

More savage and more influential is the extended subconscious dialogue Bloom carries on with his grandfather, Virag, who speaks with the accents of the stage Jew: supercalculating in a self-interested way, uninhibitedly lascivious, and wildly funny in a manner later exploited in Philip Roth's *Portnoy's Complaint*:

(Lipoti Virag, basilicogrammate, chutes rapidly down through the chimneyflue and struts two steps to the left on gawky pink stilts. He is sausaged into several overcoats and wears a brown macintosh under which he holds a roll of parchment. . . . Two quills project over his ears.)

VIRAG
(heels together, bows) My name is Virag Lipoti, of Szombathely. *(he coughs, thoughtfully, drily)* Promiscuous nakedness is much in evidence hereabouts, eh? Inadvertently her backview revealed the fact that she is not wearing those rather intimate garments of which you are a particular devotee. The injection mark on the thigh I hope you perceived? Good.

BLOOM
Granpapachi. But . . . . .

VIRAG
Number two on the other hand, she of the cherry rouge and coiffeuse white, whose hair owes not a little to our tribal elixir of gopherwood, is in walking costume and tightly staysed by her sit, I should opine. Backbone in front, so to say. Correct me but I always understood that the act so performed by skittish humans with glimpses of lingerie appealed to you in virtue of its exhibitionististicicity. In a word. Hippogriff. Am I right?

BLOOM
She is rather lean. (p. 417)

Using the frame of Homer's story of Circe, Joyce portrays Bloom in such representations as for a moment transformed into swine, as he becomes for part of the chapter the caricature of a uxorious Jewish husband. In a sequence carefully signposted as surreal, Molly's new lover Blazes Boylan enters his subconscious, and the three parties act out Bloom's humiliation and metamorphosis into a masochistic voyeur:

BOYLAN

(*to Bloom, over his shoulder*) You can apply your eye to the keyhole and play wit yourself while I just go through her a few times.

BLOOM

Thank you, sir. I will, sir. May I bring two men chums to withness the deed and take a snapshot? (*he holds out an ointment jar*) Vaseline, sir? Orangeflower . . . ? Lukewarm water . . . ? (p. 462)

The Satanic Verses contains none of the markers that Joyce inserts to suggest that such savage comedy belongs to the world of heightened or subconscious reality so that like situations are wholly within the sphere of ordinary representation. Saladin Chamcha, after his miraculous escape from an exploding plane, first encounters his metamorphosis into a satanic figure in a police van surrounded by ordinary cops:

When they pulled his pyjamas down in the windowless police van and he saw the thick, tightly curled dark hair covering his thighs, Saladin Chamcha broke down for the second time that night; this time, however, he began to giggle hysterically, infected, perhaps, by the continuing hilarity of his captors. . . .

His thighs had grown uncommonly wide and powerful, as well as hairy. Below the knee the hairiness came to a halt, and his legs narrowed into tough, bony, almost fleshless calves, terminating in a pair of shy, cloven hoofs, such as one might find on any billy-goat. Saladin was also taken aback by the sight of his phallus, greatly enlarged and embarrassingly erect, an organ he had the greatest difficulty acknowledging as his own. "What's this, then?" joked Novak . . . "Fancy one of us, maybe?" Whereupon . . . Joe Bruno, slapped his thigh, dug Novak in the ribs, and shouted, "Nah, that ain't it. Seems like we really got his goat." "I get it," Novak shouted back, as his fist accidentally punched Saladin in his newly enlarged testicles. "Hey! Hey!" howled Stein, with tears in his eyes. "Listen, here's an even better . . . no wonder he's so fucking *horny*." . . . What puzzled Chamcha was that a circumstance which struck him as utterly bewildering and unprecedented — that is, his metamorphosis into this supernatural imp — was being treated by the others as if it were the most banal and familiar matter they could imagine. (pp. 157–58)

Saladin is amazed by the lack of surprise in his captors' response and thinks he must be in an afterlife: " 'This isn't England' " (p. 158). For Rushdie, however, this England is far from surreal. Having modeled the Anglophile figure of the younger Saladin after himself, he arranges for another monstrosity in his story to explain to his alter ego (I quote from one of Rushdie's apologetic essays) "that they are all, like him, aliens and migrants, demonized by the 'host culture's' attitude to them. 'They have the power of description, and we succumb to the pictures they construct.'" Yet, Rushdie adds, to acknowledge as much is hardly to acknowledge the permanence or the enduring reality of even that which seems most quotidian, most real:

> If migrant groups are called devils by others, that does not really make them demonic. And if devils are not necessarily devilish, angels may not necessarily be angelic. . . . From this premise, the novel's exploration of morality as internal and shifting (rather than external, divinely sanctioned, absolute) may be said to emerge. The very title, *The Satanic Verses*, is an aspect of this attempt at reclamation. You call us devils? it seems to ask. Very well, then, here is the devil's version of the world, of 'your' world, the version written *from the experience* of those who have been demonized by virtue of their otherness. Just as the Asian kids in the novel wear toy devil-horns proudly, as an assertion of pride in identity, so the novel proudly wears its demonic title." (*IH*, pp. 402–3).

Frankenstein

At the center of *The Satanic Verses*'s "exploration of morality" are other familiar tales, which Joyce too drew upon in *Ulysses*. What prevents Homer's Odysseus from allowing twenty years' adversity to debase him as his shipmates are debased and from being destroyed by his own degradation? In the *Odyssey*, he is given a kind of divine grace associated with godlike intelligence and symbolized by the *molu* Hermes provides. Joyce, reimagining this question from a twentieth-century perspective, redefines it into a matter of whether Leopold Bloom can avoid being twisted by hatred stemming from his countrymen's contempt and from his wife's unfaithfulness. Amid the psychosexual descent of the "Circe" chapter and the reentry into an adulterous bed, not an extrahuman but an ultrahuman decency rescues Bloom from the self-destructive violence of the role of devil-cum-Oriental avenger assigned him. (Joyce's *molu* is a reminder of the suffering of the Irish Potato Famine, a shriveled potato skin that Bloom says "is nothing, but still, a relic of poor mamma" [p. 453].)

In "Circe," symbolically attacked by a combination of castrating female and Knight Templar (the latter's office is to guard Christian pilgrims in the holy land), Bloom's almost impossibly humane response is to insist, "Fair play, madam" (p. 451). And, confronted by the flagrant evidence of Blazes Boylan's affair with Molly, his heroism consists of conquering a desire for "retribution." At the climax of the novel's "Ithaca" chapter, we overhear a critical moment of self-dialogue:

With what antagonistic sentiments were [Bloom's "sentiments" subsequent to the sight of his soiled marriage bed] affected?

Envy, jealousy, abnegation, equanimity. (p. 602)

Bloom's "equanimity" is for Joyce the epitome of his remarkable decency. But to understand its force, we need to realize the full horror of Bloom's immigrant situation. Presented by his hosts with an image of his own monstrosity, Bloom is faced always with the question articulated by Rushdie's Saladin Chamcha:

I am the incarnation of evil, he thought. He had to face it. However, it happened, it could not be denied. I am *no longer myself*, or not only. I am the embodiment of wrong, of what-we-hate, of sin.

Why? Why me? . . .

Had he not pursued his own idea of *the good*, sought to become that which he most admired, dedicated himself with a will bordering on obsession to the conquest of Englishness? Had he not worked hard, avoided trouble, striven to become new? Assiduity, fastidiousness, moderation, restraint, self-reliance, probity, family-life: what did these add up to if not a moral code? . . .

No more of that, Saladin Chamcha told himself firmly. No more of thinking of myself evil. Appearances deceive; the cover is not the best guide to the book. Devil, Goat, Shaitan? Not I.

Not I: another.

Who? (pp. 256–57)

As it turns out, for a significant part of the action Saladin Chamcha cannot, Bloom-like, steadfastly resist the devilish role that his society imposes. Rushdie, remembering Joyce, interpolates into Joyce's model yet another paradigm, earlier and yet proleptic of postcolonial trauma. For Saladin's moral reflections are modeled closely on the defining utterance of the Frankenstein monster, modern literature's archetypal other, whose story appeared in the first self-consciousness of British imperialism:

I had admired the perfect form of my [unknowing hosts] — their grace, beauty and delicate complexions: but how was I terrified when I viewed myself in a transparent pool! At first I started back, unable to believe that it was indeed I who was reflected in the mirror; and when I became fully convinced that I who was in reality the monster that I am, I was filled with the bitterest sensations of despondence and mortification. . . .

I formed in my imagination a thousand pictures of presenting myself to them, and their reception of me. I imagined that they would be disgusted, until, by my gentle demeanour and conciliating words, I should first win their favour, and afterwards their love. . . . My person was hideous and my stature gigantic. What did this mean? Who was I? What was I? . . .

These were the reflections of my hours of despondency and solitude; but when I contemplated the virtues of the cottagers, their amiable and benevolent dispositions, I persuaded myself that when they should have become acquainted with my admiration of their virtues, they would compassionate me, and overlook my personal deformity. Could they turn from their door one, however monstrous, who solicited their compassion and friendship?[11]

So laments the maligned creature of Victor Frankenstein in Mary Shelley's classic, *Frankenstein, or the Modern Prometheus*. And like the *cri de coeur* of Leopold Bloom in *Ulysses*, this speech is unintelligible outside a colonial context. In case the horror of the monster viewing himself through the eyes of his European neighbors was not pointed enough for her readers, Shelley explicitly aligns his anguish with Europe's relations to the Orient. Having escaped his creator's revulsion, the monster finds calm in a hidden place where he can observe the discourse of a broken family in a remote forest cottage. As it happens, the family has been reduced to ruin by the dialectical evils of an Oriental immigrant and a hypocritical Western culture. A young man of noble sentiments, Felix, has fallen in love with Safie, the daughter of "a Turkish merchant [who] had inhabited Paris for many years, when . . . he became obnoxious to the government. He was seized and cast into prison the very day that Safie arrived from Constantinople to join him. He was tried and condemned to death" (p. 127). Felix "had accidentally been present at the trial; his horror and indignation were uncontrollable" (p. 127). He helps the father escape and falls in love with the daughter. But neither his country nor the Turkish merchant fashioned by Paris can tolerate Felix's effort of universalizing love and justice. France casts out Felix and his family, and the Turkish merchant attempts to thwart the match. Yet human benevolence seems to conquer all as the impoverished young lovers are united in the forest. At that point, in the excerpt just quoted, the monster, sure that if anyone can, these unfortunates will be able to judge his own sentiments, throws himself at their mercy. The result is disastrous. Felix and Safie, too, see only an inhuman other, ignoring the monster's poignant situation: "I am poor, and an exile; but it will afford me true pleasure to be in any way serviceable to a human creature" (p. 141). After their rejection, the monster, like Safie's father before him, turns to the wickedness that has been expected of him.

The last section of Shelley's modern fable concerns the monster's attempt to effect the creation of a companion other, for he recognizes that withstanding hatred and revenge are beyond his strength without the genuine fellowship that enlightenment-speaking but culturally preconditioned Europeans cannot provide. The monster fails and is driven into the murderous expression of his alienated rage. For Shelley, given the cultural dynamics, success would require a superhuman strength she cannot see the world providing.

Salman Rushdie casts his alter ego, the demonized Saladin Chamcha, into this same dilemma. Ultimately, however, Rushdie allows a more humanistic resolution. To resist turning into the demon London expects him to be, Saladin needs both the strength of his cultural identity and the protection of a genuinely cosmopolitan ethos. Instead, he has attempted to accommodate himself to a xenophobic society by exploiting his painfully acquired ventriloquism in the debased market of TV commercials. Draining his inner resources is a late twentieth-century cynicism that regards his self-exploitation as nothing more than "entertainment." In London, this cynicism passes for "postmodern" sophistication. When a partially enlightened Saladin, for example, warns his Jewish colleague Mimi not to sell herself out for a publicity fling with a "Playboy Pakistani" con artist named Billy Battuta (pp. 260–61), Mimi stiffens and retorts:

"Chamcha, listen up. . . . Comprehend please, that I am an intelligent female. I have read *Finnegans Wake* and am conversant with post-modernist critiques of the West, e.g. that we have here a society capable only of pastiche: a 'flattened' world. When I become the voice of a bottle of bubble bath, I am entering Flatland knowingly, understanding what I'm doing and why. Viz., I am earning cash. And as an intelligent woman, able to do fifteen minutes on Stoicism and more on Japanese cinema, I say to you, Chamcha. . . . Don't teach me about exploitation. We had exploitation when you-plural were running round in skins. Try being Jewish, female and ugly sometime. You'll beg to be black. Excuse my French: brown." (p. 261)

Resisting, Mimi seals her fate, and the attitudes the two shared for so long nearly ruin Saladin as well. With cynicism sapping his resolve, a sense of injustice drives him to use his finely honed mimicry to strike out at an innocent party—Gibreel Farishta. Yet, to distinguish Saladin's story from the hard inevitability of the Frankenstein fable, the climactic scene in this drama is regenerative and almost Dickensian. Rushdie, though, like Joyce before him, steeps Dickensian sentiment in an irony poised between belief and skepticism. Farishta is magnetically drawn to a blazing house in which Saladin is about to perish. But instead of repaying Saladin once and for all for his treachery, Gibreel draws back and instinctively rescues his Iago from the charred rubble, initiating Saladin's spiritual redemption:

Gibreel . . . stoops; frees Saladin from the prison of the falling beam; and lifts him in his arms. Chamcha, with broken ribs as well as arms, groans feebly. . . . "Ta. La." *It's too late*. . . . [He] gasping and fainting, with a mule inside his chest, seems to see — but will ever afterwards be unsure if it was truly so — the fire parting before them like the red sea it has become, and the smoke dividing also, like a curtain or a veil; until there lies before them a clear pathway to the door; — whereupon Gibreel Farishta steps quickly forward, bearing Saladin along the path of forgiveness into the hot night air; so that on a night when the city is at war, a night heavy with enmity and rage, there is this small redeeming victory for love.   (p. 468)

A "Humanized, Historicized, Secularized" Islam

In the passage just quoted, *The Satanic Verses* modulates from a novel about the postcolonial dialectic of identity politics into a more traditional novel concerned with the religious theme of moral redemption. Invoking the Exodus and the redemption of Israel in the parting of the Red Sea, Rushdie translates (as Joyce and Dickens had before him) a religious legend interwoven with the authority of an entrenched orthodoxy into a contemporary tale of simple decency. But because "the Story of Islam has a deeper meaning for [Rushdie] than any of the other grand narratives" (*IH*, p. 435), the tale necessarily involves the Qur'an.

In Rushdie's own account, *The Satanic Verses* juxtaposes Saladin Chamcha's predicament with Muhammad's difficulties in an earlier but equally cynical commercial world. In *The Satanic Verses*, Muhammad bears the name "Mahound" — as Rushdie acknowledges, "a Medieval European demonization of 'Muhammad.'" Why? Rushdie, quoting one of his own characters, explains: "'To turn insults into strengths, whigs, tories, Blacks all choose to wear with pride the names they were given in scorn.'" He continues: "Central to the purposes of *The Satanic Verses* is the process of reclaiming language from one's opponents. Elsewhere in the novel we find the poet Jumpy Joshi trying to reclaim Enoch Powell's notorious 'rivers of blood simile'" (*IH*, p. 402).

The Satanic Verses, however, intends to do more than rescue Islam from its European detractors. Like earlier enlightenment narratives, it rejects both the historical letter of religion and the associated power of entrenched orthodoxy. For Rushdie, it is incumbent on his generation "to develop the nascent concept of the 'secular Muslim', who, like the secular Jews, affirmed his membership in the culture while being separate from the theology" (*IH*, p. 436). To do so, the Islamic novelist must create a "humanized, historicized, secularized way of being a Muslim" (*IH*, p. 436) — in other words, to show how a contemporary Muslim like Saladin Chamcha can work out "secular Muslim" values in a postmodern world.

This is the precise Muslim equivalent of Joyce's modernist project. In *Ulysses*, the letter of Catholicism is rejected, but the possibility of a humanistic secular equivalent is presented through Stephen Dedalus's encounter with Leopold Bloom, a Chaplinesque bumbler whose human decency becomes associated in the intuition of young Dedalus with "the traditional figure of hypostasis" — the union between the human and the divine (p. 565). In *Ulysses* this matrix of Christian allusion is deliberate, elaborated, and serious, to the extent that one of the book's best readers, Stanley Sultan, has used it to interpret *Ulysses* as *The Divine Comedy* redivivus — a contemporary allegory of Christian salvation.[12] Yet Sultan, noticing the novel's allusions, gets Joyce's intention exactly backward. Instead of preserving the authority of the forms of Christian practice, *Ulysses* entertains the possibility of a humanized and secular representation of values the forms have betrayed. Both the near miracle of sympathetic imagination that Bloom unknowingly educes from Stephen and the recurring moment of love between Bloom and Molly — the resounding "Yes" with which the book concludes — ambiguously reinterpret the parable of selfless love in the story of Exodus — exactly and as self-consciously as does Rushdie's tale of Gibreel's generosity and Saladin's moral redemption. Where *The Satanic Verses* describes an urban fire parting before Saladin and Gibreel "like the red sea it has become," *Ulysses* stages its moment of greatest communion between Bloom and Stephen by way of the Psalm, *In exitu Israel de Egypto*, appropriated by the Catholic mass:

In what order of precedence, with what attendant ceremony was the exodus from the house of bondage to the wilderness of inhabitation effected? . . . With what intonation *secreto* of what commemorative psalm?

The 113th, *modus peregrinus: In exitu Israel de Egypto: domus Jacob de populo barbaro.* . . .

What spectacle confronted them when they, first the host, then the guest, emerged silently, doubly dark, from obscurity by a passage from the rere of the house into the penumbra of the garden?

The heaventree of stars hung with humid nightblue fruit. (pp. 572–73)

In *Ulysses* as later in Rushdie, however, such passages are suspended between solemnity and absurdity. Having raised by heightened lyricism the possibility of a humanistic ethos, Joyce no less dramatically takes it back. In the next moment of *Ulysses*, Stephen fades into the night's chill and the narrator represents Bloom's melancholy that the sky was "not a heaventree, not a heavengrot, not a heavenman. That it was a Utopia, there being no known method from the known to the unknown: an infinity renderable equally finite by the suppositious apposition of one or more bodies equally of the same and of different magnitudes: a mobility of illusory forms immobilized in space, remobilized in air: a past which possibly had ceased to exist as a present before its probably spectators had entered actual present existence" (p. 575). Here even "Utopia" is undermined by the interstellar void, and the narrative deliberately undermines its sentiment with a style devised to approximate the schoolbook catechism of an inept observational science.

It is possible, though, to overemphasize Rushdie's Joycean procedures. In *The Satanic Verses*, the historical forms of religion are not, as they are in *Ulysses*, entirely folded back into the figurative. Rushdie, anxiously registering the force by which religion has maintained at least a simulacrum of its literal form in the late twentieth century, directly invokes what he calls the "grand narrative, the Story of Islam" (*IH*, p. 432). Even so, for him it is not enough to interpret it in a contemporary context. The other half of his enterprise involves historicizing and thus humanizing Muhammad's story, showing how even in its origins its message was conditioned by a specific cultural context. As Rushdie points out, such a reading has long been part of the tradition of Muslim scholarship, including "my near-namesake, the twelfth-century philosopher Ibn (Rushd AverroEs), who argued that . . . 'not all the words of the Qur'an should be taken literally'" (*IH*, p. 436).

Though never mentioning Muhammad by name, Rushdie in important chapters of *The Satanic Verses* recounts the revelation of Islam, swerving away from a novel like Nikos Kazantzakis's *Last Temptation of Christ* only because he keeps the story's narrative status ambiguous. In *The Satanic Verses*, the story of "Mahound" may represent the delusions of a crazed Gibreel or a script for a theological film Gibreel's delusions have anticipated. In any case it is treated in bold historical terms, as colored by a specific set of historical interests that Rushdie elsewhere summarizes:

Arabia in the seventh century after Christ was undergoing a period of transition from the old nomadic culture to a new, urbanized, mercantile culture. What Maxime Rodinson calls the "old tribal humanism" of the Bedouins was decaying under the pressure of the new, business-based ethics of a city like Mecca. Muhammad, an orphan himself at an early age, was in an excellent position to appreciate the way in which Meccan culture failed to care for the weak as dutifully as the nomads would have. And the ethic of the revelation he received when, at the age of forty, having married a wealthy older woman and made his fortune, he climbed Mount Hira and found there the Archangel Gabriel or Gibril . . . has often been seen, at least in part, as a plea for a return to the code of the Bedouin. So we may say that the ideas of the

Qur'an are in this sense backward-looking, nostalgic, against the current. But the people on whom Muhammad's words made the strongest initial impression were the poor . . . precisely those people who knew that they would have been better off under the old nomadic system. Thus early Islam instantly acquired the character of a subversive, radical movement. . . . Muhammad's revelation [like Khomeini's revolt against history] was a revolt against his time. Yet plainly, history did move forward; nomadism did not once again become the Arab norm, nor, obviously was that truly Muhammad's aim. (*IH*, pp. 384–85)

In *The Satanic Verses*, Rushdie focuses these matters on the episode in Muhammad's career that gives his book its title. As he explains in an essay entitled "In Good Faith," "the quasi-historical tale of how Muhammad's revelation seemed briefly to flirt with the possibility of admitting three pagan and female deities into the pantheon, at the semi-divine, intercessory level of the archangels, and of how he then repudiated these verses as being satanically inspired — is, first of all, a key moment of doubt in dreams which persecute" the dreamer Gibreel (*IH*, p. 399). Rushdie allows, however, that using the fictional frame of Gibreel's delusions to explain the point of the episode may be a bit "disingenuous" (*IH*, p. 399). Gibreel's doubts answer to Rushdie's own political intuition, which accounts for the episode as a temporary political ploy in the prophet's attempt to win over a population devoted to older female deities. Rushdie's historicism also drives the skepticism of the character Salman the Persian, named, as Rushdie confesses, in "an ironic reference to the novel's author" (*IH*, p. 399). Salman the Persian, having grown suspicious of the prophet's imposing "rules for every damn thing," in his capacity as the prophet's scribe begins to alter details of Muhammad's recitation and is appalled to discover that the prophet pays no notice. Unable to live with the truth that details may not matter, he loses his faith. His namesake creator, though, seems more sanguine about Islam and less disturbed by the historical accidents of its text as long as they are understood as historical accidents and not as eternal truths. Defending not the treason of the follower but the spirit of the message, he would recover the story from fundamentalist literalism. To quote a postpublication comment, "Are all the rules laid down at a religion's origin immutable for ever? . . . What of the Islamic law of evidence, which makes a woman's testimony worth only half of that of a man? . . . Let no one suppose that such disputes about rules do not take place daily throughout the Muslim world" (*IH*, p. 400). This much and more is implicit in a narrative that understands revelation through history and then interrogates both religious and historical narrative through the self-consciousness of its own procedures.

A Struggle Between the Sacred and the Profane

The skepticism of Salman the Persian notwithstanding, Salman the denizen of a postcolonial Indian London diaspora fully appreciates the human reality of revelation and the difficulties of living in the city that is called in *The Satanic Verses* "Jahilia," which Rushdie translates elsewhere as "'ignorance,' the name given by Arabs to the period before Islam" (*IH*, p. 398). Whether we understand this mercantile community in the novel as ancient Mecca or modern London, it is a "city of sand" (*IH*, p. 398) which in important ways fails to satisfy the "explanations of the heart" that Rushdie identifies with the sacred (*IH*, p. 421). From Gibreel at the beginning of the novel, possessed by an alienated modern's imagination of such explanations, to Ayesha near the end, possessed by faith in her march to the sea, *The Satanic Verses* sets out "to explore . . . the nature of revelation and the power of faith" — "what revelation is" and "the human event of revelation" (*IH*, p. 408).

Even more than *Ulysses*, Rushdie's novel insists on the need for literature to "mediat[e] between the material and spiritual worlds . . . [and,] by 'swallowing both worlds, offer . . . something that might even be called a secular definition of transcendence" (*IH*, p. 420). In part, this is because of Rushdie's anxious awareness of the political consequences of religion's appeal to the timeless — a "revolt against history" that in the case of Muhammad or Khomeini proceeds inexorably in the path of nationalism (*IH*, pp. 383–84). Rushdie is closer to Appiah than Joyce here in acknowledging the resurgence of religious revival in the modern world and acknowledging that such resurgence does not and cannot exist outside of the context of late capitalist politics.

But *The Satanic Verses* also represents Rushdie's recognition of the genuine human need for something beyond the material and founds his justification of fiction on "the deep religious spirit with which so many of the makers of [the recent revolution against communism in Central Europe] are imbued" (*IH*, pp. 421–22). Unwilling, with Appiah, to trust in the evolving force of global cosmopolitan commodification to create a multicultural space, Rushdie insists on "the novel as the crucial art form of . . . the postmodern age" (*IH*, p. 424). It "seems probable," he writes, "that we may be heading towards a world in which there will be no real alternative to the liberal-capitalist social model (except, perhaps, the theocratic, foundationalist model of Islam)" (*IH*, p. 426). In this situation, only the novel can mediate effectively between modernizing politics and religion. For whereas both of these seek to "privilege one language above all others" (religion even "one text above others"), "the novel has always been *about* the way in which different languages, values and narratives quarrel, and about the shifting relations between them, which are relations of power." Unlike either religion or politics, "the novel does not seek to establish a privileged language, but it insists upon the freedom to portray and analyse the struggle between the different contestants for such privileges" (*IH*, p. 420).

This definition of literature is essentially derived from modernism's focus on exile, from, in Rushdie's words, "Joyce's wanderers, Beckett's tramps, Gogol's tricksters, Bulgakov's devils" (*IH*, p. 423). But in Rushdie's hands it is adapted to the crisis of politics and religion associated with the postcolonial world. The novel, that "arena of discourse . . . where the struggle of languages can be acted out" (*IH*, p. 427), is brought to bear in *The Satanic Verses* on an inexorable conflict in the postcolonial condition between the equally human and equally compelling claims "of the sacred and the profane . . . the merits of purity and those of hotch-potch, and [on the question of] how human beings really become whole: through the love of God or through the love of their fellow men and women" (*IH*, p. 395).

Conceived of in this way, both the plot of the novel and its procedures are divided and dialogical. In Rushdie's description, the novel is the story not of one but of "two painfully divided selves. In the case of one, Saladin Chamcha, the division is secular and societal: he is torn, to put it plainly, between Bombay and London, between East and West. For the other, Gibreel Farishta, the division is spiritual, a rift in the soul. He has lost his faith and is strung out between his immense need to believe and his new inability to do so. The novel is 'about' their quest for wholeness" (*IH*, p. 397).

Procedurally, the book embodies the same divisions through ambiguity, irony, openness, and dialogic form. Rushdie wishes neither to write a narrative of Third-World authenticity nor to prejudge the struggle of sacred and secular language. "Throughout the novel," he recalls, "I sought images that crystallized the opposition between the sacred and profane worlds. . . . The two struggling worlds, pure and impure, chaste and coarse, are juxtaposed by making them echoes of one another" (*IH*, p. 401). And in an action divided between two halves of a doubled protagonist, Rushdie makes a supreme effort to leave the narrative resolutions open. In the Saladin Chamcha chapters, the secular triumphs and we get a hint of the cosmopolitan tolerance of a hybrid future. But in the Gibreel Farishta–Ayesha sections, the outcome is otherwise. Gibreel without faith cannot live in the modern world and he self-destructs; his counterpart Ayesha leads a pilgrimage of the faithful to a rendezvous with death and martyrdom and on the last page of the penultimate chapter in the book overcomes the skepticism of a sympathetic doubter. The dissonance between these resolutions resonates with the ironies of the Muhammad or "Mohound" sections, where the appeal of Muhammad is as clear as the ruthlessness of his reform. Here, as Rushdie puts it, "the pure eradicates the impure. Whores and writer ('I see no difference here,' remarks Mahound) are executed. Whether one finds this a happy or sad conclusion depends on one's point of view" (*IH*, p. 401).

Establishment Violence and Postmodern Writing

Another gauge of the family difference between Joyce and Rushdie (and perhaps between modernist and postmodernist fiction) is Rushdie's concern to expose the brutalizing authority of the Western judicial system. *Ulysses* unambiguously announces its anti-imperialist politics in Stephen Dedalus's bitter assertion that he is "a servant of two masters. . . . The imperial British state . . . and the holy Roman and apostolic church" (p. 17). Near the end, the novel confirms the reality of Stephen's subjection when two belligerent British soldiers, eager to exert their authority over a rowdy Dublin vagrant, unceremoniously knock him down. The incident, apparently trivial but in fact one of the few things that actually *happen* in *Ulysses*, grew out of very deep roots in Joyce's personal experience: the soldiers are given the names of the British functionaries who harassed Joyce in Zurich during World War I and who went as far as to send him the equivalent of a draft notice, which he ignored with some pain. (The story is told at length in Richard Ellmann's biography of Joyce and tangentially in Tom Stoppard's play *Travesties*.[13])

In *Ulysses*, though, Joyce complicates and interrogates the incident with characteristic subtlety. First he blows it up to grandiloquent proportions by associating it with Dublin's Easter rising of 1916. Then he drenches both incident and history in mock-heroic ridicule. Far from making the brawl a political or emotional focal point of the action, then, *Ulysses* minimizes it, treating it as one more manifestation of a diseased colonial situation. More, Joyce uses the incident to demonstrate Stephen's growing maturity, which is exhibited in his self-disciplined refusal to be ensnared in what is clearly meant to seem a pathetic reflex of imperial-colonial authority. As the soldiers warm to their task, Stephen half-drunkenly reminds himself that though the English king "wants my money and my life . . . want must be his master, for some brutish empire of his" (p. 485). To achieve self-mastery, Stephen exhorts himself that "(*he taps his brow*) But in here it is I must kill the priest and the king" (p. 481).

Stephen's decision not to rise to the British soldiers' bait and his Hegelian perception that imperialists are mastered by their own oppression would be immediately understood by any African intellectual. Rather than a story of Fanon-like violent emergence, *Ulysses* presents in this moment of self-consciousness a recognition that bloody Irish nationalism may in the end be no more than, to quote Wole Soyinka on African counterparts, "the histrionics of wanton boys masquerading as humans." [14] Already in 1922, Joyce has felt his way toward what Appiah called "a *transnational* rather than a *national* solidity — and pessimism: a kind of post-optimism . . . that challenges earlier legitimating narratives" (p. 353).

Throughout much of *The Satanic Verses*, Rushdie follows a similar pattern. Faced with casual brutality and expected to respond with native ferocity, Saladin Chamcha makes comic and misconceived gestures at revolution. As an apparent incarnation of the devil, his fiery breath torches only wax dummies of Anglo-India's British tormentors (principally Margaret Thatcher). And as an agent of retribution, his primary effect is to drive a well-wisher and friend, Gibreel Farishta, mad with jealousy. At the end of the novel he prevails by acceptance, not revolution.

Within this postcolonial self-consciousness about the self-destructiveness of violence, though, *The Satanic Verses* presents instances of state abuse so appalling that though Saladin may find the grace to transcend them, the reader cannot. In his essays, Rushdie has observed that the realities of racism against Asians in contemporary Britain include "judges . . . who can say in court that the word 'nigger' cannot be considered an epithet of racial abuse" and a "policeman who sat in an unmarked car on Railton Road in Brixton . . . shouting abuse at passing black kids and arresting the first youngsters who made the mistake of answering back" (*IH*, pp. 134–35). In *The Satanic Verses*, their counterparts include the policemen who make rude jokes about Saladin while they are beating him senseless. When they discover he is indeed a British citizen, things get worse instead of better: they instinctively fall back on time-tested corporate and government practice:

Three and a half minutes later the Black Maria came to a halt and three immigration officers, five constables and one police driver hold a crisis conference — *here's a pretty effing pickle* — and Chamcha noted that in their new mood all nine had begun to look alike, rendered equal and identical by their tensions and fear. Nor was it long before he understood that the call to the Police National Computer, which had promptly identified him as a British citizen first class, had not improved his situation, but had placed him, if anything, in greater danger than before.

We could say, — one of the nine suggested, — that he was lying unconscious on the beach. — Won't work, came the reply. . . . Look, we can fix the tale later, first thing like I keep saying is to get him unconscious. — Right.   (pp. 163–64)

To cover themselves for what is in their minds an inadvertent technical violation of the immigration laws, they lay on Saladin, hoping that either amnesia or death will solve their problem. And when Saladin survives with his lungs full of green slime but his memory intact, one of the policemen cheerfully pays him a hospital visit and confides:

"Damn decent of you to come down with the lung thing," Stein added, with the gratitude of an author whose character had unexpectedly solved a ticklish technical problem. "Makes the story much more convincing. Seems you were that sick, you did pass out on us after all. Nine of us remember it well. Thanks."   (pp. 166–67)

Stein then advises him not to press charges. After all, he confides, "You'll forgive me for speaking plain, but with your wee horns and your great hoofs you wouldna look the most reliable of witnesses" (p. 167).

Later in the novel, when Saladin's wife discovers evidence of satanism within the very same police force, she is murdered by mysterious representatives who destroy the evidence in a fire they blame on an ethnic uprising. Afterward the establishment press echoes the official suggestion that the victims "had been bent on an act of sabotage, an 'inside job,' since one of them, the dead woman, had in fact been an employee of the organization." The police will never investigate, making sure that "the reasons for the crime" will never "come to light. . . . A tragic affair, the dead woman having been heavily pregnant" (p. 464).

Much more provocative than anything in *Ulysses,* this establishment thuggery is difficult to accept with "equanimity." The passages are as reminiscent of Dickens as of Pynchon, with the suggestion that our institutions have not outgrown their Dickensian origins. Though Rushdie, like Joyce, has no desire to sponsor nationalist revolution, his rage gets the better of him when he contemplates "the citizens of the new, imported Empire . . . the colonized Asians and blacks of Britain [for whom] the police force represents that colonizing army, those regiments of occupation and control" (*IH*, p. 132). Joyce, believing that *Ulysses*'s exposure of police spies and viceregal paternalism was more important, succeeded in excluding such rage from his work. Perhaps in Rushdie its occurrence represents a throwback and a blemish. But when we remember the prevalence of police and judicial arrogance Rushdie records, it is also possible to believe that *Ulysses* lets the brutality of the post-colonial city off just a little too easily.

NOTES

1. Salman Rushdie, *Imaginary Homelands: Essays and Criticism, 1981–1991* (New York: Penguin, 1991), p. 394. Hereafter cited parenthetically as *IH*.

2. Kwame Anthony Appiah, "Is the Post- in Postmodernism the Post- in Postcolonial?" *Critical Inquiry* 17 (Winter 1991): 336–57, see p. 344. Hereafter cited parenthetically in the text.

3. Yambo Ouologuem's *Le Devoir de violence*, for example, "seeks to delegitimate the forms of the realist African novel . . . because what it sought to naturalize was a nationalism that, by 1968, had plainly failed. The national bourgeoisie that took the baton of rationalization, industrialization, and bureaucratization in the name of nationalism, turned out to be a kleptocracy." See Appiah, "Is the Post- in Postmodernism," p. 349.

4. All page references are to Salman Rushdie, *The Satanic Verses* (1988; paperback ed. Dover, Del.: Consortium Press, 1992).

5. Page references to *Ulysses* (1922) are to the edition by Hans Walter Gabler (New York: Vintage, 1986) and are included parenthetically in the text.

6. See, for example, Vincent Cheng, *Joyce, Race, and Empire* (Cambridge: Cambridge University Press, 1995); Fredric Jameson's "Modernism and Imperialism" in *Nationalism, Colonialism and Literature*, ed. Seamus Deane (Minneapolis: University of Minnesota Press, 1990), pp. 43–66; and Kieran Quinlan's essay on the Field Day Movement's revisionary reading of Yeats, Joyce, and the Irish Renaissance in *Yeats and Postmodernism*, ed. Leonard Orr (Syracuse: Syracuse University Press, 1991), pp. 64–79.

7. For Joyce's comment to Gorman, I am indebted to John Whittier-Ferguson, who cited it in a paper given at the 1993 Irvine Joyce conference. The comment appears in Herbert Gorman, *James Joyce* (1939; rpt. New York: Rinehart, 1948), p. 234, and in Richard Ellmann, *James Joyce* (Oxford: Oxford University Press, 1959), p. 412.

8. See Ellmann, *James Joyce*, pp. 203–4.

9. See Vicki Mahaffey, "Fascism and Silence: The Coded History of Amalia Popper," *James Joyce Quarterly* 32 (1995): 501–22.

10. See Thomas Richards, *The Commodity Culture of Victorian England: Advertizing and Spectacle, 1851–1914* (Stanford: Stanford University Press, 1990), chap. 5.

11. Mary Shelley, *Frankenstein* (1818; rpt. New York: Dutton, Everyman's Library, 1963), pp. 117, 118–19, 133–34, 136–37. Subsequent page references are given in the text.

12. See Stanley Sultan, *The Argument of Ulysses* (Columbus: Ohio University Press, 1964).

13. See Ellmann, *James Joyce*, pp. 439ff., esp. pp. 471–72.

14. From Wole Soyinka, *Myth, Literature and the African World* (Cambridge: Cambridge University Press, 1976), p. 100, quoted in Appiah, "Is the Post- in Postmodernism," p. 351.

15. Cultural *Métissage* and the Play of Identity in Leïla Sebbar's *Shérazade* Trilogy

Leïla Sebbar is a contemporary Franco-Algerian woman novelist, essayist, and short story writer. Born and raised in Algeria by an Algerian father and a French mother, she grew up speaking her mother's tongue. She then moved to Paris to complete her studies in French literature and has been living and teaching there ever since. The protagonists of her novels are most often the Beurs, that is, children of Maghrebian immigrants in France who, like herself, are *croisés*, people in between worlds. Her most famous work is probably the three novels that chronicle the adventures of seventeen-year-old Shérazade, a young runaway of Algerian descent who, though always claiming to be on her way to Algeria, travels throughout Paris in the first book, *Shérazade* (1982), throughout France in the second one, *Les Carnets de Shérazade* (1985), and throughout the Middle East in the 1991 conclusion, *Le Fou de Shérazade*.

Sebbar bases a large part of her novels on Western representations of Arab people, pictorial and written. She seems to devote more space to Western representation than to works originating from the Arab world, and an obvious question arises for the reader: how are we to interpret the influence of Western representation on her works? Why is it given such importance? Are we to view her texts as either having fallen into the trap of Orientalist repetition or as engaging in oppositional dialogue with the Orientalist tradition so as to expose its imperialistic and colonialist presuppositions? Or is it impossible in her case to use such dualistic frameworks?

To all groups that have been submitted to a dominant group's hegemony, two main forms of psychological and ideological resistance are open. One is to create a framework negating the presence and power of the hegemonic dominant, centering instead on an enabling vision of one's group as strong, free, and empowered. This strategy involves mythologizing and is often built around a nostalgic, imaginary return to a prehegemonic world. The Négri-

tude movement participated in that strategy, as do separatist cultural feminism and feminist theology of the Goddess. They look back to a world without the Other's hegemony, without the "epistemic violence" of colonization
and/or patriarchal power (Spivak 1991:804). Yet this desire to mythologize an
elsewhere originates from the historical presence of a crippling force acting
on the dominated group; this desire often upholds stereotypical characteristics imposed by the hegemonic dominant over subordinate groups (i.e.,
blacks as essentially emotional and irrational, women as inherently nurturing and peacemaking). This radical strategy that would eradicate hegemony
is resorted to because of that very hegemony. Thus it is a form of oppositional
discourse.

Another strategy of resistance involves the realization that the hegemonic
dominant uses its power to enforce what gets transmitted and what gets forgotten. This hegemonic discourse can be subverted but not ignored. Therefore, this strategy, more historical than mythological, involves reappropriation. Instead of creating new myths, it exposes the old ones for what they are,
ideological constructs and not objective truths. For example, Sebbar's protagonists are too young to have direct knowledge of recent historical events such
as the Algerian war, and they are exiled from their land of origin by their
families' immigration. Therefore, their search for origins must be mediated
by historical and artistic representations of their ancestors' presence.[1]

Since Sebbar uses the strategy of reappropriation rather than that of mythologizing, she must engage Western representation rather than circumvent
it. Because French (neo)colonial discourse attempted to erase Algerian culture and history, Western sources are necessarily omnipresent in her texts.
For Sebbar's protagonists, it is a matter of gathering as many traces of their
historical presence as possible so as to create a new, mosaiclike memory out
of the fragments of the old one: Shérazade, for instance, spends hours reading books that "told an old story, the history of her tattered memory, and a
new, modern story where continents and civilizations intersect, a history that
would be her own" (Sebbar 1985b:129).[2] These tattered bits of memory are
to be found anywhere they can, throughout books, various encounters, paintings, stories, photographs, and so on.

Sebbar's sources are both Western and Arabic. Because the hegemony
could not control everything, there remain Arabic sources to use, whether in
writing (the literary tradition, written histories) or orally. For instance, the
great figure of Abd-El-Kader (who unified the tribes to fight against French
colonization in the nineteenth century), as well as the tale of the *Arabian
Nights*, are prominent in Sebbar's fiction. For her, the oral tradition comes

not only from the women of the family when they gather together (Sebbar 1982:200–203) but, more important, from the grandparents who remain in Algeria and become their grandchildren's main affective ties to their parents' land. Throughout the *Shérazade* trilogy, Shérazade remembers her grandfather's ritual purifications (see *Shérazade*, pp. 136–37, for example). The memories of the summers spent in Algeria with her sister Mériem revolve around the figure of the grandfather as transmitter of Algerian culture.

As her young protagonists' travels allow them to gather heterogeneous bits and pieces of their history, Sebbar mixes all these sources into a cultural mosaic mapping their interior landscape. By juxtaposing historical and contemporary sources, Arabic and Western, she brings together "high" and "popular" cultures. The French cultural "patrimony" (literature, nineteenth- and twentieth-century painting) mingles with photojournalism and mainstream film.

Sebbar's insistence on pictorial representation and popular culture is a way of attracting a young readership whose eclectic learning is often done outside of school, so that allusions to Marilyn Monroe will help them "digest" references to Richard Wagner. Such a pedagogical strategy is meant to ease the learning process, to make learning painless and even unnoticed, to use entertainment for pedagogical purposes. There is no hierarchy of disparate elements, only a juxtaposition, in which the reader is free to pick what she or he chooses to remember. This pedagogical process is mirrored in the ways in which the protagonists themselves learn about their cultural environment.

The learning process is geared not only at young people similar to the novels' protagonists but also at a very French readership that might profit from learning about sociological, linguistic, artistic, and historical aspects of both Beur and Arabic cultures. Part of the learning process includes gaining an awareness of the centuries of interlocked histories of the countries on both sides of the Mediterranean. For instance, in the second book of the trilogy, Shérazade puts in parallel the writings of two early eighteenth-century travelers, Turkish ambassador and historian Mehmed Efendi on France and British aristocrat Lady Montagu on Turkey (Sebbar 1985b:181–83). It is interesting that both writers comment on the freedom of the "other" women, French in the first case, Turkish in the second. These writers even met once: "The Orient meeting the West, each going back to their native countries, their luggage heavy with notes, with titillating and picturesque anecdotes from both sides of the sea" (p. 183). This quotation illustrates how the impulse to objectify the other exists on both sides. Orientalism also had an

"Eastern" counterpart. For example, blond hair functions as a sign of complete otherness which fascinates not only Efendi but also the Turks who came in contact with Montagu, as well as the Turkish immigrants Shérazade meets in France. The fascination for blond hair prevents them from seeing the person behind it (p. 183). Blond hair, for them, could be said to function in a similar way as the veil does for Westerners visiting Arab countries. The attraction exerted by the sign of absolute difference impedes the recognition of the other as subject—the Turkish immigrants are too busy looking at the German waitress Helga's hair to listen to her conversation (p. 184).

One of the characteristics of such an objectification is to focus on the least representative but most striking aspects of the "Other" world: both Efendi and Montagu neglect to describe rural areas, centering instead on the eccentricities of court life. Sebbar insists on this class clash, compensating for Efendi's and Montagu's narrow perspectives by bringing contemporary Turkish immigrants into her novel. The eighteenth-century exotic travel narratives are put in parallel with the exilic situation of poor Turks in France to shock the reader into an awareness of the distance between Orientalist fantasy and the material conditions of real people's existence.

The juxtaposition of knowledge, literary and personal (Shérazade visited the village where these Turks now live), creates a subtler, more complex picture of the reality of Turkish-French involvement. This juxtaposition occurs through an exchange between Shérazade and Gilles, the truck driver who is giving her a ride, pointing to the pedagogical purpose of such dialogue. Shérazade, the cultural *métisse*, teaches the Frenchman that he is also part of the same mixed heritage, whether he likes it or not. She reminds him of the fact—often easily forgotten by the French—that the Arabs occupied the south of France for almost three hundred years, from the eighth to the eleventh centuries, that is, longer than the French presence in Algeria. The history of conquest, loss, and cross-cultural mixing between the Arab world and Europe is a long-lasting one which repeats itself (Sebbar 1985b:264). This history lesson is not offered to justify French colonization and neocolonialism, but to unsettle French assumptions of superiority over Arab cultures as well as to work against the myth that French identity is based on racial purity.

Throughout the novel, Sebbar insists on many instances of cross-fertilization and cultural encounters between the Arab and the French worlds. Toward the end of the book, Nasser, a Tunisian historian, puts in relation two texts on the "Other," the twelfth-century *Chroniques arabes des croisades* and François de Chateaubriand's nineteenth-century *Itinéraire de Paris à Jérusalem*. He turns the tables on contemporary anti-Islamic French discourse by critiquing Chateaubriand's bias against Islam, calling him a Christian "fa-natic, a fundamentalist" (p. 270). He uses words the French usually reserve for religious Muslims. Sitting at the terrace of a café, Nasser then reads out loud (for all to hear) an Arabic ethnographic description of the European women who participated in the Crusades. The author of the *Chroniques* placed these women in two categories, the prostitute and the warrior. The text, whose tone is similar to many French books on the "Arab Woman," infuriates the bar patrons, who start a brawl.

Juxtaposing Arab texts on the French and French ones on the Arabs is a very important part of Sebbar's strategy in her novels. For her, it is crucial to make Western Orientalist representations conflate with Arab representa-tions of the West to show that the impulse to render the Other exotic is present on both sides and to destabilize both kinds of objectifications. This allows her to remind the French of a history in which they too have been conquered, dominated, and represented as Other. Gilles's impatient reaction to Shérazade's historical teachings and the riot in the café created by Nasser's reading bear witness to the fact that such history is not welcomed by many French people, some of whom, rather than discussing the Crusades, "rail about immigrants in France" (p. 272). The power of Sebbar's juxtapositions lies in the fact that they force the French to confront the reductive objectifi-cations they have engaged in by placing them in the position of objects of another's discourse.

The long history of military conquest and cultural interaction between the two regions has resulted in a *métissage*, a cross-cultural connection em-bodied not only by the characters of Shérazade and her boyfriend Julien but also by their relationship itself. As a *pied-noir* (from a family of French settlers in the Maghreb), Julien is also a cultural *métis*. His profession of faith about his work in *Shérazade* is very close to Sebbar's own project:

He worked both on colonial archives and on the archives of Arab civilization and literature. When he talked about it, people would always be amazed that he would take an equal interest in such different productions — antagonistic, they said. But these contradictions, if there were any, did not bother him. He was curious about everything that, from as far as history could go, constituted his own history as well as that of two peoples, two cultures which had been in relation since the Crusades (p. 113).

Sebbar, like Julien, thrives on these contradictions and antagonisms, refusing to reduce the richness and complexity of the Arab/French connection and foregrounding its ambiguities.[3]

This ambivalent connection is symbolized by Julien's and Shérazade's relationship. They come from "different," "antagonistic" backgrounds. The son of French colonists, Julien grew up in Algeria. After the war—in which his parents participated on the side of the Algerian National Liberation Front—he and his family were forced to seek exile in France. For Shérazade, born in France to Algerian immigrants, Algeria is the place of distant origins and summer vacations. Both characters are in between, neither completely exiled nor totally at home.

For Sebbar, this contradiction, however painful to live through, is also a source of richness. Shérazade's and Julien's relationship is a love story marked by mediation and absence. It is punctuated by Shérazade's repeated disappearing acts. Both characters are absent from Algeria, the country to which they have a strong emotional attachment. This exile is expressed linguistically: both speak Arabic with an accent (Sebbar 1991:18, 37; 1982:113). Their relationship is also marked by an important pedagogical element. As Mildred Mortimer remarks in *Journeys Through the French African Novel*, Shérazade and Julien teach each other their own fragmented knowledges of the Algerian/French historical and linguistic juncture (1990:185). For example, Shérazade teaches Julien sentences in the Algerian dialect, while he teaches her literary Arabic vocabulary (Sebbar 1982:146). The exchange is also cultural: Shérazade tells Julien popular, oral Algerian stories (p. 147); he reads to her famous Arabic poems (Sebbar 1991:116) and introduces her to Orientalist paintings (1982:13).[4]

Because of its colonial and neocolonial context, the exchange between Shérazade and Julien is fraught with danger and must be constantly renegotiated. This explains why Shérazade leaves Julien each time he is about to incorporate her into one of his colonial fantasies. Their relationship is not to be read as an apology of colonization as fruitful encounter or as the site of an unproblematic multiculturalism but, rather, as the realization that the colonial encounter, in its violence, created a hybridization that can never be erased. Such a *métisse* history must be dealt with, and the search for one's roots and identity must of necessity pass by this crossroads. This is made clear in Sebbar's treatment of French Orientalist painting.

Sebbar's protagonist experiences an ambiguous fascination for Western representations of Algerians. Sebbar focuses on Shérazade's responses (as a *métisse* at the crossroads between Algeria and France) to what Edward Said has called Orientalism. In the trilogy, she foregrounds the elements of an Orientalist discourse of representation that can be of use to her character's process of identity formation, while also addressing the violence inherent in these representations. Shérazade goes through the process of identity formation in part by grappling with Western representations, in turn subverting, overthrowing, or reappropriating them for her own purposes in a playful, parodic, and sometimes violent exchange. Masquerade is one of the means by which, to paraphrase Judith Butler, identity and the contests over its "authenticity" are produced (1990:159). In other words, it is through donning the trappings of the Odalisque, through performing the role of the "Oriental woman" and at the same time distancing herself from these representations, that Shérazade constructs her own *métisse* identity. In this repetition of Orientalist representation, a difference emerges. Whereas such representations were meant to stand in for the absent "Algerian woman," the fact that Shérazade is partially present under the Orientalist layers creates a surplus, an excess of meaning which displaces the fixed, overdetermined category of "Oriental woman." Luce Irigaray's theory of mimicry in "Power of Discourse" may be helpful here to understand the process I have just outlined. Irigaray posits that it is first through their deliberate repetition of a male discourse of female representation that women will be able to reappropriate language. This repetition will be subversive because of its difference: spoken from a different position, it might extend into the realm of parody; female mimicry will

make "visible," by an effect of playful repetition, what was supposed to remain invisible: the cover-up/recovering of a possible operation of the feminine in language. It also means "to unveil" the fact that, if women are such good mimics, it is because they are not simply resorbed in this function. *They also remain elsewhere:* another case of the persistence of "matter," but also of *"jouissance"* (1985:76, translation modified).

Beyond literary analysis, my broader purpose is to go beyond what I see as a problematic situation in feminist theory caused by the current binary opposition between essentialism and postmodernism.[5] I neither subscribe to the position that there is such a thing as a core identity formed before entry into the sociocultural structures of society nor that identity is only a performance, a mask underneath which only absence can be found. The assumption that the hegemonic dominant has always already completely overdetermined all representations is a dangerous and self-serving theory defusing the possibility of what Chandra Talpade Mohanty calls "dynamic oppositional agency":

The relations of power I am referring to are not reducible to binary oppositions or oppressor/oppressed relations. I want to suggest that it is possible to retain the idea of multiple, fluid structures of domination which intersect to locate women differently at particular historical conjunctures, while at the same time insisting on the dynamic oppositional agency of individuals and collectives and their engagement in "daily life" (1991a:13).

The *Shérazade* trilogy exemplifies such dynamic oppositional agency. Shérazade's identity is not solely constructed out of her encounters with Orientalist scholars and representations but also out of her relationships to the Maghrebian immigrant community, family ties to Algeria, and contact with marginal figures. It is through the power relations existing between these different cultural sites that she negotiates her identity and establishes her agency.

For Shérazade, disguise is experienced as a subversive gesture of identity formation. During her travels through France, she and her French friend Marie visit nineteenth-century Orientalist writer Pierre Loti's house in Rochefort. They manage to stay after hours, putting on some of Loti's outfits from his Orientalist collection: "They dressed up as Ottoman warriors, harem princesses, Odalisques, Black slaves . . . Not one thing was missing from Loti's bazaar" (Sebbar 1985b:161).

As she repeats Loti's masquerading gesture, Shérazade recognizes how reductive his construction of the Orient is for her, whereas her friend Marie does not see the difference. The stereotypes perpetuated by Loti anger Shérazade: "She had felt like breaking it all. . . . This accumulation of Orientalish stuff had exasperated her, not Marie. — This Orient is straight out of K-Mart . . . He must have found it in a cereal box, Shérazade said, laughing, before she wrapped herself in silk for her exotic night" (pp. 161–62). The use of words like "bazaar" and "Orientalish" and the references to the discount store and household product put Loti's collection in parallel with cheap, mass-produced normalizing artifacts. Shérazade resents the epistemic violence of this exotic collection that encapsulates the Orientalist impulse to appropriate, collect, possess, classify, and accumulate in an effort to conquer through stereotyping the other. She channels her anger through derision. She mocks Loti's pathetic collection, laughing at it, wearing it tongue in cheek, as a disguise.

Shérazade's gesture is all the more subversive because it is forbidden, since Loti's house, now turned into a museum to his glory, is closed at night. Role-playing Odalisques, the two women clandestinely stay in the museum overnight and play with items that are not supposed to be touched or tampered with. Shérazade is even tempted to steal a few things, although Marie convinces her that they would be too heavy for the two runaways to carry.

This would not have been the first time Shérazade engaged in theft. Like Matisse's *Odalisque à la culotte rouge*, a painting that fascinates the young protagonist (Sebbar 1982:244–45), Shérazade, playing in and out of Orientalist representation, also wears red underwear (pp. 130, 233). But her red underwear has been shoplifted, a gesture typical of her subversive spirit. Rather than being a complacent Odalisque lavished with gifts, Shérazade is a runaway who, in Hélène Cixous's words, "flies/steals through" the language of Orientalist representation (1975:49). Shérazade's fascination with the figure of the Odalisque, then, does not prevent her from measuring the distance between herself and Matisse's and Delacroix's painted women, a distance to which her Orientalist, *pied-noir* boyfriend Julien is oblivious and which once prompts her to leave him with the note, "I am no Odalisque" (Sebbar 1982:206). This message, which remains unsigned, indicates a refusal to be defined by fixed Orientalist parameters of representation. Shérazade, the runaway, not only engages in petty theft but participates in a holdup in a fancy restaurant (pp. 64–68) and a break-in (pp. 105–9) with her gang. She thus literally steals/flies not only through language but also through French society, disrupting both its representations and its material organization. Here, Sebbar is engaging and distorting yet another French stereotype of Arabs and Beurs — as thieves — by presenting her protagonist's activities as subversive of the dominant order.

After her anger and desire to destroy Loti's exotic bazaar, her laughter at his colonial fantasy as she dons some of its trappings frees her from its hold. Like the Medusa's laugh, Shérazade's laughter allows her to distance herself from the dominant representative order. In contrast, it is much harder for French people to shake the Orientalist hold over them because they lack other frames of reference. Part of Sebbar's project can thus be understood as an attempt to provide French readers with another frame of reference through her fiction. Shérazade's friend Marie, for instance, does not understand Shérazade's anger at what the French girl considers to be Loti's "innocent" whims. As for Julien, who may identify with the Orientalist writer at some level, Loti's imaginary world peoples his own: immediately attracted by Shérazade when he meets her for the first time, he compares her to Loti's Oriental lover Aziyadé (pp. 7–8).

The context in which the scene of Shérazade's masquerade takes place reinforces the reductive and naturalizing character of Loti's collection. The scene occurs directly after a passage in which Shérazade explains to Gilles that the young Beur singers they just met are *not* dressed up, *not* masquerading: "Their Turkish, Arab, Berber or African grandfathers' traditional clothing belongs to them, and European clothes belong to everyone, so their own look is about mixing it all up, but not any which way, it's very calculated" (Sebbar 1985b:159). As opposed to Loti's, this way of dressing, which is also to an extent Shérazade's, is not a disguise, although Gilles believes it to be so because it appears exotic to him. Rather than being the expression of a colonial fantasy, the Beurs' mixed clothing is a sign of what Françoise Lionnet calls *métissage:* a cultural and/or racial mixing which, turned into an aesthetic and artistic creation, reflects negatively on Loti's cheap bazaar. This aesthetics of *métissage* is also reflected in Shérazade's name.

Shérazade's first name embodies a hybridity that inscribes within itself the dynamics of loss and excess.[6] As an Orientalist marker for the exotic woman, the name is too much, too good to be true: "Her name often triggered strange, unexpected and uncontrollable reactions" (Sebbar 1985b: 140). The first novel of the trilogy opens with a scene in which Julien, who is attracted to Shérazade precisely because she reminds him of Delacroix's green-eyed woman (in the painting *Femmes d'Alger dans leur appartement*), is stunned to find reality confirming his Orientalist fantasy in such a way (Sebbar 1982:7).

Shérazade, however, is not the Sultana of *The Arabian Nights*. In the transcription of her name from spoken Arabic to the French birth certificate, the name loses what would be an excess syllable in French (because of the mute "h") but is "the sweetest, most Oriental syllable" in Arabic, according to an old Lebanese woman whom Shérazade meets in the last book of the trilogy (Sebbar 1991:164). Shérazade's name is a perfect metaphor for France's assimilation policy with regard to immigrants. What is most representative of other cultures must be cut off for the other to be accepted and assimilated into the fabric of French life. What could be viewed as the richness of difference is rejected as unnecessary excess.

The loss of the syllable marks Shérazade as a cultural *métisse*. Like Homi Bhabha's interstitial spaces, her name functions as a sign of in-betweenness that metaphorically gives her some margin for maneuver. She takes on this new identity imposed on her by the French administrative system and uses it to avoid being confused with her namesake the Sultana and thus to claim difference from her doomed model. As Gilles notes, the Sultana Scheherazade "is a gentle and flexible woman, not . . . aggressive like Shérazade" (Sebbar 1985b:104). Many of the men Shérazade encounters do not at first understand the difference between the two names and the two women, and Shérazade is always prompt to enlighten them. She claims her difference from Scheherazade by holding on to the unique spelling of her name whenever an Orientalist tries to impose his or her colonial fantasy onto her.

As part of the game of hide-and-seek she plays with those who want to incorporate her within their colonial fantasy, Shérazade also uses aliases. When she first meets Michel Salomon, a Jewish *pied-noir* photographer, she plays with/anticipates his Orientalist fantasies by pretending to be named Balkis, "like the Queen of Sheba" (Sebbar 1985b:268). When Nasser, the Tunisian scholar, joins them, she reveals her real name (p. 269). For those who cannot accept her name, she has two French alternatives to offer, sometimes Rosa and most often Camille (pp. 29, 169, 207; 1991:173). The choice of the androgynous, traditional French name Camille functions as yet another disguise.

Just as she wraps herself in Loti's silk, consciously playing along with his taste for the "exotic," Shérazade often *appears* to be complying with men's representations of the Oriental woman. She lets herself be photographed and filmed over and over by several different men, including Julien and Michel. Yet she remains highly conscious at all times that the men are creating their own fantasy of her, and she keeps on destabilizing these representations. For instance, while she lets Julien take endless rolls of pictures of her, she always chooses her own poses: "She never obeyed his orders" (Sebbar, 1982:148). She uses disobedience, escape, and laughter as strategies of refusal which allow her to subvert the men's representations of her.

In contrast to the men's seriousness about their "work" of representation, Shérazade envisions it as game-playing: "She performs the scene" (Sebbar 1991:131). She makes herself elusive, proving that none of these representations can ever define her completely. But she also resists being reinscribed as the enigmatic, mysterious, and silent Oriental woman. For instance, she teaches Julien how to change his perception of her. Throughout *Shérazade* and *Le Fou de Shérazade*, Julien alters "the [film] script that he had written for her" because Shérazade's agency forces him to confront the inadequacy of his representation of her (Sebbar 1991:180). Communication and dialogue are possible between them: "Shérazade made some remarks to which Julien listened. He modified his script to include what she had said" (Sebbar 1982:160). Although Julien pursues his inner vision of Shérazade, he proves himself open to the young woman's challenges of that vision. The space of their dialogue is thus one of constant renegotiation.

Communication does, however, break down sometimes, even with Julien. In such cases, Shérazade does not hesitate to resort to violence. She tears up the pictures of herself that Julien had posted all over his apartment when she realizes that these representations may mean more to him than she herself does: "You don't need me alive, really" (p. 158). A parallel can be drawn between Julien and Pierre Loti for in both cases, their colonial fantasies rely on the absence of the object of desire. The Other's actual presence is in excess in the economy of colonial desire. Shérazade's violent act allows her to break through Julien's colonial unconscious: "He felt that Shérazade was right" (p. 159).

In her book *Transfigurations of the Maghreb*, Winifred Woodhull analyzes other instances in which Shérazade uses violence as a response to the violence exerted upon her by men's representations of her (1993:20–22). Woodhull notes the sexualized vocabulary used to describe a photographer's camera which Shérazade breaks after he surreptitiously tries to take a picture of her at a party: "his equipment severely mutilated" (Sebbar 1982:125). The camera explicitly symbolizes the phallus. Sebbar thus exposes the libidinal investment attached to the use of photography to appropriate women's images. By attacking the camera, Shérazade hits where it hurts the most — literally, below the belt. Her violence, as a response to violence of a sexual nature exerted against her, is experienced as sexually castrating. By breaking the camera, she effectively neutralizes (neuters?) Orientalist desire, a desire which is perceived as violent because the camera, like the phallus, can be used as a weapon. Sebbar's choice of vocabulary when Shérazade is being photographed indicates the potential danger of representation: Shérazade serves as a "target for a photographic eye" (Sebbar 1985b:193).

In the colonial or postcolonial contexts, violence is inherent to the representational act, as Malek Alloula remarks in *The Colonial Harem*: "Colonialism is, among other things, *the perfect expression of the violence of the gaze*" (1986:131). Even more than Alloula, Sebbar insists that the colonial gaze is also a phallic gaze. Shérazade encounters several instances of the violence of photographic representation, including French military photographer Marc Garanger's collection of pictures of Algerian women, *Femmes algériennes 1960*. As opposed to the colonial postcards analyzed by Alloula (in which paid models were used to stand in for an absent subject, Algerian women), Garanger photographed Algerian women and men to establish identity cards for that population during the Algerian war of liberation from the French. As Shérazade leafs through that book, the narrator comments: "These Algerian women all had the same intense and fierce look in front of the shooting lens, a look so savage that the images would only be able to record it, without ever mastering or dominating it. These women all spoke the same language — her mother's language" (Sebbar 1982:220). The women's reaction to being forcibly photographed parallels Alloula's work, which is an "attempt . . . to return this immense postcard to its sender" (1986:5). Alloula remarks that the women in the postcards, even though they were willing models, often look at the camera with hostility or boredom instead of projecting enjoyment and unbridled sexuality (p. 98). Similarly, the women Garanger photographed resisted by returning the violent gaze to its sender. The photographs are in both cases representative of the general violence of French colonization of Algeria.

Sebbar's treatment of Garanger's photographs and Alloula's critique of the postcards bear testimony to the impossibility of totally mastering or dominating the Algerian people. Decades later, Garanger's violent book allows Shérazade to establish a link to her roots because she connects these women to her mother through language. In this context, this violent photo album is made to serve a positive function for Shérazade. As Woodhull shows in her book, Shérazade comes across the picture book at a critical moment (1993: 121–22). Her encounter with Garanger's *Femmes algériennes* (a book whose direct violence covers the exotic potential of these new *Femmes d'Alger*) functions as a cautionary tale which allows her to reject the moviemaker's fantasy of the Oriental woman in which she was getting entangled and to momentarily leave his film project.

In her article on Beur writer Azouz Begag, Samia Mehrez critiques Deleuze and Guattari's concept of deterritorialized minor literatures by arguing for the necessity of reterritorialization in postcolonial minor literature: "Our critical investigation should never stop at 'deterritorialization'" because postcolonial "minor" literature, rather than glorifying exile, "seeks to acquire and legitimate territory" at the same time as it "deterritorializes the dominant . . . the crucial question is indeed one of territory, one of legitimate space that cannot afford to be nomadic, that can only counteract exile" (1993:27–28, 33). Mehrez links the absence of a reflection on reterritorialization in *Kafka* to the fact that, like Julia Kristeva in *Strangers to Ourselves*, Deleuze and Guattari appear to be more interested in the "depoliticized" implications of minor literature for native speakers of major languages (p. 27). They investigate the possibility for such writers to carve their own space of difference within their language and culture. The difference in power position between such a situation and that of exiles or immigrants, especially Beurs in France, is too easily erased by Deleuze, Guattari, and Kristeva, as both Mehrez and Woodhull point out (Woodhull 1993:88–89).

Exiled minority groups fragmented by conflicting allegiances and desires are confronted with the impossibility of using a nationalistic framework to further their cause. This is particularly true of the Beur populations depicted by Sebbar. For exiles, the concept of belonging to a nation is often replaced by a desire to create an imagined territory for oneself and other exiles. In his "Reflections on Exile," Edward Said opposes exile to nationalism, and insists on exiles' "urgent need to reconstitute their broken lives" (1990:360).

In Sebbar's case, writing is used as a locus for reterritorialization. Her purpose is to "give (children of immigration) a territory in literature" (quoted in Laronde 1987–88:8). A group whose literal presence in France is denounced as excessive by too many French people, Beurs are extremely concerned with issues of territory. By weaving *métissés* texts, Sebbar attempts to reterritorialize, not at the nationalist level, but to create "imagined communities" that do not hark back to a common, mythical past.[7] Rather, they emerge through foregrounding a history of colonization and resistance. In an interview with Monique Hugon, she adds that she likes to "write in French about a reality which is not absolutely French, and to give Arabs a legitimate space in French literature" (1986:37). As Woodhull shows, this allows Sebbar to "productively alter the terms of debates about Frenchness," or, in other words, to reterritorialize the dominant by reappropriating, displacing, and challenging its self-definitions (1993:106). It is in this context that Sebbar's assertion that she is a French writer must be understood: her project is to redefine Frenchness as *métissage*, in terms inclusive of people of Maghrebian descent.

For Sebbar, the French language is what allows her "to experience exile as a territory" (1985a:10). Writing in French permits Sebbar to turn exile into a "productive" position (quoted in Hugon 1986:35). Exiled from her place of origin, she negotiates her own location through the creative act: "Writing is the privileged place, the chosen, adopted land" (quoted in Hugon, p. 35). In other words, Sebbar finds her imagined community in the space of writing. The lack of a land to call her own, her home, makes her take writing as her territory, a territory inscribed in the French language. Sebbar would concur with Said's assertion that "the only home truly available now, though fragile and vulnerable, is in writing" because "homecoming is out of the question" (1990:365, 361). This last remark is certainly true for the Beurs, as exemplified by Shérazade's journeys. As she wanders around Parisian, French, and Middle Eastern territories, Shérazade gathers a literary and cultural baggage which allows her to create her own imagined territory, a Mediterranean mosaic. In the case of Sebbar's fiction, then, Mehrez's claim that postcolonial "minor" literature seeks a "legitimate space that cannot afford to be nomadic" must be qualified. Because the space of reterritorialization is marked by preexisting, overdetermined conditions and borders, reclaiming such a territory must of necessity be at the same time a grounded and a nomadic practice constantly negotiating between fixed and objectifying representations. For Woodhull, it is a matter of both "dismantl[ing] fixed identities" and "affirm[ing] the liberatory aspect of the *gatherings* of dispersed identities" (1993:100). Mobility can be understood precisely as what grounds Shérazade's relational, fragmented identity, what allows her to piece the different parts of the mosaic together.

Shérazade thus travels in and out of Orientalist parameters, as an insider/ outsider, always on the border, in between, in flight. She reappropriates representations of herself for what she can learn from them at the same time that she returns the violent gaze to its sender by weaving her own fragmented identity over and through these representations. The roots that Shérazade, the nomadic Beur runaway, attempts to plant are not literal because she is always in flight; rather, they are imagined, cultural and literary.

NOTES

1. It was only after developing these two concepts of mythologizing and reappropriation that I became familiar with a similar distinction made by Stuart Hall in "Cultural Identity and Diaspora." Hall considers two definitions of cultural identity. The first is based on an essential, fixed view of identity that must be unearthed from the layers of colonial experience. The second presents identity in terms of mobile, shifting, historically contextualized positionings, as a "production" constructed within representations (pp. 392–95). In a recent essay on the second book of the *Shérazade* trilogy, Françoise Lionnet also develops an analogous model with respect to history: history can be suffered, acted on/inverted, or appropriated through discursive reconstruction (1995:174–75).

2. All translations from Sebbar's texts are my own.

3. I am indebted to Winifred Woodhull's analysis of Sebbar's *Shérazade* in her book *Transfigurations of the Maghreb*.

4. For a study of the influence of Orientalist paintings in Shérazade's process of identity formation, see Denise Brahimi's article "Orientalisme et conscience de soi."

5. The work of feminist theorist Chandra Talpade Mohanty has been instrumental in my thinking through these issues.

6. For a thorough analysis of the mechanisms of naming in Sebbar's works, see Michel Laronde, *Autour du roman beur*.

7. The words are Benedict Anderson's. I am following Chandra Talpade Mohanty's use of the terms to describe nonessentialist, political bases for group alliances (1991a:4–5).

WORKS CITED

Alloula, Malek. 1986. *The Colonial Harem*, trans. Myrna Godzich and Wlad God-zich. Minneapolis: University of Minnesota Press.

Anderson, Benedict. 1983. *Imagined Communities: Reflections on the Origin and Spread of Nationalism*. London: Verso.

Bhabha, Homi. 1994. *The Location of Culture*. New York: Routledge.

Brahimi, Denise. 1987. "Orientalisme et conscience de soi." In *Littérature maghré-bine d'expression française de l'écrit à l'image*, ed. Guy Dugas, pp. 29–36. Meknes, Morocco: Faculté des Lettres et des Sciences Humaines de Meknes (Maroc), Université Sidi Mohamed Ben Abdellah.

Butler, Judith. 1990. *Gender Trouble: Feminism and the Subversion of Identity*. New York: Routledge.

Cixous, Hélène. 1975. "Le Rire de la Méduse." *L'Arc* 61:39–54.

Hall, Stuart. 1994. "Cultural Identity and Diaspora." In *Colonial Discourse and Post-Colonial Theory: A Reader*, ed. Patrick Williams and Laura Chrisman, pp. 392–403. New York: Columbia University Press.

Hugon, Monique. 1986. "Leïla Sebbar ou l'exil productif" (interview). *Notre librairie* 84 (July–Sept.): 32–37.

Irigaray, Luce. 1985. "The Power of Discourse and the Subordination of the Femi-nine." In *This Sex Which Is Not One*, trans. Catherine Porter, pp. 68–85. Ithaca: Cornell University Press.

Laronde, Michel. 1987–88. "Leïla Sebbar et le roman "croisé": Histoire, mémoire, identité." *CELFAN Review* 7:6–13.

———. 1993. *Autour du roman beur: Immigration et identité*. Paris: L'Harmattan.

Lionnet, Françoise. 1989. *Autobiographical Voices: Race, Gender, Self-Portraiture*. Ithaca: Cornell University Press.

———. 1995. "Narrative Journeys: The Reconstruction of Histories in Leïla Sebbar's *Les Carnets de Shérazade*." In *Postcolonial Representations: Women, Literature, Identity*, pp. 167–86. Ithaca: Cornell University Press.

Mehrez, Samia. 1993. "Azouz Begag: *Un di zafas di bidoufile* or the *Beur* Writer: A Question of Territory." *Yale French Studies* 82:25–42.

Mohanty, Chandra Talpade. 1991a. "Cartographies of Struggle: Third World Women and the Politics of Feminism." In *Third World Women and the Politics of Femi-nism*, ed. Chandra Talpade Mohanty, Ann Russo, and Lourdes Torres, pp. 1–47. Bloomington: Indiana University Press.

———. 1991b. "Under Western Eyes: Feminist Scholarship and Colonial Dis-courses." In *Third World Women and the Politics of Feminism*, ed. Chandra Tal-pade Mohanty, Ann Russo, and Lourdes Torres, pp. 51–80. Bloomington: Indiana University Press.

Mortimer, Mildred. 1990. *Journeys Through the French African Novel*. Portsmouth, N.H.: Heinemann Educational Books.

Said, Edward W. 1978. *Orientalism*. New York: Pantheon Books.

————. 1990. "Reflections on Exile." In *Out There: Marginalization and Contemporary Cultures*, ed. Russell Ferguson, Martha Gever, Trinh T. Minh-Ha, and Cornel West, pp. 357–66. New York: New York Museum of Contemporary Art.

Sebbar, Leïla. 1982. *Shérazade, 17 ans, brune, frisée, les yeux verts*. Paris: Stock.

————. 1985a. "La langue de l'exil." *La Quinzaine littéraire* 436 (March 16–31): 8, 10.

————. 1985b. *Les carnets de Shérazade*. Paris: Stock.

————. 1991. *Le Fou de Shérazade*. Paris: Stock.

Spivak, Gayatri Chakravorty. 1991. "Three Women's Texts and a Critique of Imperialism." In *Feminisms: An Anthology of Literary Theory and Criticism*, ed. Robyn R. Warhol and Diane Price Herndl, pp. 798–814. New Brunswick: Rutgers University Press.

Woodhull, Winifred. 1993. *Transfigurations of the Maghreb: Feminism, Decolonization, and Literatures*. Minneapolis: University of Minnesota Press.

EMILY A. HADDAD

16. Fatal Nationality

Sulaymān Fayyāḍ's Novel 'Voices'

Although set a few years before Egypt proclaimed itself once and for all an independent republic in 1952, Sulaymān Fayyāḍ's *Voices* (1972/1977) is very much a novel of the postcolonial condition in Egypt.[1] It is concerned both with the practical consequences of long-standing imperialism and with the efforts of the colonized people to recognize and respond (practically and otherwise) to their disadvantaged situation. It is impossible to separate the events depicted in *Voices* either from the colonial context in which they are shown to occur or from the postcolonial consciousness that informs the novel. This is especially true of the novel's central event, the death of the character Simone. As the novel moves slowly toward this point, Fayyāḍ creates a complex picture of the many large issues which contribute to this fatal outcome: among others, global history and politics (especially imperialism), economics, gender, race, and religion.

While my reading of *Voices* alludes to each of these factors, it is my contention in this essay that the problem of nationality — national identification, national difference — is the novel's overriding concern and tends consistently to subsume the other issues raised by the novel. Fayyāḍ presents nationality as the motivating force behind the thematic development and plot of *Voices*, including the novel's tragic denouement. In particular, problems of nationality intersect with four thematic areas to which the novel draws special attention: sexuality (particularly sexual attractiveness), skin color, language, and questions of authority and dominance.

Voices is a relatively short work (116 pages; 98 pages in translation), structured as a series of first-person narratives by various of the novel's characters. The story they tell is this:[2] Thirty years after Ḥāmid al-Buḥayrī's emigration to

I wish to thank Professor Werner Sollors, Eve Troutt Powell, and David Schur for their comments on an earlier version of this paper, which was also presented in March 1994 at the American Comparative Literature Association Annual Meeting, Claremont, Calif.

Paris, he returns for a visit to his home village of al-Darāwīsh, accompanied by his French wife, Simone. Ḥāmid soon departs on a business trip to the capital, leaving Simone in the care of his brother ʾAḥmad.

During Ḥāmid's absence, a group of his mother's friends visit, hoping to see Simone, who keeps to her room. Instead, the women, including ʾAḥmad's wife, Zaynab, spend the afternoon discussing Simone. One of these women later returns and persuades Ḥāmid's mother that they, with Zaynab and two other women, should remove Simone's pubic hair and determine whether she has been circumcised. These five women enter Simone's room, overwhelm her, and undertake their task. Seeing that she is in fact uncircumcised, they proceed to perform this operation, after administering some anesthetic. To their horror, she bleeds to death as a result of the circumcision, never regaining consciousness. Local officials initiate a cover-up, ordering her buried immediately.

At almost every turn of this novel's distressing plot, the national identification of both Simone and the villagers is foregrounded. From very early on, *Voices* emphasizes the way the characters serve as representatives of their own nationality. This emphasis is most obvious in the case of Simone; from the time Ḥāmid's telegram announces her intent to visit the village to just before her circumcision, Simone's Frenchness is referred to often and emphatically.[3] It determines the villagers' preparations for her visit (e.g., the installation of European bathroom facilities), but, more important, it also defines both their understanding of her and their interpretation of her relationship with them. As the arrival of the "Frenchwoman" becomes imminent, the villagers must come to terms not only with her nationality but—for the first time—also with their own. Maḥmūd, a local student, who will later serve as Simone's guide and interpreter, explains the circumstances:

Before this surprise came upon our village without warning, everything seemed natural in our eyes, and familiar to our minds. This was life, and there was no other. . . . But now, even before anything material or tangible had happened . . . our eyes began to turn toward that imminent and astonishing new thing, tumbling down upon our village from above; we succumbed to its pressure, with feelings of backwardness and shame . . . and fear that we would see ourselves with new eyes—and that the Other would see us, that Other arriving from an invisible world known to none of us. (pp. 19–20 [10–11])

In confronting Simone's nationality and thereby becoming aware of their own, the villagers cannot avoid recognizing that France is technologically advanced and globally dominant, while their village could hardly be less so. In reaction, the villagers feel that they must make a good impression on Simone, not only to welcome her hospitably as the wife of a long-lost native son but to show her (and themselves) that they can measure up against the enormous pressure described by Maḥmūd. They try to spruce up the village, cleaning the streets and installing makeshift street lights. Ḥāmid's brother 'Aḥmad exhausts himself refurbishing both his house and his store. In the words of the mayor of al-Darāwīsh, the aim of all this renovation is "to raise Ḥāmid's head before his wife, and to raise the head of al-Darāwīsh, the district, and the whole of Egypt, before all foreigners, represented in the person of the lady Simone. . . . Al-Darāwīsh must present an appearance worthy of itself and of Egypt" (pp. 29–30 [21–22]). Thus cast firmly as representative — not only of France but of "all foreigners" rather than as an individual — Simone enters into a relationship with the village that is perceived by the villagers as competitive, even adversarial. They are always aware that Simone's nationality places her in alliance with the dominant world powers of the West, while their own status is determined by Egypt's global subordination.[4]

Only very rarely, however, does Simone herself appear to perceive this global, political dimension of her relationship with the village. At one point, for instance, she asks Maḥmūd why the peasants do not use machinery in their work. He records his reply: "I answered her as best I could, [mentioning] ignorance, overpopulation, the scarcity of capital, and British imperialism. When she saw me impassioned with what I was saying, she began to tell me how sorry she was and to apologize, as if she herself were the cause of everything that had happened, as if she had opened an old and forgotten wound in my heart" (p. 81 [79]). Simone appears here to be accepting blame for the peasants' deprivation, implicitly accepting her role as a representative of European hegemony. Yet the mere fact that she asks the question reveals an astonishing naïveté.[5] Simone's apparently sudden awareness here seems all the more peculiar given that Ḥāmid's preceding narrative recalls her asking him exactly the same question. In each of these exchanges, Simone's superficial and fleeting consciousness of her nationality's significance contrasts sharply with Maḥmūd's and Ḥāmid's recognition of their own Egyptianness. Just as the mayor presents the village of al-Darāwīsh as the representative of Egypt, so too both of these characters acknowledge any Egyptian (themselves included) as representative of Egyptians generally.

Fayyāḍ's treatment of Egyptians is varied and nuanced. He includes Egyptian characters with different levels of education, sophistication, and wealth and avoids eliding the social differences between, for instance, a virtually illiterate shopkeeper and a doctor or a district official. Yet in his own way, each character situates himself (or is situated by others) as a representative of the Egyptian nation, diverse and internally conflicted, but still a single unit in relation to the external world.[6]

By presenting the various characters as national representatives, Fayyāḍ places the question of national identity at the center of the narrative. At the same time, the author links the idea of nationality with other major themes throughout the novel so as to project a complex and multifaceted image of national identity. I will discuss the relationship between national identity and some of these themes, beginning with sexuality. As the villagers consider Simone's nationality and sexual power vis-à-vis their own, her sexual attractiveness becomes a subject of serious interest. Simply because she is French, Simone is implicated throughout in the stereotype of the French woman who is free of male control and is, as a result, sexually unrestrained.[7] Simone unintentionally acts out this role from the very beginning of her visit. For instance, she not only chooses to attend a reception to which she is the only woman invited, but she also appears there indecently dressed, according to village standards. Her host, the Mayor of al-Darāwīsh, describes the scene:

Simone came to the hall with Ḥāmid and his brother 'Aḥmad. Her appearance delighted my heart as a male, but angered me as a [respectable] man. Half of her back was bare, her hair was raised up off her long neck that looked like the neck of a gazelle, and her breasts were full and prominent, with the cleavage between them scandalously revealed. The hem of her red dress was short, above her knees. The young men of al-Darāwīsh and the surrounding countryside were yelling like crazy people outside the hall. I thought that she would corrupt them, and tempt us away from our veiled women and our virtuous girls. (p. 54 [49–50])

Much as Fayyāḍ portrays Simone as largely oblivious to her role as a representative of European political power, he shows her to be equally unaware of the likely sexual effects of her appearance, except in the most extreme instances.[8]

Simone's unwitting participation in this sexual stereotyping is reinforced by her absolute and exclusive adherence to French standards of behavior throughout her stay. She does not, for instance, wear a *gallābīya*, although that garment would be much more comfortable and practical in village life. She learns absolutely no Arabic, not even "thank you" or "good morning."[9] Most important, she attempts no modifications in her behavior to reflect village customs or expectations, despite her remarks to the contrary.[10] She is never shown to deviate from, or to make any effort to dispel, the mythological image of the Parisian that envelops her the moment Ḥāmid's first telegram arrives in the village.

This is an image with tremendous sexual appeal for most of the men in the village, from the youths outside the reception to Simone's brother-in-law 'Aḥmad to the mayor himself. Even Maḥmūd, who comes to know Simone better than anyone else in the village, is overtaken by this received image. He becomes infatuated with Simone, fascinated mainly by her difference from the village women:

Simone is not attractive, nor beautiful, nor ugly. Her skin is red, as the sun quickly scorched it along the way. Her slender physique is delicate and shapely. Together, her feathery blue dress and her complexion are charming, enchanting. Her gait is lively and her blue eyes shine with vitality. Many of the women in our village are much more beautiful than she is, and more attractive, but this woman has spirit, and a lofty and noble character. . . . In front of her I felt sorry for all our women. . . .

Simone — ah, Simone. How lovely and charming her name is, and the beauty of her eyes, and the magic of the camera which dangles from her shoulder at her slender waist. (p. 38 [30–31])

Maḥmūd's admiring description of Simone here is structured around an implied composite image of the village women. Simone's physique and way of moving her body are notable because they set her apart from the village women, who are typically heavier. Her comparatively scanty dress draws attention to the shape of her body. Even the shade of her dress stands out, as the village women wear mainly black.[11] Finally, her light coloring and her blue eyes give her an exotic look. In short, although Maḥmūd mentions the village women only briefly (and not unfavorably), they remain the standard by which he considers Simone. This is true even of Simone's less physical attributes, such as her "lovely and charming" name and her dangling camera. Neither of these attributes is shared by the women of al-Darāwīsh, and therein originates their appeal to Maḥmūd.[12]

Although the women in the village also perceive Simone's sexual power, they tend to express envy, resentment, or disapproval rather than attraction. Zaynab's response is quintessential. Because she is attracted to Ḥāmid, she becomes jealous of Simone; her realization that her husband, 'Aḥmad, is attracted to Simone only adds fuel to the fire.[13] Zaynab makes very clear, however, that her objections to Simone's sexuality have everything to do with Simone's nationality. Once Simone is circumcised, she predicts, Ḥāmid "will know that his wife is not preferable to me, nor more proper, and that an Egyptian woman is a thousand times better than a foreigner. And 'Aḥmad too will know that I am preferable to that puny Simone, and that he ought to be grateful that he got as good a catch as I, since he's [so] poor and ignorant next to his brother Ḥāmid" (p. 100 [103]). As Zaynab's defensive tirade here demonstrates, there can be no getting around nationality. Her own overwhelming sense of inferiority originates in a nationality-based comparison between Simone and herself, "an Egyptian woman" — a comparison in which the male characters (Ḥāmid and 'Aḥmad) are equally implicated.

Voices seems to link sexual status irrevocably to national identification (although, as we shall see later, Simone's circumcision will complicate this linkage). The relationship between skin color and nationality, and, in parallel, language and nationality, however, presents a more complex picture from the start. Although Simone's skin color is referred to only infrequently in *Voices* and the motif of color is relatively understated in the novel as a whole, it remains a primary marker of the characters' nationality. Through questions of color, Fayyāḍ raises and explores the problem of national identification, especially where such identification falls into doubt in some respect.

White skin color is first mentioned during the mayor's narrative, before Simone's arrival. Villagers remark that traces of French ancestry can be seen in the skin and eye color of those village inhabitants descended from Napoleon's soldiers (p. 32 [24]). This is virtually the only mention of whiteness per se until the end of the novel, when Zaynab is looking down at the anesthetized Simone: "It has occurred to me," she says, "that [Simone] pleases Ḥāmid with her spirit, and maybe also with her body, which resembles *malban* in its whiteness and softness" (p. 103 [107]).[14]

These two explicit comments on white skin frame a number of other references to skin color, whether light or dark. It is through these more complicated and nuanced references that Fayyāḍ explores the murkiness of national identification. Ḥāmid's one brief narrative offers an excellent perspective on these more intricate aspects of nationality. Ḥāmid begins by claiming Egypt as his "homeland" (p. 41 [33]) but immediately expresses his discomfort with it. In the cities of Alexandria and Cairo, he says, "the world seemed somewhat close to the world from which we had come" (p. 41 [33]) but only in its physical environment. "The people," however, "differed greatly" (p. 41 [33]). Even those who wore European clothes were distinguished by differences in behavior; in Ḥāmid's words: "They resembled Simone's people, despite their dark faces and their brown eyes. But the spirit and the culture! The cleanliness and the temperament!" (pp. 41–42 [33–34]). Here skin color serves as the initial indicator of difference; Ḥāmid's acknowledgment of the Egyptians' dark coloring is the immediate prelude to his recognition of their (distressing) divergence from his own expectations and ideals.

A few paragraphs later, Ḥāmid gives a more concrete manifestation to this association between skin color and other aspects of Egyptian national identification. As he passes through other villages on his way to al-Darāwīsh, he links the physical environment of rural Egypt with the color of the peasants' faces: "I was upset at the sight of the low, continuous mud-brick villages, and the dark, withered faces, emaciated and wan" (p. 43 [35]). The brownness of the mud-brick buildings and the brownness of the peasants' skin become visually (and symbolically) interchangeable; the clusters of buildings and the groups of people working "side by side" are images of equal degradation. Ḥāmid soon returns to this image, at his first sight of al-Darāwīsh (p. 45 [38]). In this case, he juxtaposes the low, mud-brick buildings with the layer of black dirt covering people's faces and clothes. Although he presents the obvious darkness of the villagers' skin as an external covering rather than an intrinsic characteristic (as in the previous image), the connection between the dark buildings and their inhabitants' dark skin remains at the center of the image. Whether dark in origin or darkened by circumstance, dark skin color is, in Ḥāmid's presentation, indicative of Egyptian nationality and of its debasement.

Underlying Ḥāmid's narrative here is obviously a struggle with his own national identification, but he makes little progress toward resolving it. Throughout the narrative, he consistently accepts that Egypt is his country and that the Egyptians are his people. Yet his identification with Egypt causes him an increasing sense of shame and bewilderment, as well as irritation. In the end, he is an Egyptian who does not feel Egyptian; his understanding of his situation goes no further.

As conscious as Ḥāmid is of other Egyptians' complexions, his treatment of his nationality makes no mention of his own skin color. For the villagers of al-Darāwīsh, however, the color of Ḥāmid's skin is very much at issue as they consider his national identity. Maḥmūd first raises this question as he describes the moment of Simone and Ḥāmid's arrival in al-Darāwīsh: "Suddenly I saw before my eyes two worlds: the faces of all the [village] people, and the face of Simone—and even the face of Ḥāmid, whose complexion and bearing had changed a great deal, to the point that you could not tell that he was from al-Darāwīsh stock" (pp. 36–37 [29]). Simone's nationality and color go unexamined here; they are obvious. Simone represents the European standard; both visually and connotatively, Simone's whiteness, especially as accentuated by her scanty dress and the crowd of darker faces surrounding her, emerges as her most salient feature. Similarly, the villagers' color and national identification are securely understood and bear no consideration by the narrator. Ḥāmid's status, in contrast, is uncertain from the first; historically, he is known to be from the village, but his physical appearance — including, of course, his "complexion" — no longer totally supports that identification. As a result, Ḥāmid's case casts doubt on Mahmūd's implied presumption that color accurately marks national identity, that a very "light" person is European, while a "dark" person is Egyptian.[15]

In a subsequent narrative, Mahmūd returns to this question with a clearer perspective. He explains his view: Ḥāmid "would really be Parisian, but for the fact that he's dark, and his hair is not completely combable, and his eyes are brown" (p. 76 [73–74]). Conversely, Mahmūd goes on, "He would be Egyptian, but for the healthy glow of his face, and the skin reddened as far as his throat, possibly from the quantity of wine he had drunk, and the amount of pork he had eaten, and the many hot and cold baths he had taken over the years, and the persistent effort [he had made] to consume vegetables and fruits rich in vitamins"[16] (p. 76 [74]).

While Mahmūd presents two possible national identifications for Ḥāmid here, it is clear from his ensuing reflections that he sees Ḥāmid more as Parisian than Egyptian. "But I don't feel . . . he is a son of al-Darāwīsh in any true sense," Mahmūd concludes (p. 76 [74]). Ḥāmid's French acculturation, as exemplified here in his eating, drinking, and bathing habits, overrides his Egyptian origin and his more or less Egyptian appearance. He achieves a sort of middle status; he is acknowledged as belonging visually and/or ancestrally to one category while also recognized as genuinely part of another. Ḥāmid's shift away from a pure Egyptian classification is especially notable given the villagers' initial, unquestioned assumption that he is Egyptian. Before his arrival, for instance, Ḥāmid is referred to as a "citizen" (p. 17 [7]) by the district official. So, too, virtually all the preparations for Ḥāmid's arrival have Simone as their target because she, not he, is the foreigner to be impressed. Only once Ḥāmid appears does his nationality come into question. At this point, the villagers observe that his color has changed to some extent; more important, they are forced to acknowledge the unreliability of color as marker of nationality. Rather as, in Ḥāmid's narrative quoted above, the circumstances of the villagers' nationality add an extra layer of darkness to their already dark skin, Ḥāmid's circumstances have altered his complexion while modifying his national identification.[17]

*

Although color is the most visible trait associated with nationality, language forms an important, albeit invisible, correlate. The role of language and communication is most obvious in the case of Simone, whose ignorance of the Arabic language thwarts effective communication between her and her hosts in the village, as various of the novel's narrators point out.[18] Fayyāḍ further emphasizes her linguistic exclusion by his choice of narrators; Simone is not one of the novel's numerous narrators so that anything she says is "interpreted" by one or another of the narrators. In this, the reader's position approximates the villagers', who also hear her only through an interpreter, either her husband or Maḥmūd.

Communication in *Voices* is not simply a matter of knowing the language, however; in fact, knowing the language can create problems when more complicated cultural understanding is required. In part because Ḥāmid is still able to speak Arabic, albeit clumsily, his family assumes that he is also able to remember village conventions. In most cases he does not, and serious misunderstandings result. At one point, for instance, he gives 'Aḥmad an unheard-of amount of money to distribute to their various relatives. 'Aḥmad realizes that giving out the money as intended will arouse tremendous envy within the village. He also feels that, as Ḥāmid's brother, he deserves a larger proportion of the money. Both of these complications would be immediately understood by any other villager, yet in his thirty years away, Ḥāmid has lost his sense of such matters. Similarly, although Ḥāmid is able to interpret for Simone, his disconnection from Egyptian cultural expectations prevents him from serving as her liaison in more important respects. When, for example, he gives orders that Simone not be disturbed in her room but fails to explain to her how socially unacceptable it would be for her to stay in her room while guests were visiting, he unwittingly sets the scene for her death. Much as his skin color and hair texture do, Ḥāmid's use of Arabic sends a false signal, suggesting that he is more fully Egyptian than he turns out to be.

Whereas skin color and the capacity to communicate (linguistically or culturally) serve as crucial markers of nationality in *Voices*, the ability to exercise authority is not only a marker but a consequence of national identity. Simone's case is the starkest; her ability to dominate a situation depends entirely on her national identification. For instance, her French manner of eating—the use of utensils rather than bread, the consumption of dishes in a certain order—is, as 'Aḥmad says, forced upon her hosts, to their resentment and discomfort (p. 48 [42]). Indeed, this motif of French versus Egyp-

tian table manners recurs through the novel, always with the effect of reinforcing the French model.[19] In other matters as well, Simone is able to
exercise her authority more effectively than almost any villager—and certainly any village woman—would.[20]

As the final event of *Voices* demonstrates, however, Simone is not as
invulnerable as she has appeared to be thus far. Throughout the novel,
Simone's authority has resided in her nationality, which distinguishes her
from the village women. It is in Simone's body, and specifically her clitoris,
that the village women locate the absolute origin of her difference and, con-
comitantly, her authority. Although they consider her pubic hair unclean
and remove it, its elimination is insufficient. Only the removal of her clitoris
will render her body equivalent to theirs, thus neutralizing its difference and
its power to threaten. The women's choice of Simone's clitoris makes a perverse logical sense. They perceive Simone as an unwanted intruder who
penetrates their society. They also implicitly accept the myth that an uncircumcised woman's clitoris can keep growing until it becomes like a penis.[21]
Through this myth, Simone's penetration of their society is given a physio-
logical referent, and circumcision (a symbolic removal of the phallus) becomes the sensible remedy.

Simone's clitoris is, moreover, explicitly and inextricably associated with
her national identification. Ḥāmid's mother's friend Nafīsa makes this point,
beginning with the irrefutable observation that Simone does not remove the
hair from her armpits. She speculates that Simone must not remove her
pubic hair either and then announces that "Simone . . . has not yet been
circumcised like other women" (p. 97 [100]). "How do you know?" asks
Ḥāmid's mother, to which Nafīsa responds, "That's how it is in her country"
(p. 97 [100]).

Ignoring the objections and doubts of Ḥāmid's mother, Nafīsa persists in
developing her argument, claiming that because Simone is uncircumcised,
"she becomes passionate; like a female cat [in heat] . . . she is never satisfied.
She exhausts her husband every night, and is even disloyal to him whenever
she has the chance. Simone must have done this many times before her
marriage to Ḥāmid, and afterwards too" (pp. 97–98 [100–101]). To illustrate
her point, Nafīsa cites examples of Simone's behavior in the village; she
laughs with men, she goes into strangers' homes, she sits in coffeehouses.
Thus improper behavior, which in the past has been explained on the basis
of nationality in the abstract is now confirmed according to a physical fact
determined by nationality. Nafīsa's analysis links Simone's Frenchness, her
behavior, and her uncircumcised status so closely that they become virtually

inextricable from one another. Under such circumstances, it seems reasonable to these characters that by circumcising Simone, they would eliminate the other two elements of her difference as well. With her new, "Egyptianized" physiology, Simone will have lost that which defines her as French and that which has empowered her to behave differently from the Egyptian women and to assume a standing they cannot. Zaynab makes this association explicit when she predicts that, as a result of Simone's circumcision, Ḥāmid will realize that "his wife is not preferable to [Zaynab], nor more proper, and that an Egyptian woman is a thousand times better than a foreigner" (p. 100 [103]).

One might draw a parallel between the women's effort here and the villagers' earlier attempt to Europeanize al-Darāwīsh, in that both reflect a desire to eradicate a difference which is based on nationality and which acknowledges an imbalance of power. The effort to Europeanize the village has clearly failed (the streets are once again dirty, the streetlamps have been smashed). In one sense, the women's effort is more successful. It is perhaps not coincidental in this context that, after the circumcision has begun, Simone is never again referred to as a "Frenchwoman" by any of the characters or narrators, despite the great number of such references before this event. Whatever threat Simone and her authority represent appears vanquished by her death, at least in the immediate term. Ḥāmid has been deprived of his French wife; moreover, by refusing to notify him of her death until after the burial, the officials reject his authority for the first time in the novel, in a sense confirming the extent to which his elevated status depended on his possession of "the Frenchwoman."

Overall, however, it would be very difficult to argue that *Voices* presents the women's circumcision of Simone as beneficial. The outcome of Nafīsa's plan is disastrous, not only for Simone but for the village as well. The final lines of the novel reaffirm this point. After the medical examiner, collaborating in the cover-up, has listed Simone's cause of death as "heart attack," the official who is responsible for the case takes him aside and asks:

"Tell me . . . what's the real cause of death?"
The doctor was disconcerted. [Looking] upset, with confusion visible on his face, he said, "Of course. Er . . . our death, or hers?" (p. 112 [120])

Thus Simone's death is presented as also "our death," Egyptians' death, while the question asked — "what's the real cause of death?" — remains pointedly unanswered. The answer is implied throughout the novel: nationality (specifically the conflict of national differences and the accompanying impulse to reaffirm and solidify national identity) is the cause of the death, of both "deaths." Neither Simone nor the villagers is able to accommodate to her presence in the village. Simone's solution to the situation is distance; she withdraws, carefully maintaining all that distinguishes her from her hosts, writing home about the village instead of participating in village life. The village women's solution is the opposite, an attempt to effect sameness, eradicating distance. It is important to recall, moreover, that the speakers here are the doctor and the district official, neither of them from al-Darāwīsh, which both view with contempt. That they include themselves among the "us" who die along with Simone greatly expands the significance of the village women's act. It is impossible, in this context, to conclude that their act is simply a fault of rural ignorance. These two more sophisticated male characters' inclusion of themselves among the victims inevitably frames the event in all its symbolic national importance.[22]

Fayyāḍ's point here seems to be that Simone's behavior symbolically perpetuates a wrongful power distribution between the white European and the villagers, representative subjects of imperialist oppression. But the villagers' effort to rectify the situation, though it responds directly and purposefully to the circumstances, is overall as ignorant, unrealistic, and shortsighted as Simone's approach — and certainly more malicious. Like Simone, the villagers act as their nationality and cultural experience dictate. In no case does Fayyāḍ allow individual will to take precedence over national inclination. In a global sense, the ending of *Voices* can be read as an indictment not only of a certain European attitude but even more of the Egyptian response to it. Whether by first seeking to emulate what they perceive as a European model (e.g., by "Europeanizing" al-Darāwīsh or by using knives and forks) or by later destroying what has become the quintessential symbol of Europe's threat (Simone), the villagers have gained no advantage whatsoever. Instead, as the doctor's confused final question reveals, they have caused their own "death." The eternal presence of Simone's body in the al-Buḥayrī family tomb is meant perpetually to remind the villagers of this (self-)destruction.[23]

Voices becomes at times almost allegorical in its treatment of nationality. Characters' identities depend on their gender, social class, economic status, and religion, as well as their nationality, but in *Voices* only nationality is so highly privileged as the determining element of the individual's identity. At no point in this novel is national identification a simple issue, not only because it is so intertwined with matters such as sexuality, skin color, language, and authority (complicated enough in themselves) but also because the novel always insists that national identifications exist in relation to one another and in a relationship of power with one another. By placing Simone, an individual from a globally dominant nation, in a context where her power (as an individual and as a representative) can be subverted at a local level by members of a globally subordinate nationality, Fayyāḍ establishes a situation in which the aesthetic, moral, and political distinctions that locate one national group in a certain relationship with the other become untenable, and each side subordinates the other to death.

NOTES

1. First published, as 'Aṣwāt, in Baghdad in 1972, then revised and republished in Cairo in 1977, this is Fayyāḍ's best-known work. He has also published half a dozen collections of short stories and is highly regarded as an "experimental" writer. Born in 1929, he received a mainly religious education and worked as a teacher until retiring to concentrate on research and writing. (For a brief biographical sketch, as well as a reading of *Voices* and extracts of an interview with the author, see Nadje Sadig Al-Ali, *Gender Writing/Writing Gender: The Representation of Women in a Selection of Modern Egyptian Literature* (Cairo: American University in Cairo Press, 1994], pp. 97–111.) 'Aṣwāt has been translated into English as *Voices* by Hosam Aboul-Ela (New York: Marion Boyers, 1993). I have used my own translations, based on the 1977 version, but have given the corresponding page numbers for Aboul-Ela's translation, followed by the Arabic edition page numbers in brackets.

2. This story is supposed to be based on an incident that took place in 1948 in a village in the Nile Delta; see Al-Ali, *Gender Writing/Writing Gender*, p. 108.

3. See pp. 21, 25, 29, 30, 36, 37, 38, 57, 88, 93, 94, 101 (13, 16, 21, 22, 28, 30; 31, 54, 88, 93, 94, 104); in each case, Simone is referred to as French, or Parisian specifically. There is also a much smaller number of references to Simone as European, or simply as a foreigner. The dominance of Simone's French/Parisian identification reflects the novel's more general emphasis on France's historic relationship with Egypt. Although Fayyāḍ does make both direct and oblique allusions to, for instance, British imperial involvement in Egypt, they rarely reach center stage; the novel's focus on France as the representative Western power remains consistent.

4. In a subtle, ironic twist, Fayyāḍ has Maḥmūd exclaim at the moment of Simone and Ḥāmid's arrival, "If the King himself were approaching, there would not have been such a spectacle" (p. 36 [28]). The king referred to here is Farūq, the Egyptian ruler who was deposed when Egypt was declared independent in 1952. By placing Simone above Farūq in this way, Fayyāḍ is using Simone's already established status as an emissary of European power to remind the reader once again of Egypt's subordination — an especially just reminder given Farūq's periodic capitulations to the British imperial authorities.

5. Nor is this the most naive of Simone's queries. She also asks where the forests

are and if it ever snows, questions that are too foolish for even the most ill-informed of journalists. Indeed, given her profession, Simone's gross ignorance is almost implausible and suggests that Fayyāḍ may be exaggerating her character for rhetorical or symbolic purposes.

6. Fayyāḍ's depiction of Egyptian female characters is comparatively monochromatic in this respect. Psychological differences among female characters are well developed, but all the Egyptian women portrayed belong to a relatively uniform social group (approximately, the uneducated rural lower class).

7. By the era in which this story is set, this stereotype is a well-established one, of which even these relatively isolated villagers are clearly aware. Its historical basis extends at least to 1834, when Rifāʿa Rāfiʿ al-Ṭahṭāwī reported it to the Egyptian public after a five-year stay in France. For a brief discussion of Muslim perspectives on European female sexuality and freedom, see Bernard Lewis, *The Muslim Discovery of Europe* (New York: Norton, 1982), pp. 284–94.

8. One such instance involves ʾAḥmad caressing her foot; in this case she clearly perceives the sexual element of the situation and makes her limits known.

9. On the only occasion when Simone uses an Arabic word, Maḥmūd (the narrator in this instance) makes clear that she has not learned the word during her stay in the village but had picked it up from Ḥāmid while in France (p. 86 [86]).

10. During his narrative, ʾAḥmad observes with amazement this discrepancy between Simone's French manners and her stated intention to follow local customs (p. 48 [42]).

11. Maḥmūd mentions the women's black clothes on at least two occasions (pp. 19, 34 [10, 26]); see also p. 109 (114).

12. The sexual dimensions of Simone's nationality, however, do not always stand alone in Maḥmūd's narrative. For example, as he dreams of Simone's enabling him to go to France for an otherwise impossible French medical degree, he thinks both of her economic power and of the possibility of a sexual liaison with her (p. 77 [75]). Given the "medical" disaster which befalls Simone at the end of this novel, Maḥmūd's dream inevitably has an ironic aspect.

13. In the course of Zaynab's narrative, it becomes clear that she envies Simone's whole life — her profession, her pleasures, her children. Nonetheless, Zaynab's envy both originates in and centers on her impression of Simone's sexual attractiveness to men.

14. *Malban* is a kind of sweet made of starch and sugar. Zaynab's awareness of whiteness as attractive has two likely sources. First, even Zaynab, a presumably illiterate woman living in an obscure village, would probably have some exposure to the image of the sexually attractive foreign woman, who is by tradition very white. Perhaps more important, the cultural standard of beauty favors the lighter-skinned woman over the darker. The classical Arab ideal is a woman with very light skin and very black hair, and the aesthetic preference for light rather than dark skin is persistent even in the absence of a strictly racial categorization. Nowhere does *Voices* acknowledge the possibility that a person of French origin

EMILY A. HADDAD

might be anything but white. The significance of this assumed linkage between French nationality and white skin color should not be overlooked; almost certainly, *Voices* would tell a different story if Ḥāmid's French wife were dark-complexioned. Nonetheless, despite the importance of color as a trait, nationality remains much the privileged concept. Race per se is not addressed directly.

For an overview of Middle Eastern views of color and race, see Bernard Lewis, *Race and Slavery in the Middle East: An Historical Enquiry* (New York: Oxford University Press, 1990), esp. chaps. 2, 13.

15. In Egyptian usage the Arabic word for "black" (*'aswad*) generally does not refer to people, although the word for "white" (*'abyaḍ*) is applied to both people and things. The common word to describe a "black" person is *'asmar*, which means "dark-skinned" and is used only for animate beings; this is the word Fayyāḍ uses when referring to dark-skinned Egyptians. *'Asmar* is primarily descriptive of appearance and does not necessarily imply a racial classification — rather as in white society one might say "blond" or "brunette." Where *'aswad* is used, it frequently alludes to national identity as well; people of Sudanese origin living in Egypt tend to be described in this way (often with derogatory intent).

Given the basic flexibility of these terms, it might be argued that the dichotomy evident between black and white in *Voices* is in part a Western importation, but one should also remember that the acknowledgment of color differences (and the concomitant privileging of light skin) has long existed in Arab culture (see Lewis, *Race and Slavery in the Middle East*, esp. chaps. 2, 13, 14). The question of race in modern Egyptian society is an extremely complex one to which I cannot do justice here. To present a full picture, one would need to analyze not only the position of Sudanese residents of Egypt but also that of Nubians, whose national and racial status is even less clear; both the role of Ottoman Turkish imperialism and the relationship between notions of race and developing concepts of the Egyptian nation would also need to be investigated.

16. As in Maḥmūd's description of Simone cited above (p. 38 [30–31]), the village counterpoints for this presentation of Ḥāmid are implicit but obvious. Islamic law forbids wine and pork to the villagers. Poor sanitary facilities limit bathing and contribute to disease. Fruits and vegetables are not reliably available, and the villagers may not understand the nutritional importance of eating them.

17. From both Ḥāmid's case and that of the village's Napoleonic descendants, it is clear that color is for these characters (and by extension for Fayyāḍ as well) an indication mainly of national rather than of racial identification. If race were primarily at issue, neither the Napoleonic descendants' Egyptian status nor Ḥāmid's both/and national identity could be accepted so readily (if at all), since ancestry and blood inheritance would be far more privileged than they are in *Voices*.

18. See for instance p. 51 (46; 'Aḥmad), p. 57 (53; the mayor), pp. 71, 80 (67, 78; Maḥmūd), and p. 102 (105; Zaynab).

19. See, for example, pp. 55, 84 (51, 84). In the former case, the more cosmopoli-

tan Egyptian characters comfortably join Simone in her use of knife and fork, but here as elsewhere it is she who sets the standard. While there is an evident dichotomy between rural and urban practices in this scene, the more important division still occurs along national lines.

20. Simone's relationship with 'Aḥmad offers the clearest example of her extraordinary authority; although accustomed to respected status as head of his household, 'Aḥmad routinely finds himself following Simone's orders.

21. This common perception has been well documented; for further information on this and on medical and ethical aspects of female circumcision, see Alison T. Slack, "Female Circumcision: A Critical Appraisal," *Human Rights Quarterly* 10 (Nov. 1988); Scilla McLean, ed., "Female Circumcision, Excision and Infibulation: The Facts and Proposals for Change," *Minority Rights Group* 47 (Dec. 1980): 3–21; and Fayṣal Muḥammad Makkī 'Amīn, *Khifāḍ al-Marʾa* ('Umm Durmān: Manshūrāt Maʿhad Sakīna, 1990). For a discussion of religious aspects (Jewish, Christian, and Muslim), see 'Abū Bakr 'Abd al-Rāziq, *Al-Khitān: Raʾy al-Dīn wa-al-ʿIlm fī Khitān al-ʾAwlād wa-al-Banāt* (Cairo: Dār al-Iʿtiṣām, 1989); for more recent information specific to the practice in Egypt, see Dina Ezzat, "A Savage Surgery," *Middle East* no. 230 (Jan. 1994): 35–37. As all of these note, a range of procedures are described as "circumcision" (*khitān*). On the basis of Fayyāḍ's incomplete depiction, supplemented by information about the types of circumcision most common in Egypt, I think it fairly safe to assume that the operation in *Voices* is what Slack and McLean refer to as excision or clitoridectomy, not the more extreme infibulation. The practice of circumcision is supported by various rationales, in addition to the notion that it prohibits excessive clitoral growth; circumcision is supposed to be hygienic, to comply with tradition or with presumed religious dictates, to prevent girls and women from becoming prey to sexual desire and losing their virginity before marriage (or, as in Simone's case, from being unfaithful to their husbands). Whatever the motives, the operation is often hazardous and has long-term negative effects on the health of women, in addition to limiting or entirely preventing their sexual pleasure. Female circumcision is also referred to as genital mutilation and is widely considered a violation of human rights.

22. The official's reflections foreground his awareness of this event's broad implications; see esp. pp. 108–9 (113–14).

23. This problem of nationality is to a certain degree replicated and reinforced at the level of gender. If it is Egyptians who destroy themselves, it is also women who destroy one of their own. Like Egyptians in general, women are presented in this novel as perpetuators of their own oppression. This could be interpreted as a condemnation of oppression generally, as a demonstration of the way an oppressive system engineers its own continuation; but Fayyāḍ may mean it more pointedly. In recounting her interview with Fayyāḍ, Al-Ali notes that in criticizing women for being "the guardians of traditions" he emphasizes circumcision as a case in point. See Al-Ali, *Gender Writing / Writing Gender*, pp. 108, 111.

BIBLIOGRAPHY

'Abd al-Rāziq, 'Abū Bakr. *Al-Khitān: Ra'y al-Dīn wa-al-'Ilm fī Khitān al-'Awlād wa-al-Banāt.* Cairo: Dār al-I 'tiṣām, [1989].

Al-Ali, Nadje Sadig. *Gender Writing / Writing Gender: The Representation of Women in a Selection of Modern Egyptian Literature.* Cairo: American University in Cairo Press, 1994.

'Amīn, Fayṣal Muḥammad Makkī. *Khifād al-Mar'a.* 'Umm Durmān: Manshūrāt Ma'had Sakīna, 1990.

Ezzat, Dina. "A Savage Surgery." *Middle East* no. 230 (Jan. 1994): 35–37.

Fayyāḍ, Sulaymān. *'Aṣwāt.* Baghdad: Maṭba'a al-Irshād, 1972; rev. ed. Cairo: Kutub 'Arabīya, 1977.

———. *Voices.* Trans. Hosam Aboul-Ela. New York: Marion Boyars, 1993.

Lewis, Bernard. *The Muslim Discovery of Europe.* New York: Norton, 1982.

———. *Race and Slavery in the Middle East: An Historical Enquiry.* New York: Oxford University Press, 1990.

McLean, Scilla, ed. "Female Circumcision, Excision and Infibulation: The Facts and Proposals for Change." *Minority Rights Group,* no. 47 (Dec. 1980), 3–21.

Slack, Alison T. "Female Circumcision: A Critical Appraisal." *Human Rights Quarterly* 10 (Nov. 1988): 437–86.

17. Borders, Exiles, Minor Literatures

The Case of Palestinian-Israeli Writing

Writing in 1986 of a recent trip to Egypt, Iraqi-born Israeli novelist Sami Michael reported seeing a group of youths perched on a street railing in downtown Cairo, chattering loudly and unselfconsciously in Israeli Hebrew. The scene seemed strange and out of context for him, particularly when he realized that these were not Jewish Israelis but Palestinian Arab Israelis. To Michael, their linguistic display indicated the youths' pride in their Israeli identity. "At that moment," he writes, "Hebrew was not, in their eyes, the language of the Jewish people, but that of the State of Israel. They live at one and the same time in two homelands: the Israeli homeland that exists and the Palestinian homeland that is lost, that may yet be revived. This [dichotomy] creates the fracturing of identity reflected in the pointed declaration made by the Arabs of Israel: 'My nation is at war with my country'" (1986:12).

The scene described by Michael is an appropriate metaphor for the ambivalent position of the Arab population of Israel.[1] The youths depict the split between Arab and Israeli identity, between Palestinian origins and Israeli citizenship. Theirs is a doubled identity that exemplifies the doubled poles of cultural and political opposition. At the same time, Michael's example is problematic; he defines Arab-Israeli identity from the position of a Jewish Israeli (albeit one of Arab origin), an ideological problem he does not address or reconcile. The young Palestinian Israelis of whom he writes sit not on one side or the other of Israeli identity, not on one side or the other of occupation conflict, but "on the fence" — that is, in the space between borders. Borders function like poles of opposition: the space between them is where ambivalence and hybridity are produced (Hicks 1991:xxiv). By speaking Hebrew — in an Arab country — these Palestinian Israelis point to the interstitial space that they themselves occupy by virtue of their identity. While this space might suggest emptiness, or a "no-man's-land," it primarily indicates a hybridity, a conjoining of the features of each side in a centralized cultural and linguistic arena. Hybridity suggests a solution for the split "I" of the border zone. Sitting on the fence in Cairo, the Arab-Israeli youths occupy a space between borders, between poles of linguistic and nationalistic opposition, between national (Palestinian) and civil (Israeli) identity—and in so doing, they exemplify cultural hybridity.

Minor literatures produced by border subjects frequently articulate this dialectic of doubled linguistic and national identity. The purpose of these literatures is, at least in part, to reclaim a territory for a people displaced by territorial occupation, whether colonial or otherwise. This is a literature not bound by borders, one that extends beyond questions of exile and majority versus minority culture. The literary project of border-dwelling Palestinian-Israeli writers—particularly those writing in Hebrew—is the creation of a hybrid literature located neither at home nor in exile, neither on one side of the border nor another, but in the space between them—the space of cultural hybridity. The writings of Atallah Mansour, Naim Araidi, and Anton Shammas—Palestinian Israelis who write in Hebrew—address the issues of borders, exile, and minor literature and the intersections between them.[2] An examination of their major texts will demonstrate how Palestinian-Israeli writing works to articulate issues of hybridity and interstitial space and will attempt to locate it firmly within the contemporary Israeli literary canon as a new form of Israeli writing. This new writing claims a space within the Hebrew language for the Arab writer, reaching across both linguistic and national borders and, in so doing, reconstructs (even explodes) the ideology of literary articulation and the politics of interpretation.

In his Hebrew novel *Arabesques*, Palestinian-Israeli writer Anton Shammas uses language to articulate the dialectic of doubled linguistic and national identity addressed in Michael's essay. "I know," Shammas has said, "that . . . my real homeland is the doubled homeland of language, of Arabic and Hebrew" (Shammas 1993). Citing Dante's description of Hebrew as the "language of grace," as opposed to Babel's "language of confusion," Shammas declares: "The original deterritorialization and scattering of the Palestinians in 1948 was done in the language of grace. Exile for the Palestinian refugees was a language of confusion. There was no grace in being a confused refugee" (1991:217). The language of Palestinians, Shammas argues, was deterritorialized "by another, and only later did we realize that Arabic does not even have a word for 'territory.' The act of deterritorialization, then, took place outside our language, so we could not talk, much less write, about our plight in our mother tongue. Now we need the language of the Other for that, the language . . . that can re-territorialize us, as imaginary as that might be, giving us some allegedly solid ground" (1989:56). These comments clearly articulate Shammas's reasons for writing in Hebrew. There are other Palestinian-Israeli writers, however, such as Emile Habiby and Muhammad Inaim, for whom Arabic was not only available but was, and remains, the language of choice for writing of their experience of deterritorialization. The choice of Hebrew, then, cannot be explained solely on the basis of the presence or absence of necessary words or phrases; it must be explained as a political choice. For an Israeli Arab (a minority within a regional majority) to write in Hebrew is to enter into the economy of language of his occupier. The language of the other, the step-(m)other tongue, is, for writers like Shammas, Mansour, and Araidi, a language of grace suffused with confusion. It is a territory that the Palestinian-Israeli writer of Hebrew literature must penetrate and occupy in order to articulate his or her doubled national identity and to heal the fissure of his or her split self.

The first novel published in Hebrew by an Arab is Atallah Mansour's *In a New Light* (1966), a narrative of hidden identity and internal exile, taking place in the 1950s, the period of early Israeli statehood. *In a New Light* describes the attempts of a young Arab to gain acceptance as a member of a Jewish kibbutz, using a false Jewish name and Jewish-Israeli identity. The protagonist, Yusuf, exemplifies the location of the Palestinian Israeli in an inner border zone—he is an Arab raised by a Jewish family following the murder of his father (either by Jews, Arabs, or the British—this detail is unknown to him). Yusuf eventually changes his Arab name to the Hebrew equivalent Yossi and attempts to join a kibbutz—perhaps the quintessential symbol of Jewish territorialism in Israel, particularly in the 1950s. While under consideration by the kibbutz membership committee, Yusuf/Yossi has an affair with a married American immigrant to Israel, an experience she perceives as exotic. In representing the relationship between the two, Mansour puts a new twist on the stereotype (present in early Jewish-Israeli literature) of the Arab as a dangerous, exotic native who attempts to penetrate the Jewish woman and her land. *In a New Light* makes this vision of the Arab the fantasy of the Jewish woman and suggests that he is, in actuality, a threat neither to the Jewish woman nor to the Jewish man—although the kibbutz members do perceive Yusuf/Yossi as a potential enemy once his secret is revealed. They finally agree to grant him membership in the kibbutz, but neither as a Jew nor as an Arab: they simply vote to admit a new member.

Although Yusuf/Yossi has attempted to cross the border between Arabism and Judaism, the kibbutz members will not allow the crossing over to become complete. They choose instead to position him between the categories of Arab and Jew, and his membership status reflects this in-betweenness: he is entitled to the identity of neither one nor the other but must exist in the space between them.

In a New Light documents a failure at reconciling cultural difference, a failure at producing cultural hybridity: Yusuf/Yossi is unable to negotiate the distance between Arabism and (Israeli) Judaism and is fated to dwell in the no-man's-land that separates them. Even his affair with a Jewish kibbutz member brings him no closer to his desired identity, since she herself—an American immigrant to Israel (and not a native of the land, like the protagonist)— dwells in-between borders, in-between identities.

Published in 1986, Anton Shammas's *Arabesques* is the first Hebrew Arab novel to achieve critical acclaim, both in Israel and in the United States (Vivian Eden's English translation of the novel was published in 1988 by Harper & Row). It is the fictionalized tale of the Arab Shammas family's history from the early days of the British occupation of Palestine to present-day Israel. It chronicles the personal history, too, of Anton Shammas—the author has inserted himself into his own narrative as a character—from his youth in the Galilean village of Fassuta to his journey to a writers' workshop in Iowa City, Iowa. There he confronts the specter of his affair with a married Jewish-Israeli woman and ultimately meets his double, who has haunted his life and his family's history for two generations.

Like Mansour, Shammas plants his text centrally within Israeli language and culture, thereby nullifying its (potential) peripheral status and making it the joint domain of the Palestinian-Israeli writer and the Jewish-Israeli reader. Shammas is more successful, however, at beginning to negotiate the distance between Palestinian and Jewish-Israeli culture because his narrative uses not only modern Hebrew language but Arab narrative devices to mediate between the dominating majority and the dominated minority. The result is a text that is a hybridization of Jewish-Israeli and Arab existence, a text that can only be the product of the border zone. The importance of the border zone and of the hybrid text produced within it is that it gives voice to the hybrid border dweller.

Arabesques is a border text, a hybrid text, but not only because of its language; Shammas's novel also crosses borders of intertextuality in its frequent evocation of contemporary Jewish-Israeli literature. There is a tale, in the early sections of the novel, about deaf Palestinian twins, sons of an exiled Palestinian woman who has allied herself with the Palestinian nationalist cause. This pair of twins clearly echoes another one in Amos Oz's *My Michael*, a novel dealing with a woman's sexual and national identity crisis that describes, at one point, a rape fantasy involving Arab twins from her youth. In adapting Oz's twins into his own text, Shammas evokes the intersection between national and sexual politics established in *My Michael* and moves them explicitly into the realm of Palestinian identity crisis. Oz's Hannah is transformed, in Shammas's hand, into Surayyah Said, a woman whose identity lies at the center of *Arabesques*. This woman, originally named Laylah Khoury, discovers the terrible secret of the Shammas family and so presumably is betrayed by them to the Jewish police, who force her into exile beyond the borders of her homeland. It is there, in exile, that she splits her identity, changing her name to Surayyah Said and her religion from Christianity to Islam. (And it is there that she gives birth to her twin sons.) The secret she is suspected of discovering is one of an infant stolen from a hospital and sold for adoption to the Lebanese Abyad family (for whom Laylah worked as a domestic) — an infant originally named (as is the central character in this fiction) Anton Shammas. Shammas's twins, like those of Amos Oz, point to a doubling of identity, or, more correctly, a splitting of individual identities into seemingly irreconcilable parts.

An additional example of intertextual border crossing in the novel is located in Shammas's creation of the character Yehoshua Bar-On, clearly a parody of Jewish-Israeli writer A. B. Yehoshua. Bar-On, whom Shammas's literary (and autobiographical) counterpart Anton Shammas meets at an Iowa writers' workshop, is a Jewish-Israeli writer working on a novel about a Palestinian Israeli (based on the fictional Shammas) whom he calls "my Jew." In describing his novel in progress, Bar-On declares: "My Jew will be an educated Arab. But not an intellectual. He does not gallop on the back of a thoroughbred mare . . . nor is he a prisoner of the IDF. . . . Nor is he A. B. Yehoshua's adolescent Lover" (1988:82; 91).[3] This comment by Bar-On is intertextual on several levels. It suggests, first, the stereotype of the Arab as an exotic native and a breeder of Arabian horses. Second, it alludes to S. Yizhar's well-known story "The Prisoner," in which a Bedouin is wrongfully arrested by and becomes a prisoner of the Israel Defense Forces. Third, it is clearly evocative of Yehoshua's novel *The Lover*, in which an adolescent Palestinian Israeli has a brief sexual encounter with a Jewish-Israeli girl. Finally, and most important, the reference to Yehoshua points to his (Yehoshua's) appropriation of Arab-Israeli identity for the purpose of exploring —

like Oz, but in a different venue — Jewish-Israeli sexual and domestic politics. There are other clear and even more direct intertextual borrowings in *Arabesques*. Of particular interest is Shammas's paraphrasing of A. B. Yehoshua's title *The Continued Silence of a Poet* as "the continued silence of a writer" (p. 83; 91) to describe Bar-On's contemplation of the problems of fiction. Also notable is his use of the well-known concluding phrase "Hebrew, Arabic and Death" from Yehudah Amichai's poem "Seven Laments on the War Dead" to describe Anton's feeling of desolation upon the discovery of his love letters to his Jewish-Israeli mistress: "The husband had discovered the correspondence, and the secret, so terrible in its beauty, was gone, and the world reverted to its former state of Hebrew, Arabic and Death" (p. 85; 95).

These intertextual borrowings and adaptations place Shammas squarely not only within Hebrew language but within contemporary Hebrew literature and literary history. He does not, however, stop at the borders of his own cultural arena: *Arabesques* weaves into its tapestry of language and memory threads of European and American literature that intersect with those of Israeli literary culture. The reliance on memory as a structural foundation (and flaw) in *Arabesques*, together with references to Marcel Proust and Père Lachaise (the cemetery where he is buried) recall *Remembrance of Things Past* and thereby point to the crucial role that memory plays in Shammas's novel in constructing and deconstructing history. Even more central to the structure of *Arabesques* is the seemingly incidental mention of Willa Cather's *My Ántonia* (the first novel Anton ever read), followed by a lengthy quote from the beginning of that novel. In it, Cather's Jim Burden visits the narrator — a manifestation of Willa Cather — to discuss a recent train ride across Iowa, a woman named Ántonia, and a manuscript he has written about her. Burden brings the manuscript to the narrator, a well-known American writer, and says, "'Here's the thing about Ántonia . . . I suppose it hasn't any form. It hasn't any title either.' He went into the next room, sat down at my desk and wrote across the face of the portfolio the word 'Ántonia.' He frowned at this a moment, then prefixed another word, making it 'My Ántonia.' That seemed to satisfy him" (pp. 123–24; 138–39). That this quote is the narrative key to *Arabesques* does not become apparent until the last pages of the novel, when Anton meets his double, Michael Abyad — whose identity he has shared and shadowed all his life. Toward the end of his stay in Iowa (the locus of Cather's train ride), Anton agrees to meet with Abyad, whose history mirrors the one Shammas has been telling throughout *Arabesques*. Like Cather's Burden, Abyad secretly writes an account of his early life and brings it to the narrator of the text we are reading. "Take this file," Abyad tells Anton, "and see what you can do with it. Translate it, adapt it, add or subtract. But leave me in. I didn't take time to arrange the material. I haven't even found a title for it" (p. 234; 259). The intertextual connection with *My Ántonia* becomes even stronger in the next passage: "If Michael were the teller, he would have ended it like this: 'He opened a drawer and took out a pencil and wrote on the file: My Tale. He frowned at this a moment, then he used an eraser, leaving only the single word Tale. That seemed to satisfy him'" (p. 234; 259). Shammas clearly mirrors the blurring of textual origins introduced in Cather's text, but he goes further: while Burden adds the possessive "my" to his title, Abyad erases this word from his title, effacing the concept of possessiveness from his manuscript, his representation of Palestinian history. Shammas's migration ultimately crosses not only linguistic borders but literary and national territories as well.

In addition to borders of textuality and nationality, *Arabesques* crosses borders of sexuality, class, and race. Anton's affair with Shlomit is most significant because she is both married and a Jewish Israeli. The affair crosses multiple boundaries: it defies the taboo against extramarital sexuality and that of mixing race, religion, and nationality. It also points to differences in class, as Anton originates from a poor Arab village and Shlomit is married to an officer in the Israeli army. The character of Surayyah Said also points to a border crossing, since she crosses over from Christianity to Islam after being expelled beyond the literal borders of the State of Israel. Finally, the novel traverses territorial borders, moving from the village of Anton's youth to the city of his adulthood, to the rural plains of Iowa in the United States.

The structure of *Arabesques* consists of two interlocking narratives titled "The Tale" and "The Teller." The former relays the Shammas family history, while the latter dwells on Anton Shammas's Iowa journey. Constructed around a system of doubled characters, plot devices, and narrative voices, the novel exists in the interstitial space between Israeli Arabism and Arab Hebrew—a hybrid culture and a hybrid language. By writing in Hebrew—for a Jewish-Israeli (i.e., Hebrew-reading) audience—Shammas, an Arab, enters into the economy of language of Israel and, in so doing, occupies the language of his occupier. He sees the entry into language as his means of deterritorializing, decolonizing, destabilizing that occupation. It is a means of reversing the formula of lack that defines him as a member of a colonized and displaced nation, as an other, an exile at home.[4]

At the center of his narrative, Shammas positions the tales of his Uncle Yusef as a microcosmic, metaphoric representation of that narrative. He says that his uncle's stories "were plaited into one another, embracing and parting, twisting and twining in the infinite arabesque of memory. Many of his stories he told again and again . . . while other stories were granted only two or three tellings during the whole of his lifetime. All of them, however, flowed around him in a swirling current of illusion that linked beginnings to endings, the internal to the external, the reality to the tale" (pp. 203, 226–27). The Arabian iconography of the arabesque allows the storyteller to reject the authority of unified, totalizing representation and, in so doing, focuses our attention on the internal dynamics of the political, national, and cultural images involved.

Like the arabesque of Uncle Yusef's stories, that of Shammas's novel makes no claim to represent any reality outside itself. Instead, it allows Shammas to create a hybrid literary form, that of blending oral — Arabic — and written — Hebrew — textual traditions. The sections titled "The Tale" focus on narrative — the traditional Arab oral narrative — and relate the history of the Arab Shammas family from the early nineteenth century to the present. Those titled "The Teller" focus on narrator — the written story in Hebrew/Jewish literary tradition — and follow Shammas in his quest as an Israeli representative to an international writers' workshop in Iowa City. The ideological dilemma of Shammas's identity (both as a writer and as a character in his own fiction) is thus translated into a struggle between texts and a hybridization of texts.

It is precisely this hybridization of Arab and Israeli literary traditions that allows Shammas to enter into majority culture while still representing a minority culture, thereby absolving himself of responsibilities and commitments to the master culture. By writing in Hebrew, the language of his conquerors, the Arab Shammas can realize Derrida's ideal of speaking the other's language without renouncing one's own. As Hanan Hever correctly observes, the author's use of Hebrew becomes a vehicle for minority discourse; in the hands of the Arab-Israeli Shammas, "Hebrew, the mythic language of Zionism, undergoes a process of deterritorialization — the first definitional component, according to Deleuze and Guattari, of a minor literature. Yet . . . although Shammas does carry out a process of deterritorialization of Hebrew, at the same time he is reterritorializing it as the language of the [Jewish as well as Arab] Israeli" (1990:287).

Minor literature, Deleuze and Guattari tell us, does not come from a minor language but rather is what a minority constructs within a major language. A case in point is Shammas's construction of a Hebrew novel from the position of an Arab Christian minority in Israel. Kafka, they argue, marks the impasse that bars access to writing for the Jews of Prague and turns their literature into something impossible — "the impossibility of not writing in German, the impossibility of writing otherwise. The impossibility of writing because national consciousness, uncertain or oppressed, necessarily exists by means of literature" (1986:16). Shammas turns Arab literature into something impossible, too: his novel expresses simultaneously the difficulties and underlying tensions of writing in Hebrew and the impossibility of writing in any other language. It expresses, as well, the impossibility of not writing at all. Clearly, Shammas is producing a minor literature; it is constructed within the context of a majority literature and so must be produced in the language of that culture. And to paraphrase Deleuze and Guattari, the impossibility of writing in Hebrew is the deterritorialization of the Palestinian-Israeli population itself. Arab Hebrew is a deterritorialized language, appropriate (and appropriated) for strange and minor uses. As an Arab in Israel, Shammas is a deterritorialized subject. By writing in Hebrew, he achieves a measure of reterritorialization. He chooses the language of his country — Hebrew — to reclaim a territorial space for his nation.

Like minor literature, the arabesque at the center of Shammas's text is characterized by a lack of obligation to unified, coherent representation or mythic symbolism. The arabesque undermines the dichotomy that any minor literature must address — the dichotomy between an extreme reterritorialization of language through symbols and archetypes and a radical deterritorialization of language. Faced with these two demands — an extreme deterritorialization as opposed to a concern for relative degrees of reterritorialization and deterritorialization — the arabesque can suggest a dynamic middle way, a hybrid way. Shammas's novel exemplifies the fluid concept of the nation-state through the iconography of the arabesque. "[This] paradigm concedes the importance of the concept of a nation state, but only as articulated through the arabesque: not as an absolute and rigid notion, defined once and for all, but in a much more critical and flexible sense, as something evolving and responsive to the dialectical process" (Hever 1990:289). Shammas exploits the form of the arabesque as a means of realizing his conception of the unstable Palestinian narrative; the atemporal, arabesque rhythms of his novel force linear and cyclical discourse into confrontation with one another and, in so doing, serve as a touchstone for evaluating the nondialectic attitude toward time found in Israeli public discourse as well as contemporary Palestinian fiction.

The form of the arabesque especially motivates the description, in Shammas's novel, of the oppression of Palestinian women, without minimizing the overall web of political oppression depicted in it (Hever 1990:276). Thus, for example, in describing the hardships endured by Laylah Khouri (a.k.a.

Surayyah Said), Shammas interweaves her mistreatment by Israeli soldiers in 1948 and 1981 with her misfortunes at the hands of Arab society (her betrayal by a member of the Shammas family and her sexual and financial exploitation by Mlle Sa'ada). Laylah the Palestinian is portrayed in the novel, like so many of its other women, as a commodity, passed from hand to hand, from government to government, territory to territory.

Laylah/Surayyah's existence parallels another arabesque, the cyclical course taken by Michel/Michael Abyad, the baby who was kidnapped into adoption and was himself treated as a commodity. The arabesque thereby "takes the fetishization of the individual and the dominance of exchange value and weaves them into a fabric of human relationships existing in a context of social and political repression" (Hever 1990:277).

Shammas has described Palestinians as a people who "travel light, empty-pocketed, with the vanity of those who think home is a portable idea, something that dwells mainly in the mind or within a text. Celebrating modern powers of imagination and of fiction, we have lost faith in our old idols— memory, storytelling. We are not even sure anymore whether there ever was a home out there, a territory, a homeland" (1989:56). Any use of the term "Palestinian" suggests fractured identity because the term encompasses Muslims, Christians, and Druze and both Israeli and West Bank/Gaza Palestinians—within and around the borders of Israel—not to mention the many Palestinians in other areas of the world. Smadar Lavie suggests that Palestinian-Israeli writers attempt to reconstitute their identity by exploring "their Self/Other dualism [which] is as clear to them as it is to other Israelis. They are an almost ultimate Other: they are not Jewish, nor have they immigrated to Israel from anywhere. They are articulating a linear narrative of their oppression vis-à-vis the Zionist state. The citizenship they hold in that state, however, fractures their narrative's linearity, and collapses the Self/Other dualism into multiple subject positions" (1992:89). It is this dualism that Shammas explores in *Arabesques*, mimicking it in the fracturing of the textual narrative.

Nowhere is the volatile instability of *Arabesques* so evident as in the character of Michael Abyad, the stolen child presumed dead but in fact given away to a childless Lebanese family—the child for whom the author (and his fictional counterpart) was named. This double, this Anton renamed Michel renamed Michael, provides the final twist and fracturing of Shammas's narrative. Doubling, I submit, is the mirroring of the self in the other, the other in the self.[5] The self is identified only through the double—the other. The subject, as defined by European-based philosophy, labors under the illusion of acting on its own. The subject in border writing, however, can no longer be conceived as a unified subject or as a subject who thinks it is acting on its own. *Arabesques* holds up several pairs of mirrors in which doubles may gaze at one another: Anton Shammas and Michel/Michael Abyad; the doubled identity of Laylah Khoury/Surayyah Said; Surayyah's deaf twin sons; the twinned narrative ("The Tale" and "The Teller"); even the twin spaces of the village Fassuta and the city Haifa.

In *Arabesques*, the doubled other is not only a mirror of the self but a self who is also being mirrored: Abyad and Shammas are doubles of each other. They are boundaries, poles of opposition that shift repeatedly so that it is difficult to tell who is the double of whom, who is the stable self and who is his other. "There is a man," Anton is told, toward the end of the novel, "whose name is the same as yours, and who holds half your identity in his hands." Later, while contemplating the two figures that construct his sense of self — his double and his Israeli lover (both of whom are also forms of his other) — Shammas ties them to the language of mirrors that informs his identity: "This Michael Abyad has silently woven himself into my life, where the magic thread of Shlomit has come undone and unravels in my hands: like a rope slipping through one's hands following the full bucket, whipping against the throat of the cistern and sinking into the depths. And the surface of the water ripples for a while, until it returns to the mute language of mirrors" (1988:182; 202). The past bangs against the present, threatening its stability, weaving together time, memory, and doubled selves with longing and desire — both sexual desire and desire to fill in the gaps of history and identity.

Shammas's discovery of Abyad initially destabilizes his own identity — his sense of himself. When he finally meets Abyad at the novel's end, he hears the ultimate version of the story of his own identity, and, as he says, "Michael Abyad's voice overlaps the end of my thoughts" (p. 232; 257). What he does not know is that Abyad's role as double has been destabilizing for *his* identity as well. In this version of the tale, it is not Laylah Khoury, who works for the Abyad family, but Almaza Shammas (Anton's aunt and the mother of the stolen baby) who raises and cares for the adopted child. In 1949, a woman in black comes to the Abyad house looking for her son. Michel has a nervous breakdown and is sent to the United States to recuperate. Years later, he returns to Lebanon; unable to locate his natural mother and influenced by stories of the Shammas family told to him by Anton's cousin Nur (whom he meets in Lebanon), Abyad comes to identify himself with the lost son of Almaza. Having been raised on her stories about her Anton, Abyad ultimately writes himself into the Shammas family history in the role of Anton, who actually died in infancy—at least in this version of the story. "I hear about him," Abyad tells Shammas, "and sleep on his pillow. I even have his dreams" (p. 233; 258).

Upon returning to America from his visit to Beirut, Michael Abyad begins to write an autobiography in the name of Anton Shammas—both Anton the author and Anton the lost child. Finally, upon meeting the writer in the United States, he gives him the notes for his book: "Take this file," he says, "and see what you can do with it. Translate it, adapt it, add or subtract. But leave me in. I didn't have time to arrange the material. I haven't even found a title for it" (p. 234; 259). The door to the secret has opened, the snare has been set, the rememberer—and the reader—have been caught. The double becomes the self, the self becomes the other. *Arabesques* ends with Shammas paraphrasing Jorge Luis Borges: "Which of the two of us has written this book I do not know" (p. 234; 259).

"Thirteen Ways of Looking at It" is the final poem of Shammas's collection *Shetah Hefker* (No-man's-land). In this poem (clearly derivative of Wallace Stevens's "Thirteen Ways of Looking at a Blackbird"), Shammas expresses a sense of dislocation, of belonging neither on one side of the border nor the other:

> The blackbird does not daydream.
> The blackbird knows.
> And because he knows,
> He does not tell.
>
> I do not know.
> A language on this side,
> and a language on this side.
> And I am daydreaming in the no man's land.
> (1979:46)

Home, for Shammas, is the space between borders, the space belonging neither to his Israeli self nor to his Palestinian Arab self. It is the space of exile at home.[6]

Like Shammas, poet Naim Araidi explores his fractured Arab-Israeli identity, writing and publishing in Hebrew inside Israel. Araidi is a Druze, a non-Jewish citizen of Israel, born in Palestine. He, like Shammas and other Palestinian Israelis, is in exile from a homeland that no longer exists except in nostalgia and ideological space. His home has become exile, and his exile is home. Araidi's first exile was to leave his native village in the Galilee to study in the Israeli city of Haifa. The title poem of Araidi's *Hazarti el ha-Kefar* (Back to the village) describes the poet's return to the Arab village of his youth:

> Back to the village
> where I first learned to cry
> back to the hill
> where the landscape is nature
> and there is no room for a picture
> back to my house made of stones
> which my fathers hewed from rocks
> I returned to myself—
> and this was my intention.
>
> . . . I came back to the village
> as one who flees from civilization
> and appeared at the village
> as one who comes from exile to exile.
>   (1986:7–8)

Araidi's poetry, like Mansour's and Shammas's fiction, reflects the conflict of existing between two worlds and the condition of experiencing home as exile, of being inside and outside at the same time. The poet's departure from his village indicates a movement, a border crossing, into a "spatial and cultural exile among the privileged Jewish elite" (Lavie 1992:85), and his return to it represents a turning of borders inside out, where home too becomes an exile of sorts, and the notion of home becomes elusive and unattainable.

Many of Araidi's poems are love songs laden with sexual desire that is represented as transgressive. Love is described as something forbidden, sinful. And the body of the lover is a border that he crosses, against the law, a territory that he enters in spite of the dangers and taboos involved in that act, as expressed in "You again":

> You again
> and all this sorrow and the hill that is
>   not and the Carmel
> that is not the Galilee
> which is you and me and this sorrow.
> You again
> and all this love
> Forbidden and permitted at once.

I never knew how to be so
alone
when you and I and all these hills
grow wings but do not fly
I never thought as now
of the joy of hiding from people
this fear of the forbidden
and of your green eyes that will turn
    to another
and the future
and always.

(1986:35)

The association of the Carmel mountains with the body of the lover (a forbidden territory) is reiterated in "Me, the Carmel, and Fallen Leaves," but in this poem, it is the city of Haifa that is personified as an ambivalent lover and the Carmel as a past lover recalled with nostalgia and longing:

. . . Haifa left me alone —
the first kiss will not wound me
nor the last
and not the sun setting before my eyes
in an instant.
Haifa let me drown
without a ship to give to the waves . . .

Haifa will embrace me and carry me on her back
I walk with the sorrow of human beings
waiting for salvation that will not come
for love is an inheritance. . . .

The Carmel showers kisses
on my dark body,
thorn and thistle
and I melt from all the love
and am sent upwards
to laugh aloud and the humor of fate
nursing and not saved.
Oh, my Carmel and the great Galilee
this is the great silence
that turns song into melody:

I am the wave and the north wind
I am the sign of ancient love

I am the depths of a single song
I am the fetus of the betrayed pregnancy
I am the sacrifice

and the lone lamb.

(pp. 47–50)

Araidi speaks of living between two times, languages, cultures: "Here [in the village] everyone lives on village time, and I don't like it. When I lived in Haifa, I lived on Western time. I didn't like that either. Now, back in the village, in a paradoxical conflict, I try to live in both times. But my dubious freedom in Israel's mutation of a Western democracy is better for me than my own stagnant village." And yet he stays in the village with his family rather than moving them back to Haifa because, as he says, "I owe my children their mother culture. Their mother tongue. . . . But as for myself, I'm living on a fence — one foot here, one foot there, always trying to close my legs" (Lavie 1992:84). Like Shammas and the youths of Sami Michael's essay, Araidi perches on a fence, in the space between village time and Israeli Western time, between Hebrew Arabic writing and the hegemony of non–Arab-Israeli literary tradition.

Araidi's first novel *Tevilah Katlanit* (A fatal christening, 1992), further explores the theme of cultural dislocation and fractured identity. It is the tale of a young Druze who, after completing his obligatory service in the Israeli army, arrives at university and finds himself caught between two opposing worlds: that of his Arab mother culture and that of the Israeli culture to which he finds himself drawn. Araidi, like Mansour and Shammas before him, employs the theme of forbidden love to explore that of dislocation mentioned above, but the border crossing in his novel is less transgressive than those of his predecessors: here the protagonist falls in love with a Christian woman whom he marries. It is the birth of their children that articulates clearly, in this text, the ambivalence he experiences in the space between two cultural realities, the space between borders.

Shammas, Araidi, and Mansour are part of a group identified by Smadar Lavie as Third World Israeli writers.[7] These are individuals who must continually remap their border zones so that they can maintain their exilic home in the claimed homeland of the Jews.[8] The creative force and agency of these writers arise out of their sense that their home is in exile and their exile is their home. By writing their own lived experience in new literary forms, and specifically in Hebrew, Third World Israeli authors articulate alternative worldviews: "They write using a flowing narration based on traditional Arab storytelling, but starkly juxtaposed with a spare narration revealing their alienation from the Eurocentric project of Israeli nation-building. Some authors syncretize these two narrative worlds. . . . The continual juxtapositions create borders along the contiguities, where images and ideas intersect explosively in the text — deterritorializing the Sabra culture" (Lavie 1992:92). In an interview with Lavie, Shammas declares: "I can't write in Arabic any more. I don't want to. The exile you create inside the language is a home. An exile is a home, and the Jews are the best proof of that. If my diaspora is the Jewish home, for me writing in Hebrew is like blowing it up from within" (p. 103). Although Lavie's analysis of Third World Israeli writers is useful for placing Shammas, Araidi, and Mansour within the context of border writing, it fails to recognize that by writing in Hebrew and by infusing their works with forays into Jewish-Israeli, European, and American cultural territories, these writers are, in effect, reclaiming the territory of the border for their nation. These border crossings blur the boundaries between home and exile, between center and periphery, and efface the line that separates them, thereby allowing for the emergence of a hybrid territory from within the interstitial space that lies between them. It is this interstitial space that produces Palestinian-Israeli Hebrew writing, one that might be called not only border writing but, more significantly, hybrid writing — a writing not only across borders but within and between borders.

Border writing, or hybrid writing, is by nature subversive. It disrupts the one-way flow of information in which a colonizing power produces information, and thereby controls the images of itself as well as of the powers that govern it (Hicks 1991:xxvii). These narratives not only subvert, they document and indict: historical realities are imposed on fiction to expose the political and social realities of the people represented in them. The connection between knowledge and power is crucial to border writing, which often reverses the colonial formula in which knowledge is used by those who have power to distort historical records. In Shammas's text, for example, the distortion of historical records — of the family history — is an act of self-empowerment, a claiming of knowledge to claim power.

The writing of Palestinian Israelis in Hebrew must be read as a political act of resistance — against occupation, colonization, interpretation — an act with significant ramifications for both writers and their reading public. The purpose of Palestinian-Israeli literary resistance is (at least in part) to call into question the act of interpretation and its implied politics. Shammas's *Arabesques* in particular moves Palestinian-Israeli writing forward by interrogating the politics not only of exile but of literary interpretation. It is a text that resists interpretation. It offers only ambivalence and instability, conflation of author and subject, text, subtext, and reader. Like Shammas's description of Uncle Yusef's stories, his own tales are "plaited into one another, embracing and parting, twisting and twining in the infinite arabesque of memory" (p. 203; 226). Shammas's use of the arabesque as a form of narrative experimentation calls to mind Gilles Deleuze's interrogation of the distinction between interpretation and experimentation in *Dialogues:* "The strength [of experimentation] is that each time the interpretations are dismantled and the famous signifier is eliminated. . . . Experiment, never interpret. Make programmes, never make phantasms. . . . But from fragment to fragment is constructed a living experiment in which interpretation begins to crumble, in which there is no longer perception or knowledge, secret or divination. . . . English or American literature is a process of experimentation. They have killed interpretation" (1987:49). So, it would seem, has the Arab writer of Israeli literature.

NOTES

1. In using the terms "Arab population of Israel," or "Palestinian Israeli," I am referring to Arab citizens of the State of Israel who live within the borders of the Green Line, and not to the Arab inhabitants of the West Bank or Gaza or to any part of the newly forming Palestinian authority. At the same time, I acknowledge that Arab Israelis, while identifying themselves as citizens of the state, may, at the same time, identify themselves as Palestinian nationalists.

2. One of the challenges of examining Palestinian-Israeli writing in Hebrew is that there is so little of it. Mansour, Araidi, and Shammas are a few of the major authors of Hebrew Palestinian literature.

3. References to *Arabesques* will appear with the page number in the original Hebrew text, followed by that in Vivian Eden's translation. In the process of translating the text into English, Shammas and Eden amended the original, heavily encoded Hebrew, adding explanation and embellishment where they deemed it necessary. The original Hebrew for this quote, for example, reads: "Nor is he a lost, love-sick boy" (p. 82). In his original text, Shammas clearly makes the assumption that an Israeli reader will recognize the reference to Yehoshua's novel; the reference would easily be lost in translation to an English public.

4. In a 1979 study, Elia Zureik chronicled the stages of Palestinian history according to a model of external and internal colonialism. The early stage, before 1948, is marked by British colonization of Palestine and a dual Arab-Jewish society in that colonized region. Asymmetrical power relationships are mediated in this period, by the British presence, at the same time that Zionist hegemony excludes Arabs and

eventually moves toward Palestinian dispersion with the foundation of the state. The middle stage, between 1948 and 1967, is marked by what Zureik calls "internal colonialism"—the marginalization of Palestinian peasants and confiscation of land by the new Israeli government; political manipulation and economic stagnation of the Arab population of Israel; and residential and occupational segregation. The final stage in Zureik's model, from 1967 to 1978 (when the study was completed), is marked by accelerated forms of internal colonialism in Israel, particularly regarding the colonial dependency of the West Bank and Gaza on Israel but including the further proletarianization and segregation of Palestinians within the Green Line borders of Israel (see *The Palestinians in Israel*). In discussing the politics of colonialism and occupation in Israel today, I am referring less to a formal imperial occupation of one nation by another than to Zureik's conception of the internal colonization and deterritorialization of one dweller in a territory by another in the same.

5. Freud wrote of the double as evoking feelings of dislike and "uncanniness." Lacan, in discussing Freud's notion of doubling, suggests that there is nothing more dislikable and agonizing than someone who resembles oneself (*Ecrits*, pp. 15–16). For Freud, it is the "narcissistic" or "animistic" phase that returns so strangely in the image or figure of the double. In the presence of this figure, one is positioned in an absolutely familiar relation with the "not-me," that is, with the other—but in the form of a no less absolute uncanniness, since this other self is now seen on the outside, as the result of one's repressing the narcissistic apprehension of the world (Borch-Jacobsen, p. 45). Doubling, furthermore, is invented as a preservation against extinction, as a protection against the destruction of the ego. Otto Rank calls the double "an energetic denial of the power of death" (Borch-Jacobsen, p. 45). But when this denial is surmounted, the double reverses its aspect. "From having been an assurance of immortality, it becomes the uncanny harbinger of death" (Freud 234–35). Lacan takes up the principal ingredients of Freud's concept of doubling and uncanniness in his configuration of the "mirror stage" of human psychic development: the mirror, the image, the double, narcissism, castration (imaginary fragmentation), and death. In meeting oneself in the mirror (meeting one's double), according to Lacan, one struggles simultaneously with self-love and self-hatred, projecting the self onto the double, or other, while losing the self in the double. The meeting with the double causes a sense of loss of self, for, in meeting the double, "I" is no longer "I" but becomes alienated because it begins to seek itself in its reflection and not in itself. The meeting of the double, indeed the double him/herself, represents a fragmentation of the self, which looks for affirmation and identification through the image of the double—the representation of the self—and not through the self itself (Borch-Jacobsen, p. 71).

6. *Shetah Hefker*, published in 1979, describes a far stronger sense of exclusion and exile than does *Arabesques* (1986), which suggests more of a possibility for hybridity and inclusion. It would appear that in the years between the writing of these two texts, Shammas developed the perspective that language could be used as a ve-

hicle for creating hybrid literary forms that could address the issues of the minority from within the language of the majority.

7. In using the term "Third World Israeli writers," Lavie is referring to Israelis outside Ashkenazi — European — hegemony, such as Israeli Arabs and Mizrahi Jews — Jews from the Arab world. Among these writers she lists Shammas, Naim Araidi, Shimon Ballas, and Sami Michael.

8. The remapping is intended to separate out an independent space in a border zone, one that cannot be usurped as a frontier by Israel's Eurocenter. The Israeli Third World border zone thus emerges as "the locus of re-definition and re-signification . . . of the conflicting pressures toward both exclusion and forced incorporation" (Lavie, p. 95). Palestinian and Mizrahi writers such as Shammas and Michael write in inner border zones — the space between nation and empire — rejecting the Eurocenter and refusing to remain beyond and behind the borders of Israeli literary production. But the position of Shammas, Araidi, Mansour, and other Palestinian-Israeli writers is more complex than Lavie allows: there are clear differences and points of contiguity between Palestinian and Mizrahi writers, as there are between Mizrahi and European Israeli writers. While it is true that Palestinian and Mizrahi Israelis share an Arab heritage, it is also true that, in the opposition between Israeli and Palestinian identity, "Israeli" includes "Mizrahi" — placing that category of identity in opposition to that of "Palestinian." Lavie's reading of Third World Israeli writers contains some elision between Palestinian-Israeli and Mizrahi-Israeli identity and does not carefully enough point to the acute national and cultural differences between them.

WORKS CITED

Araidi, Naim. 1986. *Hazarti el ha-Kefar* (Back to the village). Tel Aviv: Am Oved Publishers.

———. 1992. *Tevilah Katlanit* (A fatal christening). Tel Aviv: Bitan Publishers.

Borch-Jacobsen, Mikel. 1991. *Lacan: The Absolute Master.* Stanford: Stanford University Press.

Deleuze, Gilles, and Felix Guattari. 1986. *Kafka: Toward a Minor Literature,* trans. Dana Polan. Minneapolis: University of Minnesota Press.

Deleuze, Gilles, and Claire Parnet. 1987. *Dialogues,* trans. Hugh Tomlinson and Barbara Habberjam. New York: Columbia University Press.

Freud, Sigmund. 1957. "The Uncanny." In *The Standard Edition of the Complete Psychological Works of Sigmund Freud,* 17:219–56. London: Hogarth Press.

Hartsock, Nancy. 1990. "Rethinking Modernism: Minority vs. Majority Theories." In *The Nature and Context of Minority Discourse,* ed. Abdul R. JanMohamed and David Lloyd. Oxford: Oxford University Press.

Hever, Hannan. 1989. "Israeli Literature's Achilles' Heel." *Tikkun* 4 (Sept.–Oct.): 30–33.

————. 1990. "Hebrew in an Israeli Arab Hand: Six Miniatures on Anton Shammas's *Arabesques.*" In *The Nature and Context of Minority Discourse,* ed. Abdul R. JanMohamed and David Lloyd. Oxford: Oxford University Press.

Hicks, Emily. 1991. *Border Writing: The Multidimensional Text.* Minneapolis: University of Minnesota Press.

Lacan, Jacques. 1977. *Ecrits: A Selection.* Trans. Alan Sheridan. New York: Norton.

Lavie, Smadar. 1992. "Blow-ups in the Border Zones: Third World Israeli Authors' Groupings for Home." *New Formations* 18 (Dec.): 84–106.

Mansour, Atallah. 1966. *be-Or Hadash* (In a new light). Tel Aviv: Karni.

————. 1969. *In a New Light.* Trans. Abraham Birman. London: Vallentine, Mitchell.

Michael, Sami. 1986. "Arabesqot shel Tsiyonut" (Arabesques of Zionism). *Moznayim* 60 (July–Aug.): 10–17.

Shammas, Anton. 1979. *Shetah Hefker* (No-man's-land). Tel Aviv: ha-Kibbutz ha-Meuhad.

————. 1986. *Arabesqot* (Arabesques). Tel Aviv: Am Oved.

————. 1988. *Arabesques.* Trans. Vivian Eden. New York: Harper & Row.

————. 1989. "Amerka, Amerka." *Harper's* 282 (Feb.): 55–61.

————. 1991. "At Half Mast — Myths, Symbols, and Rituals of the Emerging State: A Personal Testimony of an 'Israeli Arab.'" In *New Perspectives on Israeli History: The Early Years of the State,* ed. Laurence J. Silberstein. New York: New York University Press.

————. 1993. "Azivah — ha-Shanah ha-Marah mi-Kulan" (Leaving — the bitterest year of all). *ha-Aretz,* Sept. 15.

Zureik, Elia. 1979. *The Palestinians in Israel: A Study in Internal Colonialism.* London: Routledge & Kegan Paul.

18. The Poetics and Politics of Space in J. M. G. Le Clézio's *Etoile errante*

Tu es l'étranger. Et moi?
Je suis, pour toi, l'étranger. Et toi?
L'étoile, toujours, sera séparée de l'étoile; ce qui les
rapproche n'étant que leur volonté de briller
ensemble.

You are the stranger. And I?
I am, for you, the stranger. And you?
The star, always, will be separated from the star; they
are drawn closer only by their will to shine together.
— Edmond Jabès

Two young women cross paths in May 1948 along the dusty road leading to Jerusalem: Esther, a French Jew headed for the city of light in a guarded convoy, and Nejma, a Palestinian woman headed in the opposite direction, destined for the refugee camps of Iraq. Nejma approaches Esther without a word except for her name written on the blank page of a notebook. Their brief, chance encounter will leave them with an exchange of hastily scribbled names and with the memory of their gaze fraught with fear and uncertainty yet sealed with the bond of mutual compassion and understanding that neither will ever forget. Then each continues her way toward a destiny of exile and wandering that escapes their individual control. Back in the truck, another woman tries to explain to Esther: "No one is innocent. Those are the mothers and wives of the men who kill us," to which Esther answers:

This essay was originally presented at the American Comparative Literature Association convention held at the Claremont Graduate School in March 1994. All page references to *Etoile errante* (Paris: Gallimard, 1992) are given in parentheses in the text; all translations are mine.

"But the children?" (p. 213). The novel is dedicated neither to the Israeli nor the Palestinian cause but "To the captive children," to those caught in the midst of a tragic conflict they did not create and cannot solve.

This pivotal scene in Jean-Marie Gustave Le Clézio's 1992 novel, *Etoile errante*, dramatically underscores the absurdity of the human toll that is blindly and randomly exacted upon the innocent by uncontrolled and uncontrollable forces. The arrival of Jewish refugees into the capital of the recently formed State of Israel does not alleviate the pain and suffering of either the Jews or the Palestinians. This dual displacement of Jews toward the Promised Land and Palestinians toward the refugee camps stands as just one more swing in the movement of a tragic pendulum. Like some political law of physics, every movement within such a circumscribed and coveted space leads to an equal and opposite reaction. Recent shifts in power and initiatives toward peace in the Middle East have almost inevitably been accompanied by violent flare-ups that erupt on all sides of the conflict. While refusing to ground solutions in historical debates over precedence and priority, Le Clézio succeeds in putting a human face on the confrontations that have pitted two ancient peoples against each other, often in the most inhumane and violent terms. The crossed destinies of Esther and Nejma embody the diasporic wanderings of their peoples, just as their encounter on the road to Jerusalem has the brevity and arbitrariness of stars crossing in the heavens.

The evocative, haunting title, *Etoile errante* (literally "wandering star") suggests a spliced reference to "shooting star" ("étoile filante") and "wandering Jew" ("Juif errant"). Indeed, references to stars fill the pages of the novel, creating a sensation of multitude and omnipresence throughout. The star is also an appropriate image for the title because it is shared by both Jews and Arabs as part of their popular and religious imagery. This title immediately positions the narrative on both a poetic and political level, setting the parameters of a world vision in which space is both psychic and physical. Indeed, Le Clézio superimposes nonquadrant space, which is cosmic, apolitical, and unoccupiable, above geopolitical space with its borders and boundaries. He also posits the superiority of language over politics and of dialogue over confrontation. His novel ultimately shows the need for understanding and tolerance in a region racked by strife and bloodshed. This message obviously echoed a popular sentiment because *Etoile errante* has obtained a great deal of success, both critical and popular, and was praised by readers and representatives from all sides of the political and religious spectrum. For its humanistic treatment of the Jewish-Arab question, *Etoile errante* was awarded the grand prize of the International Human Rights League in 1992.

This most recent novel by J. M. G. Le Clézio prolongs the author's life-long attention to exile and wandering as well as to issues of culture and identity, especially within an extra-European context. Le Clézio has published over thirty books in about as many years, beginning with the 1963 novel, *Le Procès-verbal*, that won the coveted Prix Renaudot and catapulted him onto the literary scene at the age of twenty-three. Besides works that profess to his strong attachment to native cultures, two other novels deserve particular mention in that they form a sort of triptych with *Etoile errante*. *Désert* (1980) recounts the conquest of southern Morocco by French troops in the early twentieth century, doubled by the contemporary story of Lalla, a Bedouin orphan descended from the legendary "blue men" of the desert. Her flight from North Africa to the immigrant slums of Marseilles raises issues of immigration and integration while crystallizing around her plight the ineluctable eradication of ancient civilizations. *Onitsha* (1991) is a partially autobiographical novel that depicts both legendary and mythical Africa alongside the reality of the colonial enterprise. The questions of a young boy's family identity are played out against the backdrop of post–World War II colonial Africa and a father's search for a legendary Egyptian queen.

Despite his considerable success in France, despite his ties to the prestigious Gallimard publishing house, Le Clézio has consistently shunned the Parisian literary scene, preferring the warmth and relative anonymity of Nice, the island of Mauritius, or Mexico, old and new. His true affinities lie more with the Amerindian populations of Central America than with the literary tribes and empires of the French capital. He also readily identifies himself as a "Franco-Mauritian writer," referring thereby to his eighteenth-century ancestors who left Britanny for the Indian Ocean island some five hundred miles east of Madagascar. Le Clézio, interestingly, means "wall" or "enclosure" in the language of his Breton ancestors, perhaps referring back to the Celtic practice of erecting stone enclosures. It is certainly a fitting ancestry for one interested in legend to be associated with a people known more for their worship of the heavens than for their conquest of the earth. Although he is understandably proud of this heritage, it is nevertheless important to stress that Le Clézio has spent more time going over, around, or under age-old boundaries than in erecting new ones of his own. In a recent article, he declares: "For someone who is an islander like me, a descendant of Breton *émigrés* who settled on the island of Mauritius, someone raised by the sea who would spend hours watching cargo ships and hanging around the docks, someone who has no roots in the earth, like a man who walks up and down the boulevards and who is neither from one neighborhood, nor from one city, but from all the neighborhoods and all the cities — the French language is my only homeland, the only place I truly live." [1]

Le Clézio's insatiable wanderlust has taken him to the four corners of the globe, making him a tireless wanderer in a world with borders, always ready to accomplish a forward flight, a Marco Polo in search of a mythical Cathay. He shares the feeling of estrangement that is expressed by Hogan, the main character in *Le Livre des fuites:* "I am a man without a land; I belong to no culture." Like a cultural nomad, he is also free to choose where he wishes to plant his roots. In his journeys, Le Clézio carries with him the memory of his ancestors, whether they be his Mauritian grandfather in *Le Chercheur d'or* [2] or the vanquished native peoples of Central America in *Le Rêve mexicain ou la pensée interrompue.* [3] Le Clézio's true universe is the language that makes it possible to tell the tales that bear witness to the range of human experience, even beyond the culture that nourished that language. In confronting issues of historical transformation, Le Clézio most often adopts a universalist point of view, giving voice to even the most vulnerable and obscure of peoples. *Haï* (1971) contrasts Central American Indian modes of communication and expression with those of Western industrialized civilizations, much to the benefit of the former. Le Clézio does not write from a national perspective, except insofar as the French language is his homeland. He has often shown concern with the ruptures and disjunctions of both ancient and modern life, usually related in terms of myth and fable. *Etoile errante* therefore marks a shift in his preoccupations in that the political and national concerns are immediate, pressing, and in constant transformation. Despite this unusual context, the treatment nevertheless remains highly poeticized even when the situation could lend itself to polemics or politics. The nature of the Jewish-Arab conflict must be considered to be the site of a larger problematic as it becomes the converging point for questions of nation, identity, language, and power.

Despite its 1992 publication date, *Etoile errante* had been in preparation for some years: a 30-page section, the diary of Nejma in the Nour Chams refugee camp, was published in 1988 in the *Revue d'études palestiniennes*. It raised discussion and speculation about Le Clézio's political sympathies for or against the Palestinian cause and led to the author's refusal to allow himself to become a political pawn in an ideological war of words. The subsequent upheaval known as the *intifada* and the long "war of stones" led him to defer an earlier publication date because he feared that the political climate would inevitably drag his novel into an arena of polemics that he refused to enter. To have engaged in this debate would have been to recognize that political and national forces were capable of solving the problem they had been responsible for creating. The ultimate decision to publish *Etoile errante* should not therefore be interpreted as a political act of *engagement*, but rather as a desire to tell the tale of a human drama that continues to create misery and suffering for all concerned. The novel neither glorifies suffering nor seeks to incriminate any one side of wrongdoing; rather, it exemplifies in moving terms Albert Camus's humanistic goal of cultivating the art of living in times of catastrophe. The novel also takes on a haunting dimension when one knows that it is largely inspired by the real-life stories of two women.

Etoile errante spans some 40 years through the crossed destinies of two female characters, Esther and Nejma. Each woman, as a result of their fleeting encounter on the road outside Jerusalem, will undertake to write a journal for the other without knowing whether that unknown other will ever actually read the words destined for her. Structurally, Esther's tale frames Nejma's, although the question of narrative economy should not be taken as a sign of greater or lesser importance. Both women, through their writings, will attain and reveal for an unknown, hypothetical reader the trials by which they come to define their identities in the context of strife and persecution. Their struggle revolves largely around their quest to regain possession of themselves beyond the identities imposed upon them by the outside world. In fact, both Esther and Nejma will ultimately move away from their civil identities that tie them to cultural and national groups in favor of a greater individuality and a stronger independence. Exiles they were, and exiles they will remain.

Esther's story begins in the summer of 1943 in the mountainous hinterland above Nice, where she and her parents, along with other Jewish refugees, are placed under relatively benevolent Italian control in the village of Saint-Martin-Vésubie. The innocence of children's games and excursions into the vibrant surrounding countryside hide a more ominous reality. Esther, a young adolescent on the verge of life, also makes the capital discovery of her Jewish identity, largely as a result of the way others identify her as such. She had shown little consciousness of her identity until that moment and thus becomes the other before she becomes herself. Indeed, Esther is known in the village as Hélène and had been forced for her own safety to conceal much of her identity and to carry false identification papers. To the outside world, she is Hélène, but to her father she is Esther or "Estrellita," little star. The infamous yellow star that had become the visible identification sign of Jews elsewhere had not come to Saint-Martin. The Jewish refugees were nevertheless required to report every day to the Italian authorities, who thereby verified that they were present and accounted for in the village. Esther had apparently lived the early years of her childhood without any strong religious upbringing. The evening that she goes to the synagogue for the first time and hears the strange and moving Shabbat ceremony is also the beginning of another journey. This spiritual discovery coincides with the forced retreat of the Italian army, leaving the entire region prey to the German tanks that come rumbling up the valley. The panic-stricken Jewish population of Saint-Martin flees in the face of overwhelming odds and certain destruction. Esther and her mother, Elizabeth, here begin an odyssey that will take them over the mountains by foot to the relative safety of Italy before they finally make their way to Israel.

Geography, at least of the political sort that gets scrambled in wars, is soon replaced by topography: a border is no longer a guarded checkpoint but a mountain pass to cross, a precipice to negotiate, a rocky trail that leads on an uncertain journey into the unknown (p. 91). The mountain is a wall that must be crossed so as to reach safety on the other side. Esther, the wandering star, the wandering Jew, feels the exaltation of climbing closer and closer to the sky and the clouds until she reaches the opening that is the mountain pass. There she finds herself suspended between two worlds at that "window" that allows her to see into the other side of the world (p. 115). Stars, in like fashion, do not obey the artificial borders that are traced by armies and politicians; rather, they move across the vast, empty space, heroines of a cosmic order that escape the bounds and boundaries of our delimited, earthly existence. Esther's father, meanwhile, remains behind to help a lagging group of "fugitives," as they are called, in their attempt to escape the onslaught of the approaching German panzer division. Her father embodies a triple marginalization: Jewish, communist, and Résistant. In a significant sense, he belongs to the underground, to those who recognize no borders or boundaries, to those who defy the political divisions that separate people. His courage and daring will cost him his life when he is gunned down by the advancing enemy. Thereby is created the first major rupture and discontinuity in the novel, one that will haunt Esther throughout her life.

Esther's brutal initiation to the world of wandering and exile has left her with an awareness that her carefree, childhood existence has ended and that only forward flight will allow survival. She and her mother continue their exodus until 1947–48, when they embark for Israel. When they return to France from Italy after the war in search of safe passage to the Promised Land, they must again cross the same mountain pass, which this time is likened to "a hole in [Esther's] center, a window through which to see the void" (p. 134). At this point the narrative switches to the first person as Esther, now seventeen and greatly aware of the problems of identity, proceeds to tell the story in her own voice. Her appropriation of language is connected with her awareness of the power of the word, especially as it conveys a religious message. Her narrative begins: "I know that I am leaving this country forever. I don't know if I will arrive safely on the other side, only that we shall soon be gone" (p. 139). Their departure is intimately linked to a desire to flee the past and its horrors; their constant displacement only reinforces the empty feeling of existence without time and space.

Space contains not only a poetic and political dimension but also a cultural one, given that the diasporic conception of space is characterized by multiple sites separated by a void. Continuity and cohesion have been lost because of the absence of a common identity. This idea of dissemination is closely linked to that of diaspora, where small pockets of culture subsist in largely alien surroundings. A common language could nevertheless serve as a connector, a bond among exiled peoples settled in foreign lands, surrounded by foreign populations. This notion of fragmentation captures perfectly the spatial experience of Esther and Nejma in *Etoile errante*. It is also important to note that the narrative structure reflects this same general tendency. Frequent shifts across space and time, sudden changes in narrative voice, fragmented subdivisions within an overarching chapter organization all make for a narrative framework that embodies exactly the discontinuities in the individual characters' tales. Such disorientation comes largely from the sense that there is no suitable place to settle and begin anew the construction of life. Even Esther's arrival in Israel does not mark the end of her diaspora because it does not resolve the psychic wandering that began at the time of Saint-Martin. Although the Greek word *diaspora* is more widely used to denote this dispersion of people, the Hebrew word *galut* more accurately suggests exile and void both psychically and physically, as well as a longing for resolution to that wandering. Esther's immediate goal of returning to the land of Israel might solve her desire for a physical home, yet nothing seems adequate to heal her psychic scars. When her thoughts turn to her father, it is with the realization that he, too, had been forced to flee in the face of an incomprehensible horror (p. 146). Her most treasured possessions, memories of the past, have sustained her in her wanderings, yet now they become a source of immense torment and pain.

The novel acquires its profound rhythm and resonance through the successive departures that take place, as if Esther's and Elizabeth's lives were defined essentially as movement away rather than movement toward. This situation will slowly change as they set their sights on Jerusalem, a city they have never seen but one they seem to have always known. Jerusalem represents "life before the destruction" (p. 155), referring to the destruction of the biblical city and the subsequent Babylonian Exile and also to the contemporary attempt once again to eradicate the Jewish people. The void in Esther stems from the loss of her father as much as from any ancestral persecution. In a long, significant section in the book where forward progress is denied as their vessel must work its way through the British blockade, death looms constantly as the price to pay for the cessation of movement. Esther will momentarily overcome the void within her by realizing the truth: "Those who kill others rob them of life; they are like savage beasts, without pity" (p. 153). Besides containing the story of Esther's struggle for survival against concerted forces of evil and destruction, *Etoile errante* traces the discovery of an identity and an individual and collective coming of age that results from the cataclysmic events of the war.

Le Clézio's novel pays extraordinary attention to the play of light and shadow that provide the cosmic dimension within which is played out a moving human drama. The light, whether of Eretz Israel or of the stars in the sky, also contains the potential to cast shadows over the land and all its people. Light, given by Elohim, is what separates night from day, creating time as well as the science of understanding. Awareness and understanding, we are led to see, can bring solace or suffering. As the settlers move closer to Israel, they read the "Book of Beginnings," the spiritual texts, which progressively take on more reality than the external world around them. The tales of Canaan, of bondage in Egypt, of the Promised Land, all contribute to the beginning of a newfound awareness that will galvanize the disparate group of Jews into citizens of a state. These readings are a crucial step in Esther's transformation and discovery of her own identity. She turns to her mother: "Now I know that we will make it to Jerusalem. When we know all that is in the book, we will have arrived" (p. 185). Books are reflections of spiritual reality, much as maps are representations of geographical and political space. Esther belongs to the people of the Word, the people who have been sustained throughout their centuries of wandering and displacement by their faith in the Book. In an intense moment of realization, she discovers how simple and clear everything has become now that she understands: "Everything has become real" (p. 186). Her people's collective journey was taking them toward the Promised Land, toward the fabled city of light, toward a new identity and a new community. Their exaltation becomes obvious as they make it through the British blockade and set foot on the land named after the people of the Covenant. The light of the name of the fabled city of Jerusalem, the light that has guided them to their destination can sometimes, however, shine so brightly that it proves blinding.

Just as the star of Esther disappears upon her arrival at the walls of Jerusalem, the star of Nejma comes into view as she and her people are forced to evacuate the newly formed State of Israel. Nejma means "star" in Arabic, making her truly another "wandering star" about to embark on her own diaspora. Her tale, which is emblematic of the plight of her people, is recounted largely in the first-person narrative contained in a journal in which she records the memory of life in the refugee camp of Nour Chams (literally, "light of the sun") beginning in the summer of 1948. Her act of writing has two audiences: on a personal level, Esther Grève, whom Nejma knows only for having had her inscribe her name in a blank notebook at a stop along the Jerusalem road and, in a more general sense, all those who might be inclined to ignore or forget the deplorable conditions of refugee life. Edward Said has commented on the ephemeral, unstable, fragmentary quality of Palestinian writing as a reflection of the discontinuities inherent in their social and political condition.[4] Said even mentions as exemplary of this need for improvisation within a disposable culture the common practice of jotting down messages on notebooks much as Nejma and Esther do in their brief encounter. The major difference in *Etoile errante* is that the page is not torn from the notebook, but rather spawns myriad other pages that bear witness to a wide spectrum of human experience. Writing becomes for Nejma the opening of a space against conquest and injustice, a plea for compassion and understanding.

Nejma seems less concerned by political reality than by fundamental questions such as the one that reappears throughout her journal: "Does the sun not shine for everyone?" When the United Nations carried them away from their farm, they left everything; they thought that they were being relocated and the camp was just a stop along the road to another life. Nour Chams, however, has become a prison, and it has every likelihood of becoming a cemetery (p. 220). The earth, parched by the hot sun, yields few crops and little water for the human beings who have been herded into this remote area and abandoned except for sporadic relief aid brought in by the United Nations. It is "the end of the earth, since there can be nothing beyond it, since its inhabitants can hope for nothing else" (p. 223). The fate of the Palestinian refugees, not unlike that of the Jews, has been determined by others, by strangers, by foreigners who seem to have decided to eradicate them from the face of the earth (p. 219). The act of writing is a combat against the devouring power of ignorance, exclusion, and forgetting.

Like Esther's village of Saint-Martin-Vésubie, the camp of Nour Chams has a geography outside of the combat zone. It is, however, more a place of internment than a refuge, situated in a no-man's-land that is not conducive to prosperous settlement. In contrast to the abundance of water that runs through the streets of Saint-Martin, the camp of Nour Chams is a patch of arid land in a remote desert. Edward Said characterizes Palestinian space in the following manner: "Thus Palestinian life is scattered, discontinuous, marked by the artificial and imposed arrangements of interrupted or confined space, by the dislocations and unsynchronized rhythms of disturbed time."[5] The physical plight of the refugees soon leads to mental and moral suffering and breakdown. As the wells dry up, the laughter and familiar chatter of everyday life recede, leaving only the daily announcement of the names of sons, brothers, and husbands who have been killed in the war. The women, children, and elderly people at the camp, meanwhile, have had even their mirrors confiscated, leaving them to rely on their reflection in the eyes of others to see themselves. Nejma's memory becomes all the more important as it bears witness to a process of debasement and degradation that few people are allowed to witness, that most of the world has chosen to ignore. The stars above, like the light of "unknown cities suspended in the sky" (p. 246), are the most faithful witnesses to the earthly sufferings of her people. On some nights, their pale, cold light makes the camp dwellers seem even more isolated, more abandoned.

A ray of hope enters the camp with the birth of a child to one of Nejma's neighbors. Soon after, however, rats bring an epidemic that spreads through the camp and kills the child's mother. This confirms the belief that there is no hope left, that there is no reason to hope, and that those who remain at Nour Chams will certainly perish. Nejma and the mysterious shepherd, Saadi, gather a bit of food and the infant child and immediately set out to flee the camp, embarking on a perilous journey across a war-torn, desert land. Like Esther's flight, their survival is dependent upon their ability to move forward without stopping in hopes of attaining the valley of Saadi's childhood, where they hope to find refuge. Their escape across the desert, in contrast to the squalor of Nour Chams, provides the idyllic center of Nejma's tale. This section is related by an omniscient narrator. Nejma and Saadi form an impromptu couple, with child, goat, and kid, crossing on foot the open, desert spaces under a star-studded sky. This tranquil interlude, besides providing relief from the despair and desolation of the camp, also stands in marked contrast to the war raging about them. Although not without a general direction, their wandering aims more at avoiding any of a great number of perils, especially armed patrols, rather than reaching any specific goal.

In contrast to Esther's arrival in Israel, signaling the end of her diaspora, Nejma's wandering has no fixed destination other than the return to her former life and land. Like the Jewish diaspora, the Palestinian dispersion supposes multiple sites that exist simultaneously yet disconnectedly across space. Nationhood leads to contestation with the newly proclaimed State of Israel under attack by its Arab neighbors; meanwhile, the displaced Palestinians have no geographical and political structure within which to construct a collective identity. Iraq, Jordan, and Lebanon are names that beckon the "fugitives" in the dark night, encouraging them to continue along their path. It seems there is, literally, nowhere to go, except to continue along the never-ending road under the sun that shines for everyone, that burns everything below (p. 284).

As the narrative shifts back to the tale of Esther, it is 1950 and she and her mother have found refuge and companionship in another sort of camp, a kibbutz, where they work in the fields until the sun drives them back indoors. There they find community with Jews of all backgrounds, all nationalities. The intense activity of life on the kibbutz fills a void; Esther knows that she must not leave an unoccupied space in her thoughts that might let in memories that she wants to hold at bay (p. 295). Connected by the land that belongs to everyone, and therefore to no one, the Israeli settlers have achieved a new beginning, as Esther's father dreamed, as the holy book promised. The drama is, of course, that the same land is contested by two rival peoples. Esther and her fellow Jews were metaphorically reborn on the sandy beach where they first set foot on the land of Eretz Israel (p. 313). "Grève," significantly, means "shore" or "bank," thus making her a littoral character even by name. Their individual nationalities are also shed in favor of a greater common identity, their Judaism, that is the vital link on which the young nation is founded.

The new beginning becomes more concrete when, at the beginning of Hanukkah, Esther and her fiancé, Jacques, conceive a child. The Festival of Lights is also the commemoration of the revolt of the Maccabees that led to the enlarged frontiers of the land of Israel in the second century B.C.E., as well as the rededication of the Temple. But the promise of a brighter future is short-lived for Esther as the cycle of violence between Jews and Arabs sets in, making their newfound freedom ominously more limited than they had hoped. When news arrives that Jacques has been killed in a border skirmish during the first Arab-Israeli War, he joins Esther's own father and the many others on both sides of the conflict who have left behind orphans. Esther decides to become an exile once again, fleeing to Montreal, where she will give birth to their son. Michel will be the "child of the sun," born at dawn in a northern land, yet endowed with the strength and agility of a shepherd (his father's last name was, after all, Berger, "shepherd," in French), with the light of Jerusalem shining in his eyes (p. 313). Esther will realize Jacques's dream of going to medical school in Canada, where she will decide to become a pediatrician and return to Tel Aviv with their son in 1966. The children, hers as well as Nejma's and countless others, will need her care. The return to Israel leads, however, to an uneasy stability, nothing that resembles peace or serenity. Wherever Esther's flight takes her, there will always be a place in her memory for Saint-Martin and her father, for Jacques and the kibbutz, for Nejma, who entered her life so briefly yet whose shadow still weighs heavy in her mind.

Esther's memory of Nejma occupies a short but essential section in the final narration of her wanderings (pp. 307–11). Their destinies converge here, at least in Esther's imagined memory, which skips at a rapid pace from scene to scene in her past. This first-person narrative serves to connect the two women as Esther writes to Nejma in a black notebook like the one the Arab woman held out to her for many years earlier along the dusty roadside. She dreams that someone has delivered to her Nejma's notebook and that she can decipher the unfamiliar script, that this dual act of writing has created a mysterious but inalienable bond. In a dreamlike sequence, Esther imagines that she will return to that same dusty road where their paths crossed and find Nejma; there, they will exchange their respective notebooks "so as to abolish time and to put an end to the burning suffering of death" (p. 308). This would somehow bring Nejma back from the harsh, forgotten land of exile and allow them to contemplate each other once more.

The interplay of memory and exile comes full circle when Esther receives word that her mother, Elizabeth, lies dying in a hospital in Nice; her return to the bedside of her mother opens the floodgates of past memories, old wounds, present doubts. It is the summer of 1982 and the outbreak of war in Lebanon; the fires over Beirut will be echoed by the massive forest fires that erupt at the same time in the south of France, especially in the hinterland above Nice. It is also the year of the massacre of Palestinians in the Sabra and Shatilla refugee camps. Fires and smoke cast a sinister shadow over the entire novel, suggesting the burning flames of war, the destruction of millions of innocent victims in the Nazi death camps, the showering of bombs over southern Lebanon. The cycle of life and death becomes more poignant as Elizabeth spends her final days recalling her past "in the words of life" (p. 323). Esther realizes: "If I don't find out where the pain comes from, I will have wasted my life and lost my truth. I will continue to wander" (p. 326). Is that truth to be found wandering through the streets of Nice with the ashes of her mother in a metal cylinder, passing in front of buildings where torture and death had taken place during the war while indifferent passersby turned their heads? Or is it the empty feeling left by the death of Jacques, whose son, Michel, now carries within him the legacy of so much wandering, so much suffering? Or could it be the memory of Nejma, who has disappeared, both from Esther's sight and from the space of the novel? Is it the natural passing of time signaled by the death of her mother? Death is clearly equated in all of these cases with silence, with the absence of words, which are agents of truth, giving both a poetic and a political charge to the act of writing.

Esther's journey into the past continues with a pilgrimage to the village of Saint-Martin, the village of exile and death, the focus of her return toward life. She feels more a stranger than ever, unable to connect fully with a past fraught with pain, unable to find solace in forgetting. The cascade of memories and sensations leads to a telescopic use of time in this final section, where so much of the past remains present, where so much of the present reminds Esther of the past. As she wanders through the once familiar streets and surroundings, she realizes that Jerusalem, her city of light, the city her father so wished to see, might very well lie on the mountainous slopes above Nice just as much as it figures on the map of Israel (p. 335). Our political maps with stars to represent capitals have only limited validity. As her personal narrative ends, Esther realizes that her promised land lies on the other side of the sea with her son and new husband; that light awaits her and shines in the eyes of those children whose sorrow and suffering she wants to alleviate. Finally, she wants to go and find Nejma, her "lost sister," who disappeared years earlier in a cloud of dust along a barren, war-torn road.

Of the many lessons that might be derived from this moving, highly poetic novel, perhaps the most important is the way psychic space supersedes physical space, even if the latter seems to impinge on life more often and more directly. Both Esther and Nejma cross human, geographical, and political borders as a condition of their survival; but these borders are artificial and arbitrary, not mental and necessary. Like the stars in the sky, they rarely follow a well-trodden path. There is no utopia here, whether on the Israeli or Palestinian side, only people who find themselves on opposing sides of a conflict, on opposing sides of a barrier to understanding and acceptance. Wherever their wanderings take them, Esther and Nejma will carry with them the memory of their common bond, the conscience of the fragile threads that connect us all one to another. Le Clézio, through the tale of these two unlikely "sisters," suggests that our human connections far exceed the political and social differences that might separate us. If borders and boundaries divide people along lines and directions pertinent to physical space, memory and language observe no such limits. Even after political and military forces have drawn up new maps and traced new borders, the tales of Esther and Nejma obey their own truth as they transcend them. The discovery of this truth is indissociably linked to the discovery of language. Such is the condition of exiled wanderers who belong nowhere, which is to say everywhere, and who carry with them the words that give meaning to their lives.

Le Clézio feels strongly that his only true country is the French language. The difficulty, he goes on to say, stems from the fact that "economic, military and colonial powers also inhabit a language":

Without a doubt, there has never been a more important question than that of borders, those cursed dotted lines that must be erased: the Rio Grande like an Acheron drowning the misery of "wetbacks," the new Iron Curtain restraining the wretched of Eastern Europe, Algeciras, the chancre of the modern world, shutting off behind barbed wire those children with eyes too dark, ghettos, camps, infamous territories and the seas where boat people capsize. Against all this, I would like for the French language to be the language of freedom and the language of hope. ("Eloge," p. 83)

Language and life are indissociable. The choice of two central female characters, alternating as they do with their personal narratives, contributes also to the sense that life might one day conquer over suffering, destruction, and death. Le Clézio, rather than allowing the cartographer's lines to determine belonging and exclusion, wealth and poverty, survival and extermination, delivers a moving plea for the eradication of those borders that divide rather than connect, that attempt to control not only earthly bodies but heavenly ones as well.

NOTES

1. J. M. G. Le Clézio, "Eloge de la langue française," *L'Express*, Feb. 14, 1993, p. 82.

2. *The Prospector*, trans. Carol Marks (Boston: David R. Godine, 1993).

3. *The Mexican Dream or, The Interrupted Thought of Amerindian Civilization*, trans. Teresa Lavander Fagan (Chicago: University of Chicago Press, 1993).

4. Edward W. Said, *After the Last Sky: Palestinian Lives* (New York: Pantheon Books, 1985, 1986), pp. 37–38.

5. Ibid., p. 20.

Reference Matter

Index

In this index an "f" after a number indicates a separate reference on the next page, and an "ff" indicates separate references on the next two pages. A continuous discussion over two or more pages is indicated by a span of page numbers, e.g., "57–59." *Passim* is used for a cluster of references in close but not consecutive sequence. Italicized page numbers denote references to figures.

Index

Index

Index

Index

Index

Index

Library of Congress Cataloging-in-Publication Data

Borders, exiles, diasporas / edited by Elazar Barkan and Marie-Denise
  Shelton.
       p.   cm. — (Cultural sitings)
    Includes bibliographical references and index.
    ISBN 0-8047-2905-0 : (cloth) — ISBN 0-8047-2906-9 :
  (pbk.)
       1. Ethnicity.   2. Identity (Psychology)—3. Ethnic relations.
  4. Ethnicity in literature.   5. Ethnic relations in literature.
  I. Barkan, Elazar.   II. Shelton, Marie-Denise   III. Series.
  GN495.6.B65   1998
  305.8 — dc21   97-16108
                                                                     CIP

♾This book is printed on acid-free, recycled paper.

Original printing 1998

Last figure below indicates year of this printing:

07 06 05 04 03 02 01 00 99 98